LONGMAN STUDY GUIDES

GCSE
German

Chris Watson

David Rogers

LONGMAN STUDY GUIDES

SERIES EDITORS: **Geoff Black and Stuart Wall**

Titles available

Biology
Business Studies
Chemistry
Design and Technology
Economics
English
English Literature
French
Geography
German
Information Technology

Mathematics
Mathematics: Higher Level
Music
Physics
Psychology
Religious Studies
Science
Sociology
Spanish
World History

Addison Wesley Longman Ltd,
Edinburgh Gate, Harlow,
Essex CM20 2JE, England
and Associated Companies throughout the World.

© Addison Wesley Longman 1997

All rights reserved; no part of this publication may be reproduced, stored in a retrieval system, or transmitted in any form or by any means, electronic, mechanical, photocopying, recording or otherwise without either the prior written permission of the Publishers or a licence permitting restricted copying in the United Kingdom issued by the Copyright Licensing Agency Ltd, 90 Tottenham Court Road, London W1P 9HE.

First Published 1997

ISBN 0582-30487-3

British Library Cataloguing-in-Publication Data
A catalogue record for this book is available from the British Library.

Set by 34 in 9.75/12pt Sabon

Printed in Great Britain by Henry Ling Ltd,
at the Dorset Press, Dorchester, Dorset

CONTENTS

Editors' preface   iv

Acknowledgements   iv

Information about this book   v

1 **GCSE and Key Stage 4 German**   1

2 **Examination techniques**   7

3 **Subject Content: Areas of Experience**   11

4 **Listening: Foundation Tier**   45

5 **Listening: Higher Tier**   67

6 **Reading: Foundation Tier**   83

7 **Reading: Higher Tier**   103

8 **Speaking: Foundation Tier – role-plays**   121

9 **Speaking: Higher Tier – role-plays**   139

10 **Speaking: Foundation and Higher conversation, presentation and coursework**   155

11 **Writing: Foundation Tier**   164

12 **Writing: Higher Tier**   180

13 **Writing: Coursework**   192

14 **Grammar**   196

15 **A checklist of language tasks**   219

16 **Vocabulary**   230

Index   252

▶ **EDITORS' PREFACE**

Longman Study Guides have been written by the people who set and mark the exams – the examiners. Examiners are aware that, due to lack of practice and poor preparation, some students achieve only the lowest grades; they are not able to show the examiner effectively what they know. These books give excellent advice about exam practice and preparation, and organising a structured revision programme, all of which are essential for examination success. Remember: the examiners are looking for opportunities to *give* you marks, not take them away!

Longman Study Guides are designed to be used throughout the course. The self-contained chapters can be read in any order appropriate to the stage you have reached in your course. The examiner guides you through the essential parts of each topic, making helpful comments throughout.

We believe that this book, and the series as a whole, will help you establish and build your basic knowledge and examination techniques. For additional help with exam practice and revision techniques, we have published a series called *Longman Exam Practice Kits*, which are available from all good bookshops, or direct from Addison Wesley Longman.

GEOFF BLACK AND STUART WALL

▶ **ACKNOWLEDGEMENTS**

I would like to thank Alasdair Mckeane for his advice about the index and Arthur Fancett for his help with the manuscript. I would also like to thank Claudia Schlottmann for reading the manuscript and making many helpful amendments and contributions to the German.

CHRIS WATSON

▶ INFORMATION ABOUT THIS BOOK

This book has been written as a course companion for use throughout your GCSE course in German.

The first two chapters provide invaluable information about studying for a GCSE in German – how the examination will be structured and assessed, details about the courses offered by the main examination boards, how to prepare for the examination and the study skills required. You should read these chapters carefully as they provide information that will be useful to you throughout your two-year course.

Chapter 3 looks at the language tasks/Areas of Experience that you will need to be familiar with, such as everyday activities, personal and social life, the world around us, the world of work and the international world. You should also study and learn the vocabulary lists (sub-divided into topic areas).

Chapters 4–13 then look at the four main methods of assessment – listening, reading, speaking and writing – for both Foundation and Higher Tiers. In each of these chapters advice is given about preparing for the assessment and tips about the types of questions you might be asked. To help you practise what you have just learnt, these chapters also include practice situations, questions and tasks with answers.

Chapters 14–16 focus on grammar and vocabulary. To achieve the best marks in the four main assessment areas you need to show that you understand and can apply the language.

- ▶ As you work through the chapter on grammar, try the exercises to practise what you have just read (Chapter 14).
- ▶ To show yourself how much you have learnt during your studies, tick the 'learnt' and 'tested' boxes for each topic area in the **Checklist of language tasks** (Chapter 15).
- ▶ Use the mini dictionary 'vocabulary lists' from German to English and from English to German for reference while using the book and for your homework (Chapter 16).
- ▶ For a list of instructions that you might come across in the GCSE examination turn to page 249.

Chapter 1

GCSE and Key Stage 4 German

GETTING STARTED

This book sets out to help you develop the skills you need as a candidate for GCSE German. It will explain the exact requirements of each examining group. It will cover in full detail the four major language skills of listening and responding, reading and responding, speaking and writing. These are the four Attainment Targets of the National Curriculum. It will provide extensive examples of questions set at both Foundation and Higher Tiers. The book also offers suggestions to help you develop your skills outside the classroom, suggestions which are entirely relevant to the examination and which can provide you with a feeling of enjoyment and achievement.

WHAT YOU NEED TO KNOW

The GCSE

When the GCSE was first introduced it was seen as an opportunity to improve syllabuses and methods of assessment in modern foreign languages for candidates of all abilities. The hope was that this would attract more candidates and this indeed has been the case. Now, under the requirements of the National Curriculum, everyone must study a modern foreign language at Key Stage 4 and the GCSE has become the means of assessment for the National Curriculum at this level. In developing their syllabuses the examining groups have made every effort to preserve the philosophy of the GCSE while meeting the requirements of the National Curriculum, National Criteria and the SCAA Code of Practice. The point of all this is to ensure that all candidates are treated equally and fairly no matter which examination they take or when they take it and that standards are maintained nationally.

The aims of GCSE

1. The fundamental aim of the GCSE examination in German is that the course should 'develop the ability to understand and use German effectively for purposes of **practical communication**'.
2. The GCSE examination is based on the idea that it should allow candidates to show what they **can do**, rather than expose what they cannot do. The requirements of the examining groups are therefore clearly set out and available to candidates, teachers and the public.
3. The examining groups produce detailed lists of the Areas of Experience, topics, vocabulary and grammar needed for their respective examinations.
4. This all means that the GCSE is a very open examination, in that everything that is required of the candidate is **laid down** in the Syllabus and Defined Content of each examining group.
5. The mark schemes are **positive**. Candidates are awarded marks for what they **actually achieve** and do not have marks deducted for every mistake. Examinations also contain sections in which everyone, whatever his or her ability, has a chance of success.

Examination content

Although examining groups are free to explore and develop their own syllabuses and examination models, they must do so within the framework of the National Curriculum and its requirements. There is therefore a large measure of common ground in the different examinations of the six major examining groups. This common ground is based on the four National Curriculum Attainment Targets in modern languages – of listening and responding, reading and responding, speaking and writing – and the five Areas of Experience specified in the National Curriculum, which define the types of language task that students must be taught. The GCSE examination in German comprises the following elements:

1

1 Foundation Tier listening and responding
2 Foundation Tier reading and responding
3 Foundation Tier speaking
4 Foundation Tier writing
5 Higher Tier listening and responding
6 Higher Tier reading and responding
7 Higher Tier speaking
8 Higher Tier writing.

All candidates must enter *either* Foundation Tier *or* Higher Tier in *each* of the four Attainment Targets. Thus a candidate may be entered for listening and reading at Higher Tier but at Foundation Tier for speaking and writing if this is felt to be in his/her best interests, having regard to his/her aptitudes and abilities. A candidate may not, however, be entered for two tiers in the same Attainment Target. In this way a candidate's examination entry can be tailored to what he/she can do and no one should be faced with an impossible and overwhelming task on the day of the examination.

Foundation Tier is targeted at grades G up to C, while Higher Tier is targeted at grades D up to A*. It is important that you are entered for the most suitable tier for you. For instance, candidates who are entered at Higher Tier and who fail to reach the required standard for a grade D will be awarded a U (unclassified). Similarly, if you were entered at Foundation Tier in all four Attainment Targets the highest grade you could achieve would be a C.

In general, questions will be in the target language, i.e. German!, and answers will be required in German too. Where it is felt to be legitimate for the task, however, the question may be in English and you may be asked to give an answer in English. There is a limit to how many questions of this kind may be included in the exam. Don't worry about this now as we shall be looking at question types in more detail later.

Some boards allow coursework either partly or wholly instead of a final examination in some of the Attainment Targets, usually writing, but also in speaking. The SEG examination is quite different to the others in that it is modular in structure and therefore contains quite a large element of coursework and continuous assessment.

Table 1.1 shows in grid form the requirements of five of the examining groups. It looks complicated but remember that you will only be involved with one examining group. Find out which one that is and ignore the rest.

Table 1.1 Course overview

	MEG F	MEG H	NEAB F	NEAB H	NICCEA F	NICCEA H	London F	London H	WJEC F	WJEC H
Listening Time allowed (minutes)	40	40	30	40	30	30	25	35	45	45
Weighting	25%	25%	25%	25%	25%	25%	25%	25%	25%	25%
Stimulus	RT	RT	RT	RT	RT	RT	RT	RT	RT	RT
Reading Time allowed (minutes)	50	50	30	50	40	40	30	45	45	45
Weighting	25%	25%	25%	25%	25%	25%	25%	25%	25%	25%
Speaking Time allowed (minutes)	10–12	12–15	8–10	10–12	10	10	8–10	10–12	10	12
Weighting	25%	25%	25%	25%	25%	25%	25%	25%	25%	25%
Role-plays	2	2	2	2	2	2	2	2	2	2
Presentation	Y	Y	Y	Y						
General conversation	Y	Y	Y	Y	Y	Y	Y	Y	Y	Y
Coursework option							✓	✓		

Table 1.1 (cont)

	MEG F	H	NEAB F	H	NICCEA F	H	London F	H	WJEC F	H
Writing Time allowed (minutes)	50	60	40	60	45	45	30	50	45	60
Weighting	25%	25%	25%	25%	25%	25%	25%	25%	25%	25%
Coursework option	✓	✓	✓	✓			✓	✓	✓	✓

Key: FT=Foundation Tier HT=Higher Tier RT=recorded tape ✓=option available
Y=yes, a requirement

▶ **SEG** The scheme for the Southern Examining Group (SEG) is very different from those above. The SEG GCSE is modular in structure. Each module lasts about 15 weeks, is topic based and covers all four Attainment Targets. Assessment is through a mixture of coursework, end of module tests and a final examination covering all four modules. Table 1.2 illustrates the structure of the SEG GCSE.

Table 1.2 The SEG GCSE

	When and how assessed	Listening	Speaking	Reading	Writing	Total
Module 1 Contact with a German-speaking country	Year 10 by February Coursework Tasks set by SEG Teacher assessed	5% RT 3 test pieces	5% Candidate records a presentation	5% 3 test pieces		15%
Module 2 Organizing a visit to a German-speaking country	Year 10 June End of module test Tasks set and marked by SEG	10% RT FT 20 mins HT 20 mins		10% FT 30 mins HT 30 mins		20%
Module 3 Holidays and travel	Year 11 December Coursework Tasks set by SEG Teacher assessed		5% Candidate records a presentation		10% FT 2 pieces of work (a) 30 words (b) 100–120 words HT 2 pieces of work each 100–120 words	15%
Module 4 The young person in society	Year 11 June Final exam Exam set and marked by SEG (covers all 4 modules)	10% RT 20 mins	15% 1 role-play General conversation: FT 5 mins HT 8 mins	10% FT 30 mins HT 30 mins	15% FT 30 mins 1 task 80 words HT 30 mins 1 task 120 words	50%
Total		25%	25%	25%	25%	100%

In Modules 2 and 4 candidates may attempt *either* Foundation Tier *or* Higher Tier. In Modules 1 and 3 there is a range of assessments at both tiers which candidates may attempt according to their abilities.

Chapter 1 GCSE and Key Stage 4 German

▷ **Short courses** MEG, NEAB, London and WJEC offer short courses similar to those described above but which do not cover all the National Curriculum Areas of Experience. The content of the examination is based on two of the Areas of Experience: B 'Personal and social life' and D 'The world of work'. The type of tasks you will have to learn to do and the tests are the same as for the full courses, but you do not have to cover as wide a range of topics and contexts. Some groups offer these short courses in combination with another short course such as Business Studies to make a full GCSE. If you are interested in any of these courses you should contact the examining group concerned for further information.

▷ **IGCSE** The International GCSE is an examination developed by the University of Cambridge Local Examinations Syndicate in co-operation with international schools and education officials from different parts of the world. If you live in the United Kingdom and you do not attend an international school, you will not be able to follow a course leading to the IGCSE.

The IGCSE follows the same aims as the GCSE and there are many areas that are common to the IGCSE and the GCSE. Although this book concentrates on the GCSE, it will also help you with the IGCSE.

There are some important differences, however, which relate to the options and the grades.

There are seven grades (A–G). There is no grade A*. There are sections of the examination to test listening, reading, speaking and writing. The examination has two levels – Core and Extended – and you have to decide before the examination which level to enter. There are then only two possibilities:

1 **Core**
Students opting for the Core can gain grades C–G only. They must sit the following papers:

Paper 1 Listening – Sections 1 and 2 (30 minutes)	33⅓%
Paper 2 Reading and directed writing – Sections 1 and 2 (1¼ hours)	33⅓%
Paper 3 or 5 Speaking (15 minutes)	33⅓%

2 **Extended**
Students opting for the Extended curriculum can gain grades A–G. They must sit the following papers:

Paper 1 Listening – Sections 1, 2 and 3 (45 minutes)	25%
Paper 2 Reading and directed writing – Sections 1, 2 and 3 (2¼ hrs.)	25%
Paper 4 Continuous writing (1¼ hrs.)	25%
Paper 3 or 5 Speaking (15 minutes)	25%

Paper 5 is coursework with school-based assessment and may not be offered by all centres.

In general, the Core is like the GCSE Foundation Tier and the Extended is like the GCSE Foundation Tier and Higher Tier combined.

All the questions are written in German and all the answers are to be written in German; as with the GCSE the emphasis is very much on **communication.**

▷ **Grades** As we have seen, if you do Foundation Tier you can gain grades G–C. If you do not do well enough for grade G, you will be unclassified and receive no certificate. If you do Higher Tier, you can gain grades D–A*, but if you do not do well enough for a grade D you, too, will be unclassified and receive no certificate. It is, therefore, of the utmost importance that you are entered for the correct tier and you should discuss this with your teacher. If you very narrowly miss grade D at Higher Tier you may be given a grade E. You should check the regulations of the group for which you are studying if you are in any doubt.

Grades are awarded using a points system, which is common to all the groups offering GCSE German. Your marks for each part of the examination (listening, reading, speaking and writing) are converted to a number of points and totalled. The total number of points is converted to a grade on the scale common to all examining groups. How many marks you have to achieve to gain a certain number of points is determined by an awards committee with reference to the overall quality of candidates' work. Each individual examining group has its own committee, which will be composed of senior examiners and officials from the examining group. The points available in each of the four language skills (listening, speaking, reading and writing) is shown in Table 1.3:

Table 1.3 Points available in each of the four language skills

Grades	Points available at Higher Tier	Points available at Foundation Tier
A*	8	
A	7	
B	6	
C	5	5
D	4	4
E	3	3
F		2
G		1

You should note that it is not possible to gain more than five points in a Foundation Tier component. At Foundation Tier the maximum number of points you can gain is 20 (4×5). Hence the maximum grade is C (see Table 1.4). You also cannot be awarded one or two points at Higher Tier. If you obtain a mark less than that needed for three points at Higher Tier you will gain no points and be deemed to be inappropriately entered for the Higher Tier in that component.

The conversion of points to final grades is shown in Table 1.4:

Table 1.4 The conversion of points to grades

Grade	Points
U	0–1
G	2–5
F	6–9
E	10–13
D	14–17
C	18–21
B	22–25
A	26–29
A*	30–32

Each board also has an appeals procedure to enable those candidates who have serious reason to think that they have not achieved the grade they deserve to have their marks looked at again. All the groups go to the utmost trouble to ensure that marking is fair to everyone. They all have systems to deal with candidates who miss a grade by a very small number of marks, who are handicapped in any way or who are ill on the day of the examination.

▷ Addresses of the exam groups

London
EDEXCEL Foundation (formerly ULEAC)
Stewart House, 32 Russell Square, London, WC1B 5DN
Tel: 0171 331 4000
Fax: 0171 331 4044

MEG
Midland Examining Group
1 Hills Road, Cambridge, CB1 2EU
Tel: 01223 553311
Fax: 01223 460278

NEAB
Northern Examinations and Assessment Board
31–33 Springfield Avenue, Harrogate, North Yorkshire, HG1 2HW
Tel: 01423 840015
Fax: 01423 523678

NICCEA
Northern Ireland Council for the Curriculum, Examinations and Assessment
Clarendon Dock, Clarendon Road, Belfast, BT1 3BG
Tel: 01232 261200
Fax: 01232 261234

SEG
Southern Examining Group
Stag Hill House, Guildford, Surrey, GU2 5XJ
Tel: 01483 506506
Fax: 01483 300152

WJEC
Welsh Joint Education Committee
245 Western Avenue, Cardiff, CF5 2YX
Tel: 01222 265000
Fax: 01222 575994

IGCSE
International General Certificate of Secondary Education
University of Cambridge Local Examinations Syndicate, 1 Hills Road, Cambridge, CB1 2EU
Tel: 01223 553311
Fax: 01223 460278

Chapter 2

Examination techniques

GETTING STARTED

As we have already established in Chapter 1, the GCSE examinations in German test the four language skills or Attainment Targets separately. In this section we look at ways of preparing yourself for tests in these skills. Here we shall concentrate on the more **general** techniques you can apply to each skill, leaving more detailed consideration to later chapters. We also look at a few techniques which are important in the **exam room** itself.

WHAT YOU NEED TO KNOW

▷ **Preparation**

Although the four skills are tested separately, they are very closely linked in real life. This means that any work you do to improve *one*, such as listening techniques, will also have a positive 'spin-off' effect on the other three.

Vocabulary-learning is a chore, but it is a necessary part of your preparation. Make sure you begin early and learn gradually, remembering to test yourself as you learn. Chapter 3 will help you to work your way through the topic areas you have to study in depth.

Grammar is an integral part of any language. Although the emphasis in the GCSE examination is less academic than in previous examinations, the more accurate you are, the higher the marks you will gain. Again, be methodical:

▶ Go over exercises you have done in class, do them again and see if you can improve on your earlier performances.
▶ Use the grammar section in Chapter 14 of this book.
▶ Draw up a practical checklist for use before and during the examination (see Chapter 15).

Working with a friend can often be a helpful change from working on your own. This is especially important for speaking and vocabulary work.

Listening

At first sight **Listening** is a difficult skill to practise on your own, but there is still plenty you can do. In the chapters on listening (Chapters 4 and 5) we go into detail about some of the things you can do, but here are some brief points as an introduction:

▶ There is an increasing number of language programmes on radio and television. Watch them whenever you can. Make recordings, where that is possible, so that you can listen to them again, but check copyright procedures. You will need to check details yourself, because the series and times of transmission are constantly changing.
▶ Most courses now have cassettes to accompany them, so make sure you hear them at school. You may be able to borrow listening material from your teacher. The cassette that goes with this book will also give you valuable practice in listening.
▶ Depending on where you live, you may be able to pick up **German** radio stations. Of course, if you have satellite or cable television, you will have access to German programmes.

The 'A step further' section at the end of Chapter 5 gives you a range of practical ways in which you can develop your listening skills.

Reading

Reading is probably the easiest skill to revise, because there is plenty of material available. At GCSE you are required to read a wide range of texts in different styles, so the more you read, the better. Chapters 6 and 7 cover reading in detail, but here are some introductory points:

7

- Make full use of your school textbook. It will no doubt contain much reading material, and the more modern courses provide an excellent range of texts suitable for GCSE. Re-read articles you have read and note down any vocabulary you do not know, without looking it up. This is an invaluable step on the way to learning vocabulary.
- There are some interesting readers in schools and libraries. Find out what there is and take advantage of what is 'on the doorstep'. There are also short magazines especially designed for foreign-language learners. Stanley Thornes Publishers Ltd, Ellenborough House, Wellington Street, Cheltenham, Gloucestershire, GL50 1YW (telephone 01242 228888) is an invaluable source of magazines, readers and puzzle books.

The 'A step further' section at the end of Chapter 7 gives you lots of practical suggestions for developing your reading skills.

Speaking

Preparations for **speaking** are dealt with in depth in Chapters 8, 9 and 10, but you should bear the following considerations in mind:

- The topic lists and language tasks in Chapter 3 will provide you with a lot of essential material for the speaking tests. Make sure you know what tests you have to do and which topic areas they cover, and try to anticipate likely activities for role-plays and probable areas for discussion.
- Stock up on key expressions, especially for the role-plays, e.g. *Ich möchte..., Was kostet das? Wie komme ich am besten...?*
- Get used to the sound of your own voice, because most of the speaking tests will be recorded.
- Get as much practice as you can with your teacher, friends – and anyone who speaks German!
- Use your textbook fully and cover all the examples it provides.

The 'A step further' sections at the end of Chapters 9 and 10 give you a large number of practical suggestions for developing your speaking skills.

Writing

Grammar and spelling will be important in **writing** tests, but the main thing is to **get the message across**. The more accurate you are, though, the more marks you will gain, especially at Higher Tier.

- Go over exercises done in class. Try them again.
- Try the exercises in this book. Check the answers and note the examiners' comments on student answers.
- Work your way through your course book again.
- Use the grammar section in this book (Chapter 14) to help you.

Writing is covered in detail in Chapters 11, 12 and 13 and the 'A step further' section contains further suggestions for developing your writing skills.

▷ Hints on the use of dictionaries

As we have seen, you are permitted the use of a dictionary in certain parts of the examination. In general you will be allowed a dictionary throughout the reading and writing examination. You may use a dictionary during any reading time you are given for the listening examination before the tape recording is played, but not during the test itself. You will also be allowed to use a dictionary during the time you are given to prepare the role-plays before you go into your speaking test. If you are doing course work outside the classroom you will obviously be able to have access to a dictionary if you wish, but if the course work is done in class you may or may not have a dictionary depending on the examination group's exact regulations. All the groups have slightly different rules, so it is as well to check what they are.

The use of a dictionary can be a great help to you both in revision and preparation for the examination, as well as in the examination room itself. If you are able to use a dictionary confidently, it will obviously help with understanding of written material as well as in your own writing, but may also be useful when preparing for the speaking test.

However, you must learn to use a dictionary. It is not an ability that you are born with! While a dictionary can be a useful tool, if used correctly, it can also cause problems, if misused. Hopefully, you will have plenty of opportunity to practise using dictionaries in class. Here are some of the many pitfalls in the use of a dictionary that you should guard against:

- Dictionaries usually list alternative meanings for one word. You must make sure you choose the correct one for the **context**. For instance, if you look up the word 'change' you will find many alternatives, depending on what you mean by it; *sich umziehen, verändern, wechseln* are just three of the verbs. Two of the nouns might be: *das Kleingeld* or *die Veränderung*.
- If you simply look words up and string them together you will end up with nonsense. For example, 'I like beans on toast' could become *Ich ähnlich Bohnen auf Gesundheit*! This would be totally meaningless to a German speaker, even a sympathetic one!
- You will find many different abbreviations in dictionaries. This can lead to misunderstandings about genders, plurals and whether words are nouns, verbs and so on. For instance, *m* usually means 'masculine', i.e. a noun that is a *der* word – *der Mann, der Wald* etc. The abbreviation *f* usually means 'feminine', i.e. a noun that is a *die* word. Hence *See m=der See*, **the lake**, but *See f=die See*, **the sea**.
- If you are using the dictionary to prepare a speaking exercise or test, you must be able to correctly pronounce the German you find. You will need to practise reading aloud to be able to do this well.
- If you want to look words up in a dictionary, you must be able to spell reasonably well first, otherwise you won't know where to look! This applies to looking things up from English to German as well as from German to English.

You must practise using a dictionary if you are to become proficient in its use. It is not within the scope of this book to teach you how to use a dictionary, but here are some useful things to remember:

- When looking up a word, read through all the alternatives given and select the most appropriate for the context from the examples.
- Having selected the German word you want from the alternatives given, look it up again in the German–English section and see what it translates back as.
- The general structure of the German language is simply different from that of English, so you cannot translate word for word. For example, the German for 'How are you?' is *Wie geht's?* A word for word translation would give, *Wie bist du?*, which is wrong. A word for word translation of *Wie geht's?* would give 'How does it go?' or 'How goes it?', which is not really what we say in English.
- If you find abbreviations you do not understand, look them up in the key.

It is vital that you do not rely on the dictionary. The dictionary is not a substitute for learning vocabulary. In all the tests you will have limited time and it is paramount that you do not waste time through overuse of the dictionary. You must regard the dictionary as an aid or tool, like a rubber or ruler, which you may also have in the examination. It is not a substitute for thorough learning and preparation.

▶ In the examination

Most of what is said here refers to **written** examinations. We consider **oral** techniques in the chapters 8–10.

Memory aids

Don't forget to use mnemonics, tables, key aids and checklists which you have developed during your preparation for the written examinations. Once you have been told you can start, make a quick note of your 'supports' before you start answering the questions.

Read the questions carefully

Make sure that you answer *all* parts of the question, and that you cover *all* the tasks. This applies to *all four skills*! Don't forget to turn the last page over if there is a question on the back.

Presentation

Whatever people may say to the contrary, a tidy, well-presented script which is easy on the eye and easy to read DOES create a favourable impression on examiners. It may not mean that they will award you more marks, but it will certainly do you no harm, and if an examiner **cannot** read clearly what you have written, then he or she cannot award marks!

Timing

Timing is critical. First make sure you know exactly how long you have for each test. You will have been working to timed exercises in your preparation for the examination, so you should have a clear idea of how long you will need for a particular exercise. Make sure you distribute your time in the examination wisely so that you don't spend too long on one question and then have to rush things at the end. You should also include in your schedule enough time to *re-read* and to *check* your answers. This is especially important for the writing tests, but is still important for the other skills. In the chapters on writing there are suggestions for drawing up your own grammar checklist and using it in the examination.

Planning answers

- In the writing papers, especially at Higher Tier, you will need to plan carefully what to write. You can do this by making notes of key vocabulary, structures and idioms, *before* you write your answer.
- You will have to keep to fairly strict word limits, and in some cases the space provided for your answer will not allow you to write much, e.g. in the case of postcards.
- You must also remember that you have to cover *all* the tasks, so you have to leave yourself words and room to do this.
- At both Foundation and Higher Tiers you will be attempting to 'show off' what you know, so it's a great help to jot down a few **interesting** items of vocabulary and some idioms before you start writing your actual answer.

Answer all the questions

There may be occasions when you are genuinely stuck on a particular question, but do not waste time over it. Write yourself a note of the question number and go on to the next question. Don't forget to come back to the unanswered question later, though.

There are always clues to help you overcome a word you do not understand:

- Look at the **other words** in the sentence and try to work out a possible meaning.
- See if there is another **German** word you know which is like the word giving you trouble, e.g. *Warteraum* is likely to have a connection with *warten*, *Spielplatz* with *spielen*.
- There may be an **English** word similar to the German word.

If all else fails, then don't just leave a blank space – make a sensible reply which seems possible, or tick a box if that is what the exercise requires. Remember, you never lose out by 'having a go'.

Re-read and check

Use time at the end of the exam wisely. Make sure you have in fact covered all you were required to.

Now you are ready to move on to Chapter 3 and to start getting down to the real work. Work your way thoroughly through the book and persevere. It will be worth it. *Good luck*!

Chapter 3

Subject content: Areas of Experience and exam topics

GETTING STARTED

As we have seen, the different examining groups have all produced differing yet similar syllabuses. A great deal of detail is available to teachers and students as to what exactly you must know and be able to do for the examination. Indeed, a glance at any of the syllabus booklets may make you think that there is too much! In this chapter we summarise some of the main tasks you will be set.

We start by considering some important expressions you will meet throughout the book and in your lessons. We pay particular attention to Areas of Experience and topics. Language tasks, grammar and vocabulary are also considered.

WHAT YOU NEED TO KNOW

▷ **Key terms** *Areas of Experience*

The National Curriculum specifies five Areas of Experience within which teaching and learning of modern foreign languages must take place. The GCSE examinations aim to assess candidates' learning within the context of these five Areas of Experience. They are:

A Everyday activities
B Personal and social life
C The world around us
D The world of work
E The international world

These five Areas of Experience are common to all the examination groups.

Topics

The Areas of Experience are subdivided into topics. The number and exact name of the topics varies from examining group to examining group, but they are all broadly similar. Table 3.1 shows how each examining group divides up the Areas of Experience.

Table 3.1 Areas of Experience and topics

	MEG	NEAB	NICCEA	London	WJEC
A Everyday activities	Language of the classroom Home life School routine Eating and drinking Health and fitness	Language of the classroom School Home life Media Health and fitness Food	Home and school life Food and drink Shopping Eating out	Life at home Food and drink Health and fitness School	Language of the classroom Home life and school Food, health and fitness
B Personal and social life	Self, family and friends House and home Personal relationships	Self, family and friends Free time, holidays and special occasions	Self, family and friends Health Holidays and leisure	Myself, family and friends Free time and social activities	Self, family and personal relationships Free time and social activities

11

Table 3.1 (*cont*)

	MEG	NEAB	NICCEA	London	WJEC
B Personal and social life	Free time and social activities Festivals and special occasions Holidays: getting around Accommodation	Personal relationships and social activities Arranging a meeting or activity Leisure and entertainment	Celebrations and special occasions		Holidays and special occasions
C The world around us	Home town and geographical surroundings Shopping Public services Natural environment Weather Finding the way Meeting people Places and customs Travel and transport	Home town, local environment and customs Finding the way Shopping Public services Getting around	House and home Town and countryside Getting around Weather	Home town and local area The environment and society	Home town and local area Natural and made environments People, places and customs
D The world of work	Further education and training Future career plans Employment and unemployment Communication Language at work	Further education and training Careers and employment Advertising and publicity Communication	Services to the public Occupations and places of work Future plans and career	Further education and work Language and communication in the workplace	Further education and training Careers and employment Language and communication in the workplace
E The international world	Tourism and travel abroad Life in other countries (e.g. customs) World events and issues (e.g. poverty, environment, war)	Life in other countries/ communities Tourism Accommodation The wider world	Travel and tourism Life in countries or communities in which German is spoken Caring for the environment	Travel at home and abroad World events and issues	Tourism at home and abroad Life in other countries and communities World events and issues

As we have already seen the SEG course is organised in a different way. Coverage of the Areas of Experience and any related topics takes place within the context of the four modules (see page 3). The Areas of Experience are exactly the same but topics from a range of areas appear in each module. Modules 1, 2 and 3 cover the five areas between them and Module 4 covers all five. Table 3.2 shows which topics appear in each module and how they relate to the Areas of Experience.

Table 3.2 Areas of Experience and topics in the SEG modular course

	Module 1	Module 2	Module 3	Module 4
A Everyday activities	Daily routine School Well-being Courtesies and conversational skills	Food and drink Getting help in an emergency	Health and welfare	School Health
B Personal social life	Personal details Family and pets	Finding a hotel room	Arranging to go out	Personal identity Personal relationships

Table 3.2 (cont)

	Module 1	Module 2	Module 3	Module 4
B Personal and social life	Interests Personal leisure pursuits	Going out for enjoyment Entertainments		
C The world around us	Home and local environment Local and leisure environment	Travel by bus Asking the way Money and banks Shopping for souvenirs and stamps	Travel and transport Public services Weather Sightseeing Directions Shopping	Spending money (fashion, shopping)
D The world of work	Personal details			Future plans At work
E The international world		Tourist information	Holidays and accommodation	The environment

No matter which examination you will be taking, you will have to cover work relating to all the Areas of Experience. The topics and tasks within them vary from group to group. Which Area of Experience a topic is covered in also varies and some topics and tasks may be required in more than one area. Although the schemes are different, the types of language task required are similar across all the boards.

▷ **Language tasks**

A comprehensive, but not exhaustive, list of things you will be expected to do is provided on pages 14 to 24, broken down by topic area. It may appear off-putting at first, but you will soon see that there are many things that you can do well already. The list will show you clearly what you need to learn. Keep referring back to it.

You need to work through the list systematically and check that you can perform all the tasks relevant to you and your tier of entry. Later in the book (Chapter 15) is a checklist on which you can record your progress. Note that there are two columns to show that you have tested yourself on two different occasions (it's no good learning something and then forgetting all about it!).

▷ **Grammar**

One of the main aims of the National Curriculum and the GCSE is to equip you to use language effectively for the purposes of **practical communication**. This means that you do not have to use perfect German to do well at speaking and writing, especially at Foundation Tier. However, the more accurate you are, the better you will communicate, so you must revise (or learn?) as much **grammar** as you can. To help you we have provided a breakdown of the grammar expected at Foundation and Higher Tier. There is also a separate grammar revision chapter with exercises at the end of the book (Chapter 14).

▷ **Vocabulary**

The examining groups provide lists of **vocabulary** that may be included in their tests. However, they reserve the right to include a certain percentage of words not included in their lists, but they are not allowed to test them. This means that you know exactly which words you have to learn. The vocabulary is listed by topic area in this chapter and in alphabetical order at the end of the book. Please remember that there is a considerable amount of overlap since some vocabulary may obviously be used in a variety of topics.

▷ **Communication**

The GCSE has, as its starting point, the need for people to be able to understand each other. Your aims are to be able to explain what you want to say or write, and to understand what **other people** say or write. So, at all stages, you should not be worried about making a mistake or two. The important thing is to be able to **get your message across** as well as you possibly can. No one is going to expect you to produce perfect German all the time, and you will be able to score very highly even if you do make some mistakes.

Dictionaries

All the examining groups allow the use of bilingual dictionaries (i.e. English–German, German–English) in various parts of the exam or in coursework assessments done under exam conditions. Details of each examining group's rules about this appear in the relevant chapters that follow. Remember, however, that there is an art to the use of a dictionary. Unless you know how to use it properly it will be of very little help to you, especially when working from English into German. In Chapter 2 there are further general hints about the use of dictionaries.

LANGUAGE TASKS BY TOPIC

Tasks are only mentioned once, but you may be required to do them in any appropriate topic. Topics may have slightly different names in the syllabuses of different examining groups, e.g. School=School life=School routine etc. Not all examining groups specify language tasks in this amount of detail, but you may assume that these are generally the sorts of task you will have to perform. Tasks have been grouped together under what are felt to be the most appropriate topic headings and according to where they appear in the examining groups' syllabuses, but individual examining groups may list them somewhat differently. Tasks are required for both tiers unless preceded by 'H', meaning that they are required at Higher Tier only. A general requirement at Higher Tier is that candidates should be able to cope with a degree of unpredictability and a wider range of potential problems. They should also be able to use and understand a wider range of vocabulary and structures, including some unfamiliar items, as well as discuss issues and give opinions. Higher Tier candidates should be able to give full descriptions and accounts.

Area of Experience A: Everyday activities

Language of the classroom, courtesies and conversation skills

You should be able to:

Learnt   Tested

- Greet and say goodbye to a German speaker.
- Ask how people are and express suitable feelings.
- Understand classroom instructions and make requests.
- Say whether or not you understand and ask for repetition and spellings.
- Ask someone to speak more slowly.
- Ask if someone speaks English or German.
- Say you speak German and how well.
- Ask whether others speak German and how well.
- Ask what things are in English or German and what they mean.
- Ask/state whether something is correct/incorrect.
- [H] Ask for explanations and pronunciation.
- Say if you agree/disagree and ask others.

School

You should be able to exchange information and opinions about:

Learnt   Tested

- Your school/college and its facilities.
- The type, size and location of your school and its buildings.
- Daily routines: when school begins and ends, how many lessons there are and how long they last, break times and lunch times, homework.

Area of Experience A: Everyday activities 15

- ▶ How you travel to and from school.
- ▶ Your school year and holidays.
- ▶ The subjects studied and your preferences.
- ▶ Clubs, sports, trips and other activities.
- ▶ Your progress at school.
- ▶ School meals.
- [H] ▶ Other types of school, making comparisons.
- ▶ The disadvantages/advantages of mixed schools/colleges.
- ▶ School rules.

Home life

You should be able to discuss where and under what conditions you and others live. In particular you should be able to do the following:

Learnt Tested

- ▶ Say whether you live in a house, flat etc. and ask others the same.
- ▶ Describe your house, flat etc. and its location.
- ▶ Find out about and give details of rooms, garage, garden etc. as appropriate.
- ▶ Mention or enquire about the essential pieces of furniture, amenities, services etc.
- ▶ Say what jobs you do around the home and whether you like or dislike them.
- [H] ▶ Discuss how much other members of your family help at home.
- ▶ Offer and ask for help with household tasks.
- ▶ Ask and say where places and things are in the house.
- ▶ Say you need and ask others if they need soap, toothpaste, towel etc. and ask about taking a bath/shower.
- ▶ Describe daily routines at home on working days and weekends.
- ▶ Give and ask for information about meals and meal times.
- [H] ▶ Express opinions about typical meals, meal times and eating habits.
- ▶ Talk about pocket money and how it is earnt/spent.
- [H] ▶ Discuss the responsibilities of running a home and compare your home to others.

Media

You should be able to:

Learnt Tested

- ▶ Understand simple information about television programmes, films, radio, music and performers.
- ▶ State which programmes, films, music or performers you have recently seen or heard.

- ▶ Express simple opinions about television and radio programmes, films, books, magazines and music. ☐ ☐
- ▶ Ask permission to use the telephone, radio or watch television. ☐ ☐
- [H] ▶ Understand and narrate plots/themes of books, television/radio programmes, films and simple news items. ☐ ☐
- ▶ Ask for and give opinions about newspapers, magazines, books, television and radio programmes, music and performers and give reasons. ☐ ☐

Health and fitness, well-being

General

           Learnt Tested

- ▶ State how you feel (well, ill, better, hot, cold, tired). ☐ ☐
- ▶ Ask others how they feel. ☐ ☐
- ▶ Refer to parts of the body where you are in pain or discomfort. ☐ ☐
- ▶ Call for help. ☐ ☐
- ▶ Warn about danger. ☐ ☐
- ▶ Say if you have any allergies. ☐ ☐
- [H] ▶ Discuss healthy and unhealthy lifestyles. ☐ ☐

Illness and injury

- ▶ Report minor ailments (e.g. temperature, cold, sunburn). ☐ ☐
- ▶ Say you have lost a filling. ☐ ☐
- ▶ Ask for items in a chemist's and ask if they have anything for a particular ailment. ☐ ☐
- ▶ Respond to an enquiry as to how long an ailment or symptom has persisted. ☐ ☐
- ▶ Say you would like to see a doctor or a dentist. ☐ ☐
- [H] ▶ Make an appointment to see a doctor, dentist or chemist. ☐ ☐
- ▶ Report injuries. ☐ ☐
- ▶ Deal with contact with the medical services. ☐ ☐
- ▶ Say whether you take medicine regularly and, if so, what. ☐ ☐
- [H] ▶ Ask advice about medicines and understand instructions about them. ☐ ☐
- ▶ Tell others about medical facilities and surgery hours. ☐ ☐
- ▶ Say if you are insured. ☐ ☐

Accident

- [H] ▶ Describe an accident and say if anyone is hurt or injured and how. ☐ ☐
- ▶ Report that there has been an accident. ☐ ☐
- ▶ Ask or say whether it is serious. ☐ ☐
- ▶ Ask or advise someone to telephone for the police, doctor, ambulance or fire brigade. ☐ ☐

Area of Experience B: Personal and social life   17

Food and drink

General

Learnt   Tested

▶ Discuss your likes, dislikes and preferences and those of others. ☐ ☐

▶ Discuss your typical meals, meal times and eating habits. ☐ ☐

▶ Buy food and drink (see also Shopping). ☐ ☐

▶ Explain what a dish is or contains. ☐ ☐

[H] ▶ Discuss dietary requirements and the preparation of specific dishes. ☐ ☐

Café, restaurant and other public places

▶ Attract the attention of the waiter/waitress. ☐ ☐

▶ Order a drink or snack. ☐ ☐

▶ Order a meal. ☐ ☐

▶ Ask for a particular fixed price menu. ☐ ☐

[H] ▶ Say how many there are in your group. ☐ ☐

▶ Ask for a table (for a certain number) and generally make enquiries about seating and state seating requirements or preferences. ☐ ☐

▶ Ask about the availability of certain dishes and drinks. ☐ ☐

▶ Ask the cost of dishes and drinks. ☐ ☐

▶ Ask for an explanation or description of something on the menu. ☐ ☐

▶ Express opinions about a meal or dish. ☐ ☐

[H] ▶ Express appreciation and pay compliments. ☐ ☐

▶ Make a specific complaint and give reasons. ☐ ☐

▶ Accept or reject suggestions. ☐ ☐

▶ Ask if the service charge is included. ☐ ☐

▶ Ask about the location of facilities (e.g. toilets, telephone). ☐ ☐

At home

▶ Ask about the time and place of meals. ☐ ☐

▶ Ask for food and table items (e.g. more, a little, fork, knife, salt, pepper etc.). ☐ ☐

▶ React to offers of food (accept, decline, apologise, express pleasure). ☐ ☐

▶ Express likes, dislikes and preferences. ☐ ☐

▶ Respond to a toast, e.g. *Prost*. ☐ ☐

▶ Area of Experience B: Personal and social life

Self, family and friends/personal relationships

You should be able to give information about yourself and others (e.g. members of your family or host family, friends) and seek information from others on the following points:

Learnt   Tested

▶ Names (including spellings). ☐ ☐

- ▸ Address (including spellings). ☐ ☐
- ▸ Telephone numbers. ☐ ☐
- ▸ Ages and birthdays. ☐ ☐
- ▸ Nationality. ☐ ☐
- ▸ General descriptions (including sex, marital status, physical appearance, character or disposition of yourself and others). ☐ ☐
- ▸ Occupations. ☐ ☐
- ▸ Pets. ☐ ☐
- ▸ How you get on with people. ☐ ☐
- ▸ Likes and dislikes (with regard to other people and other topic areas in the syllabus). ☐ ☐
- [H] ▸ Feelings about others. ☐ ☐

You should also be able to:

- ▸ Greet people and respond to greetings both formally and informally. ☐ ☐
- ▸ Make and understand introductions. ☐ ☐

Free time, leisure and entertainment, holidays and special occasions

Learnt Tested

- ▸ State your hobbies, leisure activities and interests. ☐ ☐
- ▸ Give simple opinions about hobbies, leisure activities and interests. ☐ ☐
- ▸ Ask about the hobbies and interests of other people. ☐ ☐
- [H] ▸ Discuss your interest and involvement in clubs or societies. ☐ ☐
- ▸ Agree or disagree with **other people's** opinions. ☐ ☐
- ▸ Describe and comment on the leisure facilities in your area. ☐ ☐
- ▸ Buy entry tickets for cinema, theatre, concert, swimming pool, sports centre, football match and leisure facilities. ☐ ☐
- ▸ Find out about the cost of seats or entry and about starting and finishing times. ☐ ☐
- ▸ Understand explanations of activities and invitations to participate. ☐ ☐
- ▸ Give explanations of activities and invite others to participate. ☐ ☐
- ▸ Describe recent holiday or leisure activities. ☐ ☐
- [H] ▸ Express and understand more detailed opinions about leisure activities. ☐ ☐
- ▸ Discuss preferences and alternatives for going out. ☐ ☐
- ▸ Give and ask for information about excursions and visits. ☐ ☐
- ▸ Discuss and express opinions about watching and participating in sporting events. ☐ ☐

Arranging a meeting, activity or to go out

Learnt Tested

- ▸ Make simple suggestions for going out. ☐ ☐

Area of Experience C: The world around us   19

- Invite someone to go out.
- Accept or decline an invitation.
- Ask about, suggest or confirm a time and place to meet.
- [H] Find out whether a particular activity or facility is available and discuss options.
- Negotiate arrangements for a meeting or activity.

▷ Area of Experience C: The world around us

Home town, local area and customs, people and places

You should be able to give information and simple opinions about your home town or village and surrounding areas, and seek information from others, with respect to:

Learnt Tested

- Location.
- Character.
- Amenities, attractions, features of interest.
- Population.
- Climate.
- Local history, customs, festivals etc.

You should also be able to:

- Understand weather predictions and descriptions and describe weather conditions.
- [H] Give weather predictions and understand forecasts.
- Understand and make comparisons between your home and a German-speaking country: towns, regions, climate and geographical features.
- Name parts of Germany, Austria and Switzerland or the UK you know, and talk about them.
- Understand references to countries where German is spoken.

Finding the way

You should be able to:

Learnt Tested

- Attract the attention of a passer-by.
- Ask or state where a place is.
- Ask how to get to a place.
- Ask or state if a place is near or far.
- Understand directions.
- Express thanks.
- [H] Ask for and give detailed directions to a specific place.

Shopping

You should be able to:

Learnt Tested

- Ask where specific shops are.
- Ask about opening and closing times.

- Ask for specific items mentioning colour, size, who it's for.
- Express the quantity required: weight, volume, container.
- Ask and understand about availability/non-availability.
- Understand the question 'Is that all?' and reply to it.
- Express opinions about clothes.
- Say you will/will not buy something.
- [H] Find specific goods and departments in a store.
- Discuss shopping habits, preferences and facilities.
- Give reasons for buying/not buying things.
- Return unsatisfactory goods giving reasons, and ask for a refund.
- Understand information about discounts, special offers, reductions and sales.

Public services

Post office
You should be able to:

Learnt Tested

- Ask where a post office or letter box is.
- State you would like to send letters/postcards to your home country and ask what it costs.
- Ask for stamps of particular values.
- Ask if there is a telephone nearby.
- [H] Ask about sending letters and postcards or parcels to a specific country or within the country.

Banks/currency exchange

- Say and understand numbers from 1–1000.
- Find out when banks are open.
- Exchange money or travellers' cheques.
- Enquire about rates of exchange.
- [H] Enquire about commission charges and the acceptability of eurocheques and credit cards.
- Ask for coins or notes of a particular denomination.

Lost property and theft

- Ask where a loss should be reported.
- Report loss stating what you have lost, when and where it was lost and describing the item (what it is made of, size, shape, colour, make, contents).
- [H] Report the theft of an item and give the above details.

Hire services
You should be able to:

- Obtain information about the hire of specific items (car, bicycle, wind surfing board, sun lounger etc.).
- Understand replies to the above and fill in a relevant form.

Cleaning and repairs

You should be able to:

▶ Find out where something can be cleaned/repaired. ☐ ☐

▶ Ask for something to be cleaned/repaired. ☐ ☐

▶ Find out when an item will be ready for collection. ☐ ☐

▶ Find out the cost. ☐ ☐

Getting around

You should be able to:

Learnt   Tested

▶ Give and understand information on how to get into town (means of transport, directions). ☐ ☐

▶ Ask if there is a bus, tram, train to a particular place. ☐ ☐

▶ Understand simple signs and notices. ☐ ☐

▶ Ask about the location of facilities: bus/tram stops, platforms, ticket machines, toilets etc. ☐ ☐

▶ Buy tickets, stating: destination, single or return, class, day of travel. ☐ ☐

▶ Ask and tell someone about times of departure and arrival. ☐ ☐

▶ Respond to ticket checks. ☐ ☐

[H] ▶ Ask for and give information about travel by public transport. ☐ ☐

▶ Make arrangements for travel by public transport. ☐ ☐

▶ Discuss common forms of transport. ☐ ☐

▶ Buy fuel and obtain services at a petrol station. ☐ ☐

▶ Report the location and basic details of a breakdown. ☐ ☐

▶ Report the location and basic details of an accident. ☐ ☐

▶ **Area of Experience D: The world of work**

Further education and training

You should be able to:

Learnt   Tested

▶ Understand, ask and give information about future plans. ☐ ☐

▶ Say what subjects/courses are available and state preferences. ☐ ☐

[H] ▶ Understand information about different types of further education and training. ☐ ☐

▶ Understand and discuss others' descriptions of their education/training. ☐ ☐

Careers and employment

Learnt   Tested

▶ Give information about travel to and from work. ☐ ☐

▶ Understand and say that someone is unemployed. ☐ ☐

▶ Understand details about and discuss jobs, weekend jobs and work experience. ☐ ☐

22 Chapter 3 Subject content: Areas of Experience and exam topics

- Say if you have a spare time job and give details. ☐ ☐
- Give simple opinions about jobs. ☐ ☐
- State occupation of self and family. ☐ ☐
- Understand the names of common occupations. ☐ ☐
- [H] Ask about and give reasons for future study choices. ☐ ☐
- Express hopes for the future and describe plans. ☐ ☐
- Enquire about the availability of work. ☐ ☐
- Ask about people's occupations. ☐ ☐
- Discuss the advantages and disadvantages of different occupations. ☐ ☐

Language and communication in the workplace

You should be able to:

Learnt Tested

- Ask for and give telephone numbers. ☐ ☐
- Answer the telephone. ☐ ☐
- Make telephone calls and ask to speak to someone in particular. ☐ ☐
- Take or leave a telephone message: name, numbers, time to ring back. ☐ ☐
- Ask about delivery and collection times. ☐ ☐
- [H] Make arrangements to contact and be contacted by telephone, fax or E-mail. ☐ ☐
- Obtain coins or a phone card. ☐ ☐
- Describe local industries and employment opportunities. ☐ ☐

Advertising and publicity

You should be able to do the following:

Learnt Tested

- Understand simple opinions about particular advertisements. ☐ ☐
- Understand simple publicity about leisure activities and public events. ☐ ☐
- [H] Give opinions about particular advertisements. ☐ ☐

▷ Area of Experience E: The international world

Life in other countries/communities

You should be able to:

Learnt Tested

- Understand money including written and printed prices. ☐ ☐
- [H] Discuss typical foods and how to prepare them. ☐ ☐
- Discuss important social conventions such as forms of address and eating habits. ☐ ☐

Tourism at home and abroad

You should be able to:

Learnt Tested

- Talk and ask about holidays in general with regard to: ☐ ☐

Area of Experience E: The international world

		Learnt	Tested
	– where you normally spend your holidays.	☐	☐
	– how long they last.	☐	☐
	– with whom you go.	☐	☐
	– what you do.	☐	☐
▶	Understand others giving this information.	☐	☐
▶	Describe a previous holiday, saying:		
	– where you went.	☐	☐
	– how you went.	☐	☐
	– with whom you went.	☐	☐
	– for how long.	☐	☐
	– where you stayed.	☐	☐
	– what the weather was like.	☐	☐
	– what you saw and did.	☐	☐
	– what your general impressions were.	☐	☐
▶	Give simple opinions about excursions and places of interest.	☐	☐
H ▶	Ask for and give information about excursions: cost, time, location.	☐	☐
▶	Ask for tourist information, e.g. maps, town plans, brochures, prospectuses etc.	☐	☐
▶	Discuss past and future holidays.	☐	☐
▶	Express preferences and opinions about types of holiday, excursions and places of interest.	☐	☐

Accommodation

With reference to hotels, youth hostels and campsites you should be able to:

		Learnt	Tested
▶	Ask if accommodation is available.	☐	☐
▶	Say when you require accommodation and for how long.	☐	☐
▶	Say what sort of accommodation you require.	☐	☐
▶	Ask the cost per person per night.	☐	☐
▶	Accept or reject the accommodation offered.	☐	☐
▶	Identify yourself.	☐	☐
▶	Ask about your key and the location of your room.	☐	☐
▶	Ask where facilities are: dining room, toilet, showers, bathroom, games room.	☐	☐
▶	Ask about meal times.	☐	☐
▶	Say you would like to pay.	☐	☐
▶	Make reservations.	☐	☐
H ▶	Ask for and understand information about rules and regulations.	☐	☐
▶	Arrange accommodation for other people.	☐	☐
▶	Ask about reduced rates for students/groups.	☐	☐

- Make complaints, request alternative accommodation and give reasons.
- Give and ask about opinions and preferences regarding types of holiday accommodation.

The wider world, world events and issues

Learnt Tested

- Understand the names of countries and nationalities commonly encountered.
- Understand the discussion of current issues and events of general news value and of interest to 16-year-old students, e.g. conservation, nature, lifestyles.
- Express a reaction to such items.
- [H] Discuss environmental issues of personal interest, e.g. pollution, recycling, nature, equal opportunities.
- Understand opinions and information about global issues.
- Discuss any part of a German-speaking country you know about and describe it (e.g. its history, geography, current and future developments).
- Give opinions about religion, politics and society.
- Compare UK lifestyles with German-speaking countries.

VOCABULARY BY TOPIC AREAS

Here the vocabulary required by the examining groups is broken down by **topic area**. This should help you in preparing for **all four skills** in German. The lists within each topic area are often alphabetical, **but not always**. Especially with shorter lists, it sometimes makes more sense to arrange the words in clusters of related items. You can of course find a **full** alphabetical listing of vocabulary in Chapter 16.

This list goes beyond the requirements of Foundation Tier. You should learn vocabulary with reference to the language tasks you need to do.

See page 230 for a key to symbols and abbreviations used in the vocabulary lists.

▷ Self, family and friends, personal relationships

Name
der Name (-n) *name*
der Nachname/Familienname (-n) *surname*
der Vorname (-n) *first name*
  heißen *to be called*
  nennen *to call*
  schreiben *to write*
  in Ordnung *all right*
  Herr, Frau, Fräulein *Mr, Mrs, Miss*
  (e.g. Herr Kaupsch) (e.g. Mr Kaupsch)
die Unterschrift (-en) *signature*
der Mädchenname (-n) *maiden name*
  buchstabieren *to spell*
  sich schreiben *to write one's name*
  unterschreiben *to sign*

  letters of the alphabet

Address and telephone
die Adresse (-n) *address*
die Allee (-n) *avenue*
die Anschrift (-en) *address*

der Wohnort (-e) *place of residence*
die Straße (Str.) (-n) *street*
die (Haus)Nummer (Nr.) (-n) *(house) number*
das Dorf (¨-er) *village*
die Stadt (¨-e) *town*
das Land (¨-er) *country, state (of Germany)*
der Park (-s) *park*
die Parkanlage (-n) *park*
der Platz (¨-e) *place, square*
die Postleitzahl (-en) *postal code*
der Weg (-e) *way, path*

der Brief (-e) *letter*
der Briefumschlag (¨-e) *envelope*
der Umschlag (¨-e) *envelope*
das Telefon *telephone*
das Telefonbuch (¨-er) *telephone directory*
die Telefonnummer (-n) *telephone number*
die Vorwahlnummer (-n) *dialling (STD) code*

  wohnen *to live*

Nationality
der Ausweis (-e) *identity card*
der Paß (¨-sse) *passport*

der Staat (-en) *state*
die Postleitzahl (-en) *postcode*

England/Deutschland/Österreich
  England/Germany/Austria
die Schweiz *Switzerland*
die Bundesrepublik *the Federal Republic*
  (and other countries as appropriate)
  Belgien – Belgier/-in – belgisch *Belgium – Belgian (person) – Belgian*
  Frankreich – Franzose/Französin – französisch *France –Frenchman/woman – French*
  Holland (die Niederlande) – Holländer/-in – holländisch *Holland (The Netherlands) – Dutchman/woman – Dutch*
  Italien – Italiener/-in – italienisch *Italy – Italian (person) – Italian*
  Spanien – Spanier/-in – spanisch *Spain – Spaniard – Spanish*
die (Vereinigten) Staaten/Amerika – Amerikaner/-in – amerikanisch *the (United) States/America – American*
das Ausland *abroad*
der Ausländer (-) *foreigner (male)*
die Ausländerin (-nen) *foreigner (female)*
  names of other major countries, nationalities, adjectives

Age
geboren am . . . *born on*
  (e.g. ich bin am zweiten Juni geboren) *(e.g. I was born on the 2nd of June)*
geboren in . . . *born in*
  (e.g. ich bin in London geboren) *(e.g. I was born in London)*
der Geburtstag (-e) *birthday*
das Geburtsdatum (Geburtsdaten) *date of birth*
der Geburtsort (-e) *place of birth*
das Alter (-) *age*
das Jahr (-e) *year*
der Monat (-e) *month*
  (e.g. 4 Monate alt) *(e.g. 4 months old)*
das Kind (-er) *child*
der/die Erwachsene (-n) *adult*
jung *young*
alt *old*

People
der Mann (¨-er) *man*
  Herren (H) *Gentlemen (on toilet door)*
der Junge (-n) *boy*
die Dame (-n) *lady*
  Damen (D) *Ladies (on toilet door)*
die Frau (-en) *woman*
das Mädchen (-) *girl*
die Staatsangehörigkeit (-en) *nationality*
der Engländer (-)/die Engländerin (-nen)
  Englishman/woman
  englisch *English*
der/die Deutsche (-n) *German (person)*
ein Deutscher/eine Deutsche *a German*
  deutsch *German*
  (and other nationalities as appropriate)
  von wo *where from, from where*
das Land (¨-er) *country, state (of Germany)*
der/die Jugendliche (-n) *young person, youth*

ein Jugendlicher/eine Jugendliche *a youth*
das Geschlecht (-er) *sex*
  männlich *male*
  weiblich *female*
  verlobt *engaged*
der/die Verlobte *fiancé(e)*
  verheiratet *married*
  ledig *single*
  geschieden *separated, divorced*
die Witwe (-n) *widow*
der Witwer (-) *widower*
der Österreicher (-)/die Österreicherin (-nen) *Austrian (person)*
  österreichisch *Austrian*
der Schweizer (-)/die Schweizerin (-nen) *Swiss (person)*
die Heimat *home country*

Describing people
was für (ein/eine) . . .? *what kind of (a) . . .?*
wie (e.g. Wie ist dein Bruder?) *how, what, what is . . . like (e.g. what is your brother like?)*
  freundlich *friendly*
  unfreundlich *unfriendly*
  lustig *happy, cheerful, funny*
  faul *lazy*
  fleißig *hard-working*
  intelligent *intelligent*
  dumm *stupid*
  dick *fat*
  schlank *slim*
der Bart (¨-e) *beard*
der Schnurrbart (¨-e) *moustache*
die Brille (-n) *glasses*
das Auge (-n) *eye*
das Haar (-e) *hair*
  ähnlich *similar, like*
  reich *rich*
  arm *poor*
  allein *alone*
  böse *angry, naughty*
  glücklich *happy*
  aussehen (sep.) *to look (like)*
  lachen *to laugh*
  erkennen *to recognise*
die Angst (¨-e) *worry*
  sympathisch *friendly, nice*
  ehrlich *sincere, honest*
  nervös *nervous*
  gut/schlecht gelaunt *good/bad tempered*
  neugierig *inquisitive*
  blöd *stupid*
  doof *stupid*
  dünn *thin*
  (sich) erinnern *to remind (remember)*
  lebhaft *lively*
  frech *cheeky*
  schüchtern *shy*
  nicht leiden können *not to like/to hate*
  sich vertragen *to get on with each other*
die Religion (-en) *religion*
  katholisch *Catholic*
  evangelisch *Protestant*
  (and other religions as appropriate)

The family and relatives
die Familie (-n) *family*
die Eltern *parents*

der Vater (⁻) *father*
Vati *dad*
die Mutter (⁻) *mother*
Mutti *mum*
der Mann (⁻er) *man, husband*
die Frau (-en) *woman, wife*
das Kind (-er) *child*
das Einzelkind (-er) *only child*
das Baby (-s) *baby*
der Junge (-n) *boy*
das Mädchen (-) *girl*
der Sohn (⁻e) *son*
die Tochter (⁻) *daughter*
die Geschwister *brothers and sisters*
der Bruder (⁻) *brother*
die Schwester (-n) *sister*
die Großeltern *grandparents*
der Großvater (⁻) *grandfather*
der Opa/Opi *grandad*
die Großmutter (⁻) *grandmother*
die Oma/Omi *granny*
der Onkel (-) *uncle*
die Tante (-n) *aunt*
der Neffe (-n) *nephew*
die Nichte (-n) *niece*
der/die Verwandte (-n) *relative*
der Vetter (-n) *cousin (male)*
die Kusine (-n) *cousin (female)*
der/die Älteste (-n) *the eldest*
der Freund (-e) *friend (male)*
die Freundin (-nen) *friend (female)*
der Mensch (-en) *person*
die Person (-en) *person*
die Leute *people*
heiraten *to marry, get married*
der Cousin (-s)/die Cousine (-n) *cousin*
der Ehemann (⁻er) *husband*
die Ehefrau (-en) *wife*
das Ehepaar (-e) *married couple*
der Schwager (⁻) *brother-in-law*
die Schwägerin (-nen) *sister-in-law*
Schwieger- *-in-law*
der Schwiegersohn (⁻e) *son-in-law*

▶ House, home and local environment, life at home

House
das Haus (⁻er) *house*
das Doppelhaus (⁻er) *semi-detached house*
das Einfamilienhaus (⁻er) *detached house*
das Reihenhaus (⁻er) *terraced house*
der Bungalow (-s) *bungalow*
der Bauernhof (⁻e) *farm*
die Wohnung (-en) *home, flat*
der Block (-s) *block (of flats)*
das Gebäude (-) *building*
die (Haus)Tür (-en) *(front) door*
der Schlüssel (-) *key*
klingeln *to ring*
klopfen *to knock*
schellen *to ring*
der Garten (⁻) *garden*
der Hof (⁻e) *yard, courtyard*
die Garage (-n) *garage*
die Scheune (-n) *barn, shed*

die Mauer (-n) *wall (outside)*
die Etage (-n) *floor, storey*
der Stock *floor, storey*
das Stockwerk (-e) *floor, storey*
die Terrasse (-n) *terrace*

alt *old*
bequem *comfortable*
groß *big, large*
klein *small, little*
modern *modern*
nett *nice, pleasant*
neu *new*
oben *upstairs, above*
unten *downstairs, below*

bauen *to build*
anbauen *(sep.) to extend*
kaufen *to buy*
verkaufen *to sell*
mieten *to rent*
wechseln *to change*
wohnen *to live*

Rooms
das Badezimmer (-) *bathroom*
das Eßzimmer (-) *dining room*
die Küche (-n) *kitchen*
das Schlafzimmer (-) *bedroom*
das Wohnzimmer (-) *living room*
der Raum (⁻e) *room*
das Zimmer (-) *room*
der Flur (-e) *hall*
der Keller (-) *cellar*
die Toilette (-n) *toilet*
das Klo (-s)/WC (-s) *toilet*
die Treppe (-n) *stairs, staircase*
der Lift (-e or -s) *lift*
die Decke (-n) *ceiling*
der Fahrstuhl (⁻e) *lift*
der (Fuß)Boden (⁻) *floor*
die Wand (⁻e) *wall (inside)*
das Fenster (-) *window*
das Dach (⁻er) *roof*
der Dachboden (⁻) *attic, loft*
das Erdgeschoß (-sse) *ground floor*
das Obergeschoß (-sse) *upper floor*
das Hochhaus (⁻er) *block of flats*
die Aussicht (-en) *view*
die Lage (-n) *situation, location*
die (Zentral)Heizung *(central) heating*
gemütlich *cosy*
möbliert *furnished*
(an)streichen *to paint*
tapezieren *to wallpaper*
heizen *to heat*
umziehen *(sep.) to move*

Bedroom
das Schlafzimmer (-) *bedroom*

das Bett (-en) *bed*
das Bettzeug *bedclothes, bedding*
die Kleiderbürste (-n) *clothes brush*
der Kleiderschrank (⁻e) *wardrobe*
die Kommode (-n) *chest of drawers*
die Lampe (-n) *lamp*
der Sessel (-) *armchair*
der Stuhl (⁻e) *chair*

der Tisch (-e) *table*
der Wecker (-) *alarm clock*

   eigen *own*
   teilen *to share*

die (Bett)Decke (-n) *bedcover, bedspread, quilt*
das Bettlaken (-) *sheet*
das Bettuch (¨er) *sheet*
die Bettwäsche *bedding, bed linen*
das Federbett (-en) *quilt, duvet*
die Gardine (-n) *curtain*
der Vorhang (¨e) *curtain*
das Rollo (-s) *blind, roller blind*
das Kopfkissen (-) *pillow*
der Nachttisch (-e) *bedside table*
der Spiegel (-) *mirror*
die Steppdecke (-n) *down quilt*
der Teppich (-e) *carpet*

Kitchen

die Küche (-n) *kitchen*

die Gabel (-n) *fork*
der Löffel (-) *spoon*
das Messer (-) *knife*
das Glas (¨er) *glass*
die Tasse (-n) *cup*
der Teller (-) *plate*
der Apparat (-e) *electrical appliance, machine*
der Herd (-e) *cooker, stove*
der Kühlschrank (¨e) *refrigerator*
die Waschmaschine (-n) *washing machine*
die Kaffeekanne (-n) *coffee pot*
die Teekanne (-n) *teapot*
das Licht (-er) *light*
das Wasser *water*
der (Wasser)Hahn (¨e) *tap*
der Knopf (¨e) *button, knob*

   drücken *to press*
   anmachen (*sep.*) *to turn/switch on*
   ausmachen (*sep.*) *to turn/switch off*
   ziehen *to pull*

das Geschirr (-e) *crockery*
der (Koch)Topf (¨e) *saucepan*
der Ofen (¨) *oven, stove*
die Schale (-n) *bowl, dish; scales*
die Schüssel (-n) *container, dish*
der (Abfall)Eimer (-) *(rubbish) bin*
   Elektro- *electric-*
   elektrisch *electric*
die Spülmaschine (-n) *dishwasher*
der Staubsauger (-) *vacuum cleaner*
die Tiefkühltruhe (-n) *freezer*
das Spülmittel (-) *washing-up liquid*
das Waschpulver (-) *washing powder*

   an sein (das Licht ist an) *to be on (the light is on)*
   ausschalten (*sep.*) *to switch/turn off*
   einschalten (*sep.*) *to switch/turn on*
   wegwerfen (*sep.*) *to throw away*

Bathroom

das Badezimmer (-) *bathroom*

das Bad (¨er) *bath, bathroom*
die Badewanne (-n) *bath (tub)*
die Dusche (-n) *shower*
das (Haar)Shampoo (-s) *shampoo*
das Toilettenpapier *toilet paper*
das Wasser *water*

die Zahnbürste (-n) *toothbrush*
die Zahnpasta *toothpaste*
das Handtuch (¨er) *hand towel*
der Rasierapparat (-e) *electric shaver*
das Waschbecken (-) *washbasin, sink*
der (Wasch)Lappen (-) *flannel, cloth*

Dining room, living room

das Eßzimmer (-) *dining room*
das Wohnzimmer (-) *living room*

der Aschenbecher (-) *ashtray*
das Bild (-er) *picture*
das Foto (-s) *photo*
der Fernsehapparat (-e) *TV set*
der Fernseher (-) *TV set*
der Kamin (-e) *fireplace*
die Stereoanlage (-n) *stereo*
die Uhr (-en) *clock*
die Pflanze (-n) *plant*
die Möbel (*plural*) *furniture*
das Sofa (-s) *sofa*
der Tisch (-e) *table*
die Elektrizität *electricity*
das Gas *gas*
das Holz (¨er) *wood, log*
der Knopf (¨e) *button, knob*
das Öl *oil*
die Steckdose (-n) *electric socket*
das Wasser *water*
das Kissen (-) *cushion*
das Regal (-e) *shelf*
das Tablett (-s) *tray*
die Tischdecke (-n) *table-cloth*
die Birne (-n) *(light) bulb*
die Kerze (-n) *candle*
die Kohle (-n) *coal*
der Schalter (-) *switch*
der Stecker (-) *(electric) plug*
der Strom *current, electricity*

Daily routine

   abräumen (*sep.*) *to clear up/away*
   anhaben (*sep.*) *to wear, have on*
   aufmachen (*sep.*) *to open*
   aufräumen (*sep.*) *to tidy (up), clear up*
   aufstehen (*sep.*) *to get up*
   aufwachen (*sep.*) *to wake up*
   bringen *to bring*
   decken *to cover, lay (table)*
   duschen *to shower*
   essen *to eat*
   fernsehen (*sep.*) *to watch television*
   frühstücken *to have breakfast*
   kochen *to cook*
   lassen *to leave, let*
   machen *to do, make*
   nähen *to sew*
   nehmen *to take*
   öffnen *to open*
   schlafen *to sleep*
   schließen *to close, shut*
   sich (hin)setzen *to sit down*
   sitzen *to sit*
   sprechen *to speak, talk*
   stehen *to stand*
   tragen *to carry, wear*
   trinken *to drink*
   tun *to do, make*

verlassen *to leave*
vorbereiten *to prepare*
(sich) waschen *to wash*
zumachen (*sep.*) *to close, shut*
das Frühstück *breakfast*
das Mittagessen (-) *lunch*
das Abendbrot *tea, evening meal (cold)*
das Abendessen (-) *tea, evening meal (hot)*
zu Abend/Mittag essen *to have tea/lunch*
auf die Toilette gehen *to go to the toilet*
Platz nehmen *to sit down*
sauber machen *to clean*
abspülen (*sep.*) *to wash up*
(ab)trocknen (*sep.*) *to dry (up)*
abwaschen (*sep.*) *to wash up*
(sich) anziehen (*sep.*) *to put on/get dressed*
(sich) ausziehen (*sep.*) *to take off/get undressed*
benutzen *to use*
betreten *to enter*
(sich) bewegen *to move*
bügeln *to iron*
einschlafen (*sep.*) *to go to sleep*
erwachen *to wake up (yourself)*
fallen (lassen) *to fall/drop*
füllen *to fill*
leeren *to empty*
plaudern *to chat, talk*
putzen *to clean*
reden *to talk*
stricken *to knit*
sich umziehen (*sep.*) *to change (clothes)*
wecken *to wake up (someone else)*
die Wäsche *washing (clothes)*

Garden
der Garten (¨) *garden*
die Gartenarbeit *gardening*
die Blume (-n) *flower*
der (Obst) Baum (¨e) *(fruit) tree*
das Gemüse (-) *vegetables*
das Gras (¨er) *grass*
die Pflanze (-n) *plant*
(be)gießen *to water (flowers)*
mähen *to mow*
wachsen *to grow*
die Gartengeräte (*plural*) *garden tools*
der Rasen (-) *lawn*

Animals and pets
das (Haus)Tier (-e) *animal/(pet)*
der (Gold)Fisch (-e) *(gold)fish*
der Hamster (-) *hamster*
der Hund (-e) *dog*
die Katze (-n) *cat*
die Maus (¨e) *mouse*
das Kaninchen (-) *rabbit*
das Meerschweinchen (-) *guinea pig*
die Schildkröte (-n) *tortoise*
das Pferd (-e) *horse*
das Insekt (-en) *insect*
die Kuh (¨e) *cow*
das Schaf (-e) *sheep*
das Schwein (-e) *pig*
der Vogel (¨) *bird*
der Wellensittich (-e) *budgerigar*
die Ente (-n) *duck*
die Fliege (-n) *fly*
die Gans (¨e) *goose*

das Huhn (¨er) *chicken*
das Vieh *cattle*
das Futter *food (for animals*
der Käfig (-e) *cage*
die Hütte (-n) *hut, shed*
der Stall (¨e) *stable*
bellen *to bark*
fressen *to eat (of animals)*
füttern *to feed (animals)*

Surroundings – urban/town
die Stadt (¨e) *town*

die Altstadt (¨e) *old town*
die Ampel (-n) *traffic lights*
die Autobahn (-en) *motorway*
der Bahnhof (¨e) *station*
die Bank (-en) *bank*
die Baustelle(-n) *building site*
die Brücke (-n) *bridge*
die Bundesstraße (-n) *A road*
die Burg (-en) *castle*
der Bürgersteig (-e) *pavement*
das Büro (-s) *office*
die Bushaltestelle (-n) *bus stop*
der Dom (-e) *cathedral*
die Fabrik(-en) *factory*
der Fernsprecher (-) *telephone*
der Flughafen (¨) *airport*
der Fluß (¨sse) *river*
das Freibad (¨er) *open-air swimming pool*
der Fußgänger (-) *pedestrian*
die Fußgängerzone (-n) *pedestrian zone*
die Gefahr (-en) *danger*
das Hallenbad (¨er) *indoor swimming pool*
die Hauptstadt (¨e) *capital*
die Industrie (-n) *industry*
das Kino (-s) *cinema*
die Kirche (-n) *church*
die Klinik (-en) *clinic*
das Krankenhaus (¨er) *hospital*
die Kreuzung (-en) *crossing, junction*
der Lärm (*no plural*) *noise, din*
der Markt (¨e) *market*
der Marktplatz (¨e) *market square, market place*
das Museum (Museen) *museum*
in der Nähe (von) *near, nearby*
die Neustadt (¨e) *new town*
der Park (-s) *park*
die Parkanlage (-n) *park*
das Parkhaus (¨er) *multi-storey car park*
der Parkplatz (¨e) *car park, parking space*
die Polizei *police*
die Polizeiwache (-n) *police station*
die Post *post office*
das Postamt (¨er) *post office*
das Rathaus (¨er) *town hall*
das Schloß (¨sser) *castle*
das Schwimmbad (¨er) *indoor swimming pool*
das Stadion (Stadien) *stadium*
die Stadtmauer (-n) *town/city wall*
die Stadmitte *town centre*
das Stadtzentrum (-tren) *town centre*
der Stein (-e) *stone*
die Stelle (-n) *place*
die Tankstelle (-n) *petrol station*
das Theater (-) *theatre*
die Treppe (-n) *stairs, staircase, steps*
der Turm (¨e) *tower*

der Verkehr (no plural) traffic
das Verkehrsbüro (¨-er) tourist office
der Bahnübergang (¨-e) level crossing
der Bezirk (-e) area, district
die Bibliothek (-en) library
der Briefkasten (¨-) letter box
das Denkmal (¨-er) monument
der Einwohner (-) inhabitant
das Gebiet (-e) area, region
die Gegend (-en) region, neighbourhood
der Kreis (-e) district, ward, constituency
der Ort (-e) place
das Reisebüro (-s) travel agent's
die Rolltreppe (-n) escalator
der Stadtbummel (-) town walk, wander in town
der Stadtteil (-e) part of town
der Vorort (-e) suburb
der Wegweiser (-) traffic sign
der Zebrastreifen (-) zebra crossing

    frisch gestrichen wet paint
    irgendwo somewhere or other
    bummeln to wander (e.g. when window-shopping)
    schützen to protect

Surroundings – rural/countryside

das Land the country
    auf dem Lande in the country

der Berg (-e) mountain
das Dorf (¨-er) village
das Feld (-er) field
der Fluß (¨-sse) river
der Hügel (-) hill
die Insel (-n) island
die Landstraße (-n) country road
das Meer (-e) sea
    in der Nähe (von) near, nearby
der Sand (no plural) sand
der See (-n) lake
die See sea
der Strand (¨-e) beach
das Tal (¨-er) valley
der Wald (¨-er) wood, forest
die Wiese (-n) field, meadow
der Bach (¨-e) stream
der Bahnübergang (¨-e) level crossing
der Forst (-e) forest
das Gebirge (-) mountains, mountain range
der Gipfel (-) summit
die Küste (-n) coast
die Landschaft (-en) scenery, countryside
die Natur Nature
die Talsperre (-n) dam
die Überfahrt (-en) crossing (of sea)
das Ufer (-) bank (of river)

Describing surroundings
Useful adjectives and other words.

    angenehm pleasant, attractive
    freundlich friendly
    gefährlich dangerous
    hoch high, tall
    nett nice, pleasant
    ruhig quiet, peaceful
    sauber clean
    schmutzig dirty

    still quiet, peaceful
    tief deep
    unfreundlich unfriendly

    gegenüber opposite
    links left, on the left
    rechts right, on the right
    fließen to flow
    flach flat
    steil steep

▶ School

Buildings

die Gesamtschule (-n) comprehensive school
die Grundschule (-n) primary school
das Gymnasium (-ien) grammar school
die Hauptschule (-n) secondary modern school
der Kindergarten (¨-) kindergarten, nursery
die Realschule (-n) type of secondary school between Gymnasium and Hauptschule
die Schule (-n) school

das Klassenzimmer (-) classroom
das Lehrerzimmer (-) staffroom
die Werkstatt (¨-en) workshop, studio
der Hof (¨-e) yard, playground
der Schulhof (¨-e) schoolyard, playground
die Aula (Aulen) hall
die Bibliothek (-en) library
das (Sprach)Labor (-s) (language) laboratory
die Turnhalle (-n) sports hall, gym

School routine

die Antwort (-en) answer
die Aufgabe (-n) exercise
das Beispiel (-e) example
der Bleistift (-e) pencil
das Buch (¨-er) book
der Direktor (-en)/die Direktorin (-nen) headteacher
die Ferien holidays
die Frage (-n) question
    eine Frage stellen to ask a question
der Füller (-) fountain pen
die Hausaufgabe (-n) homework
der Hausmeister (-) caretaker
das Heft (-e) exercise book
die Klasse (-n) class
die Klassenarbeit (-en) class test
der Klassenlehrer (-) class teacher (male)
die Klassenlehrerin (-nen) class teacher (female)
der Kugelschreiber (-) ball-point pen
der Kuli (-s) biro, pen
der Lehrer (-)/die Lehrerin (-nen) teacher
die Mappe (-n) briefcase, schoolbag
die Mittagspause (-n) lunch/midday break
die Frühstückspause (-n) morning break
die Pause (-n) break
    Oster- Easter . . .
das Papier (-e) paper
das Schulbuch (¨-er) school book
der Schulfreund (-e) schoolfriend (male)
die Schulfreundin (-nen) schoolfriend (female)
die Schultasche (-n) schoolbag
der Schüler (-)/die Schülerin (-nen) (school) pupil
das Semester (-) term
    Sommer- Summer . . .
die Stunde (-n) lesson, hour
der Stundenplan (¨-e) timetable
    Weihnachts- Christmas . . .

streng *strict*
sehen *to see*
ansehen (*sep.*) *to look at*
antworten *to answer*
aufpassen (*sep.*) *to pay attention*
beantworten *to answer (someone or something)*
besuchen *to visit, attend*
fehlen *to be away/missing*
fragen *to ask*
lernen *to learn*
lesen *to read*
studieren *to study*
vergessen *to forget*
zuhören (*sep.*) *to listen*
das Blatt ("-er) *piece/sheet of paper*
der Filzstift (-e) *felt-tip pen*
das Klassenbuch ("-er) *class book/form book*
der Klassensprecher (-) *class representative (male)*
die Klassensprecherin (-nen) *class representative (female)*
die Kreide (-n) *chalk*
der Lappen (-) *cloth*
das Lineal (-e) *ruler*
das Pult (-e) *desk*
der Radiergummi (-s) *rubber, eraser*
der Schwamm ("-e) *sponge*
die Strafarbeit (-en) *punishment, extrawork*
die Tafel (-n) *blackboard*
der Unterricht (*no plural*) *lessons*
der Zettel (-) *note*
das Zeugnis (-sse) *report*

hitzefrei *day off because of heat*
schulfrei *day off school*
abschreiben (*sep.*) *to copy*
ausfallen (*sep.*) *to be cancelled (e.g. due to teacher absence)*
bestrafen *to punish*
erfahren *to learn, experience*
loben *to praise*
nachsitzen (*sep.*) *to stay in/behind*
rechnen *to calculate*
schwänzen *to skip, skive, play truant*
versetzen *to transfer*

Subjects, marks, examinations, future plans
Biologie *Biology*
Chemie *Chemistry*
der Computer (-) *computer*
Deutsch *German*
Englisch *English*
Erdkunde *Geography*
das Fach ("-er) *school subject*
Französisch *French*
die Fremdsprache (-n) *foreign language*
Geographie *Geography*
Geschichte *History*
Handarbeit *Handiwork (e.g. Sewing, Needlework)*
Wirtschaftskunde *Commerce*
Werken *Woodwork and Metalwork*
Informatik *Technology/IT/Computer Studies*
Kochen *Cookery, Domestic Science*
Kunst *Art*
Latein *Latin*
Maschineschreiben *Typing*
Mathe(matik) *Maths, Mathematics*
Musik *Music*
Nähen *Sewing/Needlework*
Naturwissenschaft (-en) *Science*
Physik *Physics*
Religion *Religion*
Spanisch *Spanish*
Sport *Sport/Games*
Sport treiben *to do sport*
Technik *Technical Studies*
technisches Zeichnen *Technical Drawing*
Turnen *PE/PT/Gym*

ausgezeichnet *excellent*
gut *good*
interessant *interesting*
langweilig *boring*
leicht *easy*
mangelhaft *weak, lacking, unsatisfactory*
schwierig *difficult*
sehr gut *very good*
ziemlich gut *quite good*
das Lieblingsfach ("-er) *favourite subject*
die Note (-n) *mark*
Eins (bis) Sechs *1 to 6 (German school grades)*
die Abschlußprüfung (-en) *school-leaving examination*
die Prüfung (-en) *examination*
bestehen *to pass (an examination)*
durchfallen (*sep.*) *to fail (an examination)*
das Pflichtfach ("-er) *compulsory subject*
das Wahlfach ("-er) *optional subject*
das Abitur *Advanced Level examination*
die Oberstufe (-n) *sixth form*
die Leistung (-en) *performance, achievement*
die Berufsberatung (-en) *career guidance/advice*
die Fach(hoch)schule (-n) *technical college*
die Technische Hochschule (-n) *technical university*
der Lehrling (-e) *apprentice*
der Student (-en)/die Studentin (-nen) *student*
die Universität (-en) *university*
die Uni *university*

mündlich *oral*
schriftlich *written*
mogeln *to cheat*
sitzenbleiben (*sep.*) *to repeat a year, stay in the same class*

Occupations, employment and career
der Apotheker (-) *chemist, pharmacist*
die Arbeit (-en) *work*
der Arbeiter (-) *worker*
die Arbeitsstelle (-n) *job; place of work*
der Arzt ("-e) *doctor*
der Bäcker (-) *baker*
der Bauarbeiter (-) *builder, building worker*
{beim Bau arbeiten *to work in the building*
{auf dem Bau arbeiten *trade*
der Bauer (-n) *farmer*
der Beamte (-n) *official, civil servant*
der Beruf (-e) *profession*
der Briefträger (-) *postman*
das Büro (-s) *office*
der Busfahrer (-) *bus-driver*
der Chef (-s) *boss, head*
der Direktor (-en) *director, manager*
der Drogist (-en) *chemist*
der Elektriker (-) *electrician*
die Fabrik (-en) *factory*
der Fabrikarbeiter (-) *factory worker*
der Fahrer (-) *driver*
der Fleischer (-) *butcher*
der Friseur (-e)/der Frisör (-e) *hairdresser*

der Fußballspieler (-) *footballer*
die Industrie (-n) *industry*
der Kaufmann (¨er)/(die Kaufleute) *businessman*
der Kellner (-) *waiter*
der Koch (¨e) *cook*
die Konditorei (-en) *cake shop, confectioner's*
die Krankenschwester (-n) *nurse*
der Lehrer (-) *teacher*
der Lkw-Fahrer (-) *lorry-driver*
der Mechaniker (-) *mechanic*
der Metzger (-) *butcher*
der Musiker (-) *musician*
das Orchester (-) *orchestra*
der Pilot (-en) *pilot*
der Plan (¨e) *plan*
der Polizist (-en) *policeman*
das Postamt (¨er) *post office*
der Sekretär (-e) *secretary (male)*
die Sekretärin (-nen) *secretary (female)*
die Stewardeß (-essen) *stewardess*
der Sport (Sportarten) *sport*
das Theater (-) *theatre*
das Verkehrsbüro (-s) *tourist office*
der Zahnarzt (¨e) *dentist*
das Zimmermädchen (-) *chambermaid*

vielleicht *perhaps*
werden *to become*

der Angestellte (-n) *clerk*
der Arbeitgeber (-) *employer*
der Arbeitnehmer (-) *employee*
das Arbeitsamt (¨er) *employment office*
das Arbeitspraktikum (-praktika) *work experience*
der Betrieb (-e) *business, firm*
die Bundesbahn (-en) *Federal Railway*
bei der Bahn arbeiten *to work on the railways*
der Feuerwehrmann (¨er or -leute) *fireman*
die Firma (-en) *firm*
das Gehalt (¨er) *salary*
der Geschäftsmann (¨er or -leute) *businessman*
der Ingenieur (-e) *engineer*
der Lohn (¨e) *wage*
der Matrose (-n) *sailor*
das Reisebüro (-s) *travel agency*
der Rentner (-) *pensioner*
der Schaffner (-) *ticket collector*
der Schauspieler (-) *actor*
der Schiedsrichter (-) *referee*
der Soldat (-en) *soldier*
der Tierarzt (¨e) *vet*
der Verkäufer (-) *salesman*
das Werk (-e) *works, plant, factory*

arbeitslos *unemployed*
berufstätig *employed*
selbständig *independent, self-employed*

▷ **Free time and social activities**

Free time and hobbies
der Ausflug (¨e) *excursion, trip*
der Badeanzug (¨e) *swimsuit*
die Badehose (-n) *swimming trunks*
die Bademütze (-n) *swimming hat*
das Badetuch (¨er) *bath towel*
Badminton *badminton*
der Besuch (-e) *visit*
das Boot (-e) *boat*
der CD-Spieler (-) *CD player*

der Computer (-) *computer*
Federball *badminton*
das Fernsehen *television*
im Fernsehen *on television*
die Flöte (-n) *flute*
der (Foto)Apparat (-e) *camera*
die Freizeit *free time*
der Fußball (¨e) *football*
die Geige (-n) *violin*
die Gitarre (-n) *guitar*
der Handball (¨e) *handball*
die Hitparade *hit parade*
das Hobby (-s) *hobby*
das Instrument (-e) *instrument*
das Interesse (-n) *interest*
das Jogging *jogging*
die Karten (*plural*) *cards*
die Kassette (-n) *cassette*
der Kassettenrecorder (-) *cassette recorder*
das Klavier (-e) *piano*
die Langspielplatte (-n) *long-playing record, LP*
das Magazin (-e) *magazine*
die Mannschaft (-en) *team*
das Orchester (-) *orchestra*
das Picknick (-s or -e) *picnic*
die Platte (-n) *record*
der Plattenspieler (-) *record player*
die Popmusik *pop music*
das Programm (-e) *(TV) channel, (radio) station*
das Radio *radio*
im Radio *on the radio*
der Rucksack (¨e) *rucksack*
die Schallplatte (-n) *record*
der Schlager (-) *hit song*
das Schlagzeug (*no plural*) *drums*
die Sendung (-en) *(TV/radio) programme*
der Skilift (-e) *ski lift*
der Ski (-er) *ski*
der Skistock (¨e) *ski stick*
der Spaziergang (¨e) *walk*
der Sport *sport*
die Sportart (-en) *(kind of/type of) sport*
der Sportplatz (¨e) *sports field*
das Tennis *tennis*
das Tischtennis *table-tennis*
das Transistorradio (-s) *transistor radio*
die Trompete (-n) *trumpet*
der Verein (-e) *club*
Volleyball *volleyball*
die Wanderung (-en) *hike*
Wasserball *water polo*
das Windsurfen *windsurfing*
die Zeitschrift (-en) *magazine*
die Zeitung (-en) *newspaper*

anfangen (*sep.*) *to begin, start*
angeln *to fish*
aufhören (*sep.*) *to stop (doing something)*
ausgehen (*sep.*) *to go out*
baden *to swim*
beginnen *to begin, start*
fahren *to go, drive*
fernshen (*sep.*) *to watch television*
gucken *to look, watch*
hören *to hear, listen to*
joggen *to jog*
kleben *to stick*
knipsen *to take photographs*

laufen to run
nähen to sew
radfahren (sep.) to bike, cycle
reiten to ride (horse)
sammeln to collect
schauen to watch
schwimmen to swim
skifahren (sep.) to ski
spazierengehen (sep.) to go for a walk
spielen to play
springen to jump, dive
(sich) treffen to meet
treiben to do (sport)
wandern to hike
werfen to throw

fertig ready, finished
klassisch classical
laut loud
leise quiet
der Ansager (-)/die Ansagerin (-nen) (TV/radio) announcer
die Aufnahme (-n) recording, photograph
die Blaskapelle (-n) brass band
das Brett (-er) board, stage (slang)
das Dia (-s) slide (photographic)
im Freien in the open (air)
die Freizeitbeschäftigung (-en) hobby, leisure activity
die Illustrierte (-n) magazine
die Kapelle (-n) band
Leichtathletik gymnastics, athletics
die Messe (-n) fair
das Mitglied (-er) member
die Nachrichten (plural) news
die Nadel (-n) needle
das Netz (-e) net
der Pfadfinder (-) scout
die Reklame (-n) advertisement
der Rollschuh (-e) roller skate
der Roman (-e) novel (book)
das Ruderboot (-e) rowing boat
der Rundfunk (no plural) radio
die Sammlung (-en) collection
das Schach (no plural) chess
der Schläger (-) bat, raquet (tennis, cricket etc.)
Schlittschuh laufen to ice skate
das Segelboot (-e) yacht
die Seilbahn (-en) cable car
die Sendefolge (-n) episode (of series)
die Sendereihe (-n) series
das Taschenbuch (-̈er) paperback book
das Tonbandgerät (-e) tape recorder
das Tor (-e) goal
das Training (no plural) training
der Trainingsanzug (-̈e) tracksuit
der Umkleideraum (-̈e) changing room
das Videogerät (-e) video recorder
der Wegweiser (-) signpost

basteln to make things with your hands (e.g. models)
(sich) erkundigen to enquire
fangen to catch (fish/ball)
fotografieren to photograph
kegeln to bowl (e.g. tenpin)
klettern to climb
malen to paint
rennen to run
rudern to row
segeln to sail
senden to send, broadcast
stricken to knit
tauchen to dive
trainieren to train
(sich) trimmen to get fit

Entertainment
der Ausgang (-̈e) exit, way out
die Ausstellung (-en) exhibition
die Burg (-en) castle
der Club (-s) club
die Disco (-s) disco
die Diskothek (-en) discotheque
der Dokumentarfilm (-e) documentary (film)
der Eingang (-̈e) entrance
der Eintritt admission
das Eintrittsgeld (-er) entry cost/fee/price/ money
die Eintrittskarte (-n) (entrance) ticket
zu Ende sein to be over/finished, to end
das Endspiel (-e) final
der Fan (-s) fan, supporter
der Fanatiker (-) fanatic
der Film (-e) film
die Gruppe (-n) group
der Jugendklub (-s) youth club
die Karte (-n) card
die Kasse (-n) cash desk, box office
das Kino (-s) cinema
der Klub (-s) club
das Konzert (-e) concert
der Krimi (-s) thriller (TV/book), detective story
der Kriminalfilm (-e) thriller, detective story (TV/cinema)
das Museum (Museen) museum
der Notausgang (-̈e) emergency exit
der Platz (-̈e) place, seat
der Rang (-̈e) circle (in cinema, etc.)
die Reihe (-n) row (in cinema, etc.)
die Rundfahrt (-en) tour, round trip
der Sänger (-) singer (male)
die Sängerin (-nen) singer (female)
das Schauspiel (-e) play (in theatre)
das Schloß (-̈sser) castle
das Spiel (-e) play, game
das Stadion (Stadien) stadium
das Theater (-) theatre
das Theaterstück (-e) stage play
der Trickfilm (-e) cartoon
die Vorstellung (-en) performance, show
der Wildwestfilm (-e) western (film)
der Zoo (-s) zoo

besichtigen to visit
gewinnen to win
singen to sing
tanzen to dance
verlieren to lose

frei free (not engaged)
der Affe (-n) monkey, ape
die Aufführung (-en) performance
der Balkon (-s) balcony
die Besichtigung (-en) visit
die Bühne (-n) stage
die Bundesliga German football league
der Elefant (-en) elephant
das Ergebnis (-se) result
die Führung (-en) guided tour
die Garderobe (-n) cloakroom
der Jahrmarkt (-̈e) fair

die Kirmes (-sen) *fair*
die Komödie (-n) *comedy*
der Löwe (-n) *lion*
die Meisterschaft (-en) *championship*
das Parkett (-e) *stalls (cinema/theatre)*
der Pokal (-e) *cup (for sporting event)*
der Profi (-s) *professional*
der Punkt (-e) *point*
der Reiseführer (-) *guide (male)*
die Reiseführerin (-nen) *guide (female)*
der Reiseleiter (-) *guide (male)*
die Reiseleiterin (-nen) *guide (female)*
der Saal (Säle) *hall*
die Saison (-s) *season*
die Schlange (-n) *snake, queue*
   Schlange stehen *to queue*
der Tiger (-) *tiger*
der Treffpunkt (-e) *place to meet, meeting-place, rendezvous*
die Weltmeisterschaft (-en) *World Championship*
der Zuschauer (-) *spectator*

   ausverkauft *sold out*
   berühmt *famous*
   eins zu null (etc.) *one-nil (etc.) (score)*
   unentschieden *drawn (match)*
   beschließen *to decide*
   besorgen *to obtain*
   schießen *to shoot*

▶ **Travel and tourism**

Finding your way
die Ampel (-n) *traffic lights*
das Auto (-s) *car*
die Autobahn (-en) *motorway*
die Brücke (-n) *bridge*
die Bundesstraße (-n) *A road*
der Bus (-se) *bus*
das Dorf (¨er) *village*
die Ecke (-n) *corner*
   am/zum Ende *at the/to the end*
   entschuldigen Sie bitte! *excuse me please!*
das Fahrrad (¨er) *bicycle*
die Fahrt (-en) *journey, trip*
der Fluß (¨sse) *river*
   zu Fuß *on foot*
der Fußgänger (-) *pedestrian (male)*
die Fußgängerin (-nen) *pedestrian (female)*
die Hauptstraße (-n) *main street*
die Innenstadt (¨e) *town centre*
die Klassenfahrt (-en) *class trip, excursion*
das Krankenhaus (¨er) *hospital*
die Kreuzung (-en) *crossing*
die Landkarte (-n) *map*
die Landstraße (-n) *country road*
das Mofa (-s) *moped*
   in der Nähe (von) *near*
der Platz (¨e) *place, square*
die Post *post office*
das Postamt (¨er) *post office*
das Rad (¨er) *wheel, bicycle*
das Rathaus (¨er) *town hall*
der Reisebus (-se) *coach*
die Richtung (-en) *direction*
die Seite (-n) *side*
die Stadt (¨e) *town*
der Stadtplan (¨e) *town plan*
die Straße (-n) *street, road*
die Toiletten (*plural*) *toilets*
der Wagen (-) *car*
der Weg (-e) *way, path*
der Zug (¨e) *train*

   ander *other*
   breit *broad, wide*
   dieser *this*
   eng *narrow*
   fremd (sein) *(be a) stranger, (be) foreign*
   immer *always*
   nächst *next*
   spät *late*
   (nicht) weit (von) *(not) far (from)*
   erste/zweite/dritte (etc.) *first/second/third (etc.)*
   links *left, on the left*
   rechts *right, on the right*
   geradeaus *straight on*
   da *there*
   dahin *(to) there*
   dann *then*
   dort *there*
   dorthin *(to) there*
   drüben *over there*
   gleich *straight away, immediately*
   hier *here*
   hinauf *up*
   hinten *behind*
   hinüber *over*
   hinunter *down*
   an . . . vorbei *past*
   auf *on*
   außer *apart from, besides*
   bis zu . . . *as far as . . .*
   entlang *along*
   gegenüber *opposite*
   hinter *behind*
   neben *next to, by*
   über *over, above*
   um *around*
   unter *under, below*
   vor *in front of*
   zu *to*
   zwischen *between*
   wie komme ich (am besten) . . . ? *what's the (best) way . . . ?*

   abbiegen (*sep.*) *to turn off*
   fahren *to travel, go*
   finden *to find*
   folgen *to follow*
   gehen *to go (on foot)*
   kommen *to come*
   mitfahren (*sep.*) *to accompany, travel with (someone)*
   nehmen *to take*
die Nebenstraße (-n) *side road, minor road*
die Querstraße (-n) *junction road*
der Schülerlotse (-n) *lollipop person*
das Ufer (-) *bank (of river)*

   pünktlich *punctual*
   weg *away*

   dauern *to last*
   sich erkundigen *to enquire*
   überqueren *to cross*
   sich verfahren *to get lost (by car)*
   sich verirren *to get lost (on foot)*

sich verlaufen   to get lost (on foot)
verpassen   to miss (e.g. bus)

Getting around, travel by boat, bus, plane

die Abfahrt (-en)   departure
die Ankunft (¨e)   arrival
der Ausgang (¨e)   exit
die Auskunft (¨e)   information
der Ausstieg (-e)   exit (on bus/tram)
die Bahn (-en)   railway
der Bahnhof (¨e)   railway station
   Bhf   abbreviation of 'Bahnhof'
der Bahnsteig (-e)   platform
der Bus (-se)   bus
der Dampfer (-)   steam (boat)
die Deutsche Bundesbahn   German Railways
   DB   abbreviation for 'Deutsche Bundesbahn'
der D-Zug (¨e)   express, fast train
der Eilzug (¨e)   express, fast train
der Einstieg (-e)   entrance, way in (on bus/tram)
der Fahrer (-)   driver
der Fahrgast (¨e)   passenger
die Fahrkarte (-n)   ticket
der Fahrkartenschalter (-)   ticket office
der Fahrplan (¨e)   timetable
der Fahrschein (-e)   ticket
der Flughafen (¨)   airport
das Flugzeug (-e)   aeroplane
das Gleis (-e)   platform
die Haltestelle (-n)   stop (e.g. bus stop)
der Hauptbahnhof (¨e)   main railway station
   Hbf   abbreviation of 'Hauptbahnhof'
der Inter-City-Zug (¨e)   Inter-City train
der Kofferkuli (-s)   luggage trolley
der Krankenwagen (-)   ambulance
die Maschine (-n)   machine, locomotive
der Nahverkehrszug (¨e)   local train
der (Nicht)Raucher (-)   (non) smoker
die Nummer (-n)   number
der Passagier (-e)   passenger
die Reise (-n)   journey
der/die Reisende (-n)   traveller
die Richtung (-en)   direction
die Rückfahrkarte (-n)   return ticket
die S-Bahn (-en)   urban railway
der Schalter (-)   ticket office
das Schiff (-e)   ship
der Schnellzug (¨e)   fast train
der Speisewagen (-)   buffet car
die Station (-en)   station
die Straßenbahn (-en)   tram
das Taxi (-s)   taxi
der TEE-Zug (¨e)   Trans-European-Express (train)
die U-Bahn (-en)   underground
die Überfahrt (-en)   crossing (sea journey)
die Verspätung (-en)   delay
der Wagen (-)   car, coach (of train)
der Warteraum (¨e)   waiting room
der Wartesaal (-säle)   waiting room
der Zug (¨e)   train
der Zuschlag (¨e)   supplement

ab   from
an   to, on
direkt   direct, non-stop
einfach   single, simple
einmal/zweimal (etc.)   one/two (etc.)
hinten   behind, in the back

hin und zurück   return
langsam   slow, slowly
mitten   in the middle
schnell   quick
über (Frankfurt)   via (Frankfurt)
vorn(e)   in the front
werktags   workdays
wochentags   weekdays

abfahren (sep.)   to depart, leave
abfliegen (sep.)   to depart (of plane), take off
ankommen (sep.)   to arrive
aussteigen (sep.)   to get off/out
buchen   to book
einsteigen (sep.)   to get in/on
erreichen   to reach, arrive at, catch
festhalten (sep.)   to hold tight
kriegen   to get
landen   to land
nehmen   to take
reisen   to travel
reservieren   to reserve
rufen   to call
starten   to start
umsteigen (sep.)   to change
verlassen   to leave

der Abflug (¨e)   departure, take-off (of flight)
das Abteil (-e)   compartment
die Autofähre (-n)   car ferry
an Bord   on board
die Einzelkarte (-n)   single ticket
der Fahrausweis (-e)   travel pass, ticket
der Fahrpreis (-e)   price (of journey)
die Fähre (-n)   ferry
der Feiertag (-e)   holiday (e.g. Sunday, public holiday)
feiertags   on Sundays and public holidays
der Flug (¨e)   flight
die Gepäckannahme (-n)   left-luggage deposit
die Gepäckaufbewahrung (-en)   left-luggage office
die Gepäckausgabe (-n)   left-luggage collection area
das Gepäcknetz (-e)   luggage rack
der Hubschrauber (-)   helicopter
der Liegewagen (-)   couchette
die Linie (-n)   line, route
die Mehrfahrtenkarte (-n)   ticket valid for a number of journeys
das Reisebüro (-s)   travel agent's
der Schaffner (-)   ticket collector
der Schlafwagen (-)   sleeping car
das Schließfach (¨er)   left luggage locker
der Sicherheitsgurt (-e)   seat belt, safety strap
die Stewardeß (-ssen)   stewardess
der Treffpunkt (-e)   meeting point, rendezvous
die Verspätung (-en)   delay

erhältlich   available
gültig   valid
verspätet   delayed
zuschlagspflichtig   supplement payable

(sich) anschnallen (sep.)   to put on (one's) seat belt
dauern   to last
hinauslehnen (sep.)   to lean out
kontrollieren   to check (tickets, passports)
lösen   to buy (tickets)
melden   to report, announce
verkehren   to travel
verpassen   to miss (bus, train, etc.)
verreisen   to go on a long journey

Travel by road

Achtung! *beware! danger!*
die Ausfahrt (-en) *exit*
das Auto (-s) *car*
die Batterie (-n) *battery*
die Baustelle (-n) *building site, roadworks*
das Benzin (*no plural*) *petrol*
der Diesel (*no plural*) *diesel*
die Einbahnstraße (-n) *one-way road/street*
die Einfahrt (-en) *entry, entrance, drive*
das Fahrrad (¨er) *bicycle*
der Führerschein (-e) *driving licence*
Gas geben *to accelerate*
die Gefahr (-en) *danger*
der Lastkraftwagen (-) *lorry*
der Lkw (-s) *abbreviation for 'Lastkraftwagen'*
der Luftdruck *air pressure*
das Mofa (-s) *moped*
das Motorrad (¨er) *motorcycle*
Normal *2-star petrol*
der Notruf (-e) *emergency phone call*
das Öl (*no plural*) *oil*
das Parkhaus (¨er) *multi-storey car park*
der Parkplatz (¨e) *car park, parking space*
der Pkw (-s) *short for 'Personenkraftwagen': private car*
das Rad (¨er) *cycle, wheel*
das Rad/Hinterrad/Vorderrad (¨er) *wheel/back wheel/front wheel*
der Radfahrer (-) *cyclist*
der Rasthof (¨e) *service station*
der Rastplatz (¨e) *service area, parking area*
die Raststätte (-n) *service station*
der Reifen (-) *tyre*
der Reifendruck *tyre pressure*
die Reparatur (-en) *repair*
die Selbstbedienung/SB *self-service (SB=abbreviation)*
das Selbsttanken *self-service (petrol station)*
die Straße (-n) *street, road*
Super *4-star petrol*
die Tankstelle (-n) *petrol station*
die Umleitung (-en) *diversion*
die (grüne) Versicherungskarte (-n) *(green) insurance card*
die Vorfahrt *right of way, priority*
Vorsicht *care, precaution*
der Wagen (-) *car*
die Warnung (-en) *warning*
die Werkstatt (¨e) *garage (for repairs)*
die Zufahrt (-en) *access*

besetzt *taken, occupied, engaged (phone)*
frei *free*
gefährlich *dangerous*
gesperrt *closed (of road)*
gestattet *allowed*
kaputt *broken*
verboten *forbidden*
einordnen (*sep.*) *to order, get in lane*
erlauben *to allow*
freihalten (*sep.*) *to keep free*
nachsehen (*sep.*) *to look after/out for, to check (e.g. oil)*
parken *to park*
prüfen *to test, check*
radfahren (*sep.*) *to cycle*
reparieren *to repair*
tanken *to fill up (with petrol), to put petrol in*
volltanken *to fill the tank*
der Abschleppwagen (-) *breakdown vehicle*
Abstand halten *to keep a distance (from the car in front)*
per Anhalter fahren *to hitch-hike*
das Autobahndreieck (-e) *motorway merging point*
das Autobahnkreuz (-e) *motorway intersection*
die Autowäsche (-n) *car wash*
die Bremse (-n) *brake*
der Dienst (-e) *service*
der Durchgangsverkehr (*no plural*) *through traffic, all routes*
das Fahrzeug (-e) *vehicle*
der Fehler (-) *mistake*
die Gebühr (-en) *fee*
gebührenpflichtig *fee payable*
die Geldstrafe (-n) *fine*
die Geschwindigkeit (-en) *speed*
die Hochgarage (-n) *multi-storey car park*
die Höchstgeschwindigkeit (-en) *speed limit*
der Kofferraum (¨e) *boot (of car)*
der Lieferwagen (-) *van*
der Motor (-en) *engine, motor*
die Panne (-n) *puncture, breakdown*
der Parkschein (-e) *parking ticket*
die Parkuhr (-en) *parking meter*
das Parkverbot (*no plural*) *no parking*
die Reifenpanne (-n) *puncture*
der Roller (-) *scooter*
der Scheinwerfer (-) *spotlight, headlamp*
Schritt fahren *to drive at walking pace*
der Stau (-s) *queue, jam (on roads)*
das Steuerrad (¨er) *steering wheel*
die Strafe (-n) *punishment, fine*
die Tiefgarage (-n) *underground garage*
der Unfall (¨e) *accident*
die Verkehrsstauung (-en) *traffic jam*
die Versicherung (-en) *insurance*
die Windschutzscheibe (-n) *windscreen*
der Zusammenstoß (¨sse) *crash, collision*

abschleppen (*sep.*) *to tow away*
abstellen (*sep.*) *to turn off (engine)*
anlassen (*sep.*) *to start (engine)*
bremsen *to brake*
überfahren *to run over*

▶ Holidays

der Austausch *exchange*
der Ausweis (-e) *identity card, documentation*
der Bodensee *Lake Constance*
die Broschüre (-n) *brochure*
das Camping *camping*
der Campingplatz (¨e) *campsite*
die Donau *the Danube*
Europa *Europe*
die EU *the EU (European Union)*
die Ferien (*plural*) *holidays*
das Gasthaus (¨er) *restaurant, inn*
der Gasthof (¨e) *restaurant, inn*
das Hotel (-s) *hotel*
die Jugendherberge (-n) *youth hostel*
Köln *Cologne*
die Kosten (*plural*) *costs*
München *Munich*
Nord- *north . . .*
in den Norden *to the north*
im Norden *in the north*
die Nordsee *North Sea*
Ost- *east . . .*

in den Osten   *to the east*
im Osten   *in the east*
die Ostsee   *Baltic*
die Papiere (*plural*)   *papers, documentation*
der Paß (Pässe)   *passport*
die Paßkontrolle (-n)   *passport control*
der Plan (¨e)   *plan*
die Reise (-n)   *journey*
der Reisepaß (¨sse)   *passport*
der Rhein   *Rhine*
die Sandburg (-en)   *sandcastle*
   eine Sandburg bauen   *build a sandcastle*
der Stadtplan (¨e)   *town plan*
   Süd- *south* . . .
   in den Süden   *to the south*
   im Süden   *in the south*
der Urlaub (-e)   *holiday*
das Verkehrsbüro (-s)   *tourist office*
   West- *west* . . .
   in den Westen   *to the west*
   im Westen   *in the west*
   Wien   *Vienna*
der Zeltplatz (¨e)   *campsite for tents*
der Zoll (*no plural*)   *customs*
das Zollamt (¨er)   *customs house*
der Zollbeamte (-n)   *customs official*
die Zollkontrolle (-n)   *customs control*

   auspacken (*sep.*)   *to unpack*
   bauen   *to build*
   bleiben   *to stay*
   einpacken (*sep.*)   *to pack*
   fahren   *to travel, go*
   organisieren   *to organise*
   planen   *to plan*
   reisen   *to travel*
   verbringen   *to spend (time)*
   braun werden   *to get brown*
   zelten   *to camp (in a tent)*
der Aufenthalt (-e)   *stay*
die Grenze (-n)   *border, limit*
der Kanal   *the English Channel*
das Mittelmeer   *the Mediterranean*
das Reisebüro (-s)   *travel agent*
die Sehenswürdigkeit (-en)   *tourist sight*
die Unterkunft (¨e)   *accommodation*

   sehenswert   *worth seeing*
   verzollen   *to declare (at customs)*
   vorhaben (*sep.*)   *to plan, intend*
   vorzeigen (*sep.*)   *to show (documentation)*

▶ Accommodation

At the hotel (General)
das Abendessen (-)   *evening meal (hot)*
die Anmeldung (-en)   *booking (in)*
das Bad (¨er)   *bath(room)*
die Bar (-s)   *bar*
die Bedienung (-en)   *service*
das Doppelzimmer (-)   *double room*
die Dusche (-n)   *shower*
das Einzelzimmer (-)   *single room*
der Empfang (¨e)   *reception*
die Empfangsdame (-n)   *receptionist (female)*
das Essen (-)   *food, meal*
der Fahrstuhl (¨e)   *lift*
das Formular (-e)   *form*
das Frühstück (-e)   *breakfast*

das Gästehaus (¨er)   *hotel*
das Gepäck   *luggage*
das Hotel (-s)   *hotel*
der Koffer (-)   *suitcase*
der Lift (-e *or* -s)   *lift*
die Mehrwertsteuer (-n)   *VAT (Value Added Tax)*
   MWSt   (*short for 'Mehrwertsteuer'*) *VAT*
das Mittagessen (-)   *lunch*
die Nacht (¨e)   *night*
der Parkplatz (¨e)   *car park, parking space*
die Pension (-en)   *boarding house*
der Portier (-s)   *porter*
der Preis (-e)   *price*
der Reisescheck (-e *or* -s)   *traveller's cheque*
die Reisetasche (-n)   *suitcase*
der Scheck (-s)   *cheque*
das Schloßhotel (-s)   *castle hotel*
der Schlüssel (-)   *key*
der Speisesaal (-säle)   *dining room*
der Stock (Stockwerke)   *floor, storey*
das Telefon (-e)   *telephone*
die Übernachtung (-en)   *(overnight) stay, accommodation*
das Zimmer (-)   *room*
das Zimmermädchen (-)   *chambermaid*

   ab wann?   *from when?*
   allein   *alone*
   bequem   *comfortable*
   frei   *free (not booked)*
   pro   *for, per*
   wann?   *when?*

   ausfüllen (*sep.*)   *to fill in, complete (form)*
   bleiben   *to stay*
   essen   *to eat*
   frühstücken   *to have breakfast*
   kosten   *to cost*
   nehmen   *to take*
   parken   *to park*
   reservieren   *to reserve*
   telefonieren   *to telephone*
   übernachten   *to stay (overnight), spend the night*
   unterschreiben   *to sign*
der Aufenthalt (-e)   *stay*
die Aussicht (-en)   *view*
der Blick (-e)   *view*
das Erdgeschoß (-sse)   *ground floor*
das Fremdenheim (-e)   *boarding house*
das Fremdenzimmer (-)   *room*
die Halbpension   *half board*
die Vollpension   *full board*
der Wasserhahn (¨e)   *tap*
der Zimmernachweis (-e)   *room indication*

   inbegriffen/inbegr.   *inclusive*
   inklusiv   *inclusive*
   mit fließendem/heißem Wasser   *with running/hot water*
   warme Küche   *hot meals*
   sich anmelden (*sep.*)   *to book in*
   sich beklagen   *to complain*
   sich beschweren   *to complain*

At the youth hostel
der Gast (¨e)   *guest*
die Herberge (-n)   *hostel*
die Herbergseltern   *wardens*
die Herbergsmutter (¨)   *warden (female)*
der Herbergsvater (¨)   *warden (male)*
die Jugendherberge (-n)   *youth hostel*

die Person (-en) *person*
der Schlafraum (⁻e) *dormitory*
der Schlafsack (⁻e) *sleeping bag*

verboten *forbidden*

erlauben *to allow*
leihen *to borrow, lend*
das Mitglied (-er) *member*
das schwarze Brett *board with notices about duties*

At the campsite
die Abreise (-n) *departure*
die Ankunft (⁻e) *arrival*
die Batterie (-n) *battery*
das Büro (-s) *office*
das Camping *camping*
der Campingartikel (-) *camping equipment*
das Campinggas *camping gas*
der Campingkocher (-) *camping stove*
der Campingplatz (⁻e) *campsite*
der Dosenöffner (-) *tin opener*
das Feuer (-) *fire*
der Laden (⁻) *shop*
der Rucksack (⁻e) *rucksack*
der Schatten (-) *shade*
der Waschraum (⁻e) *washroom*
der Wohnwagen (-) *caravan*
das Zelt (-e) *tent*
der Zeltplatz (⁻e) *tent site*

zelten *to camp (in a tent)*
der Abfall (⁻e) *rubbish*
der Abfalleimer (-) *rubbish bin*
die Gebühr (-en) *fee*
der Klappstuhl (⁻e) *folding chair*
der Klapptisch (-e) *folding table*
die Luftmatratze (-n) *lilo*
die Spülküche (-n) *kitchen (for washing up)*
der Strom *electricity*

klappbar *folding*
tragbar *portable*

abbauen (*sep.*) *to take down (tent)*
aufbauen (*sep.*) *to put up (tent)*
aufschlagen (*sep.*) *to put up (tent)*

▸ Communication in the workplace, the language of the classroom
On the telephone
am Apparat *on the phone, speaking*
Hallo! *hallo!*
hier bei Neumann *this is the Neumanns*
hier Dieter *Dieter here*
wer spricht? *who's speaking*
wer ist dort? *who's there?*
(auf)Wiederhören! *goodbye (on the phone only)*
besetzt *engaged (of phone), occupied*

anrufen (*sep.*) *to telephone (someone)*
sprechen (mit) *to speak (to)*
telefonieren *to telephone*
eine (falsche) Nummer wählen *to dial a (wrong) number*
fasch wählen *to dial the wrong number*
bitte warten! *please wait!*

Postcards and letters
der Absender (-) *the sender*

Abs. *short for 'Absender'*
der Brief (-e) *letter*
der Brieffreund (-e) *pen friend (male)*
die Brieffreundin (-nen) *pen friend (female)*
(viele) Grüße (aus) *greetings (from + place)*
mit den besten Grüßen/Wünschen *(with) best wishes*
mit freundlichem Gruß *(with) kind regards, friendly greetings, yours sincerely*
mit freundlichen Grüßen *(with) kind regards, friendly greetings, yours sincerely*
herzliche Grüße *sincere greetings*
alles Gute *all the best*
hochachtungsvoll *yours faithfully*
sehr geehrter Herr, *dear Sir*
sehr geehrter/verehrter Herr... *dear Mr...*
sehr verehrte Dame, *dear Madam*
sehr geehrte/verehrte Frau... *dear Mrs...*
sehr geehrte/verehrte Herr und Frau... *dear Mr and Mrs...*
liebe Ingrid *dear Ingrid*
lieber Dieter *dear Dieter*

beilegen (*sep.*) *to enclose*
bekommen *to receive*
erhalten *to receive*
sich freuen *to be pleased*
Grüße bestellen *to send greetings, greet*
grüßen *to greet*
es grüßt... herzlich *best wishes from...*
Schluß machen *to finish, close (e.g. letter)*
schicken *to send*

Meeting people
die Ahnung (-en) *idea*
keine Ahnung *no idea*
die Einladung (-en) *invitation*
die Entschuldigung (-en)/Entschuldigung! *apology/excuse me!*
Feuer haben *to have a light*
der Freund (-e) *friend (male)*
die Freundin (-nen) *friend (female)*
die Idee (-n) *idea*
der Kollege (-n) *colleague (male)*
die Kollegin (-nen) *colleague (female)*
die Leute *people*
Lust haben *to feel like*
die Mahlzeit (-en) *mealtime*
die Party (-s) *party*

aber *but*
ach (so)! *oh (really)!*
ach (du lieber) Gott! *good God!*
also *so, that's why*
auch *also, too*
ausgezeichnet *excellent*
bestimmt *definite, certain, definitely, certainly*
bis später/nachher *see you later/afterwards*
bis gleich/morgen/dann *till soon/tomorrow/then*
bitte (schön/sehr) *please, here you are, that's OK*
danke (schön/sehr) *thank you (very much)*
dann *then*
denn *because, for*
doch *but, however*
eben *just, quite*
es freut mich *I'm pleased/glad*
es/das geht (nicht) *that's (not) fine/OK*
es ist mir egal *I don't mind, it's the same to me*
es kann (nicht) sein *it can(not) be*
es macht nichts *it doesn't matter*

es tut mir leid *I'm sorry*
frohe Ostern! *happy Easter!*
frohe/fröhliche Weihnachten! *happy Christmas*
frohes/glückliches Neujahr! *happy New Year!*
grüß Gott! *hallo (in South Germany)*
gute Besserung! *I hope you get well soon!*
gute Fahrt! *have a good journey! bon voyage!*
gute Heimfahrt! *have a good journey home!*
gute Nacht! *good night!*
guten Abend! *good evening!*
guten Appetit! *bon appétit, enjoy your food*
(guten) Morgen! *good morning!*
(guten) Tag! *good day! hello!*
komm gut nach Hause! *safe journey home!*
(auf) Wiedersehen! *goodbye!*

furchtbar *terrible, terribly*
gleichfalls *the same to you (polite not rude!)*
gut *good*
herein! *come in!*
herzlichen Glückwunsch! *congratulations!*
Himmel! *goodness!*
hoffentlich *I hope so/that*
ja *yes, indeed, really*
klasse! *great! first class!*
leider *unfortunately*
mach's gut! *all the best!*
mal *just*
mein Gott! *my God! goodness!*
Mensch! *crikey! wow! man!*
na *well*
nee *no (colloquial for 'nein')*
nein *no*
nicht *not*
nicht wahr! *isn't it! aren't they? etc.*
prima! *great!*
Prosit!/Prost! *cheers!*
Quatsch! *rubbish! nonsense!*
schlaf gut! *sleep well!*
schon *already*
schrecklich *terrible, terribly*
Servus! *hallo!*
so? *is that so (true)? really?*
so was! *well really!*
Spaß haben *to have fun*
Spaß machen *to be fun*
toll *terrific, great*
träume süß *sweet dreams*
Tschüs *or* Tschüß *bye! cheers! see you!*
vielen Dank! *thanks a lot!*
viel Glück! *good luck!*
viel Spaß! *have fun!*
wie bitte? *pardon?*
willkommen *welcome*
wunderbar *wonderful*

abholen (*sep.*) *to fetch, collect (e.g. from station)*
bekannt machen *to introduce (people)*
danken *to thank*
denken *to think*
dürfen *to be allowed*
einladen (*sep.*) *to invite*
gern/lieber haben *to like/prefer*
hat's geschmeckt? *did it taste good?*
ich hätte gern *I'd like*
ich möchte gern *I'd like*
(sich) interessieren (für) *to be interested (in)*
meinen *to think*
mitmachen (*sep.*) *to take part*

probieren *to try*
schmecken *to taste (good)*
sollen *to be supposed/due to*
Spaß haben *to have fun*
Spaß machen *to be fun*
stimmen *to be right, agree*
das stimmt *that's right*
träumen *to dream*
(sich) vorstellen (*sep.*) *to introduce (oneself)*
warten *to wait*
wünschen *to wish*
Zeit haben *to have time*
abgemacht *agreed*
der Blödsinn *madness, nonsense*
ich habe nichts dagegen *I've nothing against it/that*
einverstanden *agreed*
der Namenstag(-e) *Saint's day, name day*
Pech haben *to be unlucky*
(wie) schade! *(what a) pity!*
die Überraschung (-en) *surprise*
die Verabredung (-en) *agreement, arrangement, appointment, date*
das Vergnügen (-) *pleasure, fun*
mit (großem/größtem/dem größten) Vergnügen *with (great) pleasure*
Verzeihung! *sorry! excuse me!*
zum Wohl! *cheers! your health!*
zufrieden *content, satisfied*

ablehnen (*sep.*) *to decline, refuse*
annehmen (*sep.*) *to accept*
ärgern *to annoy*
(sich) ärgern *to annoy (get annoyed)*
begrüßen *to greet*
grüßen *to greet*
bitten *to ask, request*
duzen *to call 'du' (use familiar form when speaking)*
empfehlen *to recommend*
(sich) entschuldigen *to excuse (oneself)/(apologise)*
genügen *to suffice, be sufficient*
gratulieren *to congratulate*
klappen *to work out, to fold (e.g. of chair)*
raten *to advise*
siezen *to call 'Sie' (use polite form when speaking)*
(sich) treffen *to meet*
überraschen *to surprise*
sich verabschieden *to take one's leave, say goodbye*
vorschlagen (*sep.*) *to suggest*
vorziehen (*sep.*) *to prefer*

▷ Health and fitness, well-being

Parts of the body
der Arm (-e) *arm*
die Hand (¨-e) *hand*
der Finger (-) *finger*
das Bein (-e) *leg*
der Fuß (¨-e) *foot*
der Bauch *stomach*
der Magen *stomach*
der Rücken *back*
der Kopf (¨-e) *head*
der Hals (¨-e) *neck*
das Gesicht (-er) *face*
das Auge (-n) *eye*
der Mund (¨-er) *mouth*
der Zahn (¨-e) *tooth*

die Nase (-n) *nose*
das Ohr (-en) *ear*

das Bad (¨er) *bath*
  sauber *clean*
  schmutzig *dirty*

  baden *to bath, have a bath*
  sich duschen *to shower, have a shower*
  sich waschen *to wash, have a wash*

das Handtuch (¨er) *towel*
die Seife *soap*
das Shampoo *shampoo*
das Haarwaschmittel *shampoo*
die Zahnbürste (-n) *toothbrush*
die Zahnpasta *toothpaste*

  sich ausruhen (sep.) *to have a rest, relax*
  schlafen *to sleep*
  erkältet sein *to have a cold*
  Fieber haben *to have a temperature*
die Grippe *flu, influenza*
  Durst haben *to be thirsty*
  durstig *thirsty*
  Hunger haben *to be hungry, have an appetite*
  hungrig *hungry*
  satt *full (of food)*
  gesund *healthy*
  (un)fit *(un)fit*
  krank *ill*
  seekrank *seasick*
die Seekrankheit *seasickness*
  müde *tired*
die Blutprobe *blood test*
die Spritze (-n) *injection*
der Durchfall *diarrhoea*
die Magenverstimmung *stomach upset*
  mir ist heiß/kalt *I'm hot/cold*
  mir ist übel/schlecht/schwindlig *I feel sick/ill/giddy*
  was fehlt? *what's wrong?*
  was ist los? *what's the matter?*
  weh tun *to hurt*
  Heimweh haben *to be homesick*
die Allergie (-n) *allergy*
der Körper (-) *body*
das Herz (-en) *heart*
die Brust (¨e) *breast, chest*
das Knie (-n) *knee*
die Schulter (-n) *shoulder*
der Daumen (-) *thumb*
die Zehe (-n) *toe*
die Zunge (-n) *tongue*

die Erkältung (-en) *cold*
der Schnupfen *cold*
  verstopft *constipated*
die Verstopfung *constipation*
  blind *blind*
  stumm *dumb, mute*
  taub *deaf*
  dreckig *dirty*
  sich bürsten *to brush oneself*
  sich die Zähne bürsten/putzen *to brush/clean one's teeth*
  sich kämmen *to comb one's hair*
  sich rasieren *to have a shave*
  sich (wohl) fühlen *to feel (well)*
  sich hinlegen (sep.) *to have a rest/lie down*
  sich erholen *to recover*
  genesen *to get well*
  bluten *to bleed*

Accidents and emergencies

der Dienst (-e) *service*
der E111-Schein (-e) *E111 form*
die Erste Hilfe *first aid*
der Feuerlöscher (-) *fire extinguisher*
der Feuerwehrwagen (-) *fire engine*
die Geldstrafe (-n) *fine*
der Gips (-e) *plaster (of Paris)*
das Heftpflaster (-) *plaster (elastoplast)*
der Husten *cough*
die Krankenkasse (-n) *health insurance*
der Krankenschein (-e) *medical insurance record card*
die Kur (-en) *treatment, cure; convalescence*
der Kurort (-e) *spa resort*
die Lebensgefahr *danger to life; danger!*
das Löschgerät (-e) *fire extinguisher*
die Medizin *medicine*
der Notausgang (¨e) *emergency exit*
der Notdienst (-e) *emergency service*
der Notruf (-e) *emergency phone call*
die Operation (-en) *operation*
der Patient (-en)/die Patientin (-nen) *patient*
das Pflaster (-) *plaster (elastoplast)*
die Pille (-n) *pill*
das Rezept (-e) *prescription*
die Sprechstunde (-n) *surgery hours*
die Spritze (-n) *injection*
die Strafe (-n) *fine, punishment*
die Tablette (-n) *tablet*
der Termin (-e) *time, appointment (time)*
das Thermometer (-) *thermometer*
der Tod (-e) *death*
der Tropfen (-) *drop*
der Unfall (¨e) *accident*
der Verband (¨e) *bandage*
die Wunde (-n) *wound*
der Zeuge (-n) *witness*
der Zusammenstoß (¨e) *crash*

  atemlos *breathless*
  betrunken *drunk*
  blaß *pale*
  gebrochen *broken*
  körperbehindert *physically handicapped*
  tot *dead*
  verletzt *injured*
  verwundet *wounded*

  behandeln *to treat (illness); to deal with*
  sich das Bein/den Arm brechen *to break one's leg/arm*

  fallen *to fall*
  husten *to cough*
  ums Leben kommen *to die*

  löschen *to extinguish, put out*
  niesen *to sneeze*
  retten *to save*
  schwitzen *to sweat*
  sterben *to die*
  stürzen *to rush; crash*
  überfahren *to run over*
  überfallen *to attack*
  sich übergeben *to be sick*
  untersuchen *to examine*
  verunglücken *to have an accident*
  weinen *to cry*

Shopping

Shops

die Apotheke (-n) *chemist*
der Automat (-en) *vending machine*
die Bäckerei (-en) *baker's*
die Drogerie (-n) *drugstore*
die Fleischerei (-en) *butcher's*
der Friseur (-e) *hairdresser's*
der Frisör (-e) *hairdresser's*
der Gemüsehändler (-) *greengrocer's*
das Geschäft (-e) *shop, business*
die Geschäftszeiten (*plural*) *opening hours, shop hours*
der Händler (-) *trader, merchant*
das Kaufhaus (¨er) *department store*
der Kiosk (-e) *stand, kiosk*
die Konditorei (-en) *cake shop, pâtisserie*
der Laden (¨) *shop*
das Lebensmittelgeschäft (-e) *grocer's*
der Markt (¨e) *market*
die Metzgerei (-en) *butcher's*
die Öffnungszeiten (*plural*) *opening times*
der Supermarkt (¨e) *supermarket*
das Warenhaus (¨er) *department store*
der Zeitungsstand (¨e) *newspaper stand*

Einkäufe machen *to shop, do the shopping*
einkaufen (*sep.*) *to shop*
kaufen *to buy*
verkaufen *to sell*

die Abteilung (-en) *department, section*
der Ausverkauf *clearance sale*
die Auswahl *selection, choice*
der Einkaufskorb (¨e) *shopping basket*
der Einkaufswagen (-) *shopping trolley (at supermarket)*
das Erdgeschoß (-sse) *ground floor*
die Gebrauchsanweisung (-en) *instructions (for use)*
die Hälfte (-n) *half*
der Kassenzettel (-) *till receipt*
das Pfand (¨er) *deposit*
die Quittung (-en) *receipt*
der Rabatt (-e) *discount*
die Rolltreppe (-n) *escalator*
die Scheibe (-n) *slice*
der Sommerschlußverkauf *summer sale*
das Spülmittel (-) *washing-up liquid*
der Topf (¨e) *pot*
der Umtausch *exchange (of goods)*
das Untergeschoß (-sse) *basement*
die Wahl (-en) *choice*
das Waschpulver (-) *washing powder*

günstig *favourable*
umsonst *in vain, free*

ausgeben (*sep.*) *to spend (money)*
dienen *to serve*
schälen *to peel*
umtauschen (*sep.*) *to exchange (goods)*
wiegen *to weigh*

Clothes

der Anorak (-s) *anorak*
der Anzug (¨e) *suit (male)*
die Armbanduhr (-en) *wristwatch*
der Artikel (-) *article*
der Badeanzug (¨e) *swimsuit*
die Badehose (-n) *swimming trunks*
die Bluse (-n) *blouse*

die Brieftasche (-n) *wallet*
die Brille (-n) *glasses*
die Creme (-s) *cream*
die Damenkonfektion *ladies' wear*
die Farbe (-n) *colour*
die Größe (-n) *size*
der Gürtel (-) *belt*
die Haarbürste (-n) *hairbrush*
der Handschuh (-e) *glove*
die Handtasche (-n) *handbag*
das Hemd (-en) *shirt*
die Herrenkonfektion *menswear*
die Herrenmode (-n) *men's fashion*
die Hose (-n) *trousers*
die Jacke (-n) *jacket*
die Jeans (*either feminine singular or plural*) *jeans*
das Kleid (-er) *dress*
die Kleider (*plural*) *clothes*
die Kleidung *clothing*
die Krawatte (-n) *tie*
der Mantel (¨) *overcoat*
die Mode (-n) *fashion*
das Paar (-e) *pair*
das Papiertaschentuch (¨er) *paper handkerchief, tissue*
Plastik *plastic*
das Portemonnaie (-s) *purse*
der Pulli (-s) *pullover*
der Pullover (-) *pullover*
die Qualität (-en) *quality*
der Regenmantel (¨) *raincoat*
der Rock (¨e) *skirt*
die Sandale (-n) *sandal*
der Schlafanzug (¨e) *pyjamas*
der Schlips (-e) *tie*
der Schuh (-e) *shoe*
die Socke (-n) *sock*
die Sonnenbrille (-n) *sunglasses*
die Sonnencreme (-s) *suncream*
die Sonnenmilch *suntan lotion*
das Sonnenöl *suntan oil*
der Strumpf (¨e) *sock, long sock*
die Strumpfhose (-n) *tights*
das Taschentuch (¨er) *handkerchief*
das T-Shirt (-s) *T-shirt*
die Uhr (-en) *clock, watch*
der Wecker (-) *alarm clock*
die Zahnbürste (-n) *toothbrush*
die Zahnpasta (-en) *toothpaste*

anhaben (*sep.*) *to have on, wear*
wählen *to choose, select*

die Baumwolle *cotton*
der Büstenhalter (-) (BH) *brassière (bra)*
das Gummi *rubber*
der Hut (¨e) *hat*
der Kamm (¨e) *comb*
das Kostüm (-e) *suit, costume (female)*
der Kunststoff (-e) *synthetic material*
das Leder (-) *leather*
die Mütze (-n) *cap*
der Pantoffel (-n) *slipper*
der Regenschirm (-e) *umbrella*
der Schal (-s) *scarf*
die Seide *silk*
der Stiefel (-) *boot*
der Stoff (-e) *material*
die Unterwäsche *underwear*
die Wäsche *washing*

das Wildleder (-) *leather*
die Wolle (-n) *wool*

   echt *real, genuine*

   anprobieren *(sep.)* *to try on*
   einreiben *(sep.)* *to rub in (cream etc.)*
   reiben *to rub*
   schützen *to protect*

▷ Food and drink

Places to eat and drink
die Bar (-s) *bar*
die Bierhalle (-n) *beer hall*
das Café (-s) *café*
   Erfrischungen *(plural)* *refreshments*
das Gasthaus (¨-er) *restaurant, inn*
der Gasthof (¨-e) *restaurant, inn*
die Gaststätte (-n) *restaurant*
der Imbiß (-sse) *snack, snack bar*
der Imbißstand (¨-e) *snack stand*
die Imbißstube (-n) *snack bar*
das Kaffeehaus (¨-er) *coffee house*
der Keller (-) *cellar*
der Kiosk (-e) *kiosk, stand*
die Konditorei (-en) *cake shop, pâtisserie*
die Milchbar (-s) *milk bar*
der Rasthof (¨-e) *service station*
die Raststätte (-n) *service station*
der Ratskeller (-) *Town Hall Cellar Restaurant/Bar*
das Restaurant (-s) *restaurant*
der Schnellimbiß (-sse) *snack (bar)*
der Weinkeller (-) *wine cellar*
die Weinprobe (-n) *wine-tasting*
die Weinstube (-n) *wine bar*
der Würstchenstand (¨-e) *hot sausage stand*

   Herr Ober! *waiter!*
   Fräulein! *waitress!*
   Hallo (Bedienung)! *hallo (service please)!*
   Bedienung, bitte! *service please!*
die Rechnung, bitte! *the bill please!*
   Zahlen, bitte! *I'd like to pay please!*
die Kneipe (-n) *pub*
die Schenke (-n) *bar*
der Stammtisch (-e) *regulars' table (public house)*
die Theke (-n) *counter*
die Wirtschaft (-en) *public house*
das Wirtshaus (¨-er) *pub, inn*

Eating and drinking out
das Abendbrot *evening meal (cold)*
das Abendessen (-) *evening meal (hot)*
die Bedienung (-en) *service*
das Essen (-) *meal, food*
das Frühstück *breakfast*
die Gabel (-n) *fork*
das Glas (¨-er) *glass*
der Imbiß (-sse) *snack*
der Kellner (-) *waiter*
die Kellnerin (-nen) *waitress*
der Kinderteller (-) *children's meal/portion*
der Löffel (-) *spoon*
die Mahlzeit (-en) *meal, mealtime*
die Mehrwertsteuer *VAT (Value Added Tax)*
   MWSt *(abbreviation for 'Mehrwertsteuer') VAT*
das Menü (-s) *set menu*
das Messer (-) *knife*
   zum Mitnehmen *to take away (food)*

das Mittagessen (-) *lunch*
das Öl (-e) *oil*
die Portion (-en) *portion, helping*
der Preis (-e) *price*
der Schnellimbiß (-sse) *snack (bar)*
die Speisekarte (-n) *menu*
die Tageskarte (-n) *menu of the day, specials*
die Tasse (-n) *cup*
der Teller (-) *plate*
die Untertasse (-n) *saucer*
die Weinkarte (-n) *wine list*
die Weinliste (-n) *wine list*
der Zucker *sugar*
   frisch *fresh*
   lecker *delicious*
   sauer *bitter, sharp*
   scharf *spicy, sharp, strong*
   süß *sweet*

   beißen *to bite*
   frühstücken *to have breakfast*
   geben *to give*
   grillen *to grill*
   kauen *to chew*
   reichen *to pass (e.g. the salt)*
   riechen *to smell*
   schlucken *to swallow*
   schneiden *to cut*
das Gericht (-e) *course*
die Getränkekarte (-n) *drinks list*
der Getränkekellner (-) *drinks waiter*
der Pfeffer *pepper*
das Salz *salt*
die Schale (-n) *dish, bowl*
die Schüssel (-n) *dish, bowl*
der Senf *mustard*
der Strohhalm (-e) *straw*
das Tablett (-s) *tray*
der Weinkellner (-) *wine waiter*

   einschließlich/einschl. *inclusive*
   inbegriffen/inbegr. *inclusive*
   gebacken *baked*
   gebraten *roast*
   gemischt/gem. *mixed*
   paniert *in breadcrumbs*

   anbieten *(sep.)* *to offer*
   bieten *to provide*
   einschenken *(sep.)* *to pour*
   probieren *to try*

Things to eat

Starters egg dishes/fish/sausage and cold meat
die Gulaschsuppe (-n) *goulash soup*
die Suppe (-n) *soup*
die Tomatensuppe (-n) *tomato soup*

das gekochte Ei (-er) *(hard) boiled egg*
das Omelett (-e or -s) *omelette*
das Rührei (-er) *scrambled egg*
das Spiegelei (-er) *fried egg*

der Fisch (-e) *fish*

der Aufschnitt *cold meat(s)*
die Bockwurst (¨-e) *steamed sausage, like frankfurter but larger*
die Bratwurst (¨-e) *fried sausage*
die Currywurst (¨-e) *curried sausage*
die Leberwurst (¨-e) *liver sausage/pâté*

der Schinken (-) *ham*
die Hühnerbrühe (-n) *chicken soup*
die Ochsenschwanzsuppe (-n) *oxtail soup*
die Vorspeise (-n) *starter*
die Forelle (-n) *trout*
die kalte Platte (-n) *cold buffet*

Meat and poultry
das Brathähnchen (-) *roast chicken*
das Curry *curry*
das Fleisch *meat*
die Fleischsorte (-n) *kind/type of meat*
das Gulasch *goulash*
das Hähnchen (-) *chicken*
das Kotelett (-s) *chop/cutlet*
die Leber (-n) *liver*
das Rindfleisch *beef*
das Schweinefleisch *pork*
das Schnitzel (-) *cutlet, escalope*
das Steak (-s) *steak*
das Wiener Schnitzel (-) *Wiener Schnitzel, Vienna cutlet*
der Braten (-) *roast (dish)*
das deutsche Beefsteak *German beefsteak*
der Eintopf (¨e) *vegetable soup, potage*
die Grillplatte (-n) *(mixed) grill*
das Kalbfleisch *veal*

Vegetables and salads
die Bratkartoffel (-n) *fried potato*
der Kartoffelsalat (-e) *potato salad*
die Pommes frites (*plural*) *chips*
der Reis *rice*
der Salat (-e) *salad/lettuce*
die Salzkartoffel (-n) *boiled potato*
das Sauerkraut *Sauerkraut, pickled cabbage*
die Tomate (-n) *tomato*
der Wurstsalat (-e) *sausage salad*
der Blumenkohl *cauliflower*
die Bohne (-n) *green bean*
der Champignon (-s) *mushroom (small)*
die Erbse (-n) *pea*
die Gurke (-n) *gherkin, cucumber*
der Kartoffelbrei *mashed potato*
das Kartoffelmus *mashed potato*
der Knödel (-) *dumpling*
der Pilz (-e) *mushroom (large)*
die Zwiebel (-n) *onion*

Desserts
die Creme (-s) *cream*
der Eisbecher (-) *ice-cream sundae*
die Erdbeere (-n) *strawberry*
der Joghurt (- *or* -s) *yoghurt*
die Himbeere (-n) *raspberry*
der Käse (-) *cheese*
die Kirsche (-n) *cherry*
das Kompott (-e) *apple sauce, stewed fruit*
der Obstsalat (-e) *fruit salad*
der Pudding (-s) *pudding, dessert (custard type)*
die Sahne *cream*
die Schlagsahne *whipped cream*
die Vanille *vanilla*
die Zitrone (-n) *lemon*
  Zitronen- *lemon-flavoured*
die Nachspeise (-) *dessert, sweet*
der Nachtisch (-e) *dessert, sweet*

Bread/sandwiches/cakes
der Apfelkuchen (-) *apple cake*
das (belegte) Brot (-e) *bread/(open sandwich)*
das Brötchen (-) *roll*
das Butterbrot (-e) *sandwich*
das Graubrot (-e) *type of bread, very common*
das Käsebrot (-e) *bread with cheese*
der Kirschkuchen (-) *cherry cake*
der Kuchen (-) *cake*
das Schinkenbrot (-e) *bread with ham*
das Schwarzbrot (-e) *black (rye) bread*
die Torte (-n) *flan*
das Wurstbrot (-e) *bread with cold meat*

Drinks
der Apfelsaft (¨e) *apple juice*
das Bier (-e) *beer*
das Cola (-s) *coke*
ein Dunkles *a brown ale*
ein Helles *a bitter/lager*
die Flasche (-n) *bottle*
das Getränk (-e) *drink*
der Kaffee (-s) *coffee*
der Kakao *cocoa*
das Kännchen (-) *pot (of coffee/tea)*
die Limo *lemonade*
die Limonade (-n) *lemonade*
das Mineralwasser (-) *mineral water*
der Orangensaft (¨e) *orange juice*
das Pils *lager*
der Rotwein (-e) *red wine*
der Sprudel (-) *pop, fizzy drink, lemonade*
der Tee (-s) *tea*
das Wasser *water*
der Wein (-e) *wine*
der Weißwein (-e) *white wine*
der Schnaps (¨e) *spirits, schnaps*
der Sekt (-e) *champagne*

▶ Public services

At the post office
die Ansichtskarte (-n) *(picture) postcard*
der Brief (-e) *letter*
der Briefkasten (¨) *letter box*
die Briefmarke (-n) *stamp*
der Briefträger (-) *postman*
die Postkarte (-n) *postcard*
das Ausland *abroad*
  außer Betrieb *out of action*
der Briefumschlag (¨e) *envelope*
der Einwurf (¨e) *slot (for posting)*
das Ferngespräch (-e) *long-distance call*
der Fernsprecher (-) *telephone*
das Gespräch (-e) *conversation*
der Hörer (-) *receiver*
das Inland *inland*
die Leerung (-en) *collection (from post box)*
die Luftpost *air mail*
das Ortsgespräch (-e) *local call*
die Post *post office*
das Postamt (¨er) *post office*
die Postanweisung (-en) *postal order*
die Postleitzahl (-en) *postcode*
das Postwertzeichen (-) *postage stamp*
die Rückgabe (-n) *return (of money from coin box)*
das Rückgespräch (-e) *reverse charges call*
der Schalter (-) *counter*
die Taste (-n) *button*
die Telefonzelle (-n) *telephone kiosk*

das Telegramm (-e) *telegramme*
der Umschlag (¨-e) *envelope*
die Verbindung (-en) *connection*

    postlagernd *poste restante*

    abheben (*sep.*) *to pick up, withdraw*
    aufgeben (*sep.*) *to hand in*
    drücken *to press*
    durchwählen (*sep.*) *to dial*
    verbinden *to connect*

At the bank or bureau de change

die Bank (-en) *bank*
die Banknote (-n) *banknote*
die Brieftasche (-n) *wallet*
der Franken *Swiss franc*
das Geld (-er) *money*
der Geldwechsel *change, exchange*
der Groschen (-) *10 pfennig coin*
die Kasse (-n) *cash desk, till*
das Kleingeld *change (coins)*
die Mark *mark*
    DM *Deutschmark*
    D-Mark *Deutschmark*
das Markstück (-e) *one mark piece/coin*
der Paß (¨-sse) *passport*
der Pfennig (-e) *pfennig*
    Pf. *pfennig*
das Pfund (Sterling) *pound*
das Portemonnaie (-s) *purse*
der Reisescheck (-s) *traveller's cheque*
das Scheckbuch (¨-er) *cheque book*
der Schein (-e) *note*
der Schilling (-e) schilling *(Austrian currency)*
die Sparkasse (-n) *savings bank*
das Taschengeld (-er) *pocket money*
die Wechselstube (-n) *bureau de change*

    billig *cheap*
    ein wenig *a little*
    genug *enough*
    kostenlos *free*
    teuer *expensive*
    viel *much*

    arbeiten *to work*
    kaufen *to buy*
    kosten *to cost*
    sparen *to save*
    verdienen *to earn*
    wechseln *to exchange*
die Gebühr (-en) *fee*
das Konto (Konten *or* -s) *account*
die Kontonummer (-n) *account number*
der Kurs (-e) *exchange rate*
der Wechselkurs (-e) *exchange rate*

    einlösen (*sep.*) *to cash (cheques)*
    überweisen *to transfer*

Lost property

die Beschreibung (-en) *description*
die Enttäuschung (-en) *disappointment*
das Fundbüro (-s) *lost property office*
der Taschendieb (-e) *pickpocket*
die Überraschung (-en) *surprise*

    dankbar *thankful, grateful*
    sich bedanken *to thank*
    beschreiben *to describe*

    einreichen (*sep.*) *to hand in*
    enttäuschen *to disappoint*
    gehören *to belong*
    liegenlassen (*sep.*) *to leave (behind), lose*
    Pech haben *to be unlucky/have bad luck*
    überraschen *to surprise*
    verschließen *to lock*
    verschwinden *to disappear*
    versichern *to insure*
    Angst haben (um) *to be afraid (about)*
    Glück haben *to be lucky*
die Polizeiwache (-n) *police station*
der Polizist (-en) *policeman*

    glücklich *happy, lucky*

    aussehen (*sep.*) *to look, appear*
    danken *to thank*
    sich freuen *to be pleased*
    vergessen *to forget*
    verlieren *to lose*

▶ Weather

der Blitz (-e) *lightning flash*
der Donner (-) *thunder*
das Eis *ice*
das Gewitter (-) *storm, thunderstorm*
der Himmel *sky*
der Regen *rain*
der Schatten (-) *shade*
der Schnee *snow*
die Sonne *sun*
der Sonnenschein *sunshine*
der Sturm (¨-e) *storm*
das Wetter *weather*
der Wind (-e) *wind*
die Wolke (-n) *cloud*

    heiß *hot*
    herrlich *wonderful*
    kühl *cool*
    naß *wet*
    sonnig *sunny*
    stürmisch *stormy*
    windig *windy*
    wolkig *cloudy*

    blitzen *to flash (of lighting)*
    donnern *to thunder*
    frieren *to freeze*
    regnen *to rain*
    scheinen *to shine*
    schneien *to snow*
die Aufheiterung (-en) *bright period*
die Bewölkung *cloud, clouding over*
der Grad (-) *degree*
    Celsius *centigrade, Celsius*
der Hagel *hail*
die Hitze *heat*
der Hochdruck *high pressure*
die Höchsttemperatur (-en) *highest/maximum temperature*
die Kälte *cold*
das Klima (-s) *climate*
der Mond *moon*
der Nebel (-) *fog*
der Niederschlag (¨-e) *precipitation (rain, snow, etc.)*
das Sauwetter *awful weather*
der Schauer (-) *shower*

der Stern (-e) *star*
die Tagestemperatur (-en) *daytime temperature*
die Temperatur (-en) *temperature*
die Tiefsttemperatur (-en) *lowest/minimum temperature*
der Tiefdruck *low pressure*
der Wetterbericht (-e) *weather report*
die Wetterlage (-n) *weather report/conditions*
die Wettervorhersage (-n) *weather forecast*

   bewölkt *cloudy*
   feucht *damp*
   heiter *bright*
   mild *mild*
   neblig *foggy*
   regnerisch *rainy*
   schwül *sticky, oppressive*
   trocken *dry*
   trüb *dull*
   veränderlich *changeable*
   wolkenlos *cloudless, clear*

   hageln *to hail*

▷ World issues

die Religion (-en) *religion*
das Christentum *Christianity*
der Islam *Islam*
der Buddhismus *Buddhism*
der Krieg (-e) *war*
der Bürgerkrieg (-e) *civil war*
   kämpfen *to fight*
   zerstören *to destroy*
die Armee (-n) *army*
die Luftwaffe (-n) *air force*
die Marine (-n) *navy*

der Wehrdienst *conscription/compulsory military service*
   verteidigen *to defend*
die Verteidigung *defence*
der Verkehr *traffic*
der Auspuff (-e) *exhaust*
die Auspuffgase (plural) *exhaust fumes*
der Stau (-s) *traffic jam*
die Umwelt *environment*
die Umweltfrage (-n) *environmental issue*
der Regenwald (¨er) *rain forest*
der Ozean (-e) *ocean*
die Natur *nature, natural world*
die Luft *air*
die Atmosphäre (-n) *atmosphere*
   verschmutzen *to pollute*
die Verschmutzung *pollution*
die Wasserverschmutzung *water pollution*
die Luftverschmutzung *air pollution*
der saure Regen *acid rain*
das Ozonloch (¨er) *hole in the ozone layer*
die Ozonschicht *ozone layer*
die Energie *energy*
die Atomkraft *atomic energy/power*
der Strom *electricity/electrical current*
die Solarzelle (-n) *solar panel*
   sparen *to save*
   schonen *to protect*
   verschwenden *to waste*
   verbrauchen *to use up*
die Dritte Welt *the third world*
die Armut *poverty*
die Not *need/neediness*
der Hunger *hunger*
   verhungern *to starve*
   spenden *to donate*
die Spende (-n) *donation*

Chapter 4

Listening: Foundation Tier

> ## GETTING STARTED

'But they speak ever so fast!' How often have you heard people say that about people talking in a different language? Perhaps you have even said or thought it yourself! In fact there is no evidence to suggest that people from other countries speak their language any more quickly than you might speak English. It may, however, be true that people find it difficult to understand other people talking a language that is foreign to them. Why is this, and what can we do about it?

> ## WHAT YOU NEED TO KNOW

> **Listening skills**

To begin with we need to focus on the skill of **listening** itself: what do we listen to and why, and what is the nature of that listening? So, what do **you** listen to? It is helpful to think about the different kinds of listening that you do in the ordinary course of events. You may well find that you listen to:

- the news, weather reports, travel announcements on the radio/TV
- announcements at a bus/train station, an airport or a port
- an interview on radio/TV
- a commentary about a particular event of interest
- the football results
- friends making plans or talking about recent events
- someone giving you a message on the telephone
- family and friends dealing with everyday matters, e.g. 'pass me the sauce!'

These are just a few of the common situations where you find yourself listening. In each case, though, you will not expect to remember **everything** you have heard. We all make a selection and remember what we need to or want to. (Sometimes we might even conveniently forget something we do not wish to hear: 'Don't sniff, child! How many times do I have to tell you?!')

You should try this out – listen to what someone is saying quite normally and then, say five minutes later, try to remember what he or she actually said. You will almost certainly not remember the exact words used, nor will you remember all that was said, but you will remember the **key points** or pieces of information that were important to you.

By the same token, if you want to find out what the weather is going to be like, you listen to the forecast in a certain frame of mind. First you know that the person is going to be talking about the weather (and not about the latest fashion), and second, you will be listening out for key pieces of information, e.g. hot, cold, wet.

So we can conclude that we do **not** need to understand every single word we hear, and that there are often certain expectations that can actually help us to understand. The same applies to foreign languages, including German.

So remember the following:

1 You do not have to understand every word.
2 You should not be discouraged if you do not understand every word.
3 You should try to build on your knowledge of key words and expressions.
4 You should also get as much practice in listening to German as you can.

In this chapter we work through what you can expect to encounter in the Foundation Tier examination. This is best done by looking first at the Assessment Objectives of the examining groups, then seeing what they mean in terms of the examination questions themselves.

Chapter 4 Listening: Foundation Tier

Assessment Objectives

An Assessment Objective is quite simply a statement by the examining group about what exactly it aims to test. That is to say, what abilities will be expected on the part of candidates for the examination. The six examining groups all have roughly the same objectives, since they must comply with a lot of regulations, laid down in the main by the National Curriculum.

In Listening (Attainment Target 1 of the National Curriculum) the chief objective is, not surprisingly, that candidates should demonstrate 'the ability to understand and respond to spoken language.' Some examining groups spell this out in greater detail, but even if they don't you may assume that what you will have to do at Foundation Tier is generally as follows:

1. understand and note details/the main points in what you hear
2. extract specific details/information from what you hear
3. identify points of view
4. identify attitudes, opinions and emotions
5. understand references to past, present and future events
6. summarise the main points in what you hear
7. understand different registers and deal with familiar language in unfamiliar contexts.

Points 4–7 will generally be required from those candidates gaining grades D and C, but not below these grades.

At Foundation Tier the test will be made up of items of varying length such as announcements, instructions, short news items, short conversations and telephone messages, advertisements and short narratives or descriptions. There will be some longer items aimed at those candidates who will gain grades D and C, but none of the material is allowed to place an undue burden on the memory. Everything is recorded on tape and is spoken by native speakers at near normal or normal speed. Only material that is realistic and intended to be heard may be included. You will hear everything twice and there will be plenty of pauses to allow you time to read questions and write answers.

You will meet various types of question. Some will require a non-verbal response, for instance a tick in a box to indicate the correct answer, or a matching exercise. There may be true/false type tests or grid completion. For the most part the instructions and questions will be **in German** and if you have to write an answer this too will be **in German**. Don't worry about this! What is required is that you show that you have understood what you have heard, not that you can use perfect German. In the example questions that follow you will see that single word answers are generally sufficient. Some questions will be in English and you will be able to answer in English if you are specifically told to do so, but this is not the rule and you will only come across this type of question where the situation would in reality require this kind of question and answer, for example in an interpreting situation. We will see examples of this later. Finally, all the questions must be within the context of the Areas of Experience and topics listed earlier in Chapter 3.

Exam group requirements

As we saw in Chapter 1, each of the examining groups is required to set out in detail what candidates are expected to prepare for the examination. As we have seen above, the exam groups must also set out the nature of the tests to be used. A useful source of information is the **syllabus** which tells you about the length of the examination, the topic areas tested and the type of answer expected. You will also find detailed lists of the vocabulary and grammar the examination may include. Much of the information is included in Chapters 14 and 16 of this book.

- For all the examining groups the Foundation Tier listening tests last between 20 and 30 minutes.
- In all the tests there will be some brief announcements and instructions, some monologues and some dialogues. You will need practice in listening to as wide a variety of these as possible.
- You may be given reading time to read through all the questions on the paper before you hear the tape. You may be allowed to use a dictionary during this time, but not during the test itself. You should check the rules for your examining group.

Approaching the tests

The questions in the examination, as we have already noted, will test your ability to understand the **key points**. In this section we will look at the kind of things that can reasonably be asked.

In many cases the questions will be seeking an answer about:

1 Who?   *Wer?*
2 What?   *Was?*
3 Where?   *Wo? Wohin?*
4 When?   *Wann?*
5 How long? *Wie lange?*
6 How many? *Wieviele?*
7 How much? *Wieviel?*
8 Why?   *Warum?*

We need, then, to check which items could be included under these categories and you need to make sure that you are familiar with them and that you understand them when you hear them. Make certain that you know your vocabulary.

1 **Who?** people
   (a) family and friends
   (b) professions
   (c) descriptions, physical appearance, size, age etc.
2 **What?**
   (a) items relating to topic areas
   (b) what you have to do
   (c) instructions
3 **Where?** location
   (a) position: prepositions
   (b) places: buildings, landmarks, countries
   (c) directions
   (d) distances
4 **When?**
   (a) time of day
   (b) 24-hour clock
   (c) days, weeks, months, years
   (d) dates
   (e) moments in time: midday, midnight
   (f) length of time
   (g) frequency
   (h) expressions of time: today, yesterday etc.
   (i) seasons, important holiday periods: Christmas, New Year etc.
   (j) beginning, continuity, end
5 **How long?** duration
   (a) minutes, days, weeks, months, years
   (b) until + time/point in time/day/week/month/year
6 **How many?**
   (a) numbers
7 **How much?** quantity
   (a) numbers
   (b) weights and measures
   (c) size: big, small
8 **Why?**
   (a) reason

The reason for concentrating on the above subheadings will be more obvious when we consider some sample questions.

When practising listening it is a good idea to make some **notes** as you hear the passage or extract. This is especially true of numbers – e.g. times, dates, ages – but it is also true of other key points. Remember that you will hear everything twice, that there will be ample pauses and that nothing is allowed to place an undue burden on the memory. Longer items may, therefore, be split into sections with pauses between them. It is a good idea to make notes in the pauses after the first hearing but not actually while you are trying to listen. Then listen again, confirm or add to your notes and make a complete answer. You should remember to cross out neatly anything you do not want the examiner to consider. Always **read the questions carefully**, with a view to planning the information you will be

Practice with tape recordings

Listening, as we have already established, is a separate skill. To help improve your listening skills it goes without saying that you must above all have practice in listening. You will need to listen to as wide a range of voices as possible, and that of course means listening to recordings. Although that might at first seem easier said than done, let's just try to put things into perspective:

- Most people these days have a cassette player or walkman.
- Blank cassette tapes are cheap.
- Your teacher will probably have cassette tapes you can borrow.
- You can probably borrow German tapes from your local library.
- There is a cassette available with **this** book.
- There are many programmes on television and radio that you can in many cases record.
- If you are using your own tape recorder you can stop and re-listen as many times as you like.
- You can also spend as long as you like listening and then stop; it is generally a good idea to listen in short spells at first and gradually develop your ability to concentrate for longer periods. Intensive listening is hard work!
- If you have headphones you can listen without being disturbed (or disturbing others!)

So no more excuses! Make **listening** a regular part of your homework and planned revision!

EXAMINATION QUESTIONS

The following extracts are on the **cassette**, which can be bought together with the book. All the extracts are written out in full in the text, so if you have not bought the cassette get a friend from your course to read out the extracts and then try to answer the questions.

Extract 1

The first extract on the cassette is about the topic area 'school'. It gives a selection of items similar to those you might hear in the exam. We shall use the extract to practise your **skill** in listening. Play the extract (or listen to your friend reading it) and imagine that your German friend is talking to you. Try to **note down** the key words and phrases in each item.

- Play extract 1 (or have your friend read out items 1–20 below).

Answers are given in the 'Examination answers' section at the end of the chapter (see page 60).

1 „Hast du deinen Wecker mitgebracht?"

Du bist bei deiner Brieffreundin in Deutschland. Was fragt sie? Kreuze ein Kästchen an.

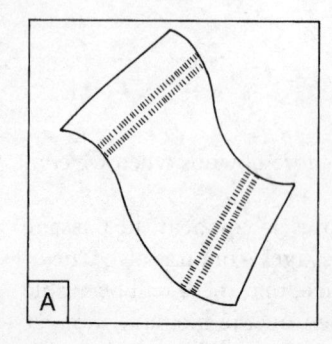

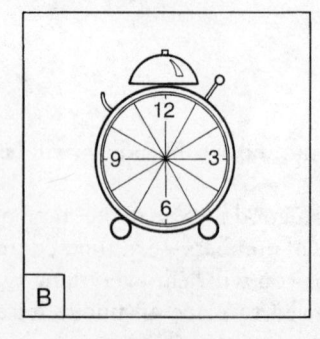

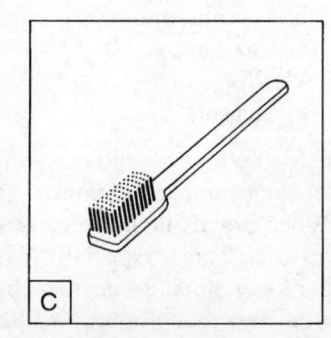

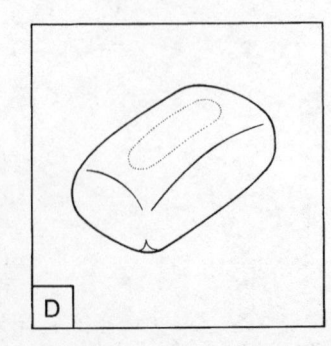

2 „Normalerweise frühstücken wir um Viertel nach sieben. Also müssen wir um sieben Uhr aufstehen."

Bei deiner Brieffreundin in Deutschland. Wann mußt du aufstehen? Kreuze das Richtige an.

- [ ] 6.45
- [ ] 7.15
- [ ] 7.04
- [ ] 7.00

3 „Wir fahren heute mit der Straßenbahn in die Schule."

Bei deiner Brieffreundin. Wie fahrt ihr in die Schule? Schreibe die Antwort auf deutsch.

4 „Du freust dich; die erste Stunde ist Englisch."

In der Schule. Was sagt deine Brieffreundin? Kreuze ein Kästchen an.

- [ ] Englisch ist die erste Stunde.
- [ ] Die erste Stunde ist Mathe.
- [ ] Englisch ist die vierte Stunde.
- [ ] Sie hat Hausaufgaben in Englisch.

5 „Die Englischlehrerin ist sehr nett. Sie spricht aber sehr schnell."

In der Schule. Wie ist die Englischlehrerin? Richtiges ankreuzen.

6 „Der Mathelehrer ist sehr streng. Ich mag ihn gar nicht."

In der Schule. Deine Brieffreundin spricht. Wie findet sie den Mathelehrer? Richtiges ankreuzen.

7 „Ich lerne Englisch schon seit vier Jahren. Wie lange lernst du Deutsch?"

In der Schule. Deine Brieffreundin spricht. Wie lange lernt sie Englisch? Richtiges ankreuzen.

- [ ] seit 14 Jahren
- [ ] seit 4½ Jahren
- [ ] seit 4 Jahren
- [ ] seit 4 Monaten

8 „Mein Lieblingsfach ist Biologie. Ich mache auch gern Kunst und Sport, aber Mathe habe ich gar nicht gern, und ich hasse Musik."

In der Schule. Deine Brieffreundin spricht. Was macht sie gern und was nicht gern? Kreuze die richtigen Kästchen an. ☺=gern ☹=nicht gern

	Biologie	Kunst	Mathe	Musik	Sport
☺					
☹					

9 „Bei uns beginnt die Schule um 8 Uhr, und um 9.25 Uhr haben wir eine Pause. Um 11 Uhr ist die zweite Pause, und um 1.30 Uhr ist die Schule aus."

Der Tag in der Schule. Wann ist was? Füllen Sie die Tabelle aus.

Beispiel: 7.30 Uhr		9.25 Uhr		
Schulbus kommt	Schulbeginn		Zweite Pause	Schule aus

10 „In der Pause kann man beim Hausmeister Cola und Orangensaft kaufen. Er verkauft auch Bonbons und Schokolade, aber kein Kaugummi. Das ist verboten. Heiße Getränke bekommt man am Automaten."

In der Schule. Was kann man beim Hausmeister kaufen? Kreuzen Sie **nur vier Kästchen** an.

- ❏ heiße Getränke
- ❏ Kaugummi
- ❏ Limonade
- ❏ Schokolade
- ❏ Brötchen
- ❏ Cola
- ❏ Bonbons
- ❏ Orangensaft

11 „Mein Klassenzimmer ist im dritten Stock. Zimmer Nummer 114. Das ist eigentlich ein Chemielabor. Unser Klassenlehrer, Herr Gottlieb, ist Lehrer der Naturwissenschaften."

In der Schule. Deine Brieffreundin spricht. Was ist richtig und was falsch? Fülle die Kästchen so aus: ✓ = richtig, ✗ = falsch.

- ❏ Das Klassenzimmer ist Zimmer Nummer 101.
- ❏ Das Klassenzimmer ist im ersten Stock.
- ❏ Das Klassenzimmer ist ein Sprachlabor.
- ❏ Herr Gottlieb lehrt Biologie und Physik.

12 „Hier ist also unser Klassenzimmer. Ich sitze in der Mitte links, neben dem Fenster."

Im Klassenzimmer. Wo sitzt deine Brieffreundin? Kreuze den richtigen Platz an.

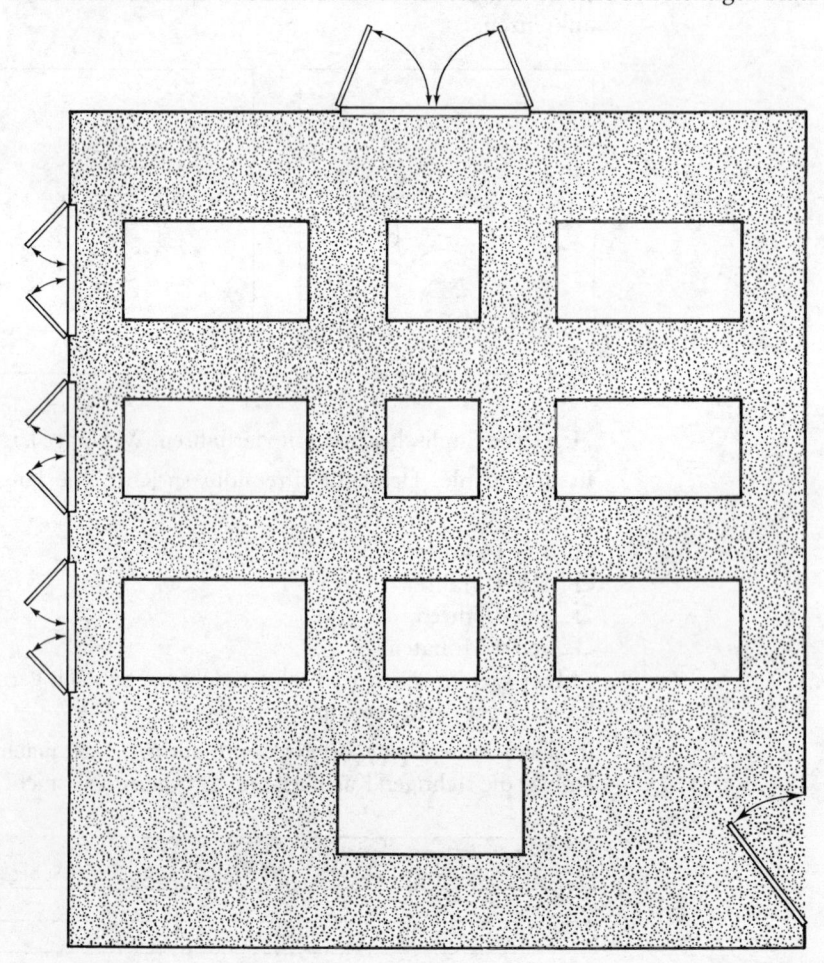

13   „Die Musiklehrerin fehlt heute. Also haben wir in der zweiten Stunde Vertretung."

You are in your German exchange school with an English friend who speaks no German. Explain what your exchange partner says. Tell your friend:

   a) what the second lesson is
   b) what the problem is

14   „Wir schreiben heute nach der zweiten Pause eine Klassenarbeit in Erdkunde. Ihr müßt also in eine andere Klasse gehen. Du kannst vielleicht mit meinem Freund Bodo gehen. Der hat Kunst, glaube ich."

In der Schule. Dein Brieffreund spricht. Fülle die Lücken aus.

In .... schreibt er eine Klassenarbeit. Das ist nach der zweiten .... Du kannst mit .... gehen. Er hat ....

15   „Wir haben gestern Zeugnisse bekommen. Das war für mich nicht so schlimm. Ich habe in Erdkunde, Latein und Englisch eine 2 bekommen. Und in Deutsch sogar eine 1. In Chemie, Physik und Biologie aber bin ich schwächer, da habe ich nur eine 3."

Deine Brieffreundin spricht über ihr Zeugnis. Welche Noten hat sie? Schreibe die Noten (1, 2, 3, 4 usw.) in die Kästchen.

Biologie	Chemie	Deutsch	Englisch	Erdkunde	Latein	Physik

16   „Heute haben wir Schwimmen. Vergiß also deine Badesachen nicht."

Bei deiner Brieffreundin. Was sollst du nicht vergessen? Kreuze das richtige Kästchen an.

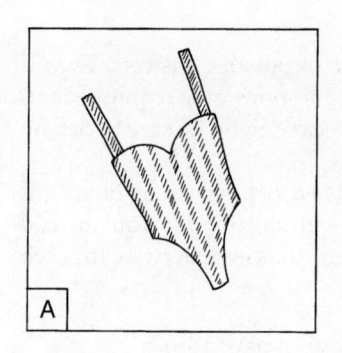

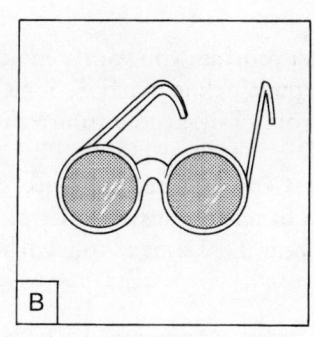

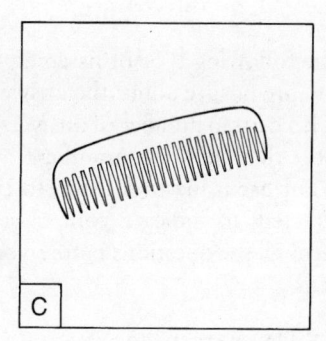

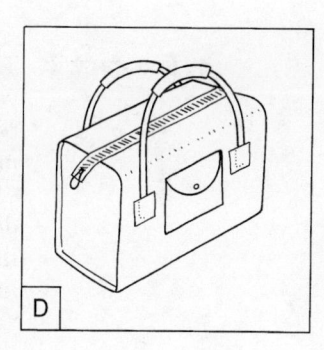

A   B   C   D

17   „Zimmer Nummer 115. Moment mal. Das ist hier rechts neben dem Sprachlabor."

In der Schule. Wo ist Zimmer Nummer 115? Kreuzen Sie das richtige Kästchen an.

18   „Guck mal. Das ist Herr Bachmann, der Mathelehrer. Da, der große Herr mit dem komischen Schnurrbart und der Brille."

In der Schule. Wer ist Herr Bachmann? Kreuzen Sie das richtige Kästchen an.

52 Chapter 4 Listening: Foundation Tier

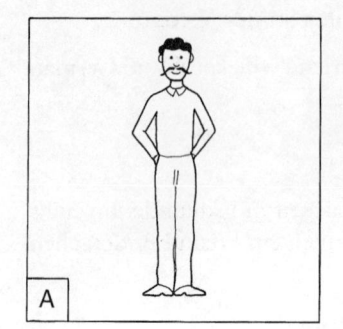

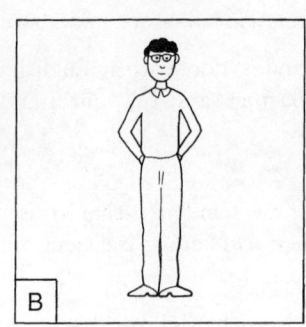

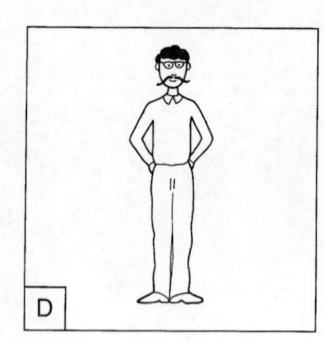

|A|B|C|D|

19 „Ach, weißt du, die Religionstunden sind stinklangweilig."

In der Schule. Deine Austauschpartnerin spricht. Wie findet sie die Religionstunden? Kreuze **ein** Kästchen an.

❑ ☺
❑ 😐
❑ ☹

20 „Ich finde meine Schule eigentlich gut."

In der Schule. Dein Austauschpartner spricht. Wie findet er seine Schule? Kreuze **ein** Kästchen an.

❑ ☺
❑ 😐
❑ ☹

You can see from the above examples that the same kind of stimulus in German can be tested using a variety of different question types. You must be prepared to encounter all of these. More than one item may also be tested from one stimulus.

▶ **Extract 2** The following type of listening test provides you with a choice of possible answers. Even if you are unsure about the answer, put a tick in one box. Some questions may require you to tick a certain number of answers from a list, say four from a choice of eight. Be sure to tick no more than the stated number.

For each question listen to the German statement twice. Then tick a box or boxes (as directed) to indicate your choice of answer/answers. There will be time for you to read through the questions before you hear the German. You will hear the German **twice** for each item.

▶ **Play extract 2** (or have a friend read out numbers 1–10 below on page 58).

1 The train you are travelling on with your parents arrives in Cologne. You hear an announcement. Tell your parents when the train will leave. Tick the correct box.

❑ in 5 minutes
❑ in 10 minutes
❑ in 15 minutes
❑ in 20 minutes

2 Die Wettervorhersage. Was brauchst du? Kreuze das richtige Bild an.

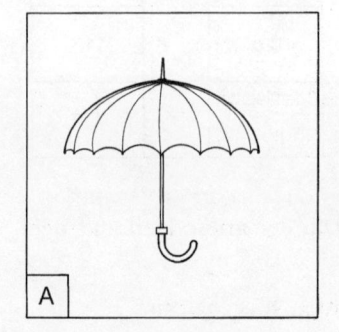

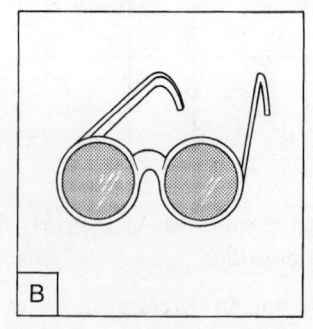

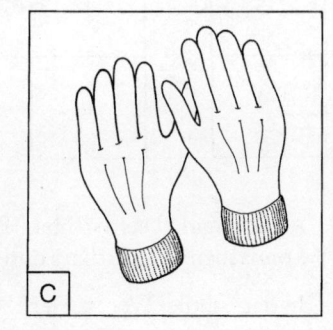

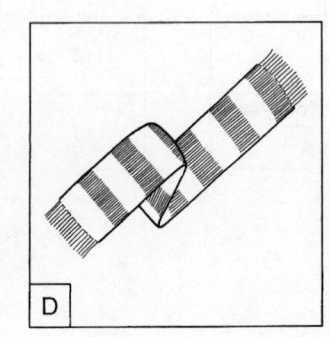

|A|B|C|D|

3 Auf der Post. Was kosten die Briefmarken? Kreuzen Sie die richtige Antwort an.
- ❑ DM 2,80
- ❑ DM 2,18
- ❑ DM 12,80
- ❑ DM 8,20

4 Im Supermarkt. Was ist im Sonderangebot? Kreuzen Sie ein Kästchen an.

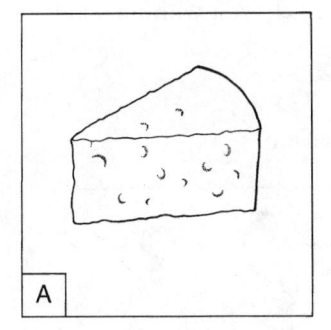

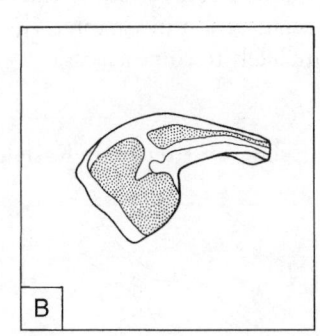

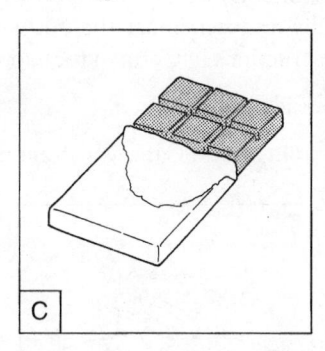

A B C D

5 Im Kino. Wann beginnt der Film?
- ❑ 8.30
- ❑ 7.30
- ❑ 7.15
- ❑ 8.45

6 Your parents are lost and receive directions. Tell them where the chemist's is. Tick the correct answer.
- ❑ 200 metres on the left
- ❑ 100 metres on the right
- ❑ 100 metres on the left
- ❑ 150 metres on the left

7 Im Informationsbüro. Wann ist das Museum geöffnet? Kreuzen Sie ein Kästchen an.
- ❑ montags
- ❑ dienstags
- ❑ mittwochs
- ❑ donnerstags

8 Bei deinem deutschen Freund. Wo ist das Konzert? Kreuze ein Kästchen an.

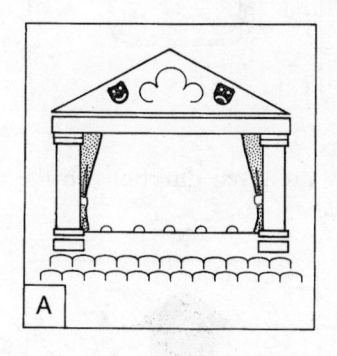

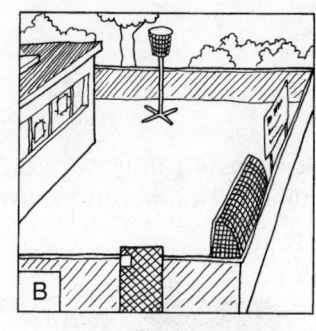

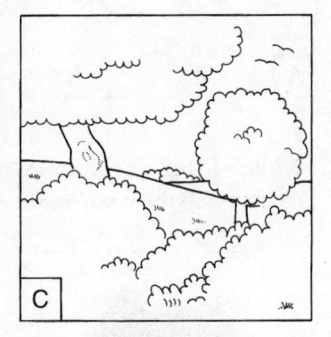

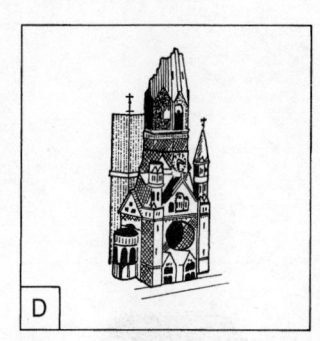

A B C D

9 Dein Brieffreund ruft an. Was hat er verloren? Kreuze **zwei** Kästchen an.
- ❑ eine Schulmappe
- ❑ ein Portemonnaie
- ❑ eine Aktentasche
- ❑ einen Regenschirm
- ❑ ein Schulbuch

10 Your parents want to go to the town centre and receive directions. Tell them how to get there. Tick the correct box.
- ❑ by train
- ❑ by bus
- ❑ by taxi
- ❑ by tram

Answers to each question are given in 'Examination answers' at the end of this chapter (see pages 60–61). To help you check your listening, a **written** version of the extract is provided on page 58.

▶ **Extract 3** In the following extract you will again meet a variety of test types. Read the questions carefully and remember there is a special section in Chapter 16 to help you with the kinds of instructions in German that you are likely to come across.

▶ Play extract 3.

1 Du bist im Café. Was fragt die Kellnerin? Kreuze ein Kästchen an.

2 You are travelling by train in Germany to Boppard with your parents. Tell them:
   (a) what platform the train goes from
   (b) what they must do to get to Boppard

3 Im Geschäft. Du kaufst Postkarten. Was kannst du noch kaufen? Kreuze die richtige Antwort an.

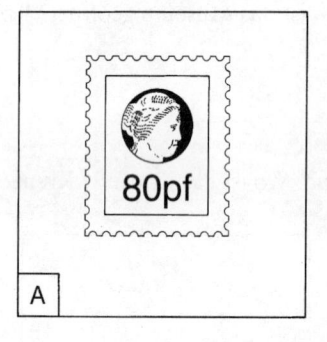

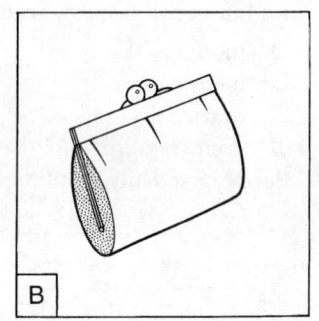

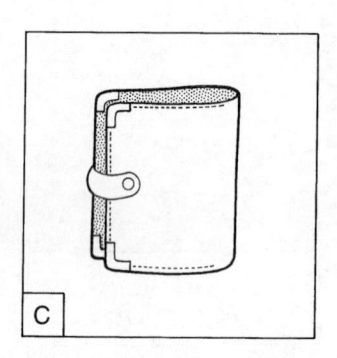

4 While on holiday your parents have lost their way. They are given directions to the station. Tell them where the station is. Tick the correct answer.

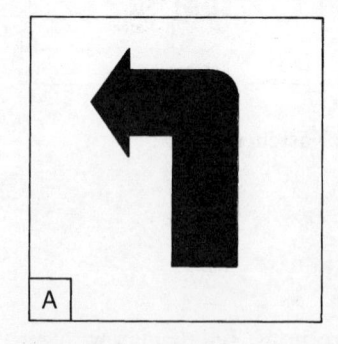

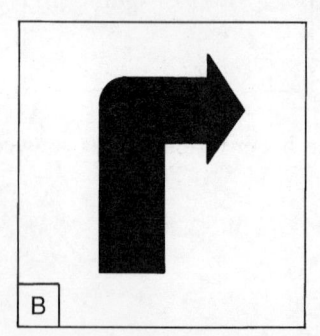

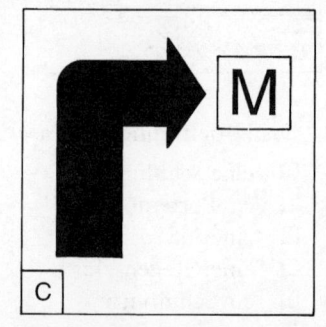

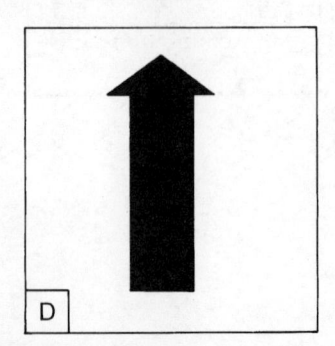

5 Dein Freund Gerd ruft an. Richtig oder falsch? (✓ = richtig, ✗ = falsch)
   ❑ Gerd kann ins Kino gehen.
   ❑ Gerd muß Hausarbeit machen.
   ❑ Gerd muß Hausaufgaben machen.
   ❑ Gerd kann nicht ins Kino gehen.

6 Am Strand. Was hat deine Freundin vergessen? Kreuze **ein** Kästchen an.

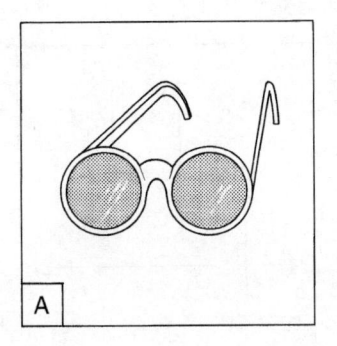

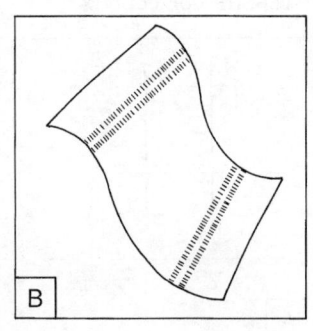

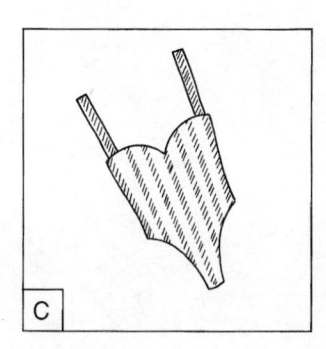

7 Bei deinem Brieffreund. Was mußt du machen? Kreuze **ein** Kästchen an.

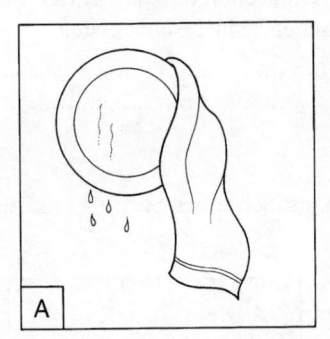

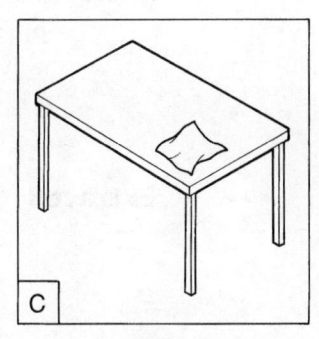

8 In der Drogerie. Was kostet das alles? Fülle die Tabelle mit den Preisen aus.

Beispiel: Seife	Aspirin	Handcreme	Tropfen	Zahnpasta	zusammen
DM 2					

The German conversations you hear in extracts 4–13 are rather longer. A **written** version of these extracts is provided on pages 58–60, with answers on pages 61–62.

▶ **Extract 4** Im Radio. Hören Sie gut zu. Füllen Sie die Lücken aus.

1 Die Dampfer fahren alle .... Minuten.
2 Die letzte Fahrt ist um .... Uhr.
3 Das kostet DM .... hin und zurück.

▶ **Extract 5** You go to the post office with your penfriend. Circle the correct answer.

1 What sort of stamps does she buy?   18 Pf   8 Pf   80 Pf
2 What does she send to Canada?   parcel   postcard   letter
3 What does it cost?   DM 52,50   DM 25,50   DM 50,25

▶ **Extract 6** 1 You want to travel to Frankfurt am Main. You are told when the next train goes. When does it leave? Tick the correct box.
❑ 12.55
❑ 15.55
❑ 15.25
❑ 12.25

2 What platform does the train leave from? Tick the correct box.
❑ 2
❑ 12
❑ 20
❑ 6

56 Chapter 4   Listening: Foundation Tier

3 You want to go to the airport. You are told where to catch the bus. Where is the bus stop? Tick the correct box.

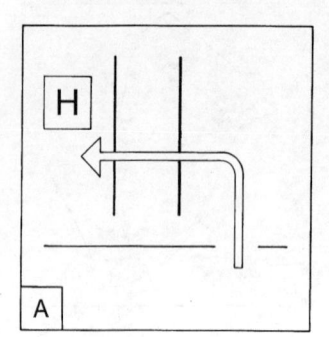

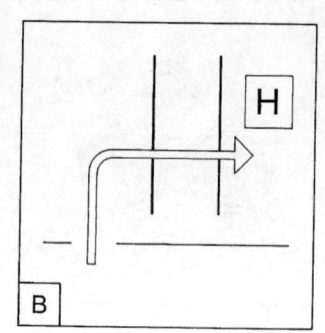

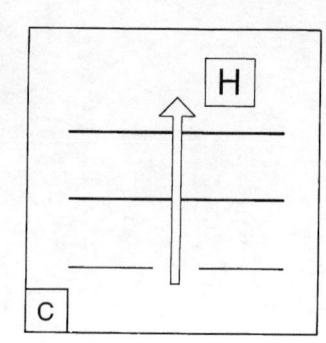

▶ **Extract 7**   1 Bei deinem Brieffreund in Deutschland. Die Mutter deines Brieffreunds spricht. Was kannst du vom Fenster aus sehen? Mache eine Liste.

....
....
....

▶ **Extract 8**   1 Sonderangebote im Warenhaus. Schreiben Sie die Preise zu den richtigen Bildern.
DM 25   DM 35   DM 250

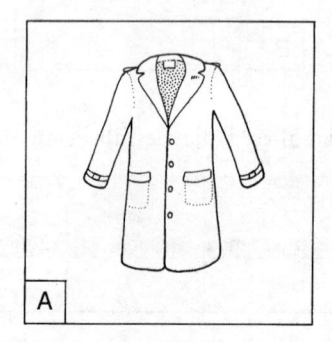

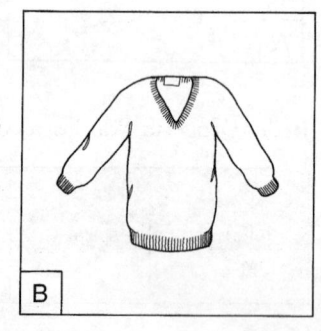

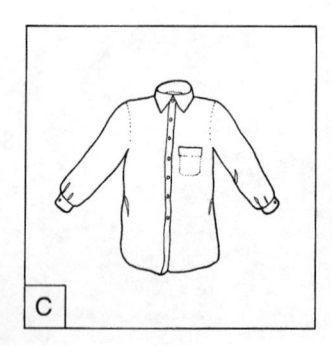

2 You are shopping with your parents. Where is the menswear department?

❏ 1st floor   ❏ 3rd floor
❏ 2nd floor   ❏ 4th floor

▶ **Extract 9**   1 Im Café. Was wird bestellt? Mache einen Kreis um die richtige Nummer, wie im Beispiel.

Beispiel: Erdbeertorte	1	②	3	4
Kirschtorte	1	2	3	4
Kirschtorte mit Sahne	1	2	3	4
Himbeertorte	1	2	3	4
Himbeertorte mit Sahne	1	2	3	4
Tasse Kaffee	1	2	3	4
Kännchen Kaffee	1	2	3	4

2 Deine Brieffreundin spricht. Wie war der Urlaub auf dem Campingplatz? Kreuze die richtigen Kästchen an.

	☺		☹
Brieffreundin		☺	
Mutter			
Vater			
Bruder			

Extract 10 1 Wie ist das Wetter morgen? Kreuzen Sie die richtigen Kästchen an.

	☁️🌧️	☀️	⛅🌧️	🌡️
Beispiel	✓			
Am Vormittag				
Am Nachmittag				
Am Abend				

▷ **Extract 11** 1 You are working on the reception in an English hotel when a German guest rings up to make a booking. Fill in the booking form in English.

```
Date ..................................................

..................................................

Double        with bath

Single        with shower

(Circle room type booked)

Number of guests ................................

Room rate (per night) ...........................

Name ................................................
```

▷ **Extract 12** 1 Im Verkehrsbüro. Sie wollen ins Museum gehen. Füllen Sie die Tabelle aus.

HEIMATMUSEUM

Öffnungszeiten:
Von........................bis........................

Jeden Tag geöffnet, außer ....und
....

Eintrittspreise: Erwachsene   DM....................
                     Kinder bis 16 DM....................

Eintrittskarten im ....und im
.... erhältlich.

58 Chapter 4 Listening: Foundation Tier

▷ **Extract 13**   1   Inge spricht über ihren Stundenplan. Schauen Sie den Stundenplan an. Füllen Sie die Lücken 1, 2, 3, 4 und 5 aus.

Stunde	Zeit	Montag	Dienstag	Mittwoch
1	8.00	Kunst	Englisch	Erdkunde
2	8.45	Kunst	Mathe	Geschichte
	9.30	Pause	Pause	Pause
3	9.50	1	2	Mathe
4	10.35	Physik	Französisch	3
5	11.35	Französisch	Erdkunde	Mathe
6	12.15	Mathe	4	Biologie
7	13.00	Frei	5	Frei

▷ WRITTEN VERSION OF EXTRACTS

▷ **Extract 2**
1. Achtung auf Gleis 4. Der Zug nach Berlin fährt in fünf Minuten ab.
2. Und jetzt die Wettervorhersage bis heute abend: überwiegend sonniges Wetter mit Temperaturen um 10 Grad.
3. Also, vier Briefmarken zu siebzig Pfennig ... macht zusammen zwei Mark achtzig.
4. Heute, meine Damen und Herren, haben wir in der Lebensmittelabteilung ein Sonderangebot: italienischen Rotwein, vier Mark zehn die Flasche.
5. Die Vorstellung beginnt um halb acht.
6. Es gibt eine Apotheke nur hundert Meter von hier, auf der linken Seite.
7. Das Museum ist nur donnerstags geöffnet.
8. Am Freitagabend ist ein Popkonzert im Park.
9. Hallo, hier Jürgen. Ich komme später. Ich muß zum Fundbüro, weil ich mein Portemonnaie und ein Schulbuch verloren habe.
10. Am besten fahren Sie mit der Straßenbahnlinie dreizehn.

▷ **Extract 3**   For checking purposes:

▷ The extract is printed below.

▷ Answers are provided in the 'Examination answers' at the end of the chapter (see page 61).

1. *Kellnerin:* Und zu trinken?
2. *Beamter:* Der nächste Zug von Gleis vier fährt nach Wiesbaden. Für Boppard in Bonn umsteigen.
3. *Verkäufer:* Hätten Sie auch gern Briefmarken dazu?
4. *Fußgänger:* Hier geradeaus. Der Bahnhof liegt am Marktplatz.
5. *Gerd:* Ich kann leider nicht ins Kino gehen. Ich muß meine Hausaufgaben für morgen machen.
6. *Freundin:* Ach! Ich habe mein Badetuch vergessen!
7. *Frau Schmidt:* Ach wie nett! Könntest du vielleicht abtrocknen? Birgit wäscht ab.
8. *Verkäuferin:* Also ... Eine Tube Zahnpasta, DM 3,25
                 Aspirin, DM 12,50
                 Tropfen gegen Ohrenschmerzen, DM 4,99
                 Handcreme, DM 6,50
                 Macht zusammen DM 27,24

▷ **Extract 4**   Warum nicht einen Ausflug mit dem Dampfer nach Königswinter machen? Die Dampfer der KD-Linie fahren alle 45 Minuten von Bonn ab. Fahrtdauer eine Stunde fünfundzwanzig Minuten. Letzte Fahrt um 18 Uhr. Die einfache Fahrt kostet nur 12 Mark, oder 18 Mark hin und zurück. Genießen Sie den romantischen Rhein mit der KD-Linie!

▷ **Extract 5**
 – Geben Sie mir bitte drei Briefmarken zu 80 Pfennig.
 – So, bitte sehr. Sonst noch etwas?

- Ja. Ich möchte auch noch dieses Päckchen nach Kanada schicken. Was kostet das, bitte?
- Moment, bitte! 600 Gramm nach Kanada kosten DM 25,50. Macht zusammen DM 27,90.

▶ **Extract 6** 1 Der Zug nach Frankfurt am Main fährt um 12.55 von Gleis 6 ab.
2 Achtung auf Gleis 12. Bitte einsteigen und Türen schließen. Der Zug fährt gleich ab.
3 Zum Flughafen? Das ist ganz einfach. Gehen Sie hier aus dem Haupteingang raus und dann links über die Straße. Da gibt's eine Bushaltestelle für die Flughafenbusse. Das ist die Linie 30.

▶ **Extract 7** Hier ist dein Zimmer. Du hast eine schöne Aussicht auf den Park. Komm hier zum Fenster. Siehst du, du kannst die Bäume sehen, und dort drüben ist das Rathaus. Hier links ist die Kirche und dahinter der Fluß. Schön, nicht wahr.

▶ **Extract 8** Meine Damen und Herren! Wir haben heute in der Herrenabteilung im Sonderangebot: preiswerte Pullover zu DM 35, Hemden zu DM 25 und englische Regenmäntel zum Superpreis von DM 250. Besuchen Sie also die Herrenabteilung im dritten Stock.

▶ **Extract 9** 1 - Fräulein, wir möchten bestellen.
- Ja, bitte.
- Also, zweimal Kirschtorte mit Sahne, zweimal Himbeertorte und vier Kännchen Kaffee.
- Möchten Sie die Himbeertorte mit Sahne?
- Nein, danke.
2 Letztes Jahr haben wir auf einem Campingplatz Urlaub gemacht. Das war im Juli, und das Wetter war sehr gut. Für mich war der Urlaub O.K. Meinem Bruder hat der Campingplatz gut gefallen, und für meine Mutter war es dort auch schön, aber Vater war gar nicht zufrieden. Ihm hat es zu viel Mühe gemacht.

▶ **Extract 10** Und jetzt, meine Damen und Herren, die Wettervorhersage für morgen. Am Vormittag überwiegend sonnig und warm mit Temperaturen um 22 Grad. Später am Nachmittag wolkig mit Schauern. Am Abend andauernder Regen, und die Temperaturen sinken bis auf 16 Grad.

▶ **Extract 11** - Hallo. The George Hotel?
- Ja, hallo. Kann ich Ihnen helfen?
- Haben Sie ein Zimmer für zwei Nächte?
- Für wann, bitte?
- Für den zwölften und dreizehnten Juni.
- Moment bitte. Was für ein Zimmer möchten Sie?
- Ein Doppelzimmer mit Bad.
- Also für zwei Personen?
- Ja.
- Ja, das haben wir. Möchten Sie das Zimmer reservieren?
- Ja, was kostet das?
- Fünfundvierzig Pfund pro Nacht. Wie ist Ihr Name?
- Hubert.
- Also, H-U-B-E-R-T.
- Ja. Danke schön.
- Danke schön, Herr Hubert. Die Reservierung ist schon gemacht. Auf Wiederhören.

▶ **Extract 12** Unser Heimatmuseum ist jeden Tag von 10.30 Uhr bis 17.30 Uhr geöffnet, außer sonntags und mittwochs. Die Eintrittspreise sind für Erwachsene drei Mark und für Kinder bis 16 Jahre eine Mark fünfzig. Sie können die Eintrittskarten hier im Verkehrsbüro oder im Museum kaufen.

▶ **Extract 13**   Die Schule beginnt um 8 Uhr. Montags habe ich in der ersten und zweiten Stunde Kunst. Um halb zehn beginnt die Frühstückspause, und ich esse meine Butterbrote. In der dritten Stunde, um neun Uhr fünfzig, habe ich Englisch, dann Physik, Französisch und Mathe. Die Schule ist um dreizehn Uhr aus.

Dienstags beginne ich mit Englisch und Mathe. Nach der Frühstückspause habe ich Geschichte, dann Französisch und Erdkunde und schließlich in der sechsten und siebten Stunde Musik – eine Doppelstunde.

Mittwochs habe ich Erdkunde in der ersten und Geschichte in der zweiten Stunde. Nach der Frühstückspause habe ich Mathematik – eine Doppelstunde, in der fünften Stunde Deutsch und in der sechsten Biologie.

▶ EXAMINATION ANSWERS

▶ **Extract 1**
1. B alarm clock
2. 7.00
3. mit der Straßenbahn
4. Englisch ist die erste Stunde.
5. B
6. A
7. seit 4 Jahren
8.

	Biologie	Kunst	Mathe	Musik	Sport
☺	x	x			x
☹			x	x	

9.

7.30 Uhr	8 Uhr	9.25 Uhr	11 Uhr	1.30 Uhr
Schulbus kommt	Schulbeginn	Pause	zweite Pause	Schule aus

10. Bonbons
    Schokolade
    Cola
    Orangensaft
11. ☒ Das Klassenzimmer ist Zimmer Nummer 101.
    ☒ Das Klassenzimmer ist im ersten Stock.
    ☒ Das Klassenzimmer ist ein Sprachlabor.
    ☑ Herr Gottlieb lehrt Biologie und Physik.
12. The seat on the left next to the window.
13. a) music
    b) the teacher is absent/there is a substitute teacher
14. Erdkunde
    Pause
    Bodo
    Kunst
15.

Biologie	Chemie	Deutsch	Englisch	Erdkunde	Latein	Physik
3	3	1	2	2	2	3

16. A swimming things
17. C
18. D
19. ☹
20. ☺

▶ **Extract 2**
1. in 5 minutes
2. B sunglasses
3. DM 2,80

Examination answers: Extract 3   61

    4 D wine
    5 7.30
    6 100 metres on the left
    7 donnerstags
    8 C in the park
    9 ein Portemonnaie
        ein Schulbuch
   10 by tram

▶ **Extract 3**
1. B 'What would you like to drink?'
2. platform 4
   change trains in Bonn
3. A stamps
4. D straight ahead (in the market place)
5. ☒ Gerd kann ins Kino gehen.
   ☒ Gerd muß Hausarbeit machen.
   ☑ Gerd muß Hausaufgaben machen.
   ☑ Gerd kann nicht ins Kino gehen.
6. B towel
7. A dry up the dishes
8.

Beispiel: Seife	Aspirin	Handcreme	Tropfen	Zahnpasta	zusammen
DM 2	DM 12,50	DM 6,50	DM 4,99	DM 3,25	DM 27,24

▶ **Extract 4**
1. 45
2. 18
3. 18

▶ **Extract 5**
1. 80 Pf
2. a parcel
3. DM 25,50

▶ **Extract 6**
1. 12.55
2. 12
3. A

▶ **Extract 7**
Park   Kirche
Bäume   Fluß
Rathaus

▶ **Extract 8**
1. rain coat DM 250
   pullover   DM 35
   shirt   DM 25
2. 3rd floor

▶ **Extract 9**
1.

Kirschtorte	1	2	3	4
Kirschtorte mit Sahne	1	②	3	4
Himbeertorte	1	②	3	4
Himbeertorte mit Sahne	1	2	3	4
Tasse Kaffee	1	2	3	4
Kännchen Kaffee	1	2	3	④

2

	☺	😐	☹
Brieffreundin		✓	
Mutter	✓		
Vater			✓
Bruder	✓		

▶ **Extract 10**

	Rain	Sun	Showers	Hot
Beispiel	✓			
Am Vormittag		✓		✓
Am Nachmittag			✓	
Am Abend	✓			

▶ **Extract 11**   Date: 12.6 and 13.6
Room: Double with bath
Guests: 2
Room rate: £45
Name: Hubert

▶ **Extract 12**

HEIMATMUSEUM

Öffnungszeiten:
Von............*10.30*............bis............*17.30*............

Jeden Tag geöffnet, außer ....*mittwochs*........und
........*sonntags*........

Eintrittspreise: Erwachsene   DM............*3*............

Kinder bis 16   DM............*1.50*............

Eintrittskarten im ....*Verkehrsbüro*............und im
............*Museum*............ erhältlich.

▶ **Extract 13**

Stunde	Zeit	Montag	Dienstag	Mittwoch
1	8.00	Kunst	Englisch	Erdkunde
2	8.45	Kunst	Mathe	Geschichte
	9.30	Pause	Pause	Pause
3	9.50	1 *Englisch*	2 *Geschichte*	Mathe
4	10.35	Physik	Französisch	Mathe
5	11.35	Französisch	Erdkunde	3 *Deutsch*
6	12.15	Mathe	4 *Musik*	Biologie
7	13.00	Frei	5 *Musik*	Frei

TESTS WITH STUDENT ANSWERS

Here are some examples of Foundation Tier listening tests with student answers. An experienced examiner has marked them and added comments. Notice that the total marks available are given in brackets after some questions. This should indicate if and when two or more items are required in the answer. If your answer only has one item, and several marks are available for the answer, it is likely that your answer is incomplete.

Test 1

This is what the student heard:

Aufgabe eins. Jürgens Familie. Schreiben Sie Ihre Antworten auf deutsch.
Hören Sie jetzt zu.

– Also, Jürgen, du bist vierzehn Jahre alt, nicht?
– Ja, das stimmt.
– Und hast du Geschwister?
– Ja, zwei Brüder und eine Schwester. Mein älterer Bruder ist sechzehn, mein jüngerer Bruder ist elf, und meine Schwester ist zwanzig Jahre alt.
– Und lebt deine Schwester noch zu Hause?
– Nein, meine Schwester arbeitet als Sekretärin in Wiesbaden, und meine Brüder gehen noch in die Schule.
– Hast du Haustiere?
– Ja, ich habe einen Hund namens Boris und zwei Meerschweinchen. Boris ist braun und weiß und ganz alt. Die Meerschweinchen sind schwarz und haben weiße Nasen.

Question and student answer

Jürgens Familie. Schreiben Sie Ihre Antworten auf **deutsch**.
Füllen Sie die Tabelle aus. Hören Sie gut zu.
Beispiel: NAME: Jürgen

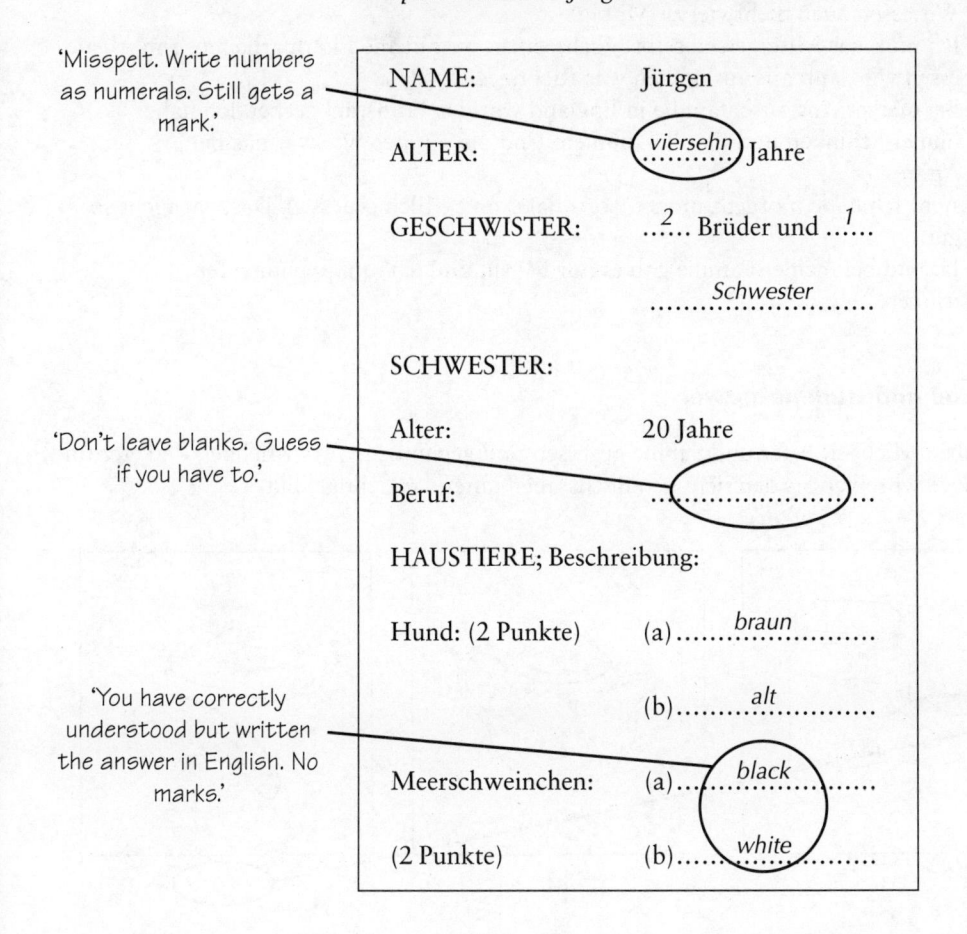

NAME:	Jürgen
ALTER:	*viersehn* Jahre ← 'Misspelt. Write numbers as numerals. Still gets a mark.'
GESCHWISTER:	...2... Brüder und ...1... Schwester
SCHWESTER:	
Alter:	20 Jahre
Beruf:	.... ← 'Don't leave blanks. Guess if you have to.'
HAUSTIERE; Beschreibung:	
Hund: (2 Punkte)	(a) *braun*
	(b) *alt*
Meerschweinchen:	(a) *black* ← 'You have correctly understood but written the answer in English. No marks.'
(2 Punkte)	(b) *white*

Chapter 4 Listening: Foundation Tier

▷ **Test 2** This is what the student heard:

1 Den Big Mac gibt es jetzt zum Superpreis von DM 2,89. Hamburger haben nie so gut geschmeckt!
2 Fahrkosten müssen nicht unbedingt so hoch sein. Kaufen Sie Ihr Benzin jetzt bei Aldi, wo alles preiswerter ist!
3 Sauberer denn je! NEF hat für Sie die besten Waschmaschinen!
4 Telefonieren Sie 60 Minuten gratis, wenn Sie vor Weihnachten ein neues Telefon kaufen. So leicht war es nie!

Question and student answer

You are listening to the radio and hear four advertisements. Tell your English friend what is being advertised.

1	Product	Hamburger
2	Product	*Benzin*
3	Product	washing machine
4	Product	telephone

'Yes. But the answer should be in English, i.e. Petrol' — (pointing to Benzin)

▷ **Test 3** This is what the student heard:

P Mensch! Ich habe einen Riesenhunger!
M Hast du heute morgen kein Frühstück gehabt, Peter?
P Nein, ich habe wieder keine Zeit gehabt, und in der Pause habe ich nur eine Tüte Chips gegessen.
M Ich habe heute morgen Brötchen mit Marmelade gegessen und auch etwas Käse. In der Pause habe ich nur eine Apfelsine gegessen. Zu Mittag esse ich Suppe.
P Wir essen auch nicht viel zu Mittag.
M Ich muß das Mittagessen selbst vorbereiten, weil meine Eltern arbeiten. Am Abend essen wir dann alle zusammen was Richtiges.
P Bei meiner Austauschfamilie in England war das Frühstück lecker. Ich habe immer Schinken und Eier bekommen. Und du Sabine? Wie war das bei Andrew?
S Ach! Ich habe morgens immer Corn-flakes mit Milch gegessen. Das war nicht so gut.
M Ja, und bei meiner Familie gab es nur Müsli, und ich mußte immer Tee trinken.

Question and student answer

Was haben Michael, Peter und Sabine gegessen und getrunken? (M=Michael, P=Peter und S=Sabine) Schreiben Sie den richtigen Buchstaben unter das richtige Bild.

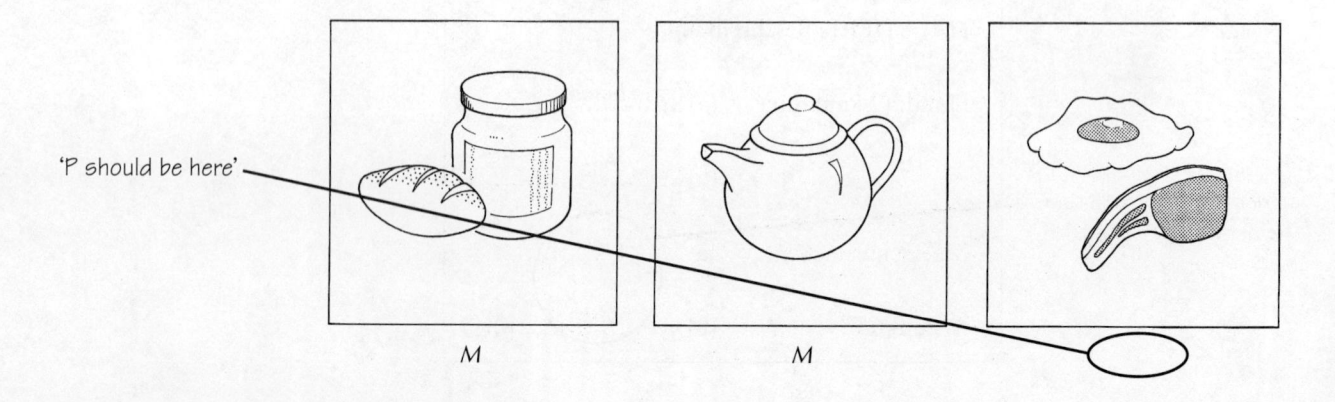

'P should be here' — (pointing to the third image)

| M | M | (blank) |

'Wrong. It should be egg & bacon.' — S

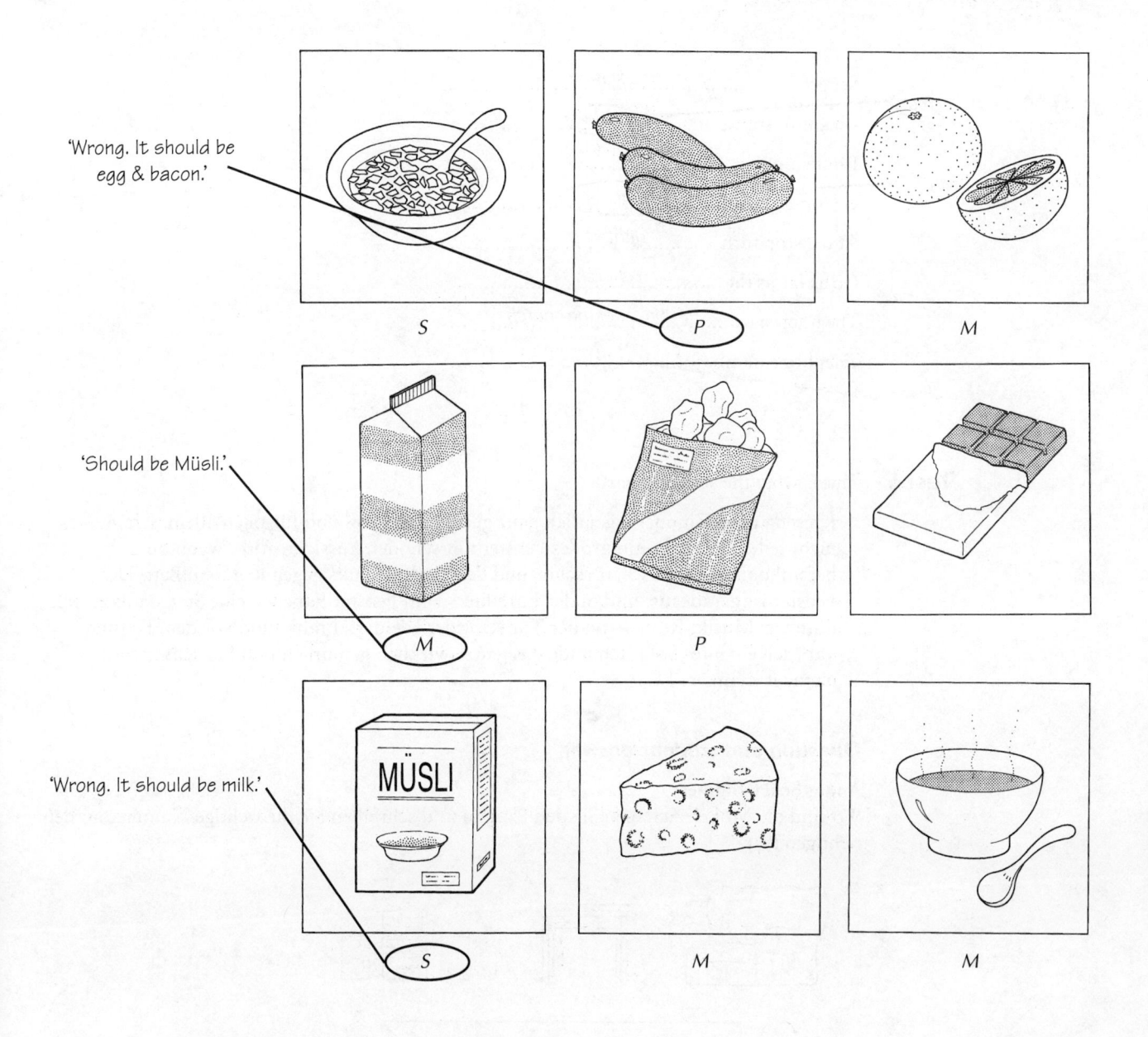

P (circled, pointing to cereal bowl)

'Should be Müsli.' — M (circled, pointing to milk carton)

'Wrong. It should be milk.' — S (circled, pointing to Müsli box)

Top row: S — P — M
Middle row: M — P — (chocolate)
Bottom row: S — M — M

> **Test 4** This is what the student heard:

– Hast du Lust, am Freitagabend bei mir zu essen? Wir können dann nachher ins Kino gehen.
– Ja, das wäre nett. Wie komme ich denn am besten zu dir? Ich habe deine Adresse, aber ich weiß nicht genau, wo das ist.
– Das ist einfach. Hast du was zum Schreiben da?
– Ja, O.K., los.
– Also, du bist schon in der Nähe des Bahnhofs. Vom Bahnhof nimmst du die Straßenbahn Linie 18. Das ist Richtung Universität. Du steigst am Kino in Neuwald aus. An der Haltestelle gehst du rechts und dann geradeaus bis zur Kirche. Unser Haus ist 100 Meter hinter der Kirche.
– Gut, das habe ich.
– Wenn du dich verirrst, kannst du anrufen. Die Nummer ist 45 12 20. Bis dann.
– Tschüß. Und danke.

Question and student answer

While you are in Germany a friend phones with an invitation. How do you get to his house?

Write your answers in English.

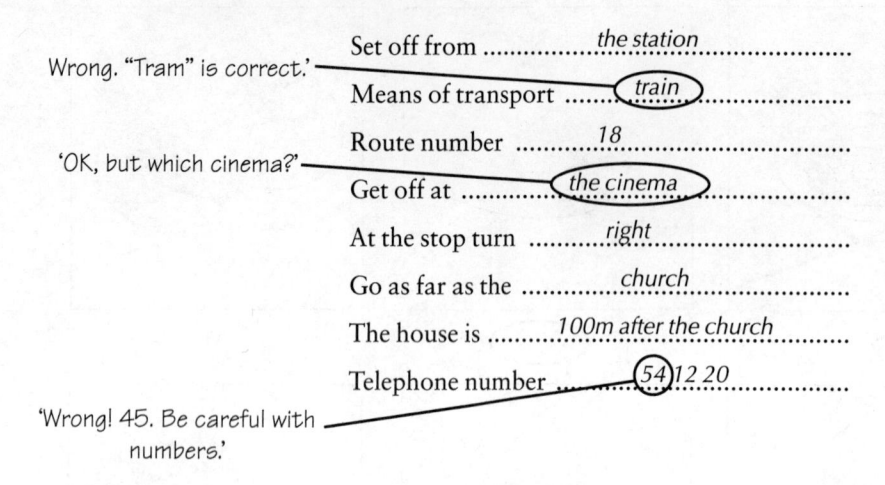

Wrong. "Tram" is correct.'	Set off from .... *the station* ....
	Means of transport .... (*train*) ....
'OK, but which cinema?'	Route number .... *18* ....
	Get off at .... (*the cinema*) ....
	At the stop turn .... *right* ....
	Go as far as the .... *church* ....
	The house is .... *100m after the church* ....
	Telephone number .... (*54*)*12 20* ....
'Wrong! 45. Be careful with numbers.'	

▶ **Test 5**   This is what the student heard:

> Ich mag mein Zimmer eigentlich ganz gern. Es ist groß und für mich allein. Ich muß es nicht teilen. Ich habe ein großes Fenster mit schöner Aussicht. Also, wenn du hereinkommst, ist das Bett rechts, und der Tisch ist links gegenüber dem Bett. Das Fenster ist geradeaus, und in der Ecke links vom Fenster habe ich eine Stereoanlage. Ich höre viel Musik. Rechts von der Tür steht der Kleiderschrank, und vor dem Fenster habe ich ein altes Sofa. Ich finde das ganze wirklich gemütlich und bin sehr gern in meinem Zimmer.

Question and student answer

Anitas Schlafzimmer.
Wo sind die Möbel? Schauen Sie den Plan an und schreiben Sie die richtige Nummer an den richtigen Platz.

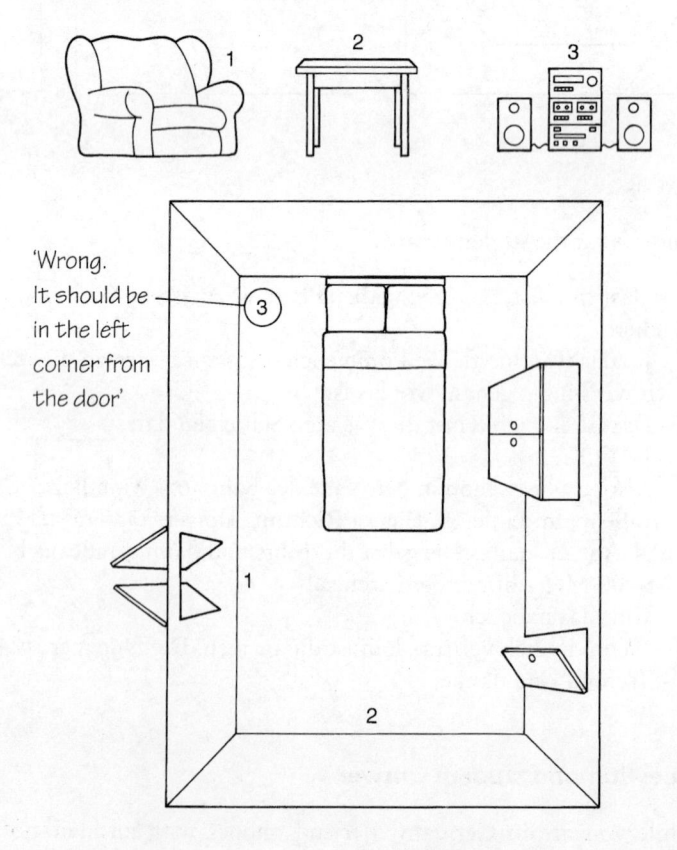

'Wrong. It should be in the left corner from the door'

Suggestions for improving your listening skills can be found in 'A step further' at the end of the next chapter.

Chapter 5

Listening: Higher Tier

▶ **GETTING STARTED**

The Higher Tier listening tests for all the examining groups are based on the same fundamental principles as the Foundation Tier tests. Higher Tier Listening overlaps to some extent with the Foundation Tier. That is to say that the easier questions at the start of the Higher Tier examinations may have formed the harder questions at the end of the Foundation Tier examination. MEG sets three exam papers (Sections 1, 2 and 3). Section 2 is common to both Foundation and Higher Tiers. Remember that you can only sit one tier. This means that you will have to give careful thought to which tier to enter. You must remember that unless you reach the standard at Higher Tier required for a grade D, you will only get a U (unclassified) in this part of the exam. This in turn may have serious consequences for your overall grade. If you are confident and successful with the more difficult questions at Foundation Tier you should be able to cope with Higher Tier.

▶ **WHAT YOU NEED TO KNOW**

▶ **Requirements**

What do you have to do?

You will be expected to demonstrate the skills required for the Foundation Tier and in addition perform the extra tasks defined in the topic areas as being for Higher Tier only (see Chapter 3).

In general you will be expected to show that you can:

- identify the **important points** or **themes** of the material
- understand the **attitudes, emotions** and **ideas** of the speakers
- **draw conclusions** from what you hear
- identify the **relationship** between the ideas expressed
- **infer meanings** from the extracts.

As with Foundation Tier all the material must be authentic and intended to be for listening to. The extracts may well contain natural hesitation, spontaneous repetition or rephrasing of sentences and a certain amount of background noise.

All extracts will be recorded by native German speakers. Extracts will be heard twice. You will be able to make notes during the test. Longer extracts will be broken down into shorter sections so as not to place too heavy a burden on your memory, though the sections may well be longer than at Foundation Tier.

You will be given reading time before the beginning of the test itself, during which you may consult a dictionary as you read through the questions. You may **not** consult a dictionary during the test itself.

▶ **Themes**

What kind of extracts can you expect?

As we saw in Chapter 4, the main sources for testing **listening comprehension** are likely to be:

- **public announcements**, e.g. in public places, shops, on the radio or television
- **news, weather, traffic reports, advertisements**
- **telephone calls**
- **guided tours**
- **interviews**, on radio or television, **surveys**
- **conversations, dialogues, discussions**, both **formal** and **informal**.

Some of the extracts, such as announcements, will be quite short, while others, such as discussions and interviews, are likely to be longer.

Obviously your understanding of a wide range of vocabulary is going to be put to the test. But it is always helpful to know where to start and what to expect. It is, then, worth considering in more detail the themes mentioned above.

Public announcements

You could expect to hear any of the following:

- **announcements at a railway station, bus station, airport, ferry terminal** – these will inevitably deal with travel arrangements, such as times of departure and arrival, changes to timetables (e.g. delays), a reminder to change trains, requests to get off, board, to go to gate 3, to report to reception
- **announcements at a campsite, hostel, hotel** – these will tend to be about facilities offered (e.g. 'campers are reminded that fresh milk and groceries can be bought in the camp shop'), special events such as evening barbecues, trips to places of local interest, excursions to local beauty spots, requests to come to reception, messages passed on from people telephoning or visiting, emergencies
- **announcements in shops** – mostly in department stores, e.g. advertising goods, special offers, bargains, sales, cheese tasting, wine tasting, café/restaurant menus, holidays etc.
- **announcements on the radio or television** – these announcements could well include commercial advertisements (e.g. for goods or services), or local features (e.g. what's on in the region, diary of coming events such as films, plays, sports events, exhibitions etc.).

News, weather, traffic reports, advertisements

You can expect these to include:

- **reports of current, topical news items** such as visits, accidents, disasters, industrial unrest, strikes, protests, famous personalities, sports, special events, occasional 'funny' stories
- **weather forecasts** mentioning temperatures, general conditions, trends, special conditions for holiday makers or skiers, natural disasters such as floods
- **road conditions, motorway reports** mentioning traffic jams (very common on German motorways), road works, diversions, accidents, advice/hints, features for holiday makers.

Telephone calls

These could include:

- messages of all kinds for someone who is not present
- a pen friend ringing you up to make arrangements, pass on information
- someone ringing you to report reasons for delay
- recorded messages, e.g. when you telephone a tourist information service and get a pre-recorded message.

Guided tours

These will obviously relate to places and features of interest. You are likely to be asked for information about dates, ages, descriptions, special features, traditions, history, famous people, stories of interest.

Interviews on the radio or television, surveys

These could well include:

- famous people talking about their lives, interests, careers
- experts talking about their specialist areas
- features of general interest, e.g. holidays, jobs, fashion, education, music, entertainment, sport, politics, the environment and 'green' issues
- ordinary people talking about any of the above and giving opinions and points of view
- open-call programmes.

Conversations, dialogues, discussions (formal and informal)

These could cover any of the areas mentioned above in interviews, but:

- **formal** discussions could include more serious matters and people, e.g. politicians
- **informal** conversations could well take place in the home environment, e.g. parents and children talking about holidays, free time, school, TV etc. The tone is likely to be rather different.

Remember that at Higher Tier you will be expected to understand details, such as facts, in the same way as at Foundation Tier, but you will also have to show that you can understand people's more complex views or feelings about things and the reasons for them. This goes beyond understanding likes and dislikes and other simple opinions that you may encounter at Foundation Tier. The specimen questions that follow will help to focus attention on this.

EXAMINATION QUESTIONS

As with Foundation Tier you can expect a variety of question types. These are best summarised as follows:

- questions in English requiring answers in English (this type is only allowed to form a small part of the test)
- questions in German requiring answers in German
- completing a table/form/note/grid in German or English or with ticks etc.
- true/false questions in German.

Again you can play extracts on the tape. Each extract is written out in full, so if you have bought the book separately, you can listen to your friend reading the extract to you. Sometimes the reader will need to play more than one role.

Extract 1 Your sister's German boyfriend rings. Pass on the message to your sister. Write the message in **English**.

```
                    TELEPHONE MESSAGES

    To: ............ Kelly ..........................................................

    From: ........ Wolfgang ....................................................

    Message: .......................................................................

    ..................................................................................

    ..................................................................................

    ..................................................................................

    ..................................................................................
```

Extract 2 Dein Brieffreund ist krank. Du gehst für ihn zur Apotheke. Beantworte die Fragen deines Brieffreundes auf **deutsch**.

Beispiel: Was haben die Tabletten gekostet? .... DM 12

1 Was soll ich essen, wenn ich Hunger habe? ....(1)
2 Und wenn ich Durst habe? ....(1)

3 Wie oft muß ich die Tabletten nehmen? ....(2)
4 Und wenn es mir nicht besser geht? ....(1)

▷ **Extract 3** You take a telephone call from the father of your brother's pen friend. Pass the message on to your parents. Write your answers in **English**.

```
                    TELEPHONE MESSAGE

 Wolfgang will arrive in ...........................................................................

 at ..........................................................................................................

 That is next ...........................................................................................

 He will be wearing ..........................................................................and

 ..........................................and carrying ..............................................

 If you're late collecting him ...................................................................

 ...............................................................................................................

 ...............................................................................................................

 ...............................................................................................................
```

▷ **Extract 4** Bei deiner Brieffreundin. Warum hat Dieter angerufen? Sag es Karin und ihren Eltern. Beantworte die Fragen auf **deutsch**.

1 Warum kommt Dieter später? ....
2 Wo ist er? ....
3 Wie geht es Dieter? ....
4 Was ist mit seinem Auto? ....
5 Warum mußte er stark bremsen? ....
6 Was macht er im Moment? ....
7 Wie kommt er nach Hause? ....

▷ **Extract 5** Im Radio. Sie hören die Wettervorhersage. Was ist richtig, und was ist falsch? Beschriften Sie die Kästchen mit F=falsch, oder R=richtig.
Beispiel: Heute abend sinken die Temperaturen im südlichen Bergland auf 1 bis 4 Grad. R.

1 ☐ Morgen vormittag wird es im Norden Nebel geben.
2 ☐ Dann gibt es Sonne.
3 ☐ Am Vormittag wird es im Süden und Osten wolkig sein.
4 ☐ Der Wind wird überall stark sein.
5 ☐ Fürs Wochenende sollen Sie nichts im Freien planen.

▷ **Extract 6** Dein Brieffreund und seine Schwester sprechen über das Fernsehprogramm. Beantworte die Fragen auf **deutsch**.
1 Was kommt heute abend im Fernsehen? ....
   ....(3)
2 Wie haben Anna und Martin die Serie gefunden? ....(1)

3 Warum ist Martin unglücklich? ....(1)
4 Wie reagiert Anna darauf? ....(1)

▷ **Extract 7** Umweltfragen zu Hause. Markiere die folgenden Sätze richtig (✓) oder falsch (✗).

1 Die Familie muß den Müll sortieren.
2 Am Wochenende fährt die Familie viel mit dem Auto.
3 Die Mutter achtet nicht auf Verpackungen beim Einkaufen.
4 Die Familie spart Energie.
5 Energie sparen heißt auch Geld sparen.
6 Die Familie braucht Bioabfälle für den Garten.
7 Die Ökoprodukte sind billig.

▷ **Extract 8** Lotte und Heinz sprechen über die neue Autobahn.
Markiere die folgenden Sätze richtig (✓) oder falsch (✗).

1 Die Autobahn reduziert den Verkehr auf der Bundesstraße in Waldhausen.
2 Der Verkehr in Waldhausen ist nicht so schlimm.
3 Heinz steht jeden Morgen im Stau.
4 Die Autobahn schadet der Umwelt.
5 Heinz findet die Autobahn gut.

Beantworte die folgenden Fragen auf **deutsch**.

6 Was denkt Lotte über die Autobahn? ....
....
7 Warum ist der Wald für Heinz wichtig? ....
....

▷ **Extract 9** Du machst eine Stadtrundfahrt durch Berlin. Höre der Stadtführerin zu.

1 Was ist richtig? Kreuze A, B oder C an. (✗)

A Die Stadtrundfahrt dauert drei Stunden. ❏
B Die Stadtrundfahrt beginnt am Reichstag. ❏
C Die Stadtrundfahrt endet am Bahnhof Friedrichstraße. ❏

2 Was ist richtig? Kreuze A, B oder C an. (✗)

A Das Mittagessen ist im Preis inbegriffen. ❏
B Die Stadtrundfahrt endet vor ein Uhr. ❏
C Die Touristen können im Funkturm essen. ❏

3 Was siehst du bei der Stadtrundfahrt? Schreibe A, B, C und D in der richtigen Reihenfolge.

	A, B, C oder D
1st	
2nd	
3rd	
4th	

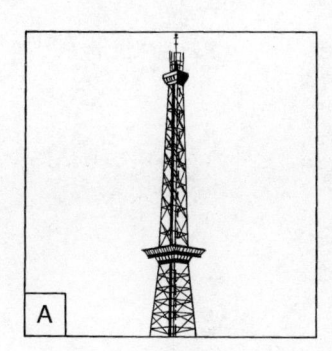

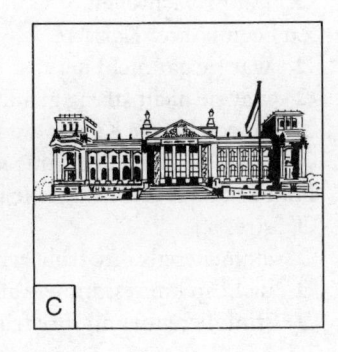

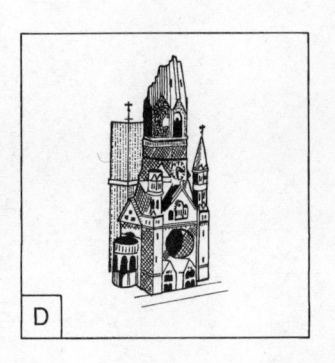

Chapter 5 Listening: Higher Tier

▷ **Extract 10** Im Fernsehen. Eine Sendung über Ferien. Markieren Sie die Sätze falsch (✘) oder richtig (✓).

1. ❏ Rügen liegt an der Nordseeküste.
2. ❏ Die Reise dorthin ist nicht sehr anstrengend.
3. ❏ Man muß die Fähre nach Schweden nehmen.
4. ❏ Familien können gut auf Rügen Urlaub machen.
5. ❏ In der Nähe der Insel kann man nicht viel machen.
6. ❏ Man fährt nicht wegen des Wetters nach Rügen.

▷ **Extract 11** Interviews über Urlaub. Füllen Sie die Tabelle auf **deutsch** aus.

	Beispiel	A	B
Beruf?	Verkäufer		
Familie?	ein Sohn		
Wieviel Ferien?	vier Wochen		
Deutschland oder Ausland?	Ausland		
Wohin?	Italien		
Warum?	interessant historisch		
Unterkunft	Hotel		

▷ **Extract 12** Interviews am Arbeitsplatz. Füllen Sie die Lücken in den Sätzen auf **deutsch** aus.

Beispiel: Anneliese ist in .....*Bremen*....geboren.

1. (a) Anneliese ist .... von Beruf.
   (b) Sie arbeitet bei .... in ....
   (c) Sie findet ihre Arbeit .... weil es ....
   ....
2. (a) Berthold arbeitet seit .... als ....
   (b) Normalerweise ist er ....
   (c) Auf der Baustelle repariert er ....
   (d) Früher arbeitete er .... und war auch eine Weile ....
   ....

▷ **Extract 13** Frau Becker spricht über ihre Karriere. Was ist richtig? Kreuzen Sie die richtige Antwort an.

1. Frau Becker ist Lehrerin geworden, weil
   ❏ ihre Großmutter Lehrerin war.
   ❏ ihre Freunde Lehrer geworden sind.
   ❏ ihre eigenen Lehrer ihr geholfen haben.
   ❏ sie immer Lehrerin werden wollte.
2. Sie arbeitet lieber
   ❏ als Chemielehrerin.
   ❏ als Lehrerin im Kindergarten.
   ❏ als Sportlehrerin.
   ❏ mit Erwachsenen.
3. Zu Beginn ihrer Karriere
   ❏ war sie gar nicht nervös.
   ❏ war sie nicht streng genug.
   ❏ gingen ihr die Kinder auf die Nerven.
   ❏ hatte sie keine Probleme mit den Kindern.
4. Frau Becker findet ihre Stelle im Kindergarten
   ❏ stressig.
   ❏ einfacher als ihre früheren Stellen.
   ❏ nicht so interessant wie am Gymnasium.
   ❏ stimulierender als ihre früheren Stellen.

> **Extract 14** The weather forecast. You hear the weather on the radio. Summarise the forecast using the table.

	North. *Example*	West	South	Centre
Weather	1 cloudy 2 showers 3 cold	1	1 2	1 2
Temperature	2 °C			
Wind	1 moderate 2 from North	1 2	1 2	1 2

> **Extract 15** Jürgen, Hans und Maria sprechen über das Rauchen. Beantworten Sie die folgenden Fragen auf **deutsch**. Schreiben Sie nur ein paar Wörter.

1 Wie alt war Jürgen, als er angefangen hat zu rauchen? ....
2 Wo hat es begonnen? ....
3 Wie fühlt er sich jetzt, da er aufgehört hat? ....
4 Wo hat Hans begonnen zu rauchen? ....
5 Wie reagierten seine Eltern darauf? ....
6 Wie hat Hans über das Rauchen gedacht? ....
7 Wer gab Maria die erste Zigarette? ....
8 Warum hat sie sie akzeptiert? ....

WRITTEN VERSION OF EXTRACTS 1–15

> **Extract 1** Also gut, kannst du bitte Kelly sagen, daß ich jetzt später nach Manchester fliege? Ich komme am Mittwoch erst um 22.00 Uhr am Flughafen an. Hast du verstanden? Die Flugnummer ist LH 7809. Ich treffe sie also so um Viertel nach zehn vor Terminal eins. Ist das okay? Also, Mittwoch um 22.15 Uhr am Flughafen von Manchester vor Terminal eins.
>
> Wenn es ein Problem gibt, soll sie mich heute anrufen. Aber bitte vor acht Uhr. Alles klar? Sie muß mich heute vor acht Uhr anrufen, wenn das mit dem Treffen am Mittwoch nicht in Ordnung ist. Vielen Dank! Tschüß!

> **Extract 2** Ihr Freund hat also Magenschmerzen und Durchfall. Am besten helfen diese Tabletten, glaube ich. Ja, die kann ich empfehlen. Aber wenn er Durchfall hat, rate ich ihm, daß er bis morgen abend, das heißt vierundzwanzig Stunden lang, nichts ißt. Er soll aber viel Wasser trinken und diese Tabletten hier viermal am Tag nehmen. Wenn es ihm am zweiten Tag noch nicht besser geht, muß er zum Arzt. Verstehen Sie? Und die Packung Tabletten hier kostet DM 12.

> **Extract 3** Hallo. Hier spricht Herr Ulrich, der Vater von Wolfgang. Kannst du bitte deinen Eltern folgendes ausrichten? Wolfgang kommt wie geplant am nächsten Montag. Und zwar kommt die Fähre um 18.25 Uhr in Harwich an. Das ist alles so wie vorher abgemacht. Ihr habt ein Foto von Wolfgang, also wird er leicht zu erkennen sein. Er wird einen roten und grünen Anorak tragen, wahrscheinlich eine Jeans und schwarze Stiefel. Auf dem Foto hat er kurze Haare, aber die sind jetzt länger geworden. Er hat auch einen Rucksack bei sich. Alles klar? Wenn niemand da ist, wird er am Hauptausgang warten. Okay? Auf Wiederhören. Grüß deine Eltern auch von mir!

> **Extract 4** Hallo, hier Dieter, Karins Bruder. Kannst du bitte Karin und meinen Eltern etwas ausrichten? Ich komme zu Besuch, wie du weißt, aber leider habe ich einen Unfall gehabt. Sag ihnen, daß es nicht schlimm ist. Ich komme also später. Ich bin auf der B 56, ungefähr 30 km von zu Hause. Ein Auto ist so schnell um eine Kurve gefahren, daß der Fahrer auf die andere Fahrbahn gekommen ist. Er kam mir entgegen, und ich mußte so stark bremsen, daß ich ins Schleudern geraten und von der Straße gerutscht bin. Mir geht es gut. Ich bin noch einmal

davongekommen, aber mein Auto ist schwer beschädigt. Man muß es abschleppen. Ich warte im Moment auf den Abschleppwagen und erstatte der Polizei Bericht. Die Polizei bringt mich auch nach Hause.

▷ **Extract 5** Das waren die Nachrichten, meine Damen und Herren, und jetzt ist es 18.10 Uhr. Es folgt die Wettervorhersage für das ganze Bundesgebiet bis morgen abend.

Über dem Ostatlantik und den britischen Inseln liegt ein Tief mit Ausläufern und einem breiten Wolkenband. In der kommenden Nacht breitet sich das Wolkenband über Deutschland aus. Das bringt Abkühlung auf 6 bis 9 Grad, im südlichen Bergland auf 1 bis 4 Grad. Im hohen Bergland Schneeschauer. Die Höchsttemperaturen für morgen vormittag betragen 12 bis 16 Grad. Im Süden von Bayern aber nur 11 Grad.

Morgen vormittag im Norden Deutschlands zuerst Nebel und dann wolkig mit Schauern. Im Rheinland südlich des Mains und im Osten bedeckt, aber niederschlagsfrei.

Am Nachmittag im Norden andauernder Regen und im Süden und Osten gelegentlich Schauer. Starker Wind aus nordwestlichen Richtungen.

Und die Vorhersage für das kommende Wochenende: überall heiterer und trockener mit Tageshöchsttemperaturen um 18 Grad.

▷ **Extract 6** Martin Kommt heute abend etwas Gutes im Fernsehen, Anna?
Anna Nein, gar nichts. Es gibt einige Wiederholungen und die Fortsetzung der englischen Serie von gestern abend. Das war stinklangweilig! Du hast auch gesagt, daß du sie uninteressant gefunden hast.
M Ich möchte trotzdem was angucken. Ich bin müde und will eigentlich nichts anderes machen. Gibt's den keine Filme?
A Doch, einen amerikanischen Krimi. Der handelt von einem Bankraub. Ich würde lieber Musik hören.
M Ach, dann lassen wir's. Ich kann ja mit meinem Computer spielen, aber ich finde es echt mies, daß ich nie fernsehen kann, wenn ich will.
A Mensch! Ich lache mich tot! Normalerweise hockst du den ganzen Abend vor der Glotze.

▷ **Extract 7** Sie fragen, was wir bei uns für die Umwelt machen? So zu Hause? Also, wir in unserer Familie machen eigentlich ganz viel. Erstens muß man hier in der Stadt den Müll sortieren, sonst wird er nicht abgeholt. Das heißt, daß Glas, Papier und Bioabfälle in verschiedene Mülleimer kommen. Dann kann das alles recycelt werden. Bioabfälle kompostieren wir für den Garten. Mein Vater hat zwar ein Auto, aber am Wochenende fahren wir meistens mit öffentlichen Verkehrsmitteln oder mit dem Rad. Ich fahre immer mit dem Rad in die Schule oder gehe zu Fuß.

Meine Mutter kauft umweltbewußt ein. Das heißt, sie kauft keine Produkte mit viel Verpackungsmaterial. Und Joghurt und solche Sachen kauft sie normalerweise im Glas, nicht im Plastikbecher. Sie findet aber, daß diese sogenannten Ökoprodukte ziemlich teuer sind. Wir achten auch auf die Zentralheizung und senken die Temperatur, wenn es nicht so kalt ist. Dabei spart man nicht nur Energie, sondern auch Geld.

▷ **Extract 8** – Sag mal, Lotte, hast du auch in der Abendzeitung gelesen, daß man plant, eine Autobahn um Waldhausen zu bauen?
– Ach ja, es ist auch höchste Zeit, daß sie das machen. Denk daran, Heinz, der Verkehr auf der Bundesstraße ist wirklich furchtbar. Da hat doch Bärbel den Unfall gehabt. In Waldhausen gibt es immer Unfälle und Staus, weil so viele durch das Dorf fahren müssen.
– Meiner Meinung nach ist das eine Schande. Die Autobahn soll direkt durch den Wald führen. Dort, wo so viele Leute am Wochenende spazierengehen. Wir haben in den letzten Jahren schon so viel Wald verloren! Und jetzt sollen wir noch mehr verlieren, nur um fünf Minuten schneller am Ziel zu sein. Das nervt mich, ehrlich.
– Du stehst nicht jeden Morgen im Stau wie ich. Ich würde gerne morgens zehn Minuten sparen und ruhig zur Arbeit kommen. Dann könnte ich auch das Wochenende mehr genießen.

Extract 9

Guten Morgen, meine Damen und Herren. Ich heiße Monika. Ich bin Ihre Stadtführerin und begleite Sie heute morgen auf dieser Tour durch Berlin. Unser Ausgangspunkt ist hier am Bahnhof Friedrichstraße. Die ganze Tour dauert ungefähr drei Stunden. Gegen ein Uhr werden wir in einem typischen alten Lokal das Mittagessen einnehmen. Die Kosten sind schon im Preis der Stadtrundfahrt enthalten.

Wir besichtigen zuerst die Gedächtniskirche, die uns an die Zerstörungen des Zweiten Weltkriegs erinnert. Wir fahren dann zum Brandenburger Tor, von wo Sie Unter den Linden genießen können. Dann gehen wir zum Funkturm im ehemaligen Ostberlin. Vom Turm haben Sie einen herrlichen Blick über die ganze Stadt. Danach besuchen wir den Reichstag, der von erheblicher Bedeutung für die Geschichte unserer Stadt und unseres Landes ist.

Extract 10

Wenn wir Urlaub in Deutschland machen, dann fahren wir meistens nach Rügen. Das ist eine Insel in der Ostsee, in der Nähe von Stralsund. Dorthin kann man von uns aus in knapp vier Stunden fahren, also ist die Reise nicht sehr anstrengend. Man braucht auch keine Fähre zu nehmen, da es eine Brücke gibt. Es gibt aber Fähren nach Schweden, und man hat die Gelegenheit, ein Wochenende oder so in Schweden zu verbringen. Das haben wir das letzte Mal getan.

Rügen selbst ist sehr schön. Die Insel hat schöne Strände, und im Sommer ist das Wetter meistens sehr gut. Man kommt auch leicht wieder ans Festland und nach Stralsund, eine schöne historische Stadt. Man kann also viel unternehmen, wenn man will, oder sich nur am Strand ausruhen. Das ist ideal für Familien. Früher haben wir immer gezeltet, aber seitdem die Kinder nicht mehr mit uns fahren, gehen meine Frau und ich ins Hotel. Maria hat keine Lust mehr, im Urlaub zu kochen. Also ist es im Hotel viel entspannender.

Extract 11

A

– Was sind Sie von Beruf?
– Ich bin Arzt.
– Und haben Sie Familie?
– Ja, ich bin seit sechs Jahren verheiratet und habe zwei Töchter von fünf und drei Jahren.
– Wieviel Ferien haben Sie im Jahr?
– Normalerweise insgesamt sechs Wochen.
– Fahren sie ins Ausland, oder bleiben Sie in Deutschland?
– Wir bleiben in Deutschland, weil das mit zwei Kindern viel einfacher ist.
– Wie verbringen Sie dieses Jahr Ihren Urlaub?
– Wir fahren dieses Jahr in die Berge, nach Bayern.
– Und wo wohnen Sie im Urlaub?
– Wir mieten dort ein Ferienhaus, weil das billiger und auch besser für die Kinder ist.

B

– Wieviel Ferien haben Sie im Jahr?
– Gewöhnlich habe ich drei Wochen im Jahr.
– Was sind Sie von Beruf?
– Ich bin Sekretärin in einem Steuerberaterbüro.
– Und was machen Sie normalerweise in den Ferien?
– Also, ich bin verheiratet und habe zwei Jungen. Einer ist vierzehn, und der andere ist sechzehn Jahre alt. Wir fahren meistens ans Mittelmeer oder auf die Kanarischen Inseln. Da hat man natürlich das beste Wetter, und dort brauchen wir uns nicht um die Jungen zu kümmern. Für sie gibt es unheimlich viel zu machen, und wir können uns ausruhen. Wir machen immer Urlaub am Meer.
– Und wo wohnen Sie normalerweise?
– Immer im Appartement. Da haben wir Platz, und wir können essen, wann und wo wir wollen.

Extract 12

1

– Wie heißen Sie?
– Anneliese Rothenberger.

– Woher kommen Sie?
– Ich bin hier in Bremen geboren.
– Und was machen Sie hier auf der Baustelle?
– Also, ich bin Architektin und muß daher die Baustellen von Zeit zu Zeit besuchen.
– Wie finden sie Ihre Arbeit?
– Ich arbeite bei einer Firma in Hamburg. Wir haben immer viele verschiedene Projekte, also ist es immer interessant, und es gibt viel Abwechslung. Im Winter auf die Baustelle zu kommen, ist aber nicht so schön!

2

– Wie heißen Sie?
– Berthold Müller.
– Und was machen Sie hier auf der Baustelle?
– Ich bin Mechaniker. Ich arbeite normalerweise in der Werkstatt, aber es gibt ein Problem mit dem Lastkraftwagen hier. Die Baufirma hat uns angerufen.
– Wie lange arbeiten sie schon als Mechaniker?
– Erst seit einem Jahr. Vorher habe ich im Hafen gearbeitet, aber die Stelle habe ich verloren. Dann war ich eine Zeitlang arbeitslos und habe am Abend in der Volkshochschule gelernt, um Mechaniker zu werden. Jetzt habe ich eine feste Stelle, und die Arbeit gefällt mir gut.

▶ **Extract 13** Ich bin seit fünfzehn Jahren Lehrerin. Als Kind hatte ich die Lehrer und Lehrerinnen eigentlich nicht so gern, und damals habe ich nicht gedacht, daß ich selbst Lehrerin werden würde. Meine Großmutter war Lehrerin, aber sie hat selten darüber gesprochen. Ich habe mich dazu entschieden, weil viele meiner Freunde Lehrer geworden sind.

Ich habe nicht immer im Kindergarten gearbeitet, wie jetzt. Zunächst habe ich an einem Gymnasium gelehrt. Ich bin in Naturwissenschaften ausgebildet und habe dort Chemie gelehrt. Inzwischen habe ich auch mit Erwachsenen an der Volkshochschule gearbeitet, aber das habe ich nie gern getan. Ich muß sagen, daß ich es vorziehe, mit Kindern zu arbeiten.

Als ich zum ersten Mal vor einer Klasse stand, war ich sehr nervös. Ich glaube aber, daß ich streng war, und die Kinder haben meine Nervosität nicht bemerkt. Vielleicht war ich zu streng. Es gab immer Probleme mit Kindern, die nicht zugehört oder miteinander gequatscht haben. Das hat mich sehr irritiert.

Meine Stelle im Kindergarten ist total anders. Mit den Kleinen ist es nicht gerade einfach, aber viel lockerer, und sie sind immer begeistert. Im Vergleich zu meinen früheren Stellen ist es weitaus angenehmer. Es gibt nicht so viel Streß, und ich freue mich, daß die Kinder immer so bereit sind, Neues zu unternehmen und zu lernen. Das ist wichtig für mich.

▶ **Extract 14** Und jetzt der Wetterbericht für ganz Deutschland bis morgen abend.

Im Norden meist bedeckt mit Schauern und sehr kalt. Tageshöchsttemperaturen um 2 Grad. Starker bis mäßiger Wind von Norden.

Im Westen heiter. Tageshöchsttemperaturen bis 8 Grad. Mäßiger Wind aus nordwestlichen Richtungen.

Im Süden am frühen Vormittag Nebel und später sonnig. Tageshöchsttemperaturen um 10 Grad. Schwacher Wind von Westen.

In Mitteldeutschland bleibt es morgen den ganzen Tag regnerisch, oberhalb 800 Metern fällt Schnee. Tageshöchsttemperaturen um 1 Grad. Mäßiger Wind von Norden.

Soweit der Wetterbericht, und jetzt kommen die Verkehrsmeldungen.

▶ **Extract 15** **A**

– Jürgen, wann hast du begonnen zu rauchen?
– Mit vierzehn, glaub' ich. Also, in der Schule war es für mich immer problematisch. Rauchen gehörte zu den Sachen, die ich gemacht habe, um anders zu sein, und weil ich immer Unsinn machen wollte. Ich habe jetzt aber damit aufgehört, weil ich viel Fußball spiele und fit bleiben will.

B

– Hans, wie lange rauchst du schon?
– Ich glaube, ich war 11 oder 12. Meine ganze Familie raucht. Ich habe drei ältere Brüder. Sie ließen immer Zigaretten überall im Haus herumliegen. Es war ganz natürlich, daß ich eine Zigarette versuchen wollte. Meine Eltern haben nichts dagegen gemacht. So hat es angefangen.

C

– Maria, seit wann rauchst du eigentlich?
– Ich weiß nicht mehr genau, wann das war. Ich glaub', schon als ich 12 oder 13 war. Einige meiner Schulfreundinnen hatten angefangen zu rauchen. Die waren älter als ich und haben mir die ersten Zigaretten gegeben. Ich wollte mich anpassen. Ich habe gedacht, daß ich das machen mußte, um ihre Freundin zu bleiben.

▶ EXAMINATION ANSWERS

▷ **Extract 1**   Message: he is coming later than planned
arriving 22.00 on Wednesday at Manchester airport
flight number LH 7809
meet him in front of terminal one at 22.15
if there is a problem ring back today before 8 o'clock

▷ **Extract 2**
1. nichts (für 24 Stunden)
2. viel Wasser trinken
3. viermal am Tag
4. du mußt zum Arzt

▷ **Extract 3**

TELEPHONE MESSAGE

Wolfgang will arrive in .... *Harwich* ....

at .... *18.25* ....

That is next .... *Monday* ....

He will be wearing .... *a red and green anorak* .... and

.... *jeans* .... and carrying .... *a rucksack* ....

If you're late collecting him .... *he will wait by the main entrance* ....

▷ **Extract 4**
1. Er hat einen Unfall gehabt.
2. etwa 30 km von zu Hause/auf der B56
3. Es geht ihm gut/nicht schlecht.
4. schwer beschädigt
5. Ein Auto kam ihm entgegen./Ein Auto kam schnell um eine Kurve.

Chapter 5 Listening: Higher Tier

6 Er wartet auf den Abschleppwagen./Er spricht mit der Polizei.
7 Die Polizei bringt ihn.

▷ **Extract 5** 1 richtig
2 falsch
3 richtig
4 richtig
5 falsch

▷ **Extract 6** 1 eine Wiederholung
eine (englische) Serie
ein (amerikanischer) Krimi
2 stinklangweilig/uninteressant
3 er kann nicht fernsehen, wann er will
4 sie ist nicht der Meinung/sie ist zornig

▷ **Extract 7** 1 richtig
2 falsch
3 falsch
4 richtig
5 richtig
6 richtig
7 falsch

▷ **Extract 8** 1 richtig
2 falsch
3 falsch
4 richtig
5 falsch
6 es ist eine gute Idee/sie ist dafür
7 viele Leute gehen dort spazieren/man hat viel Wald verloren

▷ **Extract 9** 1 A Die Stadtrundfahrt dauert drei Stunden. ☒
2 A Das Mittagessen ist im Preis inbegriffen. ☒
3

	A, B, C oder D
1st	D
2nd	B
3rd	A
4th	C

▷ **Extract 10** 1 falsch
2 richtig
3 falsch
4 richtig
5 falsch
6 falsch

Extract 11

	Beispiel	A	B
Beruf?	Verkäufer	*Arzt*	*Sekretärin*
Familie?	1 Sohn	*2 Töchter*	*2 Jungen*
Wieviel Ferien?	4 Wochen	*6 Wochen*	*3 Wochen*
Deutschland oder Ausland?	Ausland	*Deutschland*	*Ausland*
Wohin?	Italien	*Bayern, in die Berge*	*Mittelmeer, Kanarische Inseln*
Warum?	interessant historisch	*leichter mit Kindern*	*gutes Wetter, besser für die Jungen*
Unterkunft?	Hotel	*Ferienhaus*	*Appartement*

Extract 12

1. (a) Architektin
   (b) einer Firma ... Hamburg
   (c) interessant ... verschiedene Projekte/Abwechslung gibt
2. (a) Mechaniker ... einem Jahr
   (b) in der Werkstatt
   (c) einen Lastkraftwagen
   (d) im Hafen ... arbeitslos

Extract 13

1. ihre Freunde Lehrer geworden sind.
2. als Lehrerin im Kindergarten.
3. gingen ihr die Kinder auf die Nerven.
4. stimulierender als ihre früheren Stellen.

Extract 14

	North. *Example*	West	South	Centre
Weather	1 *cloudy* 2 *showers* 3 *cold*	1 *bright*	1 *early fog* 2 *sunny later*	1 *rainy* 2 *snow over 800 metres*
Temperature	2 °C	*8 °C*	*10 °C*	*1 °C*
Wind	1 *moderate* 2 *from North*	1 *moderate* 2 *from Northwest*	1 *light* 2 *from West*	1 *moderate* 2 *from North*

Extract 15

1. 14
2. in der Schule
3. fitter/gesünder
4. zu Hause/in der Familie
5. Sie haben nichts dagegen gemacht.
6. Es war für ihn natürlich.
7. die Schulfreundinnen
8. Sie wollte sich anpassen, um ihre Freundin zu bleiben.

TEST WITH STUDENT ANSWERS

Here is an example of a Higher Tier listening question. A student has answered the question and an examiner has marked it adding comments.

This is what the student heard:

> Damals nach dem Krieg war es für uns schlimm. Wir hatten gar nichts. Mein Mann hat damals 14 Stunden am Tag gearbeitet und bekam nur fünf Tage Urlaub im Jahr. Wir

sind erst 1949 zum ersten Mal in den Urlaub gefahren. Ich kann mich auch daran erinnern, daß sein Gehalt sehr niedrig war. So um 200 Mark, vielleicht 250 Mark. Wir mußten damals alles für Essen und Obdach ausgeben. Sparen konnten wir kaum, und ein Auto oder eine Waschmaschine waren ausgeschlossen. Sogar Essen zu besorgen, war nicht leicht, weil Fleisch, Butter und Vollmilch so teuer waren. Im Vergleich mit damals ist es für uns im Alltag viel leichter geworden. Wir essen, was wir wollen, und haben unseren Wagen, Waschmaschine, Spülmaschine, Mikrowelle, Farbfernseher, alles. Alles können wir jetzt haben. Aber ich sage Ihnen eines! Damals waren die Familienmitglieder und die Nachbarn enger miteinander verbunden. Alle mußten einander helfen. Sonst kam man einfach nicht durch. Das haben wir heutzutage verloren.

Question and student answer

Erika ist jetzt 80 Jahre alt. Sie beschreibt ihr Leben vor fünfzig Jahren und heutzutage. Was sagt Sie über:

- die Arbeit
- die Ferien
- das Geld
- die Familie
- den Lebensstandard

Vor fünfzig Jahren:

Die Arbeit – 14 Stunden am Tag – viel

Die Ferien – 5 Tage im Jahr – nicht viel

'All good answers, even though not in sentences.'

Das Geld – um 200–250 Mark im Monat, nicht viel

Die Familie – eng

Der Lebensstandard – nicht gut – das Essen war teuer, kein Auto, keine Waschmaschine

Heutzutage:

'Not really precise enough. You have to infer answers even if they aren't there specifically.'

Die Arbeit – besser

'Don't leave gaps! Always put something.'

Die Ferien –

Das Geld – sie haben nicht viel

'Wrong. She has everything she needs.'

Die Familie – nicht mehr eng

'good answer'

Der Lebensstandard – haben Auto, essen was sie wollen

▶ A STEP FURTHER (FOUNDATION AND HIGHER TIER)

Listening ought to be easy, but we are not very good at it. Every day we hear a great deal to which we pay no attention: radio, TV, lessons in school, people talking, traffic, birds, the wind and so on.

But in learning a foreign language, listening is the most important of the four skills, because all the others depend on it. We cannot speak a language unless we first hear it and understand it. Reading is made easier if we can hear in our heads the sounds of the printed word. And the ultimate test of the accuracy of what we write is whether or not it sounds right if we say it out loud.

So don't treat listening as a soft option which you can just absorb as you go along. That may have worked when learning to speak your own language, but look how long it took you! We haven't got that amount of time, so we have to take short cuts.

Here, then, are a few suggestions for positive listening.

▷ **The classroom**   Everything starts here. All language courses now have cassettes to go with them and they are usually of excellent quality. No doubt your teacher uses them often. But if not, then ask him or her to let you hear more German. Similarly, if you are not satisfied with the sound quality of the equipment used, then say so. Your teacher may well be glad of your support in pressing for better resources. A small single-speaker cassette recorder is not usually adequate for a classroom unless it has extension speakers. Some schools now have extension speakers on a wall or on a shelf and they make a great difference.

You may of course have access at school to small cassette recorders with headsets, or even a language laboratory. If this is the case, then there should be facilities to allow you to use them individually, either in lesson time or in free time. Perhaps the school has cassettes belonging to a course it no longer uses. Ask if you can borrow them to listen to on your own.

If you have a German assistant at school, then he or she may be prepared to record some German for you. If so then there is no copyright problem, and the school could make multiple copies for pupils to use at home.

▷ **Walkman**   Have you got a personal stereo? Why not use it for German as well? If you haven't got one then someone may be persuaded to buy one for you. If someone has helped you to buy this book, then clearly you have friends or relatives on your side!

▷ **Commercial language courses**   There are some excellent German courses available in bookshops for people learning at home or in evening classes. Your teacher will probably know about them. Even if they are fairly basic – such as *Get by in German* – they provide a lot of very good language practice, recorded by German speakers, probably on themes that are relevant to our course. You are sure to pick up new vocabulary too. Remember, however, that many of these courses will not be designed specifically to cover the requirements of GCSE.

▷ **Radio and television**   There are almost always German courses of various levels on radio and television, aimed specifically at schools or the general public. Some will even be specifically for GCSE. Sometimes they are at inconvenient times of day, but you may be able to record them and watch them when you are in the right frame of mind. Remember that schools programmes nearly always continue in your half-term week, and if you are mildly ill and have to be off school, the long, boring day can be relieved with some of the excellent radio and television programmes.

Several German radio stations can be received very clearly in Britain. It would be worth searching for them on the radio. If you have cable television or satellite then you will have access to various German channels. If you have a PC and are on the internet you will be able to access a great deal of German information.

▷ **Films**   German films are frequently shown on television or at some cinemas. Look out for them, but check carefully that they are subtitled. A dubbed version may be entertaining but it is not going to help your German.

▷ **Pen friends**   If you have a link with a German boy or girl, have you considered exchanging tapes as well as letters? This is excellent language practice for both sides and can keep you both up to date with sport and pop music and anything else you may have in common. If your school has an exchange school, this might even be done on a class basis.

▷ **Family and friends**   Revision is always more enjoyable if you can do it with someone else. An obvious area to practise with a member of the family or with a friend is numbers. They are a constant stumbling block in foreign languages and require a lot of practice. One person reads out numbers in German and the other writes down the figures. Make the numbers gradually bigger and bigger and read them out faster and faster. Include prices (Marks, Schillings and Swiss Francs), telephone numbers, weights, distances and times of day.

▶ Other sources

Does your teacher make use of Inter Nationes? This is a German organisation which produces a large amount of high-class German language material for use in schools and colleges outside Germany. Much of the material is free! Many of the cassettes would be suitable for class or individual use.

The Goethe Institut is an organisation which promotes German language and culture abroad. There are branches in London, Manchester, York and Glasgow. As well as library facilities with books, magazines, tapes and videos they also organise courses to support pupils aiming for GCSE and other activities in conjunction with schools. Your teacher should have more details.

So you see there are plenty of ways of improving your listening skills, and much of what is suggested here will help you in your other language skills as well. Do not worry if your progress seems slow. It is difficult to measure progress in listening skills. Every bit of practice will help and you will find that you are gradually understanding more and more, that you need to concentrate less and less on meaning, and that you are thinking less and less in English.

Chapter 6

Reading: Foundation Tier

GETTING STARTED

Most students seem to find reading the easiest skill to cope with. This is probably because it is the easiest skill to develop on an **individual** basis. To begin with, we all read at different speeds and we don't all understand the same words. So we usually read and learn at our **own** pace. Another important reason why reading may seem easier is that there is more material readily available.

The system for examining the skill of reading is the same as for the other skills. As we saw in the previous two chapters, Foundation and Higher Tier overlap somewhat, but you can only enter one or the other.

WHAT YOU NEED TO KNOW

Reading skills

Before we consider reading German, it is worth spending some time looking at the skill of reading itself. What do you read in English, and why? You probably read quite a variety of things and you probably read them with a variety of purposes and intentions.

You may well find that you read some or many of the following: newspapers, magazines, advertisements, brochures, public notices, messages, postcards, letters, novels, plays, poetry, reference books and much more. In each case, though, you will not expect to **understand** every word and you will certainly not **remember** every detail that you have read. You may be reading for **specific information**, e.g. to find out the time of your favourite television programme, and you will skip over or ignore information that is not relevant. On the other hand you may be reading a novel where you are **interested** in the story, but again you will sift out the information that you think is important for the story. You could try this out by doing some reading and then seeing how much you remember, and why. You will certainly not remember the exact words used! However, you will remember the key points or information relevant to you.

If you are reading a holiday brochure, you will approach the reading with a fair amount of **knowledge**. For instance, you have a reasonable idea of the likely content of the brochure: you expect to find information about accommodation, leisure activities and facilities, travel arrangements, prices, excursions, weather etc. You won't expect to find the football results! You will be looking out to make a selection of what is, for you, the relevant information, e.g. double rooms with shower, full board, deep-sea fishing, wind surfing, flight times.

We can conclude that we do not need to understand every word we read, and that there are often certain expectations which can actually help us to understand. The same applies to German.

So remember:

▶ You do not need to understand every word.
▶ You should not be discouraged if you do not understand every word.
▶ You should try to build on the knowledge of key words and expressions.
▶ You should get as much practice in reading German as you can.

Assessment objectives

As we saw in Chapter 4 the examining groups must be open about what they aim to test and must comply with all the regulations governing the National Curriculum and the GCSE. In Reading and Responding (Attainment Target 3 of the National Curriculum) candidates are expected to:

▶ read, understand and respond to written language.

Again, some examining groups spell this out in greater detail, but it is safe to assume that they will all expect candidates to:

- show that they understand main points and specific details
- understand and identify simple opinions and points of view
- show some understanding of a limited range of unfamiliar language
- understand simple references to past, present and future events.

Remember that the Areas of Experience within which your teaching and learning must have taken place are common to all examining groups and each group clearly sets down how they divide these areas up into topics. The minimum vocabulary you will need is also published, though you should expect to meet some unfamiliar words. There will be a variety of reading material including:

- signs, notices, short advertisements, instructions
- messages, lists
- letters (both printed and handwritten)
- information leaflets, brochures, guides
- short magazine and newspaper extracts.

The material may be authentic or made up but it must be realistic and it must be material that is intended to be read. At the beginning of the test items will be very short and as the test progresses you will have to deal with gradually longer items. At Foundation Tier, however, nothing will be of any great length and you will not be overburdened with reading.

Now the good news! You are allowed to use a bilingual dictionary in this part of the exam. For more information about the use of dictionaries you should refer to the relevant section in Chapter 2 (see page 9).

The length of the tests varies from examining group to examining group but is generally from 25 to 45 minutes. You can check this in Table 1.1 on page 2.

Detailed lists of the words you will be expected to understand are provided by all the examining groups – there are some differences between the groups. In the **topic areas** in Chapter 3 and in the **alphabetical** list in Chapter 16 we have attempted to include those words which are most common. Although the list is not exhaustive, it contains most of the words you will need to know. Make sure you check the requirements of your group.

Learning vocabulary is a chore but unfortunately it is an essential one for foreign languages. However, let's be positive: you know the **topics** to be covered, you know the **words** on which you can be tested, you know that you don't need to understand **every word** and you are allowed the use of a **bilingual dictionary**. Don't think, however, that because you can use the dictionary you won't need to bother with vocabulary learning. You won't have time to look up every word in the reading test, and in other parts of the exam you cannot use one! What you need to do is develop ways of taking the pain out of vocabulary learning and to make it a regular part of your revision programme.

▷ Learning vocabulary

You may find the following suggestions helpful:

- It's better to have regular, short bursts of learning rather than longer periods. Ten minutes a day is much better than one spell of fifty minutes.
- Every time you learn vocabulary you must test yourself.
- You may like to give yourself a small reward for reaching your targets.
- Learning with someone else can be a change, but you need to test each other.
- Be systematic about what sections of vocabulary you learn and when.
- Develop some ways to put some interest into your vocabulary learning, e.g. by timing yourself and improving your speed and accuracy. Use the lists to help you.
- You can make your own lists. If you have access to a computer with a word processor, you can use it to help you with your German. It's a great revision asset if it's used wisely.

▷ Approaching the tests

Most of the items are short, so the length won't be off-putting.

- Read the instruction carefully; very often there will be a title or short sentence to set the scene, and these can be very helpful.
- Study any examples carefully and write your answers in a similar way.

- There will be a variety of question types such as: questions and answers in German, questions and answers in English, multiple choice, matching, true/false in German or English, pictorial tick box answers etc.
- If you have to write an answer it will not need to be long. Often one word or a few words will suffice, but be sure to give all the information required.
- There may be an indication of the number of marks for each question. This will give you an idea of the number of points you need to mention in your answer.

Themes

You can expect any of the following reading materials to be included in the examination:

Public notices and signs

- Advertising posters, e.g. announcing coming events
- Traffic signs, e.g. highway code, places in town, motorway signs
- Signs in public places, e.g. at the railway station or supermarket
- Instructions, e.g. when to take medicine
- Warnings, e.g. Beware of the dog!
- Price lists, e.g. at a hotel, campsite, shop
- Menus, e.g. in a restaurant, café, snack bar
- Timetables, e.g. train, bus
- General, e.g. handouts about promotional activities, events

Simple brochures

- Holidays, e.g. resorts, tourist activities
- Accommodation, e.g. hotels, apartments, campsites
- Leisure activities, e.g. sports, excursions
- Special events, e.g. exhibitions, festivals
- Special offers, e.g. holidays, clothes, fares

Guides

- Places of interest, e.g. sights, buildings
- Monuments e.g. *Kölner Dom*
- Towns, e.g. sightseeing tours
- Regions, e.g. a trip along the Rhine

Letters

- Informal, e.g. from a pen friend
- Formal, e.g. from a hotel
- Semi-formal, e.g. letters page from a magazine
- Postcards

A wide range of topics may be covered in letters.

Imaginative writing

- Descriptions, e.g. of an interesting event
- Interviews, e.g. with a famous person

Remember, though, that there are many other possibilities for each of these headings, so get as much practice as you can in reading all kinds of German.

Exam hints

The questions in the exam will test your ability to understand the key points. In this section we look at the kinds of things that can reasonably be asked. In many cases the questions will be seeking an answer about:

- Who?
- What?
- How long?
- How many?

- Where?
- When?
- How much?
- Why?

So we need to check what items could be included under these categories, and you need to make sure that you are familiar with them and that you recognise them when you meet them.

Who?

People:

- family and friends
- professions
- descriptions: appearance, age, character

What?

Items relating to the full range of Foundation Level topic areas:

- what you have to do: instructions, requests, payments etc.
- what other people do/will do/have done, e.g. likes, dislikes, simple opinions, school, work, free time activities

Where?

Location:

- position: prepositions
- places: buildings, landmarks
- places: countries
- directions
- distances

When?

- time of day
- 24-hour clock
- days, weeks, months, years
- dates
- moments in time: midday, midnight
- length of time
- frequency, sequence, speed
- expressions of time: today, yesterday, tomorrow etc.
- seasons, important holidays, e.g. Christmas, New Year
- beginning, continuity, end

How long?

Duration:

- minutes, days, weeks, months, years
- until + time/point in time/day/month/year

How many?

- numbers

How much?

Quantity:

- numbers
- weights and measures
- size

Why?

▶ reasons

The importance of these subheadings will be more apparent when you look at some sample questions.

▶ EXAMINATION QUESTIONS

Shorter items

The first questions in the examination will usually be short. You may only have one word to read in some cases, disregarding the instructions. Typically the early sections will deal with signs and notices you would be likely to see around and about in Germany. Read the instructions carefully before answering. Remember that help is given with German instructions in Chapter 16.

▶ **Question 1** You are on the motorway and need petrol. Which sign do you look for?

- ❏ A UMLEITUNG
- ❏ B AUSFAHRT
- ❏ C TANKSTELLE
- ❏ D NOTRUF

▶ **Question 2** You want to park the car. Which sign do you look for?

- ❏ A PARKEN VERBOTEN
- ❏ B PARKHAUS
- ❏ C STADTPARK
- ❏ D STADTMITTE

▶ **Question 3** You want to buy aspirin. Which shop do you look for?

- ❏ A Apotheke
- ❏ B Bäckerei
- ❏ C Fleischerei
- ❏ D Modegeschäft

▶ **Question 4** In a German newspaper you see the following advertisement in the 'Lost and Found' section. Which pet is lost?

> # Haben Sie eine Schildkröte gefunden?
> ## Tel: 0221–275686

- ❏ A cat
- ❏ B dog
- ❏ C guinea pig
- ❏ D tortoise

Question 5

You read the following announcement in a German newspaper.

> *Ulrich und Sabine Fassbinder*
>
> freuen sich sehr über
>
> die Geburt ihres Sohns
>
> **CHRISTOF JOSEF**
>
> am 12. Juni.

What is being announced?

- A a death
- B a marriage
- C a birth
- D a wedding anniversary

Question 6

Which day is the restaurant closed?

> **Täglich von 08.00 bis 17.00 Uhr geöffnet**
>
> **Von 12.30 bis 13.30 Uhr geschlossen**
>
> **donnerstags Ruhetag**

- A Wednesdays
- B Thursdays
- C Tuesdays
- D Saturdays

Question 7

Am Flughafen.

> *Ab dem 13. September*
>
> **TÄGLICH**
>
> *nach Chicago*
>
> **MIT LUFTHANSA**

Was ist richtig?
Nach Chicago fliegt die Lufthansa

- ❏ A jeden Tag
- ❏ B einmal in der Woche
- ❏ C zweimal in der Woche
- ❏ D dreimal in der Woche

▷ **Question 8** Am Bahnhof.

Was bedeuten die Symbole? Schreiben Sie den richtigen Buchstaben in die Kästchen.

A Geldwechsel   D Erfrischungen
B Toiletten   E Fundbüro
C Fahrkarten   F Auskunft

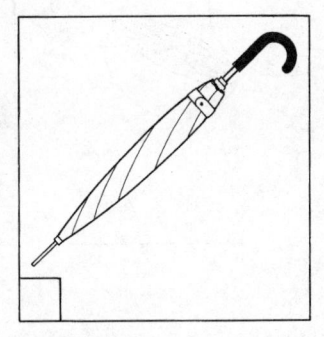

▷ **Question 9** Im Einkaufszentrum

Wo kauft man
A Aspirin?   ❏ ZEITSCHRIFTEN
B Pizza?   ❏ BLUMEN
C Briefmarken?   ❏ ANDENKEN
D Comics?   ❏ POSTAMT
E Geschenke?   ❏ IMBISSTUBE
F Rosen?   ❏ DROGERIE

▷ **Question 10**

Einkaufsliste

Kartoffeln   *Milch*
Apfelsinen   *Käse*
Butter   *Schokolade*

Was kaufst du? Schreibe Ja oder Nein.

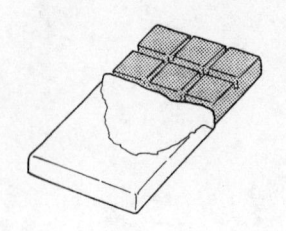

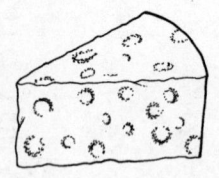

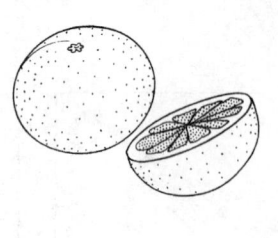

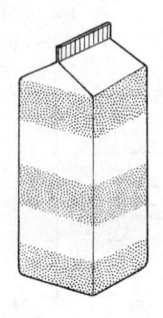

_____   _____   _____

_____   _____   _____

▷ **Question 11** Reklame.

IN UNSEREM GLÜCKSSPIEL

JEDEN MONAT

EINEN URLAUB ZU GEWINNEN!

Was kann man gewinnen? Kreuzen Sie A, B oder C an.

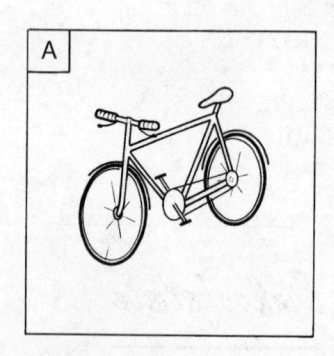

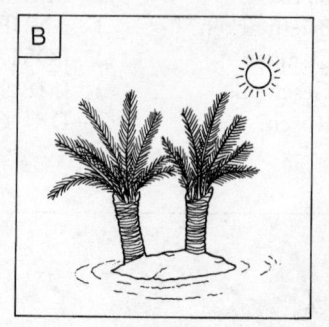

| A | B | C |

▷ **Question 12** Schilder.

A DAMENMODE

B HEISSE WURST

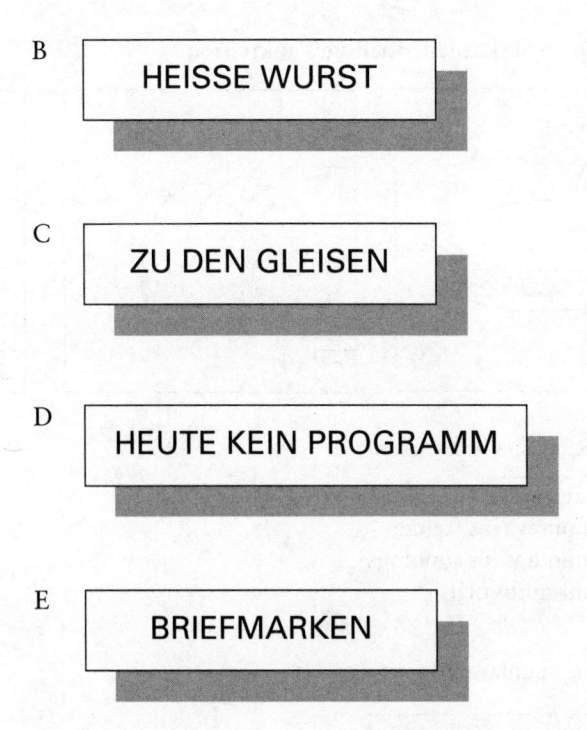

C ZU DEN GLEISEN

D HEUTE KEIN PROGRAMM

E BRIEFMARKEN

Wo kann man diese Schilder sehen? Schreiben Sie A, B, C, D oder E.

- ❏ Am Bahnhof
- ❏ Im Kino
- ❏ Auf der Post
- ❏ Im Warenhaus
- ❏ In der Imbißstube

▶ **Question 13** Hier ist eine Einkaufsliste. Wo kannst du die Dinge kaufen?

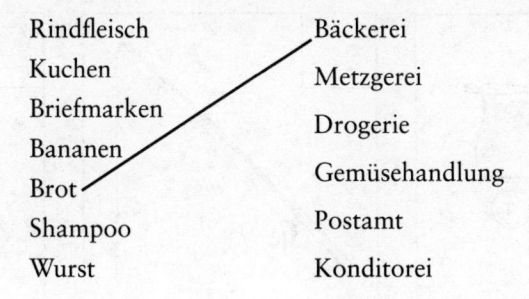

Rindfleisch   Bäckerei
Kuchen   Metzgerei
Briefmarken   Drogerie
Bananen   Gemüsehandlung
Brot   Postamt
Shampoo
Wurst   Konditorei

▶ **Question 14** Auf dem Markt.

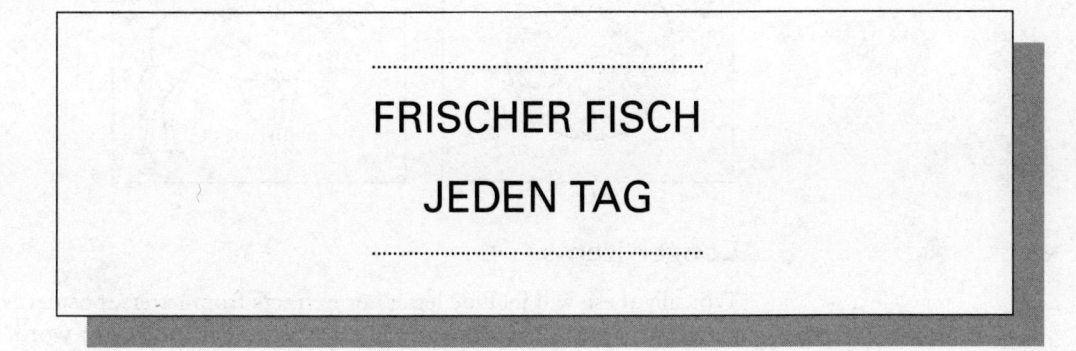

FRISCHER FISCH

JEDEN TAG

Chapter 6   Reading: Foundation Tier

(a) Was können Sie kaufen? Richtiges ankreuzen.

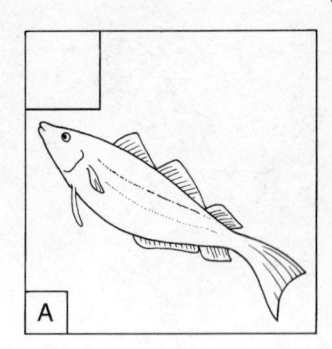

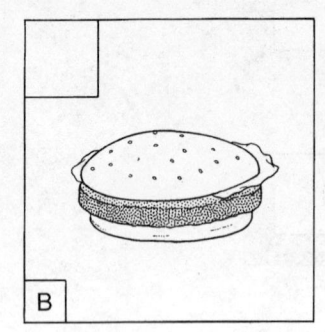

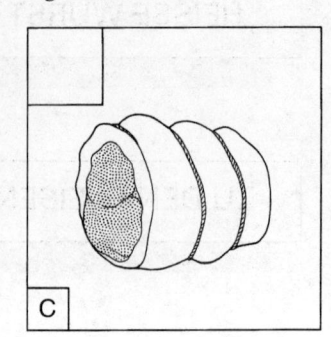

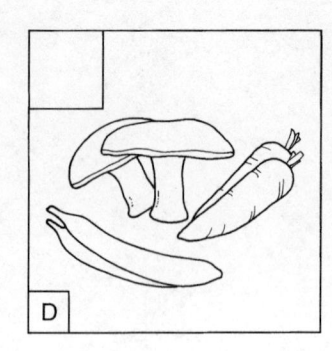

A   B   C   D

(b) Wann? Richtiges ankreuzen.

- ❏ A samstags und sonntags
- ❏ B montags bis freitags
- ❏ C montags bis sonntags
- ❏ D nur mittwochs

▷ **Question 15**   Auf dem Campingplatz. Aktivitäten.

Samstag	Aktivitäten
9.00	Fußballspiel
10.00	Radfahren
11.00	Tennis
12.00	Angeln
2.00	Schwimmen
3.00	Rollschuhlaufen
4.00	Handball
5.00	Reiten

Wann kannst du diese Aktivitäten machen? Schreibe die richtige Uhrzeit ins Kästchen.

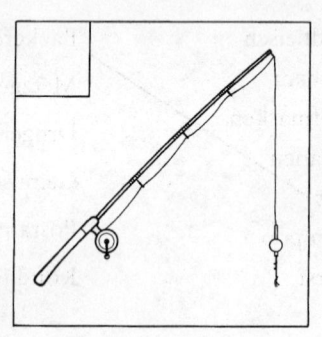

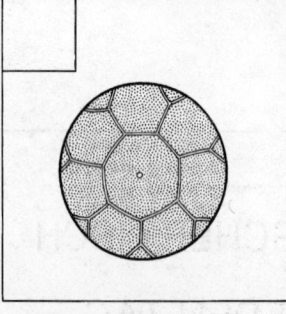

Longer items

Typically these will include letters or extracts from letters, postcards, brochures, advertising material. Remember that you do not need to understand every word. Remember too that you can look up unfamiliar words in a dictionary. If you do this, make a note of the words you look up and learn them. Do not rely too heavily on the dictionary since time in the actual test is limited. Read and study the following questions carefully before answering them.

▶ **Question 16** Lesen Sie den Brief.

> ... Dienstags ist meine erste Stunde Französisch. Sie beginnt um 8.30 Uhr. Dann um 9.30 Uhr habe ich eine Stunde Englisch. Um 10.30 Uhr habe ich Naturwissenschaften und um 11.30 Uhr beginnt Mathe.
> Das ist eine Doppelstunde. Um 1.30 Uhr haben wir eine Stunde Musik.
> Das ist mein Lieblingsfach....

Füllen Sie den Stundenplan auf deutsch aus.

Uhrzeit	Montag	Dienstag
8.30	Erdkunde	
9.30	Erdkunde	
10.30	Mathe	
11.30	Geschichte	
12.30	Englisch	
13.30	Latein	

▶ **Question 17** Du kaufst für die Familie deines Brieffreundes im Warenhaus Geschenke. Hier ist eine Liste von deinem Freund, um dir zu helfen.

> Für meine Mutter – Ohrringe?
>
> Für meine Schwester – ein T-Shirt?
>
> Für meinen Vater – einen Schlips?
>
> Für meine Großmutter – eine Schachtel Pralinen?
>
> Für meinen Bruder – einen Fußball?
>
> Für mich – eine Kassette?

Wo kaufst du die Geschenke? Schreibe das Geschenk neben die richtige Abteilung im Warenhaus.

Stock	Abteilung	Geschenk
Dritter Stock	Schmuck Lebensmittel	
Zweiter Stock	Damenmode Schuhe	
Erster Stock	Herrenmode	
Erdgeschoß	Musik Elektrogeräte	
Untergeschoß	Spielwaren Sportartikel	

▷ **Question 18** Du gehst mit deiner deutschen Freundin in ein Restaurant in Deutschland. Hier ist die Speisekarte.

Menü DM 18

Ochsenschwanzsuppe
oder
Aufschnitt
oder
Bohnensalat

Halbes Hähnchen mit Pommes frites
oder
Wiener Schnitzel mit Bratkartoffeln
oder
Jägerwurst mit Sauerkraut

Gemischtes Eis
oder
Apfelkuchen mit Sahne
oder
Käsekuchen

(a) Deine Freundin ist Vegetarierin. Welche Vorspeise nimmt sie? Kreuze die richtige Antwort an.

❏ Ochsenschwanzsuppe
❏ Aufschnitt
❏ Bohnensalat

(b) Du magst keine Kartoffeln. Was nimmst du als Hauptgericht?

- ❏ Wiener Schitzel
- ❏ Hähnchen
- ❏ Jägerwurst

(c) Deine Freundin ißt gern Obst. Was ißt sie als Nachspeise?

- ❏ Kuchen
- ❏ Käsetorte
- ❏ Eis

▸ **Question 19**

Wie sieht's mit dem Taschengeld aus?

Wolfgang, 11
Ich bekomme 10 Mark im Monat von meinen Eltern und 10 Mark von meinen Großeltern. Das ist mehr als die meisten meiner Freunde bekommen. Also bin ich damit ganz zufrieden. Ich spare im Moment für Computerspiele.

Meike, 14
Also, bei mir ist es so, daß ich nicht jeden Monat dasselbe bekomme. Ich muß meinen Vater fragen, wenn ich was brauche. Normalerweise gibt er mir, was ich will, aber es geht mir auf die Nerven, daß ich immer fragen muß. Ich möchte auch gern mal was sparen.

Torsten, 16
Ich bekomme im Monat 50 Mark, aber für 10 Mark muß ich im Haushalt helfen und das Auto von meinem Vater waschen. Das macht mir eigentlich nichts aus. Wenn ich ins Kino gehe oder Getränke will, muß ich selbst bezahlen, aber wenn ich neue Kleider brauche oder etwas Teureres, dann muß ich das nicht. Wenn ich alles ausgegeben habe, bekomme ich nichts mehr. Das passiert manchmal.

Wer spricht? Trage den richtigen Namen ein.

Beispiel: ....Wolfgang............ bekommt auch von den Großeltern Taschengeld.

(a) .... gibt ab und zu alles aus.
(b) .... bekommt keine feste Summe im Monat.
(c) .... ist mit dem Taschengeld nicht zufrieden.
(d) .... muß für das Taschengeld arbeiten.
(e) .... gibt normalerweise nicht alles aus.

▸ **Question 20** Leserbriefe. Lesen Sie den Brief von Marianne an eine Zeitschrift für Teenager. Lesen Sie dann die Antwort.

Ich bin in der sechsten Klasse und zwölf Jahre alt. Viele meiner Freundinnen haben schon einen festen Freund, aber ich noch nicht. Die Jungen an meiner Schule interessieren sich nicht für mich. Ich verstehe das nicht! Ist mein Aussehen schuld daran? Ich muß eine Brille tragen. Oder bin ich noch zu klein? Ich möchte auch gern mit einem Freund gehen. Es ärgert mich, daß ich niemanden finde. Gib mir bitte eine genaue Antwort.

Marianne.

> *Liebe Marianne,*
>
> unserer Meinung nach hast Du noch viel Zeit. Du bist erst zwölf Jahre alt, und das finden wir ein bißchen jung, um einen festen Freund zu haben. Freunde bringen auch Probleme! Vor allem sollst Du mit Deiner Familie eng zusammenbleiben. Wenn Du mehr Kontakt mit anderen Kindern außerhalb der Schule suchst, könntest Du vielleicht in irgendeinen Verein oder Klub eintreten.
>
> *Die Redaktion.*

(a) Wie fühlt sich Marianne? Kreuzen Sie nur 3 Adjektive an.

- ❏ nervös
- ❏ geduldig
- ❏ traurig
- ❏ zufrieden
- ❏ einsam
- ❏ wütend
- ❏ unglücklich
- ❏ unbequem
- ❏ glücklich

(b) Wie kann man die Antwort der Zeitschrift beschreiben? Kreuzen Sie nur 3 Adjektive an.

- ❏ unklar
- ❏ zornig
- ❏ verständnisvoll
- ❏ hilfreich
- ❏ ungeduldig
- ❏ nutzlos
- ❏ lächerlich
- ❏ praktisch
- ❏ langweilig

▶ **Question 21** Teenager im Urlaub. Lies den folgenden Artikel aus einem Magazin für Teenager.

> Michael ist 18 Jahre alt und wohnt in Chemnitz. Er hat letzten August mit seinen zwei Freunden Bodo (17) und Mustafa (18) einen Campingurlaub im Thüringer Wald gemacht. Sie fuhren mit dem Zug nach Suhl und wanderten von einem Campingplatz zum anderen. Bei schönem Wetter wollten sie 10 Tage Urlaub machen.
>
> Die drei Jungen waren sehr gut ausgerüstet, was für so einen Urlaub wichtig ist. Sie hatten alles dabei: Zelt, warme Schlafsäcke, einen Gaskocher mit Gasflaschen, Geschirr und Besteck. Ein paar Lebensmittel nahmen sie mit. Aber weil sie so schwer mitzuschleppen waren, kauften sie das Essen meistens unterwegs. Vorher hatten die drei immer Urlaub mit der Familie gemacht. Das war das erste Mal zusammen. Michael sagte: „Es hat prima geklappt. Wir sind gut miteinander ausgekommen und haben unsere Freiheit gehabt. Ich würde gerne größere Reisen ins Ausland machen, aber leider habe ich nicht genug Geld."

Beantworte die Fragen auf **deutsch**.

(a) Wann hat Michael Urlaub gemacht?

....(1)

(b) Was für ein Urlaub war das?
....(1)

(c) Wie reisten die drei Jungen in den Thüringer Wald?
....(1)

(d) Wie kamen sie zu den Campingplätzen?
....(1)

(e) Wie lange wollten sie Urlaub machen?
....(1)

(f) Warum kauften sie das Essen meistens unterwegs?
....(1)

(g) Wie haben sie früher Urlaub gemacht?
....(1)

(h) Warum gefiel der Campingurlaub Michael besser?
....(1)

(i) Wohin möchte Michael fahren?
....(1)

(j) Warum ist das problematisch?
....(1)

▶ EXAMINATION ANSWERS

Shorter items

▶ **Answer 1**   C Tankstelle – petrol station

▶ **Answer 2**   B Parkhaus – multi-storey car park

▶ **Answer 3**   A Apotheke – chemist's

▶ **Answer 4**   D Tortoise

▶ **Answer 5**   C a birth

▶ **Answer 6**   B donnerstags – every Thursday

▶ **Answer 7**   A täglich – every day = jeden Tag

▶ **Answer 8**   A = bureau de change   D = snacks
                 B = toilets   E = lost property
                 C = tickets   F = information

▶ **Answer 9**   A = Drogerie   D = Zeitschriften
                 B = Imbißstube   E = Andenken
                 C = Postamt   F = Blumen

▶ **Answer 10** You buy (ja!):   You do not buy (nein!):
                    chocolate (Schokolade)   apples (Äpfel)
                    cheese (Käse)   bananas (Bananen)
                    oranges (Apfelsinen)
                    milk (Milch)

Chapter 6 Reading: Foundation Tier

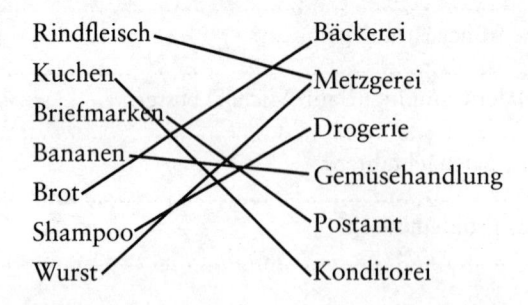

▷ **Answer 11** B a holiday

▷ **Answer 12**
A Im Warenhaus
B In der Imbißstube
C Am Bahnhof
D Im Kino
E Auf der Post

▷ **Answer 13**
Rindfleisch — Metzgerei
Kuchen — Konditorei
Briefmarken — Postamt
Bananen — Gemüsehandlung
Brot — Bäckerei
Shampoo — Drogerie
Wurst — Metzgerei

▷ **Answer 14**
(a) A fish
(b) C montags bis sonntags, i.e. every day

▷ **Answer 15**
Rollerskating – 3.00
Fishing – 12.00
Cycling – 10.00
Football – 9.00
Riding – 5.00

▷ **Answer 16**

Uhrzeit	Montag	Dienstag
8.30	Erdkunde	Französisch
9.30	Erdkunde	Englisch
10.30	Mathe	Naturwissenschaften
11.30	Geschichte	Mathe
12.30	Englisch	Mathe
13.30	Latein	Musik

▷ **Answer 17**

Stock	Abteilung	Geschenk
Dritter Stock	Schmuck Lebensmittel	Ohrringe Pralinen
Zweiter Stock	Damenmode Schuhe	T-Shirt
Erster Stock	Herrenmode	Schlips
Erdgeschoß	Musik Elektrogeräte	Kassette
Untergeschoß	Spielwaren Sportartikel	Fußball

▷ **Answer 18**
(a) Bohnensalat – bean salad
(b) Jägerwurst – it comes with Sauerkraut!
(c) Kuchen – it is Apfelkuchen = apple flan

▷ **Answer 19** (a) *Torsten* gibt ab und zu alles aus.
(b) *Meike* bekommt keine feste Summe im Monat.
(c) *Meike* ist mit dem Taschengeld nicht zufrieden.
(d) *Torsten* muß für das Taschengeld arbeiten.
(e) *Wolfgang* gibt normalerweise nicht alles aus.

▷ **Answer 20** (a) traurig　　　　　　　　　　(b) verständnisvoll
　　　　　　　　einsam　　　　　　　　　　　　　hilfreich
　　　　　　　　unglücklich　　　　　　　　　　praktisch

▷ **Answer 21** (a) letzten August　　　　　　(f) es ist schwer (mitzuschleppen)
(b) ein Campingurlaub　　　(g) mit der Familie
(c) mit dem Zug　　　　　　(h) er hatte seine Freiheit
(d) sie wanderten/sie gingen zu Fuß　(i) ins Ausland
(e) 10 Tage　　　　　　　　(j) er hat nicht genug Geld

▷ **TESTS WITH STUDENT ANSWERS**

The following two tests have been answered by a candidate. An examiner has marked them and added his comments.

▷ **Test 1** Hotels.
Lesen Sie diese Seite einer Broschüre. Dann lesen Sie über die Gruppen, die eine Reservierung machen wollen. Welches Hotel ist für welche Gruppe am besten?
Schreiben Sie die richtige Hotelnummer in die Kästchen.

1 **HOTEL SCHÖNFELDER**	2 **HOTEL STAUFFENBERG**
30 Zimmer	35 Zimmer, 2 Familienzimmer
Restaurant mit bayerischen Spezialitäten	Kinderspielplatz im Garten
Alle Zimmer mit Bad oder Dusche	Spielzimmer mit Tischtennis und Billard
Beheiztes Schwimmbad	Fernsehraum
Fernsehraum	Ruhig am Stadtrand gelegen
Im Herzen der Stadt	*In der Nähe:* Hallenbad und beheiztes Freibad, Eisbahn, Kino
Hunde nicht gestattet	Hunde nicht gestattet

3 **HOTEL ZUM LÖWEN**	4 **HOTEL ALTERSWEIDE**
70 Zimmer	10 Zimmer
Alle luxuriös mit Bad u. Dusche	Bad u. Dusche in jedem Stock
Ruhig, landschaftlich schön gelegen	Kleines Familienhotel
Restaurant	Nur Übernachtung mit Frühstück
Tennisplätze	Preiswert und bequem
In der Nähe: Wandermöglichkeiten, Rundfahrten in die Berge	Zentral gelegen
	In der Nähe: Restaurants, Sehenswürdigkeiten, 5 Minuten vom Bahnhof
Kinder unter 14 Jahren nicht erwünscht	Hunde nicht gestattet

5 **HOTEL LINDENSEE**	6 **HOTEL BERINGER**
40 Zimmer mit Bad oder Dusche	12 Zimmer mit Bad u. Dusche
Übernachtung mit Frühstück	Vegetarisches Restaurant
Direkt am See gelegen	Ruhig am Stadtrand gelegen
Eigener Strand mit Bade- und Wassersportmöglichkeiten	Wandermöglichkeiten am See
Auch Angeln	Kegelbahn
In der Nähe: Restaurants	15 Gehminuten zur Stadtmitte
20 Autominuten von der Stadtmitte	
Hunde und Kinder willkommen	Keine Hunde und keine Kinder

Die Gruppen:

'Good. They are vegetarians.'

A Familie Wagner — Hotel Nummer [6]

Meine Frau und ich wollen zusammen mit unserer Tochter und ihrem Mann ein ruhiges Wochenende genießen. Restaurants mögen wir nicht gern, weil wir alle kein Fleisch essen. Tagsüber möchten wir gern in der Nähe spazierengehen.

'Correct. It's cheap and handy for the disco.'

B Drei Studenten — Hotel Nummer [4]

Wir kommen mit dem Zug von Frankfurt an und haben kein Auto. Wir wollen die Stadt sehen und abends irgendwo essen gehen und dann was trinken oder vielleicht in eine Disco.

'Good. There are family rooms and a play area.'

C Familie Strauss — Hotel Nummer [2]

Wir haben zwei kleine Kinder und sind also lieber in einem Zimmer zusammen. Wir brauchen unbedingt Unterhaltung für die Kinder, besonders wenn das Wetter nicht so gut ist.

'Good. It's quiet. They can play tennis and there won't be any small children.'

D Herr und Frau Henze — Hotel Nummer [3]

Wir möchten uns ein bißchen verwöhnen lassen! Wir sind nicht mehr so jung und brauchen unsere Ruhe. Das heißt, keine Kinder, schöne Spaziergänge, und morgens wollen wir zusammen Tennis spielen können.

'Correct. There is a restaurant and a pool for the children.'

E Familie Gluck — Hotel Nummer [1]

Für uns ist es einfach. Wir wollen etwas Typisches aus der Region essen, die Stadt sehen und unsere zwei Teenager vergessen. Die wollen nur schwimmen und fernsehen.

'Correct. Dogs are welcome! He can go fishing.'

F Herr und Frau Stamitz — Hotel Nummer [5]

Wir wollen zusammen ein langes Wochenende verbringen. Ich möchte ein bißchen angeln, und meine Frau möchte sich in der Sonne ausruhen. Wir wollen auch nicht von Fifi, unserem lieben Hündchen, getrennt sein!

Test 2 Ferien. Lesen Sie diese drei Auszüge aus Briefen.

Katharina

> In den Sommerferien bin ich bei meiner Großmutter in Berlin geblieben und habe auch zwei Wochen in Südfrankreich verbracht. Es war sehr heiß und wir sind geschwommen und sind gesegelt. In Berlin bin ich geritten und bin auch mit meiner Großmutter an den Strand von Müggelsee gegangen. Meine Großmutter wohnt nicht weit vom See und hat eine Reitschule am Stadtrand. In Südfrankreich bin ich viel mit meiner Familie auf dem Lande spazierengegangen.
> Das waren schöne Ferien.

Bärbel

> In den letzten Sommerferien bin ich nach Spanien gefahren, weil meine Eltern ein Appartement in der Nähe von Alicante haben. Man fliegt zwei Stunden von München und das Appartement ist eine Stunde vom Flughafen entfernt. Es gibt einen wunderschönen Strand und das Meer ist prima! Ich bin auch reiten gegangen, weil es in der Nähe eine Reitschule gibt. Ich habe auch Freunde dort. Wir treffen uns meistens am Strand. Dieses Jahr war das Wetter sehr heiß. Es war sehr angenehm in der See zu baden aber sehr unbequem auf einem Pferd zu reiten. Ich liebe aber die Pferde!

Dorothea

> Ich bin dieses Jahr während der Sommerferien nach Köln gefahren. Ich habe dort einen Monat bei Freunden verbracht. Schön einen Monat weg von der Familie zu verbringen! Wir haben fast jeden Tag im Freibad gebadet und haben in der Sonne gelegen. Ich habe einige Österreicher kennengelernt, die sehr sympathisch waren. Sie haben mich eingeladen, bei ihnen zu bleiben. Ich habe viel Eis gegessen und viel Cola getrunken. Der ganze Monat war toll und ich hatte am Ende keine Lust nach Hause zu fahren

Lesen Sie jetzt die folgenden Sätze. Markieren Sie in der Tabelle, für wen die Sätze richtig sind.

1. Ich habe die Ferien an der See verbracht.
2. Ich bin geschwommen.
3. Ich habe neue Freunde gefunden.
4. Ich war mit meiner Familie im Urlaub.
5. Ich habe alles schön gefunden.
6. Ich bin geritten.
7. Ich habe meine Freunde jeden Tag gesehen.
8. Das Wetter war gut.

	Katharina	Bärbel	Dorothea
1		x	
2	x		x
3		x	x
4	x	x	
5			x
6		x	
7		x	
8	x	x	x

Examiner's comment:
On the whole well answered. There are just two errors:

Number 2 Bärbel – should be crossed. At least, she goes to the beach and says that the water is good, so presumably she swam!

Number 3 Bärbel – there should be no cross. She knows the people already, because she has often been to her parents' apartment. They are not **new** friends.

Chapter 7

Reading: Higher Tier

▶ **GETTING STARTED**

As was mentioned in Chapter 5 (Listening: Higher Tier) you cannot do both Foundation and Higher Tier in any one skill, so you will have to give very careful consideration to whether or not you enter for Higher Tier. If you are confident about the longer items in the Foundation Tier tests then you should probably try Higher Tier. The advice of your teacher will be most helpful here. Remember, however, that if you fail to reach a high enough standard in the Higher Tier Reading you will be given an unclassified grade for this part of the examination and this may have serious consequences for your overall grade.

▶ **WHAT YOU NEED TO KNOW**

▶ **Requirements** The Higher Tier reading tests for all the examining groups are based on the same fundamental principles as for the Foundation Tier tests (see Chapter 6). Again, the tests overlap somewhat. The most difficult questions at the end of the Foundation Tier paper may form the easier questions at the beginning of the Higher Tier test. Again, MEG has three sections, Section 2 forming part of both tiers.

If you have not worked your way through Chapter 6, then you should do so now before progressing to the detail of the Higher Tier requirements.

What do you have to do?

▶ You will be expected to show the skills listed under Foundation Tier over a wider range of clearly defined topic areas, which cover the same five Areas of Experience of the National Curriculum. Check which examining group you are studying for and what the exact requirements are.

▶ In addition, you will be expected to show that you can:

   – identify and summarise the important points or themes in the material
   – understand references to past, present and future events
   – understand attitudes, emotions, personal feelings and ideas
   – draw conclusions and inferences
   – identify the relationship between ideas and make comparisons
   – understand various forms of German in authentic texts containing complex sentences and some unfamiliar language in a range of registers, formal and informal, printed and handwritten, factual and non-factual (including possibly imaginative or narrative pieces). Some of the subject matter may be unfamiliar
   – select and make appropriate use of reference materials.

▶ **Themes** What kind of themes or extracts can you expect?

As we saw in Chapter 6, the main sources for testing reading comprehension are likely to be:

   ▶ public notices and signs
   ▶ brochures
   ▶ guides
   ▶ news, weather and traffic reports
   ▶ letters and messages
   ▶ interviews, magazine articles and surveys
   ▶ imaginative writing

At Higher Tier the full range of topics and vocabulary will be covered, extracts will be longer, there will be more complicated language, more extended pieces from newspapers and magazines, and generally longer pieces of formal and informal writing. Remember, though, that there are also other possibilities for each of these sections, so get as much practice as possible reading all kinds of German.

Obviously your understanding of a wide range of vocabulary is going to be put to the test. It is always helpful to know where to start and what to expect. It is, then, worth considering in more detail the themes mentioned above.

Public notices and signs

You can expect any of the following:

- **signs relating to getting about** – as a pedestrian, cyclist, motorist or tourist
- **notices, signs and other information at stations, bus stations, airports and ferry terminals** – e.g. departure and arrival times, delays, timetable alterations, special offers, tours etc.
- **notices, signs and other information at hotels, campsites and youth hostels** – about facilities, emergencies, warnings, special events, trips and excursions, messages passed on from people telephoning or visiting
- **notices and posters in shops** – perhaps in department stores, e.g. advertisements, special offers, bargains, sales, menus, holidays etc.

Brochures and guides

These could include:

- **commercial advertising** – e.g. by department stores, tourist offices, travel agents, local groups publicising activities and events
- **local features** – what's on in the region, diary of coming events such as films, exhibitions, plays, sports events, festivals etc.
- **guided tours** – these will relate to places and features of interest. You are likely to be asked to select information about dates, ages, descriptions, special features, traditions, history, famous people, stories of interest.

News, weather and traffic reports

You can expect these to include:

- **reports of current, topical news items** – visits, accidents, disasters, industrial unrest, protests, famous personalities, sports and special events
- **weather forecasts** – temperatures, general conditions and future trends, special reports for holidaymakers and skiers, natural disasters
- **road conditions** – accidents, road works, diversions, advice and hints for motorists, holiday bottlenecks etc.

Written messages

These could be messages of all kinds for someone who is not present, such as:

- a pen friend giving details of arrangements, passing on information
- someone outlining reasons for a delay or change of plan
- a written message giving details of a phone call you were unable to take
- a note asking you to do something, e.g. a job or errand.

Letters

Letters could be formal or informal, printed or handwritten. Remember to practise reading German handwriting.

- **Formal letters** will tend to relate to accommodation, holidays and jobs, but other topic areas could be included. The most obvious themes would be details of reservations for hotels, campsites and youth hostels, lost property (left while on holiday), job application correspondence.

▶ **Informal letters** will cover a wide range of material and topics, just as you would in a letter you might write in English. The most obvious themes will be current 'news', school, free time, recent activities (party or trip), future plans and making arrangements.

▶ **Semiformal letters** could also figure in this part of the examination. These are likely to be from someone you know or have a connection with but who is not actually a close friend. A parent of your exchange partner may write to your parents with details of a visit. The other kind to expect are those you might read, for instance, on the problem page of a magazine.

Interviews, magazine articles and surveys

These could include:

▶ famous people talking about their lives, interests and careers
▶ experts talking about their specialist fields
▶ features of general interest, e.g. holidays, jobs, fashion, education, music, entertainment and sport, environmental issues such as pollution, social problems
▶ ordinary people talking about any of the above as well as likes, dislikes, school, work, personal problems, social problems, the environment, world events and issues.

Imaginative writing

This could include:

▶ an extract from a story
▶ a single poem

Remember that at Higher Tier you will be expected to understand details such as facts and simple opinions in much the same way as at Foundation Tier, but you will also have to show that you can understand people's more complex feelings and opinions and reasons for them. You will also be expected to draw conclusions and make comparisons between ideas and emotions.

▶ EXAMINATION QUESTIONS

As at Foundation Tier, you can expect a variety of question types. These are best summarised as follows:

▶ questions in English with answers in English (the number of such questions is strictly limited and they may only be used where the situation is a real interpreting one)
▶ questions in German requiring answers in German
▶ multiple choice questions in German or English (see comments above)
▶ completion of forms, tables, grids etc. in German or English
▶ true/false questions in German.

As a rule it will not be necessary for you to write your answers in sentences. You will not be penalised for poor German (or English!) so long as communication of the required answer is not hindered. The clearer your answer, the easier it will be for the examiner to understand.

Some of the extracts will be quite short, while others will be longer. You must recognise that at Higher Tier there will be a greater degree of unpredictability and greater emphasis on understanding the gist as well as drawing conclusions and inferences.

Shorter items

▶ **Question 1** While on holiday with your parents you see this sign at the tram stop. They want to know what it is telling you. Summarise it in English for them.

Chapter 7 Reading: Higher Tier

> **FAHRAUSWEISE BEKOMMEN SIE AM AUTOMATEN**
>
> **BETRETEN DER STRASSENBAHN OHNE GÜLTIGEN FAHRAUSWEIS VERBOTEN.**
>
> **SCHWARZFAHRER MÜSSEN EINE GELDSTRAFE VON DM 50 BEZAHLEN**

....
....
....(3)

▶ **Question 2** Am Bahnhof. Lesen Sie das Poster. Was ist richtig und was falsch? Kreuzen Sie die richtigen Kästchen unten an.

> ### NEU BEI DER BAHN!
>
> *JUNIORPASS*
>
> FÜR ALLE UNTER ACHTZEHN JAHREN UND STUDENTEN UNTER DREIUNDZWANZIG. FÜR NUR DM 50 BEKOMMEN SIE 50% ERMÄSSIGUNG!
>
> *SENIORENPASS*
>
> FÜR ALLE RENTNER ÜBER SECHZIG JAHREN. NUR DM 40! FAHRKARTEN ZU 50% ERMÄSSIGUNG.
>
> *FAMILIENPASS*
>
> FÜR EINEN SUPERPREIS VON DM 175 FÄHRT EINE FAMILIE MIT ZWEI ERWACHSENEN UND ALLEN KINDERN UNTER ACHTZEHN EIN GANZES JAHR LANG ZUM HALBEN PREIS.
>
> *Juniorpaß, Seniorenpaß und Familienpaß sind an allen Bahnhöfen erhältlich. Studenten müssen einen gültigen Studentenausweis vorlegen. Alle müssen einen Personalausweis vorlegen.*
>
> *Alle Pässe sind im ganzen Bundesbahngebiet in allen Zügen, auch in der ersten Klasse, zwölf Monate lang gültig.*
>
> *Für TEE- und Inter-City-Züge müssen die erforderlichen Zuschläge normal bezahlt werden.*
>
> *Mit dem Juniorpaß sind Ermäßigungen bis zu 30% in anderen europäischen Ländern möglich. Weitere Informationen bekommen Sie an allen Bahnhöfen.*

(a) Der Juniorpaß ist für alle unter dreiundzwanzig Jahren.
(b) Der Seniorenpaß ist ein Jahr gültig.
(c) Den Familienpaß kann man am Schalter kaufen.
(d) Nur Rentner dürfen erster Klasse fahren.
(e) In TEE- und Inter-City-Zügen sind alle Pässe ungültig.
(f) Studenten fahren auch im Ausland billiger.
(g) Mit dem Familienpaß dürfen nur zwei Kinder billiger mitfahren.

	Ja	Nein
a)		
b)		
c)		
d)		
e)		
f)		
g)		

> **Question 3** Am Bahnhof. Your parents pick up a leaflet. Answer the questions in English. The following information is given to passengers who wish to take their bicycles with them on suburban trains:

> An Sonntagen, Feiertagen und samstags ab 14.00 Uhr können Sie ein Fahrrad (normale Bauart) in der U- and S-Bahn mitnehmen. Das geht aber nur in den Linien U1 bis U4, S1 bis S6 und S14/S15.
>
> Für Ihr Fahrrad brauchen Sie einen gültigen Fahrschein. Der kostet 2,00 DM. Sie kaufen ihn vor Fahrtbeginn am Automaten: 'Zuschlag 1. Klasse' (Erwachsene).
>
> Die Fahrrad-Einstiegtüren sind mit einem Symbol markiert. Nur hier gibt es Stellplätze–für maximal 2 Fahrräder.
>
> Aus Sicherheitsgründen und um andere Mitreisende nicht zu belästigen, müssen die Fahrräder während der Fahrt festgehalten werden. (Nicht vergessen: Kinder unter 12 Jahren brauchen zum Fahrrad eine Begleitperson über 18!)
>
> Fahrgäste ohne Fahrrad haben Vorrang. Nehmen Sie bitte Rücksicht.

(a) What are passengers under 12 with bicycles required to have?
....
....(1)

(b) What special regulation applies on trains on Saturday mornings?
....(1)

(c) What must you do with your bicycle during the journey, and why?
....
....(2)

(d) How do you know which door of the train you must use?
....(1)

Newspaper reports of events or interesting/unusual stories are likely to be common sources at Higher Tier. Usually, however, the articles will be reasonably short. Here is an example covering the report of a news item.

▸ **Question 4** In der Zeitung.
Lesen Sie diesen Artikel.

ÜBERFALL IN HELMDORFER METZGEREI

In der Nacht zum Samstag haben gegen 1 Uhr zwei bewaffnete Männer eine Metzgerei in Helmdorf überfallen. Der 35jährige Metzger und seine 30jährige Frau wurden beim Eindringen der Diebe wach. Sie wurden mit Pistolen bedroht und gefesselt.

Die zwei Einbrecher erbeuteten DM 8000 aus dem Tresor und machten sich auch noch mit fünf Kilo Jägerwurst und etwa zehn Kilo Hackfleisch davon. Bisher hat die Polizei keine Spur von den zwei Männern, bittet aber alle, denen billige Fleischwaren angeboten werden, sich zu melden.

Ordnen Sie diese Sätze. Schreiben Sie die richtige Nummer – 1, 2, 3 usw.

❏ Man hat die zwei Überfallenen gefesselt.
❏ Sie verschwanden auch mit Fleischwaren.
❏ Sie haben den Inhaber und seine Frau geweckt.
❏ Die Räuber sind nachts in die Metzgerei eingedrungen.
❏ Die Diebe haben Geld erbeutet.
❏ Niemand weiß, wohin sie geflohen sind.

Extracts from articles about celebrities and stars are also likely.

▸ **Question 5** Zeitschriften. Lesen Sie den Artikel.

Nach dreijährigem Hollywood-Aufenthalt ist Dietrich Bender, der bekannteste Rock-Sänger Österreichs, wieder in Deutschland.

Vor einem Jahr von seiner französischen Frau geschieden, wohnt er jetzt mit seinem Sohn Norbert, einem englischen Schäferhund und drei Katzen in Berlin.

Er schockiert immer noch seine Nachbarn und viele Eltern mit seinem geschminkten Gesicht und der grünen Punkfrisur.

An Geld fehlt es bei den Benders nicht. Er hat so viele Millionen in Amerika verdient, daß er sich jetzt seinen lebenslangen Traum erfüllen kann, einen Radiosender für Rockmusik in seinem Heimatland zu gründen.

Die Verhandlungen darüber sind geheim, und man weiß auch nichts über sein Privatleben, da er nie mit den Medien spricht. Man meint aber, daß der auf der Bühne schreiende, aggressiv wirkende Punk zu Hause ein liebevoller Vater ist.

Beantworten Sie die Fragen auf deutsch.

(a) Wie lange war Dietrich in Amerika?
....(1)

(b) Wann hat er sich scheiden lassen?
....(1)

(c) Wo lebt er jetzt und mit wem?
....(2)

(d) Wie sieht Dietrich aus?
....(2)

(e) Was will Dietrich jetzt machen?
....(1)

(f) Warum ist sein Privatleben ein Geheimnis?
....(1)

(g) Was wissen wir über Dietrichs Charakter?
   (i) in der Familie? ....(1)
   (ii) im Beruf? ....(1)

Letters, whether formal or informal, are likely to be made use of at Higher Tier. Study this example of an informal letter.

▶ **Question 6** Read the letter below and answer **in English** the questions that follow.

> Kassel, den 11. November
>
> Liebe Carol!
>
> Vielen Dank für Deinen Brief, den ich vor drei Wochen bekommen habe. Entschuldige bitte, daß ich erst heute schreibe. Ich bin ja sehr schreibfaul! Du auch, nicht? Oder schreibst du gern Briefe?
>
> Bei mir war in letzter Zeit ziemlich viel los. Wir haben nämlich in unserer Stadt ein neues Sportzentrum, wo ich dreimal in der Woche hingehen darf. Da kann man allerlei Sport treiben. Man zahlt natürlich Eintritt, aber das ist eigentlich ganz günstig, und wenn man Sportartikel braucht, gibt es sie dort zu mieten. Das finde ich gut, denn ich könnte es mir sonst nicht leisten, Federball, Tischtennis und dergleichen zu spielen. Mein Lieblingssport aber – was wir leider bei uns nicht treiben können – ist Skilaufen. Dieses Jahr fahre ich zum dritten Mal mit der Klasse nach Österreich.
>
> Ich finde es klasse, daß Du Gitarre spielst. In meiner Freizeit spiele ich öfters Klavier. Später will ich in einer Jazzband spielen.
>
> Zum Schluß habe ich eine Bitte. Ich sammle eifrig Briefmarken und habe bis jetzt nur wenige aus England. Hast Du vielleicht welche, die Du mir zuschicken kannst?
>
> So, Schluß für heute. Viele Grüße,
> Deine Karin

(a) When did Karin receive Carol's letter?
....(1)

(b) What does Karin say about writing letters?
....(1)

(c) What does Karin say about the cost of using the sports centre?
....(1)

(d) What facility does the sport centre offer?
....(1)

(e) What is Karin's regret about the sports centre?
....(1)

(f) What does Karin say about her musical interests?
....
....(2)

(g) What request does Karin make at the end?
....(1)

Question 7 Lesen Sie das Programm für eine Woche Urlaub.

EINE AKTIVE WOCHE FÜR ALLE

Samstag	Ankunft am Abend
Sonntag	Tag zur freien Verfügung
Montag	Vormittag: Segeln für Anfänger oder Fortgeschrittene Nachmittag: frei
Dienstag	Vormittag: Einführung ins Fliegen Nachmittag: frei
Mittwoch	Ausflug mit dem Reisebus zum Schloß Marienhof
Donnerstag	Vormittag: Angeln von Forellen am Teich Nachmittag: frei
Freitag	Vormittag: Wandern im Wald und nachher Mittagessen im Bootsrestaurant auf dem See Nachmittag: frei
Samstag	Tag zur freien Verfügung. Abfahrt am frühen Abend

Alle Aktivitäten werden von unserem Personal geleitet.

Schreiben Sie den richtigen Tag zu den Verkehrsmitteln.

Verkehrsmittel	Tag	Verkehrsmittel	Tag
(bus)		(shoes)	
(train)		(car)	

Verkehrsmittel	Tag	Verkehrsmittel	Tag

Question 8 In der Zeitschrift. Lesen Sie den Artikel und füllen Sie die Lücken in den Sätzen aus.

TRÄUME

Carsten ist 14 Jahre alt und geht auf eine Realschule. Eigentlich geht er nicht sehr gern in die Schule. Am liebsten spielt er Tennis, und er ist Fan des schwedischen Spielers Björn Borg. Nachmittags, wenn er in seinem kleinen Zimmer Hausaufgaben macht, sieht er oft die vielen Poster von Tennisstars an, die er an die Wände geklebt hat.

Sein Zimmer mag er überhaupt nicht gern, weil er es mit seinem jüngeren Bruder teilen muß. Das geht ihm auf die Nerven. „Alles ist zu eng und zu dunkel. Viele meiner Freunde haben ein großes Zimmer mit allem möglichen drin. Meine Eltern würden auch gern eine größere Wohnung haben, aber Wohnungen sind schwer zu finden und auch teuer."

Manchmal träumt Carsten von einem schönen, hellen Zimmer mit einem Computer und einem Lehnstuhl. „Letzten Endes ist mein Zimmer nur Schlafplatz", sagt er. Eine größere Wohnung können sich Carstens Eltern nicht leisten. Sie haben vier Kinder, und Carstens Vater ist arbeitslos.

(a) Tennis ist Carstens ....
(b) Sein Lieblings .... ist Björn Borg.
(c) Er kommt aus ....
(d) Im Moment arbeitet sein Vater ....
(e) Carsten hat .... Geschwister.
(f) Er findet sein Zimmer sehr .... und ....
(g) Die Zimmer seiner Freunde sind ....
(h) Er möchte gern .... im Zimmer haben.
(i) Es ist nicht ...., eine größere Wohnung zu finden.
(j) Carsten kann in seinem Zimmer nur ....

Longer items

▷ **Question 9** Life in Germany.
Read this magazine article. It describes the experiences of the son of a Turkish immigrant worker in Germany.

> Ali ist der zehnjährige Sohn eines türkischen Gastarbeiters, der jetzt in Berlin wohnt. Sein Vater ist schon vor dreizehn Jahren nach Deutschland gekommen. Der Vater hat kein Heimweh mehr. „Hier habe ich Arbeit und Geld. Alles ist viel besser als vorher in der Türkei", meint er. Er kennt sich jetzt in Berlin besser aus als in seiner Heimatstadt. Der Sohn hat auch kein Heimweh. Mit zwei Jahren sind er und seine Mutter und seine Schwester nach Berlin umgezogen. Ali ist stolz darauf, daß er schon besser Deutsch kann, als sein Vater.
>
> Als er angekommen ist, konnte er natürlich kein Wort Deutsch sprechen. Mit sechs Jahren durfte er aber sogleich mit den deutschen Kindern in die Grundschule gehen. Das war ein großer Vorteil. Viele ältere Gastarbeiterkinder mußten zunächst in Vorbereitungsklassen für Ausländer gehen und finden es immer noch schwer, Anschluß an ihre deutschen Schulkamaraden zu finden. Ali war von Anfang an mit deutschen Kindern zusammen.
>
> Für Ali gab es aber auch Probleme. Vor der Grundschule hatten die meisten seiner Mitschüler einen Kindergarten besucht. Da er damals kein Deutsch konnte, durfte er das nicht. Es hat seinen Vater viel Geld gekostet, seinem Sohn einen Privatlehrer zu bezahlen, damit er zunächst ein bißchen Deutsch lernte.
>
> Es fällt Ali aber immer noch schwer, daß er nicht so viel Kontakt zu seinen Schulkameraden hat wie seine deutschen Mitschüler. Seine Eltern können ihm auch unmöglich mit den Hausaufgaben helfen, weil sie nicht genug Deutsch sprechen. In der Familie wird immer Türkisch gesprochen. Es nervt Ali, daß er Deutsch noch nicht perfekt beherrscht und zugleich auch kein perfektes Türkisch kann.

What does Ali think about life in Germany. Explain this to someone who does not speak German.
Make a list of three positive aspects of life in Germany:
....
....
....(3)

Make a list of **three** negative aspects of life in Germany:
....
....
....(3)

▷ **Question 10** Lesen Sie den Artikel über Schulprobleme in Deutschland und beantworten Sie die Fragen auf **deutsch**.

> In Deutschland bekommen die Kinder Schulzeugnisse wie in den meisten anderen Ländern, obwohl das deutsche Schulsystem vielleicht mehr Gewicht auf Zeugnisse legt, als zum Beispiel das Schulsystem in

(continued)

(*continued*)

Großbritannien. Daher haben deutsche Schüler viel Streß. Die Schulzeugnisse sind in Deutschland überall gleich. Die beste Note ist eine eins und die schlechteste eine sechs. Schüler bekommen zweimal im Jahr ein Zeugnis, normalerweise am Ende jedes Halbjahrs. Das heißt im Dezember und im Juli oder August. Viele Schulen sind heutzutage barmherzig und geben die ersten Zeugnisse erst im Januar aus, damit die Weihnachtsferien nicht verdorben werden. Nur in den Waldorfschulen ist das anders. In diesen Schulen bekommt man keine Zeugnisse, sondern einen Bericht.

Viele Schüler haben Angst davor, ihr Zeugnis zu bekommen, weil sie wissen, daß die Lehrer und auch die Eltern so viel Wert darauf legen. Besonders am Ende des Schuljahrs ist das so. Wenn ein Schüler im Sommer eine fünf oder sechs in zwei oder mehr Fächern bekommt, dann bleibt er sitzen. Das heißt, daß er nicht ins nächste Schuljahr versetzt wird und ein ganzes Jahr wiederholen muß.

Die Schüler leiden unter dem Streß wegen ihrer Zeugnisse so sehr, daß jedes Jahr einige verschwinden oder sich sogar umbringen. Das passiert nicht sehr oft, Gott sei Dank. Man tut jetzt mehr, um den Schülern zu helfen. In manchen Orten gibt es ein Sorgentelefon. Das ist eine Nummer, die die Schüler oder ihre Eltern anrufen können, wenn es Probleme gibt. Der Anruf kostet nichts und kann auch anonym sein. Da haben die Anrufer die Möglichkeit, einfach mit jemandem über ihre Probleme zu sprechen.

(a) Wann bekommen die deutschen Schüler Zeugnisse?
....(1)
(b) Was ist in einer Waldorfschule anders?
....(1)
(c) Wie sind die Weihnachtsferien für manche Schüler besser?
....(1)
(d) Was heißt „sitzenbleiben"?
....(1)
(e) Warum haben Schüler Angst vor Zeugnissen?
....
....(2)
(f) Was passiert manchmal, wenn Schüler zu sehr gestreßt sind?
....
....(2)
(g) Nennen Sie **zwei** Vorteile des Sorgentelefons.
....
....(2)

▶ EXAMINATION ANSWERS

Shorter items

▶ **Answer 1** Buy your tickets from the machine
do not board a tram without a ticket
if you travel without a ticket there is a DM 150 on the spot fine

Answer 2

	Ja	Nein
a)		✗
b)	✗	
c)	✗	
d)		✗
e)		✗
f)	✗	
g)		✗

Answer 3

(a) Somebody over 18 must accompany them.
(b) No bicycles allowed.
(c) You must hold it for safety reasons and so as not to annoy other passengers.
(d) The door is marked with a symbol.

Answer 4

3 Man hat die zwei Überfallenen gefesselt.
5 Sie verschwanden auch mit Fleischwaren.
2 Sie haben den Inhaber und seine Frau geweckt.
1 Die Räuber sind nachts in die Metzgerei eingedrungen.
4 Die Diebe haben Geld erbeutet.
6 Niemand weiß, wohin sie geflohen sind.

Answer 5

(a) 3 Jahre
(b) vor einem Jahr
(c) in Berlin, mit seinem Sohn, einem Hund und 3 Katzen
(d) Er hat grüne Haare. Er hat ein geschminktes Gesicht.
(e) Er will einen Radiosender (für Rockmusik) gründen.
(f) Er spricht nie mit den Medien.
(g) (i) Er ist liebevoll.
    (ii) Er ist/wirkt aggressiv auf der Bühne.

Answer 6

(a) 3 weeks ago/within the last month
(b) She is lazy.
(c) It is quite reasonable.
(d) It hires out equipment.
(e) You cannot ski there.
(f) She plays the piano and wants to play in a jazz band.
(g) Could Carol send her some English stamps?

Answer 7

Verkehrsmittel	Tag	Verkehrsmittel	Tag
(bus)	Mittwoch	(shoes)	Freitag

Verkehrsmittel	Tag	Verkehrsmittel	Tag
(train)		(car)	
(sailboat)	Montag	(airplane)	Dienstag
(bicycle)		(boat)	Freitag

▶ **Answer 8** (a) Lieblingssport
(b) ... spieler
(c) Schweden
(d) nicht
(e) 3
(f) eng ... dunkel
(g) größer
(h) einen Computer/einen Lehnstuhl
(i) leicht/einfach
(j) schlafen

Longer items

▶ **Answer 9** Three positive aspects:

(a) His father can earn more money.
(b) There is work to be had.
(c) He has learnt to speak German.

Three negative aspects:

He does not have much contact with German school friends.
His parents cannot help much with school work, because they do not speak enough German.

116 Chapter 7 Reading: Higher Tier

He is frustrated that he cannot speak perfect German and also cannot speak perfect Turkish.

▶ **Answer 10** (a) im Dezember und im Juli oder August
(b) Man bekommt keine Zeugnisse.
(c) Sie bekommen das Zeugnis erst im Januar.
(d) ein ganzes Schuljahr wiederholen
(e) Die Eltern/die Lehrer legen viel Wert darauf. (1 mark)
Man bleibt vielleicht sitzen. (1 mark)
(f) Einige Schüler verschwinden. (1 mark)
Einige Schüler bringen sich um. (1 mark)
(g) Es ist kostenlos/gratis./Es kostet nichts. (1 mark)
Es ist anonym./Man kann über Probleme sprechen. (1 mark)

▶ **TESTS WITH STUDENT ANSWERS**

▶ **Test 1** Here is an example of a Higher Tier question answered by a candidate and marked by an examiner.

The following account appeared in a North German newspaper. Read it carefully and then answer, **in English**, the questions which follow.

Putzfrau in Fahrstuhl steckengeblieben

Die 48jährige Putzfrau Marthe Sirola hat vierzehn Tage im Fahrstuhl eines Hamburger Hochhauses verbracht. Der Fahrstuhl war zwischen Erdgeschoß und Keller steckengeblieben, ohne daß jemand merkte, daß sich Frau Sirola darin befand. In dieser Zeit hat sie 3500 DM „verdient".

Frau Sirola hat nur überleben können, weil sie eine Flasche Limonade bei sich hatte. So konnte sie ihren Durst löschen. Als die arme Frau nicht zur Arbeit erschien, nahm man an, sie sei krank und sei zu Hause geblieben. Deshalb suchte man sie nicht. Am 28. Mai entdeckte ein Mechaniker die bewußtlose, aber noch lebende Frau endlich im Fahrstuhl.

Die Firma, bei der die Putzfrau arbeitet, hat ausgerechnet, was Frau Sirola mit Über- und Sonntagsstunden „verdient" hat. Die Zeit im Fahrstuhl gilt als Arbeitszeit, denn sie hatte einen Besen und einen Eimer Wasser bei sich, als das Unglück geschah. An den beiden Sonntagen, die sie in dem Fahrstuhl verbrachte, „verdiente" sie sogar 300 Prozent mehr als an den gewöhnlichen Werktagen.

Questions and student answers

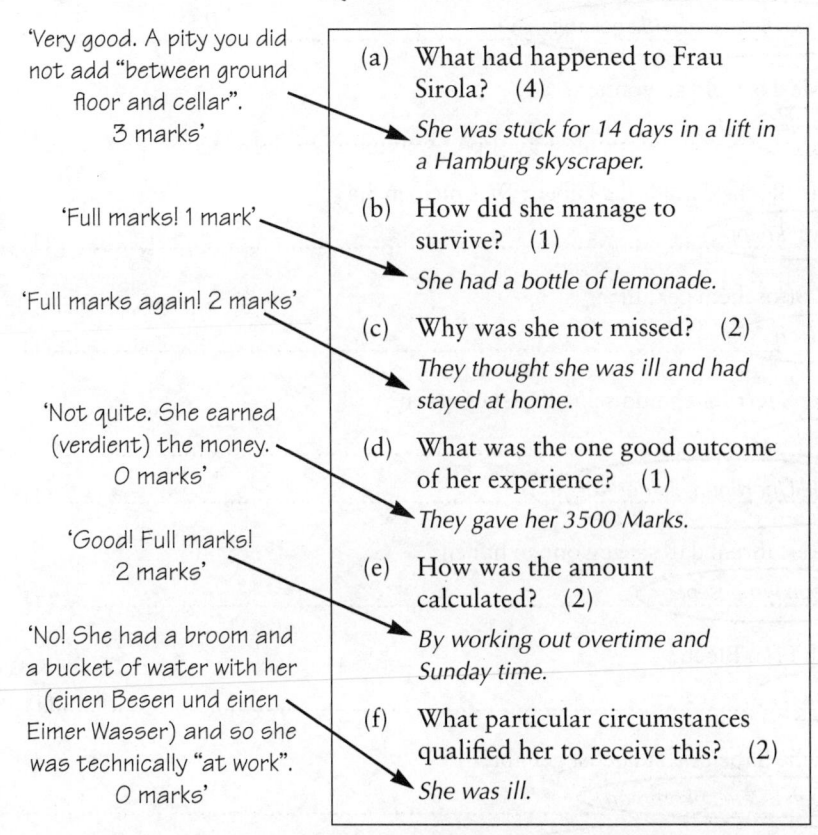

(a) What had happened to Frau Sirola? (4)
She was stuck for 14 days in a lift in a Hamburg skyscraper.

'Very good. A pity you did not add "between ground floor and cellar". 3 marks'

(b) How did she manage to survive? (1)
She had a bottle of lemonade.

'Full marks! 1 mark'

(c) Why was she not missed? (2)
They thought she was ill and had stayed at home.

'Full marks again! 2 marks'

(d) What was the one good outcome of her experience? (1)
They gave her 3500 Marks.

'Not quite. She earned (verdient) the money. 0 marks'

(e) How was the amount calculated? (2)
By working out overtime and Sunday time.

'Good! Full marks! 2 marks'

(f) What particular circumstances qualified her to receive this? (2)
She was ill.

'No! She had a broom and a bucket of water with her (einen Besen und einen Eimer Wasser) and so she was technically "at work". 0 marks'

'Good. **Eight** out of a possible **twelve**'

▶ **Test 2** Here is an example of a further Higher Tier question answered by a candidate and then marked by an examiner. This question required answers in German.

In der Zeitung. Lesen Sie den Artikel und beantworten Sie die folgenden Fragen auf **deutsch**.

> Während sie neben dem Schwimmbad im Garten ihrer Münchener Luxusvilla sitzen, erinnern sich Petra und Helmut Bloch an den Tag vor fünfzehn Jahren, als sie 850.000 Mark im Lotto gewonnen haben. Damals wohnten sie mit ihren zwei Kindern, den Söhnen Hartmut und Wolfgang, in einer Dreizimmerwohnung. Platz war knapp, und Geld hatten sie auch nicht genug, da Herr Bloch seine Stelle verloren hatte.
>
> „Wir haben furchtbar gestritten", sagt Herr Bloch. „Die Küche war in Unordnung, weil die Kinder und ich gemalt hatten. Petra sah außerdem, daß ich einen Lottoschein gekauft hatte, obwohl wir damals kaum Geld zum Leben hatten".
>
> Erst am Samstag, nachdem er den Schein weggeschickt hatte, saß er vor dem Fernseher und erfuhr, daß er alle Gewinnzahlen hatte. „Zunächst war ich eigentlich schockiert", erinnert sich Frau Bloch. „Ich konnte es einfach nicht glauben. Erst als der Scheck vor mir lag und ich die Summe schwarz auf weiß lesen konnte, habe ich wahrgenommen, was das bedeutete."
>
> Als die Nachbarn und andere Leute erfuhren, daß die Blochs so viel Geld gewonnen hatten, bekam die Familie einige Probleme. Jemand hat gedroht, ihr Auto zu beschädigen, wenn sie ihm kein Geld gäben. Sie bekamen auch viele Briefe von Menschen, die um Geld bettelten. Aber nichts ist ihnen passiert, und nachdem sie in einen anderen Stadtteil umgezogen waren, hörte das alles auf.

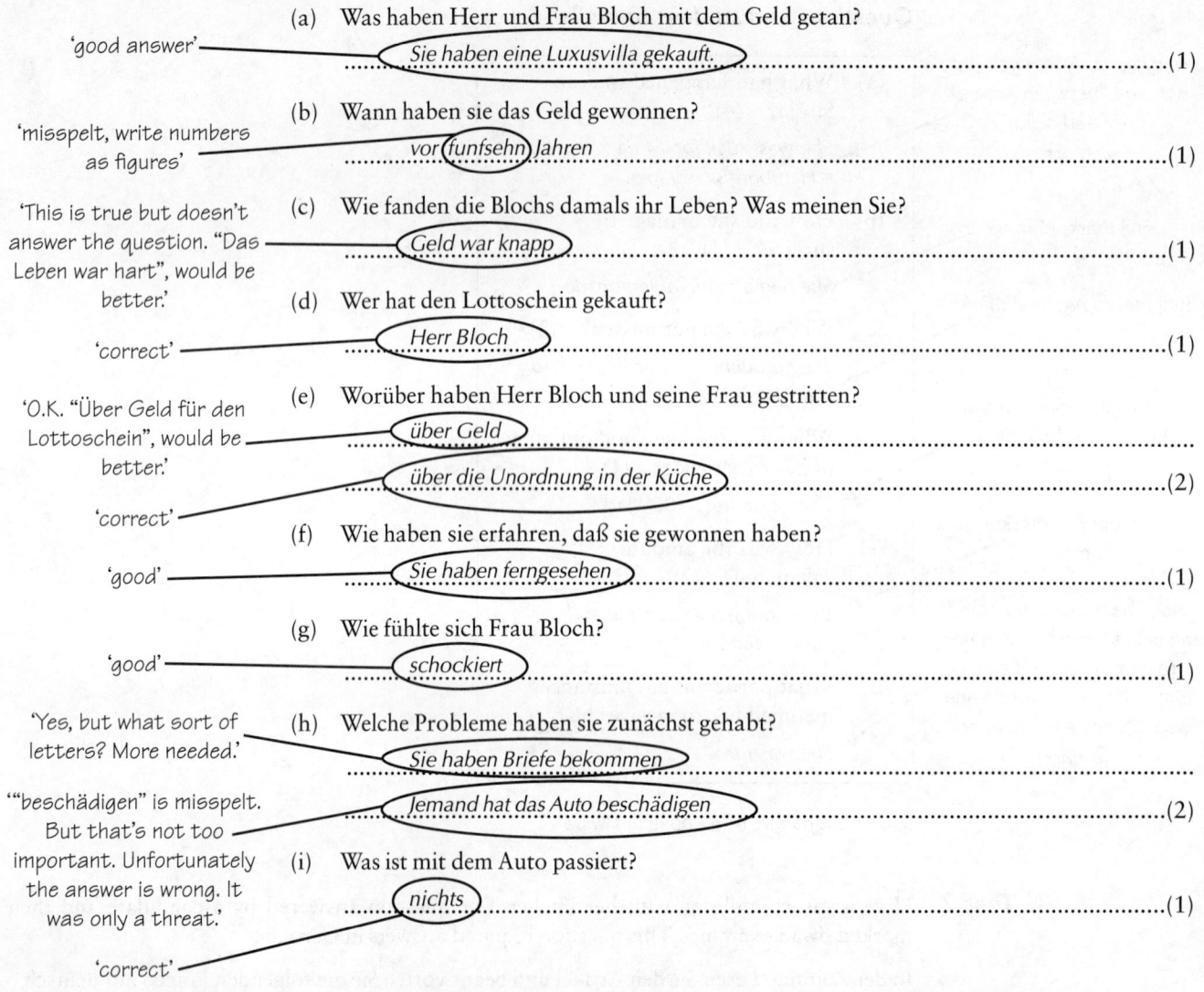

'good answer'	(a) Was haben Herr und Frau Bloch mit dem Geld getan? *Sie haben eine Luxusvilla gekauft.*	(1)
'misspelt, write numbers as figures'	(b) Wann haben sie das Geld gewonnen? *vor funfsehn Jahren*	(1)
'This is true but doesn't answer the question. "Das Leben war hart", would be better.'	(c) Wie fanden die Blochs damals ihr Leben? Was meinen Sie? *Geld war knapp*	(1)
'correct'	(d) Wer hat den Lottoschein gekauft? *Herr Bloch*	(1)
'O.K. "Über Geld für den Lottoschein", would be better.'	(e) Worüber haben Herr Bloch und seine Frau gestritten? *über Geld*	
'correct'	*über die Unordnung in der Küche*	(2)
'good'	(f) Wie haben sie erfahren, daß sie gewonnen haben? *Sie haben ferngesehen*	(1)
'good'	(g) Wie fühlte sich Frau Bloch? *schockiert*	(1)
'Yes, but what sort of letters? More needed.'	(h) Welche Probleme haben sie zunächst gehabt? *Sie haben Briefe bekommen*	
'"beschädigen" is misspelt. But that's not too important. Unfortunately the answer is wrong. It was only a threat.'	*Jemand hat das Auto beschädigen*	(2)
	(i) Was ist mit dem Auto passiert? *nichts*	(1)
'correct'		

Examiner's comment

'Quite well answered on the whole. As you can see, complete sentences are not always necessary, but you must be precise and clear, especially when asked how people feel and what they think.'

▶ A STEP FURTHER (FOUNDATION AND HIGHER TIER)

Much of the reading material at Foundation Tier is taken from notices, signs, menus and leaflets. Your course books will have some examples of these things, or you may have copies of Harrap's *German Sign Language* at school. But it should be possible to get hold of authentic material without too much trouble. After all, it is easy enough to pick up free leaflets in Britain – at the station, theatre, travel agency, information office and so on. This is where your contacts with Germany come in useful. If you have a pen friend, you could exchange packets of leaflets. Or if you know someone who is going to Germany, you could ask them to look out for suitable material.

Don't throw away any letters you may have which are written in German. It is important to get used to German handwriting (how is it different from English handwriting?) and the kind of expressions which are common in letters.

But understanding what you read is basically a matter of knowing the words. If you don't know the days of the week, then you cannot tell on which days the stop is closed. If you don't know the meaning of the word *Auskunft* then you cannot know what is on offer there. (Actually it means 'information'.)

So words simply have to be learnt, and it's no good hoping they will sink in without your making any effort. Lack of vocabulary is a constant barrier to success at exam time, so we have got to devise ways of learning lists of words in as painless a fashion as possible. Here, then, are a few suggestions for ways of taking some of the drudgery out of learning vocabulary.

1. Take the number **ten** as your norm and **find ten words** on one subject. For example, think about **transport**:

das Auto, der Wagen	das Flugzeug
das Fahrrad, das Rad	das Motorrad
der Bus	das Schiff
das Taxi	die Fähre
der Zug	das Luftkissenboot

   Now **make up a sentence** for each one, e.g. *Ich fahre mit dem Zug nach Bremen.*

   Other subjects to tackle in this way could be:

   - clothes
   - weather
   - school subjects
   - countries
   - towns in Germany
   - furniture
   - shops
   - professions
   - fruit and vegetables
   - sports
   - hobbies other than sports
   - food you like
   - buildings other than shops

   No doubt you can think of plenty more by looking at your topic lists and vocabulary lists.

2. Use a **vocabulary book**. Make sure you write carefully and neatly. Nothing is worse than revising from a grubby notebook which is full of mistakes. Give yourself plenty of space, putting the German on one side of the page and the English on the other. Then you can cover up one side and test yourself. Alternatively, put the meaning on the next page, so that you always have to make the effort of turning the page to find the answer.

3. Another simple way of learning vocabulary is to take a **rough piece of paper** and to **fold it** into four or six like this:

   You then write out, say, twenty difficult German words in column one. Then write out the English in column two. Now fold back column one so that you cannot see it. Now you only have the English in front of you. Try to write out the German again in column three. Then check with column one and fill in the gaps. Now continue in the same way.

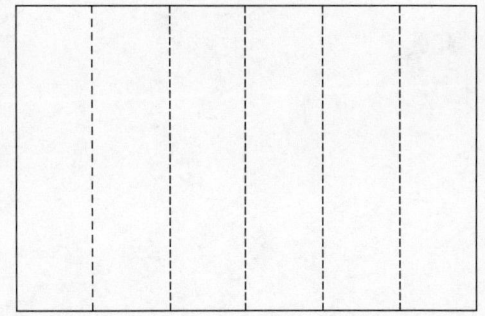

   But beware! It is quite easy to learn words on a short-term basis like this. The real test is whether you still remember them in a few weeks' time.

4. Some people develop a habit of writing **lists** of words on pieces of paper or card about the size of a postcard. They use these cards as bookmarks or pin them on the wall, prop them up by a mirror or leave them anywhere they are bound to notice them.

5. Here is another suggestion for those with an orderly mind. Find a small long, deep box, the sort of box which After Eights come in. Cut up lots of small cards (you can cut up old Christmas cards) to fit into the box like filing cards. Write the German word(s) at the top of the card, and write the English in the same way on the back.

   You can then work your way through the cards either from the German side or from the English, gradually replacing the words you know with new ones. You can also write on the bottom of the cards and turn the whole set upside down. This scheme could clearly be developed to include phrases and sentences, or questions and answers, just as in Trivial Pursuit!

6   Do not forget that words have little meaning until they are put together into sentences. So **read** German whenever you can. If you have worked through the *Lesekiste* sets, the school probably has readers to follow that. There may well be discarded textbooks in school too, which could provide excellent reading practice. And what about the school library or the local library? One school I know had an excellent scheme for providing cheap reading material. Every English member of an exchange group took to Germany a paperback which he or she no longer needed. The German group brought books to England, so that each school was able to build up a small collection of books in the foreign language.

In all your revising, remember that learning does not have to be done sitting at a table. Try speaking German as you walk about the room. Work out German phrases in your mind as you watch TV or as you cycle to school. Identify each article as you tidy your room or as you lay the table. Prop your vocabulary book up in front of you as you do the washing up.

If you can't get to sleep at night, go over groups of words in your mind. The possibilities are endless! But above all make the language something alive, something to be used, something to be enjoyed.

Chapter 8

Speaking: Foundation Tier – role-plays

GETTING STARTED

All the examining groups require you to take part in role-plays at both Foundation and Higher Tiers. This is hardly surprising since one of the aims of the GCSE and the National Curriculum is to help you to cope with the German needed in everyday situations.

WHAT YOU NEED TO KNOW

Speaking

The role-plays will require you to take the initiative, so be prepared to speak! You will need to be able to:

- ask for goods, e.g. in a shop
- ask for information, e.g. in a tourist office
- give information, e.g. in a lost property office
- make arrangements, e.g. on the telephone
- understand and answer the questions of others
- give simple opinions, likes, dislikes etc.

You will perform the role-plays with your teacher, who will take the part of a helpful and 'sympathetic' native speaker of German. The test will be recorded, so it is a good idea to practise speaking into a microphone. Depending on the examining group whose examination you are studying for, the test will be marked by your own teacher or sent away to an external examiner for marking.

You will have to do **two** role-plays. If you are studying for the SEG modular GCSE you will only do one role-play in the Module 4 end of course examination. (You will have had to do other types of speaking assessments in previous modules, which will be dealt with later.) You will need to arrive at the examination room in plenty of time before the test, allowing also for the preparation time that you will be given. Make sure that you do not have to rush at the last minute; it is important to be as calm as you can be in the circumstances. You will either be given the role-play cards on which you will be tested or you will be able to choose them yourself from a number offered. You will not be able to see what is on them, however! You are allowed to use a dictionary during the preparation time but **not** during the test itself. You may be allowed to make notes while preparing. It is important that you check the exact regulations of the exam group you are studying for.

You are not expected to use perfect German. The main point is for you to make yourself understood. This means you need to speak as clearly as you can and pronounce the words as well as you can, so that the other person can understand. At all stages your teacher will try to be as helpful as possible, to allow you to show exactly what you can do. Remember that in the GCSE you always gain credit for what you **can** do. The examination is not designed to trip you up and expose your weaknesses. So be positive from the start!

Topics and situations

The role-plays will be based on the Areas of Experience and the topics listed for Foundation Tier. It is vital, then, that you know the material relevant to you. Check exactly what your examining group states and study carefully the **language tasks** and **vocabulary** in Chapter 3.

Remember that the material listed in one topic area may be tested in other topic areas and in many different situations. As a reminder, some topics, and examples of possible situations or settings in which the role-plays might take place, are listed in Table 8.1.

Table 8.1 Topics and possible role-play situations

Topics	Possible situations/settings
Personal details	In town/on telephone
Life at home	At home/pen friend's home
School life	Places of work
Entertainment	At the cinema
Getting around	Public transport, asking the way
Holidays	Information office/hotel/campsites
Friends and family	At home/leisure facilities
Shopping	Markets, stores, kiosks, clothes shop
Food and drink	At home, restaurants, cafés
Public services	Post office, bank, cleaners
Health and fitness	At the doctor, dentist, chemist
Weather	On holiday, making arrangements

Some topics and situations/settings lend themselves more readily to role-plays than others, so listed below are some of the most common situations you are likely to meet in this part of the examination. You must prepare yourself to cope in situations which may involve:

- asking the way
- shopping
- cafés and restaurants
- booking accommodation
- petrol stations, garages
- places of entertainment
- leisure facilities
- in a German family
- school
- trains, buses, trams, stations
- banks, post offices
- tourist offices
- customs
- minor illnesses and complaints
- reporting lost property
- making arrangements to go out
- meeting new people.

Please remember that this list only represents the most likely situations to be covered. It is not an exhaustive list and you should be prepared to deal with other possibilities.

▷ **Format of the role-plays**

The role-plays will be printed on cards and each will have a sentence or two in English to set the scene. The first role-play will be relatively straightforward while the second will generally contain an element of unpredictability. The instructions for what you have to do will be either pictorial or in German or a combination of the two. Below are some examples of the types of role-play you may come across with an indication as to whether they are type 1 or type 2 role-plays. You will notice that they are not of equal difficulty. The type 2 role-play is generally more difficult than the type 1 role-play, either because of the unpredictable element, or the instructions in German rather than pictorial stimuli, or both!

▷ **Approaching the role-plays**

Now that you are more confident about what to expect, it is time to look at the role-plays in detail, and how best to prepare for them.

As with all tests, a **systematic** approach is sensible.

The first thing you need to do is read the scene-setting and any instructions carefully. Take note of who will start the conversation, you or the examiner. Look carefully at any symbols and work out what task you are being asked to do. Read carefully any German instructions and, with the help of your dictionary if this is allowed, work out the task you have to perform. Let's look at some examples.

Example role-plays

Example A: Type 1 role-play
Im Restaurant. Sie gehen mit einem Freund/einer Freundin essen.
Situation: You are in a restaurant in Germany and you want to have a meal with a friend. Your teacher will play the part of the waiter/waitress. He/she will start the conversation.

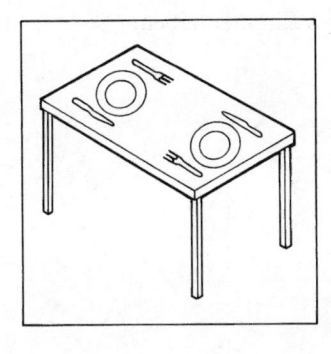

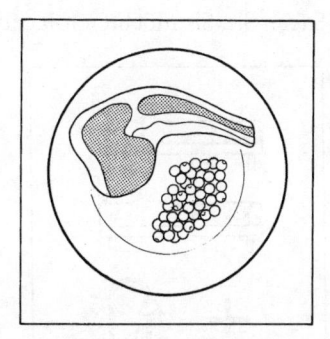

First, note that the examiner will start. Then work out the things you need to say. If you were to write out the tasks in English, this is probably how they would look:

1 Ask for a table for two.
2 Ask for a chop/cutlet/steak and peas.
3 Ask for some chips.
4 Ask for a glass of wine.
5 Ask if there is a telephone.

If you are allowed to make notes while preparing you may want to write them down in English.

There is no unexpected element in this one, so what the examiner says isn't vital for you to be able to do your part. However, if you are in any doubt as to what to do at any point, then what the examiner says will probably help you.

The next stage is to think of the German you will need to use to convey and ask for the information required. If you are allowed to make notes, jot down key words and/or phrases. Remember that there may be many different ways of saying the same thing and it does not matter which one you use as long as you get your message across. Try to think in terms of the **task** you have to do and the **end result** you want to achieve. **Do not** think of a task in English and try to translate it word for word.

For the tasks in this example you will probably end up saying something like this (key words or phrases are in bold, alternatives in brackets):

1 *Ein **Tisch für zwei**, bitte.*
2 *Ich möchte ein **Schnitzel (Kotelett, Steak) mit Erbsen**, bitte.*
3 *Eine Portion **Pommes frites**, bitte.*
4 *Ein Glas **Wein (Weißwein)**, bitte.*
5 *Wo gibt es ein **Telefon**?*

The next example is presented in a slightly different way in that there are some instructions in German as well as pictures and symbols. This makes no difference to the way you should approach it as described above.

Example B: Type 1 role-play
You arrive at a hotel in Germany and want to book rooms. Your teacher will play the part of the receptionist. **You begin the conversation.**

1 Begrüßen Sie die Empfangsdame!

2 Sagen Sie, Sie möchten folgendes Zimmer haben:

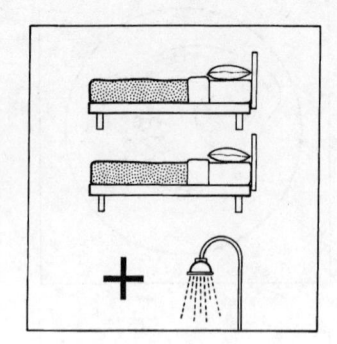

3 **JULI**

So	Mo	Di	Mi	Do	Fr	Sa
		1	2	3	4	5
6	7	8	9	⑩	⑪	⑫
13	14	15	16	17	18	19
20	21	22	23	24	25	26
27	28	29	30	31		

4 Fragen Sie nach dem Preis.

DM ?

5 Fragen Sie, wo man parken kann.

What tasks do you have to do?

1 Say hello.
2 Ask for a double room with shower.
3 Say from the tenth to the twelfth of July.
4 Ask what it costs.
5 Ask where you can park.

You should have ended up with something like this:

1 *Guten Tag! (Guten Morgen, Guten Abend, Grüß Gott)*
2 *Ich möchte ein Doppelzimmer mit Dusche, bitte.*
3 *Vom zehnten bis zum zwölften Juli.*
4 *Was kostet das?*
5 *Wo kann ich parken?*

The next example is of a role-play with an unexpected element. In this type of role-play it is vital that you listen very carefully to what the examiner asks or says, so that you can respond to the unexpected element correctly. In practice, as you will see, the context of the whole role-play gives clues as to what the unexpected element may be. Again, make a note of who begins and this time also, where the unexpected part comes.

Example C: Type 2 role-play
Am Bahnhof.
You are at a ticket office in a station in Germany and speak to the clerk. You want to travel to Berlin. You also need to find out if you need to change trains and you want to ask where somewhere else is in the station. The examiner will play the part of the clerk. He/she will start the conversation.

Make a note, mental or otherwise, of the tasks you must do:

1 Ask for a second class return ticket to Berlin. ('Berlin' is in the introduction.)
2 ?
3 Ask if you have to change trains.
4 Ask where the post office/information office/restaurant is (any one will do).

After you have completed task 1, the examiner asks: *'Raucher oder Nichtraucher?'*
For the unexpected element, therefore, you would have to say whether you wanted a seat in a smoking or no smoking carriage. For the four tasks you should have come up with something like the following:

1 *Nach **Berlin** hin und zurück, zweiter Klasse, bitte.*
2 ***Nichtraucher**, bitte.' (or 'Raucher, bitte')*
3 *Muß ich **umsteigen**?*
4 *Wo ist hier **die Post/das Informationsbüro/das Restaurant**?*

In the final example your instructions are for the most part written out in German. Remember that there may very well be words in the instructions that you can use in doing your task. Again, item 2 is unexpected. You will have to listen carefully to what the examiner says.

Example D: Type 2 role-play
You are staying at your German pen friend's house in Germany. You are talking about plans for the weekend. Your teacher will play the part of your pen friend and will begin the conversation.

1 Fragen Sie nach dem Wetter am Samstag.

2 Beantworten Sie die Frage und sagen Sie warum.
3 Erklären Sie, was Sie am Sonntagnachmittag machen wollen.
4 Sagen Sie, wann Sie am Sonntag normalerweise essen.
5 Beschreiben Sie ein typisches Wochenende zu Hause.

The messages you must convey are:

1 Ask what the weather will be like on Saturday.
2 ? Answer the examiner's question and give a reason.
3 Say what you want to do on Sunday afternoon.
4 Say when you normally eat on Sundays.
5 Describe a typical weekend at home.

After task 1 the examiner says: *Bedeckt und nicht so warm. Willst du ins Hallenbad gehen?*
So for the unexpected item, task 2, you could say:

2 No thanks. I don't like swimming in the indoor pool.

So, altogether, you should have produced something like the following:

1 *Wie wird das Wetter am Samstag sein?*
2 *Nein danke. Ich schwimme nicht gern im Hallenbad.*
3 *Ich möchte am Sonntag radfahren.*
4 *Um ein Uhr nachmittags normalerweise.*
5 *Samstags spiele ich Fußball, und sonntags mache ich meine Hausaufgaben.*

Remember that there are many ways to get your message across. You do not always need to use full sentences, but the message must be put across clearly. You should also make an effort to be polite. In other words only use *du* to people your own age or younger, or others you are related to or know very well. Use *Sie* to people older than you or who you do not know, e.g. officials, adults who are not relatives. If you make a mistake, don't worry, just correct yourself, as you would in English.

As we have seen, in some of the role-plays you must listen very carefully to what the examiner says. If you don't hear it or fully understand it, don't panic, simply ask for a repetition: *Wie bitte?*.

The next section provides a number of different role-plays of each type (type 1 or type 2) for you to work through. Get as much practice as you can. Perhaps you can work with a friend or someone at home. Make up your own role-plays and test each other. The more fun ideas you come up with, the easier you will find it to make progress.

▶ EXAMINATION QUESTIONS

The following examples are presented as they would be on the role-play cards in the examination. Work through them as we did with the examples in the previous section. In the type 2 role-plays the examiner's prompt is given, so that you are able to do the unexpected element. Suggested German for the candidate's parts together with the examiner's parts are provided in the Examination answers section at the end of the chapter (see page 135). Remember that there is no one correct answer, but many different ways to say the same thing. If what you have come up with does not match exactly what is in the key, it is not necessarily wrong. The examples cover a range of formats, the intention being to give an idea of the role-plays you will encounter in the examinations of different examining groups. Each group has its own 'style' of role-play, but they all contain the same sort of tasks.

Number 1 type role-plays

▶ **Role-play 1A** Im Hotel. Sie sind mit Ihrer Familie in Deutschland. Sie wollen im Hotel übernachten.
Situation: You want to book into a German hotel with your family. Your teacher will play the part of the receptionist. He/she will begin the conversation.

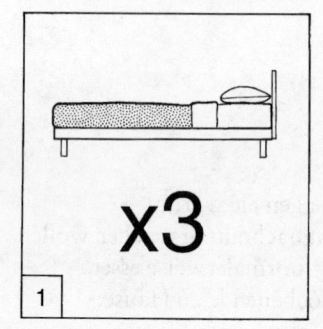

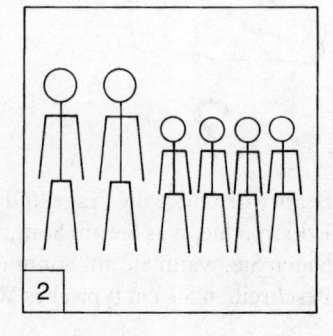

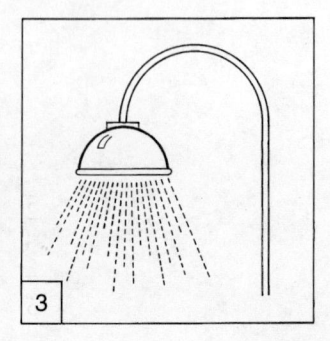

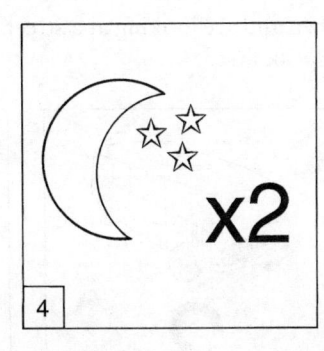

Examination questions: Role-play 1B   127

▶ **Role-play 1B**   Am Bahnhof. Sie fahren mit dem Zug.
Situation: You go to the railway station in Germany to catch a train. Your teacher will play the part of the booking office clerk. He/she will begin the conversation.

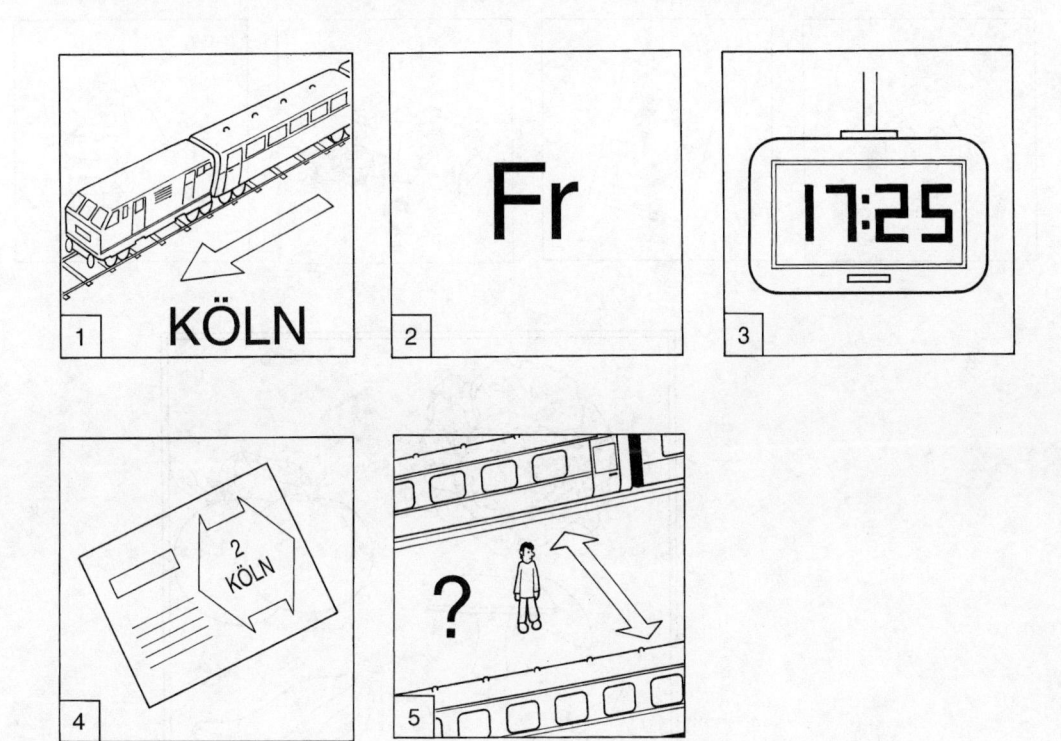

▶ **Role-play 1C**   You are at a campsite in Germany with your family and you want to stay for four nights. Your teacher will play the part of the campsite owner and will speak first.

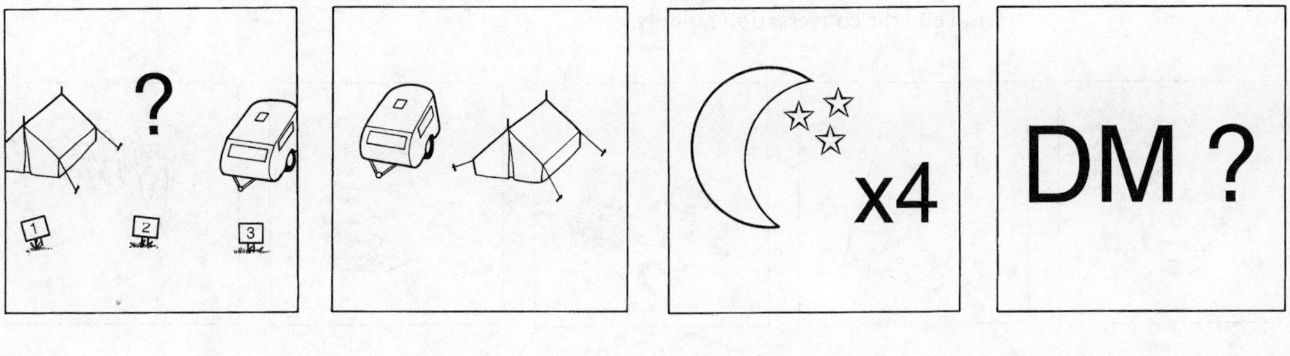

Chapter 8 Speaking: Foundation Tier – role-plays

▷ **Role-play 1D** You are in the street in a German town and are looking at a street map. Your teacher will play the part of a passer-by. He/she will speak first.

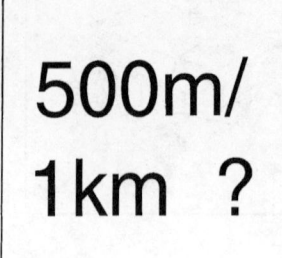

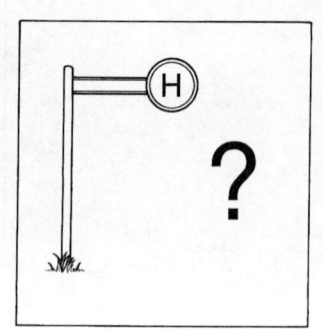

▷ **Role-play 1E** Auf dem Markt
You go to the market. You need to buy two items. Remember to greet the market trader and end the conversation politely.

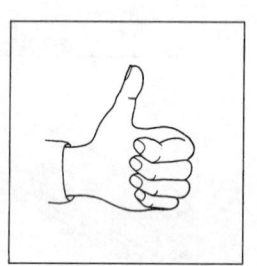

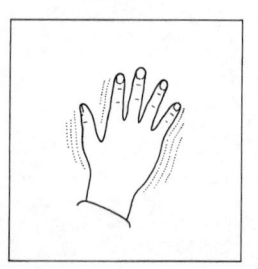

▷ **Role-play 1F** In der Metzgerei.
You are in a butcher's shop and need to buy two items. Remember to greet the shopkeeper and end the conversation politely.

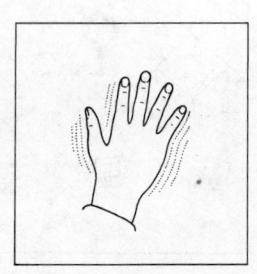

▷ **Role-play 1G** You arrive at a youth hostel and want to stay overnight. The examiner will play the part of the hostel warden. You speak first.

1. Begrüße den Herbergsvater/die Herbergsmutter.

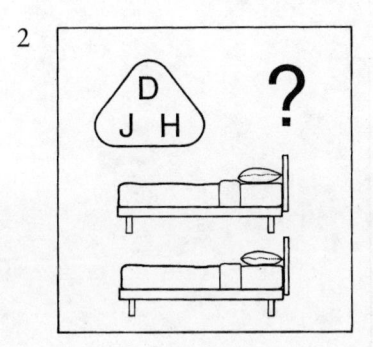

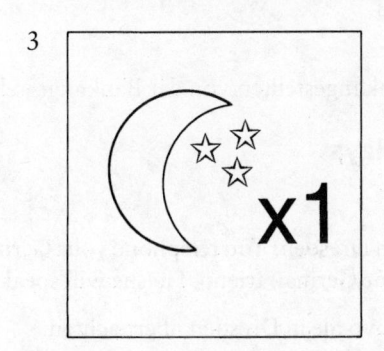

2.

3.

4.

5. Verabschiede dich vom Herbergsvater/von der Herbergsmutter.

Chapter 8 Speaking: Foundation Tier – role-plays

▶ **Role-play 1H** You go to a bank in Germany. You want to change a traveller's cheque. The examiner will play the part of the bank clerk. You start the conversation.

1 Grüße den Bankangestellten/die Bankangestellte.

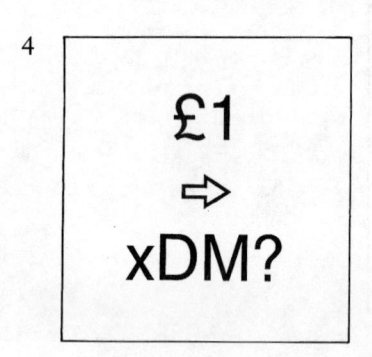

2
£10
£ ⇨ DM

3
£20
£20
£10

4
£1
⇨
xDM?

5 Verabschiede dich vom Bankangestellten/von der Bankangestellten.

Number 2 type role-plays

▶ **Role-play 2A** Am Telefon.
Situation: You are on holiday in Dresden. You telephone your German friend in Leipzig. Your teacher will play the part of your German friend. He/she will speak first.

1 Sagen Sie, wer Sie sind und wo Sie in Dresden übernachten.
2 Sagen Sie, wie lange Sie schon in Dresden sind.
Examiner: Was machst du denn in Dresden?
3 Beantworten Sie die Frage.
4 Sagen Sie 'ja' und fragen Sie nach Zügen.
5 Verabreden Sie einen Treffpunkt in Leipzig.

▶ **Role-play 2B** Am Telefon.
Situation: You would like a job in Germany. Your teacher has given you a manager's telephone number. You ring the number. Your teacher will play the part of the manager and will speak first.

1 Nennen Sie Ihren Namen und Ihren Wohnort.
2 Sagen Sie, wie lange Sie schon Deutsch lernen.

Examiner: Wann können Sie für uns arbeiten?
3   Beantworten Sie die Frage.
4   Sagen Sie, wo Sie im Moment arbeiten.
5   Fragen Sie nach dem Geld.

▷ **Role-play 2C**   You are staying with your German exchange partner in Germany. You make arrangements to go out one night. Your teacher will play the part of the friend. You must agree where to go and on what day. Agree on a time and a place to meet. Here is your diary to help you remember when you are free.

Mo	13. März	
Schule 8.15–13.00		
Di	14. März	
Schule 8.15–12.00		14.00 Freibad
Mi	15. März	
Schule 8.15–13.00		Party bei Bodo 20.30 bis spät
Do	16. März	
Schule 8.15–13.00		18.00 Fußball im Sportzentrum
Fr	17. März	
Schule 8.15–13.00		Abschiedsdisco 20.30–24.00

Teacher: Am Montag und Dienstag kann ich nicht. Ich muß Hausaufgaben machen und babysitten.

▷ **Role-play 2 D**   You go to a chemist's in Germany. You ask for something for a cough, the cost and how to use what is recommended. Remember to answer the assistant's question. Your examiner will start.

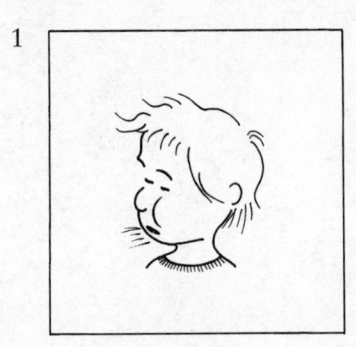

1

Examiner: Wie lange haben Sie schon den Husten?

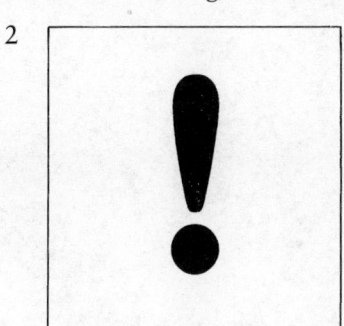

2

!

132 Chapter 8 Speaking: Foundation Tier – role-plays

3

4

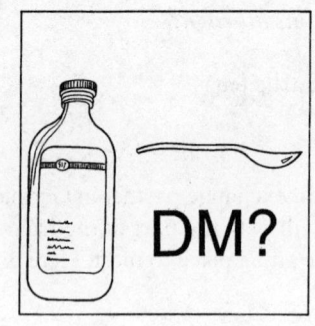

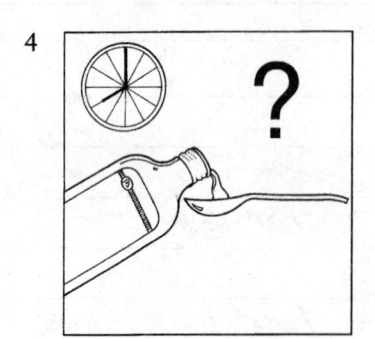

▷ **Role-play 2E** You are staying with your German pen friend. You want to arrange to go out to the cinema and to have a drink. The examiner will start.

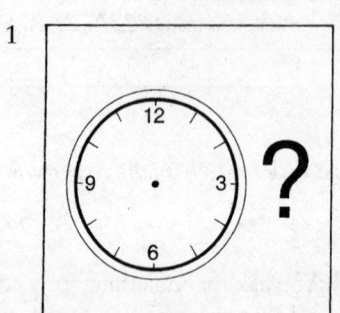

1

2

Examiner: Natürlich. Wo treffen wir uns?

3

4

▶ **Role-play 2F**   Im Fundbüro.
Situation: You have lost your camera while on holiday in a German town and go to a lost property office. Your teacher will play the part of the attendant. He/she will start.

1 Erklären Sie das Problem.
Teacher: Können Sie ihn beschreiben?
2 Beantworten Sie die Frage.
3 Sagen Sie, wann es passiert ist.
4 Sagen Sie, wo es passiert ist.
5 Sagen Sie, was er wert ist.

▶ **Role-play 2G**   While on holiday in Germany with your parents you go out for a meal. You ask for a table. Remember to answer the waiter's/waitress' question. The examiner will play the part of the waiter/waitress. He/she will begin.

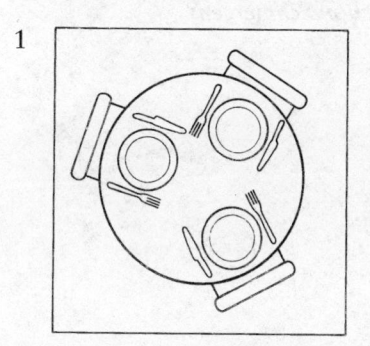

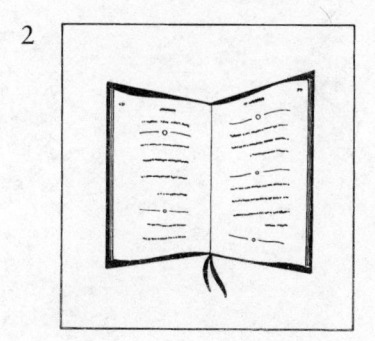

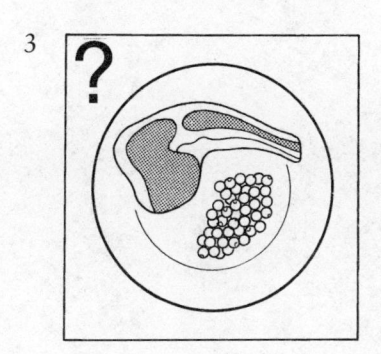

1

2

3

Examiner: Und zu trinken?

4 [!]

▶ **Role-play 2H** Beim Arzt.
Situation: While on holiday in Germany you develop ear-ache and have to go to the doctor. Your teacher will play the part of the doctor. He/she will begin the conversation.

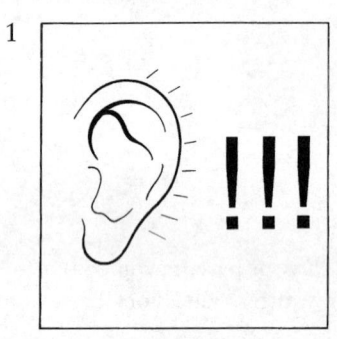

1 [ear !!!]

Teacher: Wie lange haben Sie schon Schmerzen?

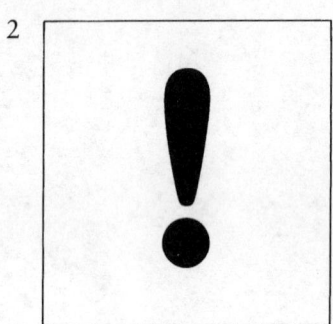

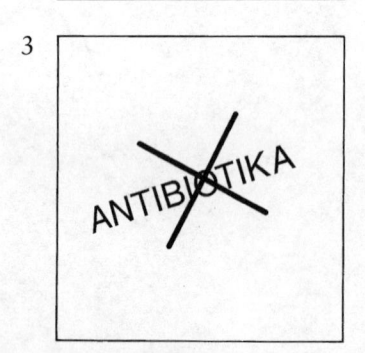

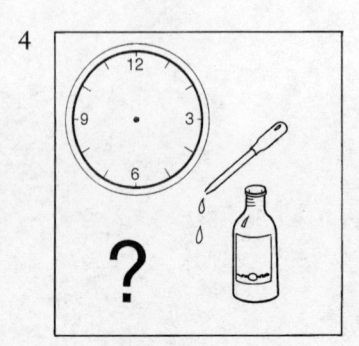

2 [!]

3 [ANTIBIOTIKA crossed out]

4 [clock, dropper with bottle, ?]

> # EXAMINATION ANSWERS

In the following role-play dialogues C stands for candidate (you) and E stands for examiner (teacher). Additionally, the examiner's part is in italics.

> **Role-play 1A**

E *Guten Tag. Kann ich Ihnen helfen?*
C Ich möchte drei Zimmer, bitte.
E *Für wieviele Personen?*
C Zwei Erwachsene und vier Kinder.
E *Möchten Sie Bad oder Dusche?*
C Mit Dusche, bitte.
E *Für wie lange?*
C Zwei Nächte, bitte.
E *Also drei Doppelzimmer für zwei Nächte. In Ordnung.*
C Was kostet das?
E *Achtzig Mark pro Zimmer pro Nacht.*

> **Role-play 1B**

E *Bitte schön?*
C Ich möchte nach Köln fahren.
E *Wann möchten sie fahren?*
C Am Freitag.
E *Um wieviel Uhr?*
C Um siebzehn Uhr fünfundzwanzig.
E *Ja, das geht.*
C Eine Rückfahrkarte nach Köln bitte.
E *So, bitte schön. Achtundzwanzig Mark.*
C Muß ich umsteigen?
E *Nein, der Zug fährt durch.*

> **Role-play 1C**

E *Guten Tag.*
C Haben Sie einen Platz frei?
E *Ja, wir haben noch Plätze.*
C Wir haben einen Wohnwagen und ein Zelt.
E *Wie lange wollen Sie bleiben?*
C Vier Nächte.
E *Alles in Ordnung.*
C Was kostet das?
E *Insgesamt zwanzig Mark pro Nacht.*

> **Role-play 1D**

E *Kann ich Ihnen helfen?*
C Wie komme ich am besten zum Bahnhof?
E *Hier immer geradeaus. Den Bahnhof sehen Sie links am Ende der Straße.*
C Ist es weit?
E *Einen Kilometer oder so.*
C Gibt es einen Bus?
E *Nein. Aber Sie können mit der Straßenbahn Linie sieben fahren.*
C Wo ist die Haltestelle?
E *Dort drüben.*

> **Role-play 1E**

C Guten Tag.
E *Guten Tag. Was hätten Sie gern?*
C Ich möchte ein Kilo Äpfel und einen Blumenkohl, bitte.
E *So, bitte schön.*
C Was kostet das?
E *Drei Mark fünfzig.*

C Danke schön.
E *Bitte schön.*
C Auf Wiedersehen.
E *Auf Wiedersehen.*

▶ **Role-play 1F**

C Guten Tag.
E *Guten Tag. Was hätten Sie gern?*
C Ich möchte fünfhundert Gramm Bratwurst und eine Dose Currysoße, bitte.
E *So, bitte schön.*
C Was kostet das?
E *Sieben Mark vierzig.*
C Danke schön.
E *Bitte sehr.*
C Auf Wiedersehen.
E *Auf Wiedersehen.*

▶ **Role-play 1G**

C Guten Abend.
E *Guten Abend.*
C Haben Sie Betten frei?
E *Ja. Wie lange möchten Sie bleiben?*
C Eine Nacht.
E *Ja. Das geht in Ordnung.*
C Was kostet das?
E *Acht Mark pro Nacht.*
C Danke. Tschüß.
E *Bitte. Tschüß.*

▶ **Role-play 1H**

C Guten Tag.
E *Guten Tag. Was kann ich für Sie tun?*
C Kann ich einen Reisescheck einlösen?
E *Natürlich. Ein Scheck über wieviel?*
C Fünfzig englische Pfund.
E *In Ordnung.*
C Wie ist der Kurs heute?
E *Für ein Pfund zwei Mark zweiundfünfzig. Sie bekommen hundertvierundzwanzig Mark.*
C Danke. Auf Wiedersehen.
E *Bitte. Auf Wiedersehen.*

▶ **Role-play 2A**

E *Hallo. Hier Dinkelmeyer, Bodo/Brünhilde am Apparat.*
C Hallo, hier . . .: Ich übernachte in der Jugendherberge hier in Dresden.
E *Das ist eine schöne Überraschung, von dir zu hören.*
C Ich bin schon drei Tage hier in Dresden.
E *Was machst du denn in Dresden?*
C Ich bin auf Urlaub.
E *Schön. Willst du uns besuchen?*
C Ja. Kann ich mit dem Zug fahren?
E *Natürlich. Die Züge fahren alle dreißig Minuten. Du kannst morgen kommen.*
C Wollen wir uns am Bahnhof in Leipzig um elf Uhr treffen?
E *Ja. Das geht. Bis dann.*

▶ **Role-play 2B**

E *Hier Schmidt. Sie suchen eine Arbeit? Wie heißen Sie und woher kommen Sie?*
C Ich heiße . . ., und ich wohne in . . . in England.
E *Sie können gut Deutsch. Wie lange lernen Sie schon?*

C Seit vier Jahren.
E *Wann können Sie für uns arbeiten?*
C Ich möchte im Sommer, im Juli und August arbeiten.
E *Ja. Das ist eine Möglichkeit. Arbeiten Sie im Moment?*
C Ich arbeite samstags in einem Supermarkt.
E *Gut. Haben Sie vielleicht eine Frage?*
C Wieviel Geld verdiene ich?
E *So ungefähr vierzehnhundert Mark im Monat.*

▷ Role-play 2C

C Hast du Lust auszugehen?
E *Ja, gerne, Wollen wir ins Kino gehen?*
C Ja. Gut! Wie wäre es mit Montagabend?
E *Am Montag und Dienstag kann ich nicht. Ich muß Hausaufgaben machen und babysitten. Ist Donnerstag gut?*
C Ich spiele am Donnerstag Fußball.
E *Wann spielst du?*
C Um achtzehn Uhr.
E *Wir könnten vielleicht am Donnerstag in die Spätvorstellung gehen. Die beginnt um zweiundzwanzig Uhr.*
C Ja. Das ist in Ordnung.
E *Wo treffen wir uns?*
C Vor dem Kino, um Viertel vor zehn. Geht das?
E *Ja, prima! Bis dann.*

▷ Role-play 2D

E *Guten Morgen. Kann ich Ihnen helfen?*
C Haben Sie etwas gegen Husten?
E *Wie lange haben Sie schon Husten?*
C Seit gestern.
E *Wir haben diese Hustenbonbons, oder ich kann Ihnen diesen Saft empfehlen.*
C Was kostet der Hustensaft?
E *Acht Mark die Flasche.*
C Wie oft muß ich den Saft einnehmen?
E *Dreimal täglich.*

▷ Role-play 2E

E *Wollen wir ins Kino gehen?*
C Wann wollen wir uns treffen?
E *So um sieben Uhr.*
C Können wir vorher etwas trinken gehen?
E *Natürlich. Wo treffen wir uns?*
C Am Marktplatz?
E *O.K.*
C Wie komme ich am besten zum Marktplatz?
E *Du kannst laufen. Es sind nur zehn Minuten.*

▷ Role-play 2F

E *Kann ich Ihnen helfen?*
C Ich habe meinen Fotoapparat verloren.
E *Können Sie ihn beschreiben?*
C Das ist ein Yaschica. Er ist klein und schwarz. Er ist in einem Beutel aus Leder.
E *Wann haben Sie den Apparat verloren?*
C Heute morgen. Ungefähr um elf Uhr.
E *Wo war das?*
C Ich glaube, vor dem Dom.
E *Wieviel hat der Apparat gekostet?*
C Zweihundertfünfzig Mark.

Role-play 2G

E Bitte schön?
C Haben Sie einen Tisch für drei?
E Ja, hier am Fenster.
C Wir möchten die Speisekarte, bitte.
E Bitte schön.
C Zweimal Wiener Schnitzel mit Bratkartoffeln und einmal Hähnchen mit Pommes frites, bitte.
E Und zu trinken?
C Drei Gläser Wein, bitte.
E Kommt sofort.

Role-play 2H

E Was kann ich für Sie tun?
C Ich habe Schmerzen im linken Ohr.
E Wie lange haben Sie schon Schmerzen?
C Seit zwei Tagen.
E Ich verschreibe Ihnen diese Tabletten.
C Ich darf keine Antibiotika nehmen. Ich bin allergisch dagegen.
E Also, diese Tropfen sind dann besser.
C Wann muß ich die Tropfen nehmen?
E Alle vier Stunden, viermal am Tag.

A STEP FURTHER

Here are two more examples, but this time without suggested dialogues as in the section above. See how you get on with them!

1 Am Telefon.
Situation: You speak to your German pen friend and want to arrange to visit him/her. Your teacher will play the part of your friend. He/she will start the conversation.

1 Begrüßen Sie Ihren Brieffreund/Ihre Brieffreundin.
2 Erklären Sie, wann Sie ihn/sie besuchen wollen.
Teacher: Dann geht's leider nicht. Wir sind auf Urlaub. Kannst du irgendwann anders kommen?
3 Beantworten Sie die Frage.
4 Sagen Sie, wie Sie reisen.
5 Fragen Sie nach einem Treffpunkt.

2 Am Flughafen.
Situation: You arrive at the airport in Germany to check in for your flight back to England. Your teacher will play the part of the attendant. He/she will start the conversation.

1 Begrüßen Sie den Angestellten/die Angestellte.
Teacher: Wieviel Gepäck haben Sie?
2 Beantworten Sie die Frage.
3 Fragen Sie nach anderen Flügen.
4 Fragen Sie nach Eßmöglichkeiten.
5 Verabschieden Sie sich vom Angestellten/von der Angestellten.

Chapter 9

Speaking: Higher Tier – role-plays

GETTING STARTED

Remember that you may only do one tier in speaking, *either* Foundation *or* Higher. You may not do both. If you choose to enter the Higher Tier, it is therefore very important that you are able to cope with the requirements. If you do not reach a high enough standard for the award of a grade D, you will be given an unclassified grade in this part of the exam, which will seriously affect your overall grade. As we have seen in previous chapters, there is overlap between the two tiers. The type 2 role-plays from the Foundation Tier (the ones with an unexpected element) form the first and easiest role-play in the Higher Tier. If you have been coping well with these as you worked through Chapter 8, you will probably want to attempt Higher Tier. Remember, however, that your ability to perform well in other parts of the speaking test, such as the Presentation and/or General Conversation, will also influence your decision. These aspects of the speaking test are dealt with in the next chapter. In this chapter we shall only look at the second, more difficult role-plays encountered at Higher Tier.

WHAT YOU NEED TO KNOW

Requirements

As in the Foundation Tier, if you enter the Higher Tier, you will be given preparation time for the role-plays. During this preparation time you will be allowed to have access to a dictionary and to make notes. You may not take the dictionary into the test with you. Again, the tests will be recorded and either marked by your teacher or sent away to be marked by the examining group. Generally you will have to do **two** role-plays, but if you are studying for the SEG modular GCSE you will only do one in the Module 4 end of course assessment. In this case there will have been other speaking assessments in previous modules, done as you went along.

As with Foundation Tier, **communication** is the key. You should be able to pronounce the sounds of German accurately enough for a native speaker to understand without difficulty, and to speak with a certain degree of correct intonation and stress. Note that at Higher Tier the degree of accuracy required is greater than at Foundation Tier, but the important thing is still '**getting the message across**'. The more accurate your German is, though, the easier it is for the examiner to understand.

So what is different about the second, more difficult Higher Tier role-plays?

▶ You will be expected to cope with role-plays from the full range of topics and situations indicated in your examining group's syllabus for both Foundation and Higher Tier.
▶ The role-plays will contain more elements of unpredictability than just the one in the first role-play (which is also the second for Foundation Tier). There may be elements of problem solving and the format of the role-play may well be looser and more open-ended, meaning that you will have to use your initiative more.
▶ The subject of the role-play may not be merely transactional, i.e. not just asking for things and information, making arrangements etc., but may take the form more of a discussion, in which you have to give more involved opinions and justify them. For instance you may be discussing holidays or school uniform with your pen friend or his/her parents.
▶ You may be required to talk about things in the present, future and past.

Make sure you check exactly what topics may be covered in the Higher Tier role-plays for your examining group.

The length of the individual role-plays will vary from one examining group to another. The number and complexity of the tasks may be different. In general the stimuli or instructions will require more thought on your part. In the main there will be an English outline, which may contain important elements of the tasks you have to do. The examiner may read out to you an introductory sentence or two in German to set the scene. In general this will merely restate what you already have in English or German on the role-play card. There may also be some kind of visual stimulus such as a town plan, photograph or page from a calendar.

Approaching the role-plays

So how do you go about preparing for these second, more difficult Higher Tier role-plays?

As always, a methodical approach will pay dividends. Because of the overlap between the two tiers, a thorough preparation of the material covered in Chapter 8 means that you will have prepared half of the role-play requirements for the Higher Tier. Assuming that you have coped well enough with the contents of that chapter, these further steps should help you:

- Make sure you know what topics will be covered in the role-playing situations.
- Check the language tasks in Chapter 3 and that you are familiar with the German required to do them. Remember these lists are not exhaustive, so cross-check with the requirements of your examining group.
- Study as many role-playing situations from previous years as you can and practise. You can do this with a friend or on your own. Use your checklists.
- There are often useful courses on the television and radio. Watch or listen to as many as possible. There are many courses with tapes available in bookshops or which you may be able to borrow from the local library. Courses on video are also plentiful as are CD-ROM titles, assuming that you have access to a multimedia PC. Remember that, while they may contain useful material, not all these courses will be designed specifically to prepare you for the requirements of GCSE.
- Try making up your own role-play situations and thinking of as many awkward questions or remarks as possible, that the examiner/teacher may ask or say. Most of you will have little difficulty imitating an awkward teacher!

During the preparation time you will be able to study the role-play carefully. Don't spend too much time preparing the first one. Allow time for the second more difficult one. Remember that you may have access to a dictionary during the preparation time, but not in the examination itself, and that you may make notes. When studying the role-play the following points should be helpful:

- Read everything carefully! Note the **key** tasks you have to do and any **key word/phrases** in German that come to mind. Work out what you are going to say.
- Try to think what the examiner might say and the possible 'twists' to the dialogue. In many cases these may be reasonably predictable from the context of the role-play. If, for example, you have to describe your school uniform, say that you think it's a good idea and persuade the other person of this. It will be reasonably safe to assume that the person you are speaking to is going to disagree for some reason. You therefore need to have thought of a number of good reasons for your opinion.
- Don't panic. Remember you can use a dictionary, but don't rely on this as the time you have to prepare is limited and overuse of the dictionary will very quickly use up all your preparation time. There may well be something that at first you do not understand, but that doesn't really matter. You may ask the examiner to repeat something, speak more slowly or explain something again, as you would in an English conversation.

Example role-plays

The two examples that follow are intended to give you an idea of what the role-plays may look like. One has a visual stimulus and the other has only written instructions. The end result, however, is much the same. The explanations are intended to help you work your way through the preparation process.

Example A

While in Germany on holiday you become unwell and decide to telephone a doctor for an appointment. You are due to return home the day after tomorrow. Your teacher will play the part of the doctor's receptionist. He/she will begin the conversation.

Approaching the role-plays 141

> **Dr. med. Helmut Kinkel**
>
> Arzt für Allgemeinmedizin
>
> MO. 08.00–11.30
>
> DI.–DO. 09.00–11.00 UND 16.30–18.30
>
> FR. 08.00–11.30
>
> Tel. 27 56 86
>
> Im Notfall Tel. 54 18 23

- Persönliche Details
- Warum haben Sie angerufen?
- Was fehlt Ihnen?

First note that the examiner will start. Now look at the bullet points and decide what tasks you are going to have to do. If we list them in English for the sake of clarity they will probably boil down to this:

(a) Give your name and (since you are on holiday abroad) your nationality, perhaps also your age (this may be useful to the doctor).
(b) Say why you have rung. In other words, say you are ill and that you want to see the doctor/make an appointment.
(c) Describe your symptoms.

Remember that there must also be more than one unpredictable element. In other words, the receptionist will ask you two (or more) questions, which will require details from you, that are not contained in the instructions above. In fact, if you think about it, you can probably predict these 'unpredictable' elements. You should try to list possibilities. For instance:

(d) Spell your name (since it will be foreign to the receptionist).
(e) Decline the offer of an unsuitable appointment (very likely because if you look carefully again at the English introduction that sets the scene, you will see that you are going home the day after tomorrow and so need an appointment before then).
(f) Reply to enquiries about further details of symptoms or the length of time you have been ill.
(g) Reply to an enquiry about insurance or how you propose to pay (this can sometimes happen when abroad).

Now try to think of the German you will need to use to get the messages across, jotting down key words and phrases. Remember again that there will be more than one way to do this. If you are unsure of any grammar or word order, try to keep things as straightforward as possible. Try to think of the end result that needs to be achieved rather than thinking of tasks in English and then trying to translate word for word. You should have come up with something like this:

(i) Hallo! Ich heiße Christopher/Christine Fancett. Ich bin sechzehn und bin hier auf Urlaub.
(ii) Ich möchte einen Termin ausmachen.
   or
   Ich möchte den Arzt sehen.
(iii) Ich habe fürchterliche Schmerzen im rechten Ohr.
   or
   Ich habe seit vier Tagen Magenschmerzen und Durchfall.

Now do the same for the unpredictable elements you have thought of:

(iv) Mein Nachname lautet: F-A-N-C-E-T-T.
(v) Das geht leider nicht. Ich muß übermorgen wieder nach England fahren.
or
Könnte ich früher kommen? Ich fahre übermorgen nach Hause.
(vi) Ich bin schon seit drei Tagen krank, und es ist sehr schmerzhaft.
or
Ich bin besorgt. Ich bin zu krank, um zu reisen, glaube ich.
(vii) Ich bin versichert.
or
Ich bin Engländer/Engländerin und habe einen E-111-Schein.
or
Was kostet eine Untersuchung? . . . Ich habe genug Geld.

Here is a suggested dialogue for the role-play in Example A. For the purposes of this example we shall assume that the 'unpredictable' elements were as in (d) and (e) above.

E *Hallo! Hier Praxis Doktor Kinkel.*
C Hallo! Ich heiße Christopher/Christine Fancett. Ich bin sechzehn und bin hier auf Urlaub.
E *Wie kann ich Ihnen helfen?*
C Ich möchte einen Termin ausmachen.
E *Ja. Könnten Sie bitte Ihren Nachnamen buchstabieren?*
C Mein Nachname lautet: F-A-N-C-E-T-T.
E *Vielen Dank, Herr/Fräulein Fancett. Sie könnten eventuell am Freitag um 8.30 Uhr kommen.*
C Das geht leider nicht. Ich muß übermorgen nach Hause fahren.
E *Das ist schwierig. Was ist denn das Problem?*
C Ich habe fürchterliche Schmerzen im linken Ohr.
E *Wie lange haben Sie die Schmerzen schon?*
C Seit zwei Tagen. Es ist sehr schmerzhaft.
E *Das glaube ich. Also, am besten kommen Sie sofort.*
C Ja, gut. Vielen Dank.
E *Bitte schön. Auf Wiederhören.*

Example B
Du bist bei deinem/deiner deutschen Brieffreund/Brieffreundin. Ihr sprecht über Freizeit. Dein Lehrer/deine Lehrerin ist der Freund/die Freundin. Er/sie beginnt.

1 Beantworte die Frage und sage warum.
2 Erkläre, was du in deiner Freizeit machst.
3 Beantworte die Frage und sage warum.
4 Frage nach Freizeitmöglichkeiten dort, wo dein Brieffreund/deine Brieffreundin wohnt.
5 Sage, wie du seinen/ihren Wohnort findest und warum.

Note that the examiner will start, this time with an unpredictable item. Look at the other instructions and see what tasks are expected. The following seems to be what's required:

(a) Say what you do in your free time.
(b) Ask about what leisure activities it is possible to do where your friend lives.
(c) Express an opinion about where your friend lives and justify it with a reason.

Predicting the 'unpredictable' is a little more difficult in this example because the context of 'free time activities' is rather more wide ranging than the scenario in Example A. It might be possible to come up with the following:

(d) Reply to a question about a particular hobby or interest.
(e) Reply to a question about membership of a club or team.
(f) Reply to a question about leisure facilities where you live.
(g) Reply to a question about a favourite activity.
(h) Reply to a question seeking clarification of something you have already said or justification of an opinion already given.

Again, make jottings of key words and phrases you will need to use. Then try and organise them into good German. Remember too, that you do not need to tell the truth when talking about yourself and where you live! All you have to do is impress the examiner with your German! You could have thought of the following:

   (i) Ich sammle Briefmarken!
  (ii) Was kann man in deiner Stadt/deinem Dorf machen?
       or
       Was kann man in der Freizeit machen, wo du wohnst?
 (iii) Ich finde deine Stadt sehr interessant, weil es so viel gibt, was man tun kann.
       or
       Ich finde dein Dorf stinklangweilig, weil es gar nichts gibt, was man machen kann.

For the unpredictable elements you may have thought of some of the following:

  (iv) Mein Hobby ist Malen.
       or
       Ich interessiere mich für Musik. Ich spiele Geige.
   (v) Ich bin Mitglied in einem Fußballverein/einer Theatergruppe.
       or
       Ich bin Mitglied in einem Jugendklub.
  (vi) In meiner Stadt gibt es ein modernes Schwimmbad, eine Eisbahn und viele Kinos.
 (vii) Am liebsten treibe ich Sport.
       or
       Mein Lieblingshobby ist Leichtathletik.
(viii) Ich treibe gern Sport, weil ich gern im Freien bin.

There follows a suggested dialogue for Example B. Remember this is only a suggestion, in order to give you an idea of what to expect. The possibilities for doing most of the tasks in this example are almost endless. For the purposes of this example it is assumed that the unexpected items were as in (e) and (f) above.

   E *Bist du Mitglied in einem Klub?*
   C Ja, ich bin im Sportverein, weil ich gern Leichtathletik treibe.
   E *Was machst du sonst in deiner Freizeit?*
   C Ich interessiere mich sehr für Musik, und ich spiele Klavier.
   E *Wie findest du die Freizeitmöglichkeiten, wo du wohnst?*
   C Ich finde meine Stadt stinklangweilig, weil es nichts gibt, was man tun kann. Es gibt Pubs und ein Sportzentrum. Das ist alles. Nichts für junge Leute.
   E *Schade! Das ist schlimm.*
   C Was kann man in der Freizeit hier in deiner Stadt machen?
   E *Es gibt viel, was man tun kann. Jugendklubs, Sportvereine, Kinos, eine Kegelbahn, alles mögliche.*
   C Ich finde deine Stadt echt prima! Es gibt viel für junge Leute, und die Atmosphäre ist besser als bei uns.

▶ EXAMINATION QUESTIONS

The examination questions that follow are set out as you would encounter them on the examining groups' role-play cards. Work through them in the same way as the two examples in the previous section. Remember that these role-plays are examples of the second type that you will do at Higher Tier only and that the first type of role-plays are dealt with in Chapter 8, since they also double up as the type 2 role-play at Foundation Tier. In the 'Examination answers' at the end of this chapter you will find suggested dialogues for the examination questions here, together with two questions in italics before each, which are the unpredictable elements. When working through the questions, try to do so as we did with the examples, without looking up these unpredictable elements. The questions that follow are intended to give an idea of the range of formats of the different examining groups, but you should be prepared to deal with other formats too, since the examples here cannot be exhaustive.

Role-play A

Du bist bei deinem Freund/deiner Freundin in Deutschland und sprichst mit dem Vater/der Mutter über die Schule. Dein Lehrer/deine Lehrerin ist der Vater/die Mutter.
Er/sie beginnt.

1. Beantworte die Frage und sage warum.
2. Sage, wie du deine Schule findest und warum.
3. Beantworte die Frage.
4. Sage, was dein Lieblingsfach ist und warum.
5. Frage nach den Schulen bei deinem Freund/deiner Freundin.

Role-play B

Sie sind auf Urlaub in Österreich. Sie gehen zum Fundbüro. Ihr Lehrer/Ihre Lehrerin ist der/die Angestellte. Er/sie beginnt.

1. Sagen Sie, warum Sie gekommen sind.
2. Beantworten Sie die Frage.
3. Beschreiben Sie den Gegenstand.
4. Beantworten Sie die Frage, sagen Sie, wie Sie sich fühlen und warum.
5. Fragen Sie nach dem Weg.

Role-play C

Sie sind auf Urlaub in der Schweiz und haben etwas gekauft. Das funktioniert nicht, und Sie gehen wieder zu dem Geschäft. Sie fahren morgen nach Hause. Ihr Lehrer/Ihre Lehrerin ist der Verkäufer/die Verkäuferin.

1. Erklären Sie, warum Sie gekommen sind.
2. Antworten Sie dem Verkäufer/der Verkäuferin.
3. Beantworten Sie die Frage und sagen Sie, wie Sie sich fühlen.
4. Beantworten Sie die Frage und sagen Sie warum.
5. Erklären Sie, was Sie wollen.

Role-play D

You are talking to your German friend about your parents, with whom you get on well. Ask your friend if he gets on well with his/her parents. You must describe your parents' characters, say whether you like them and why. Try to persuade your friend that his parents are not so bad. You begin.

- Frag, wie er/sie mit den Eltern auskommt.
- Beschreibe den Charakter deiner Eltern.
- Sag deine Meinung über sie.
- Versuche ihn/sie zu überreden, daß seine/ihre Eltern nicht so schlimm sind.

Role-play E

You are talking to your German friend about school rules, which you agree with. Ask your friend about rules at school in Germany. You must mention two rules and say why you think that they are a good idea. Try to persuade your friend that the rules are sensible. You begin.

- Frag nach Schulregeln in Deutschland.
- Erkläre zwei Regeln bei dir in der Schule.
- Sag deine Meinung dazu.
- Versuche ihn/sie zu überreden, daß die Regeln eine gute Idee sind.

▶ **Role-play F** You are talking to your German friend about environmental issues, which you think are important. Ask your friend what he/she thinks about these issues. You must describe what you do for the environment and why. Try to persuade your friend that environmental questions are important. You begin.

- ▶ Frag, was er/sie über Umweltfragen denkt.
- ▶ Beschreibe, was du für die Umwelt tust.
- ▶ Sag deine Meinung dazu.
- ▶ Versuche ihn/sie zu überreden, daß Umweltfragen wichtig sind.

▶ **Role-play G** You are in Germany and go to a travel agency to book a break in Switzerland. The examiner will play the part of the assistant and will begin the conversation.

REISEBÜRO ACKERMANN

Pauschalreisen	Städtereisen
Flüge	Hotels

Ausflüge

Täglich von 8.00 bis 17.30 Uhr geöffnet

- ▶ Wann und wohin?
- ▶ Übernachtung?
- ▶ Aktivitäten?

Role-play H

You see this poster while on an exchange visit to Germany and would like to visit the place. While speaking to your exchange partner you suggest going. The examiner will play the part of your exchange partner and will start the conversation.

VERGNÜGUNGSZENTRUM HELMSTEDT

Spaß für die ganze Familie!

FREIBAD MIT LIEGEWIESEN

TENNISPLÄTZE

ROLLSCHUHBAHN IM FREIEN

SAUNA UND DAMPFBAD

TISCHTENNIS UND SQUASH

Täglich 08.00 bis 22.00 Uhr

- Was machen?
- Was mitnehmen?
- Verkehrsmittel?

Role-play I

While on holiday with your parents in Berlin you see this poster and decide to go to the opera. You telephone to make the booking for yourself and your parents.

SCHAUSPIELHAUS

MONTAG DEN 12. JUNI

NUR EINE AUFFÜHRUNG: *La Bohème von Puccini*

AB MITTWOCH DEN 14. JUNI FÜR 3 ABENDE

DIE UNGARISCHE STAATSOPER MIT:
Norma von Bellini

- Was und wann?
- Preise?
- Zeiten?

Role-play J

Situation: Below are notes giving an outline of a journey you made to Germany on an exchange visit. Tell the examiner about the journey, answer any of his/her questions and respond to any comments he/she makes.

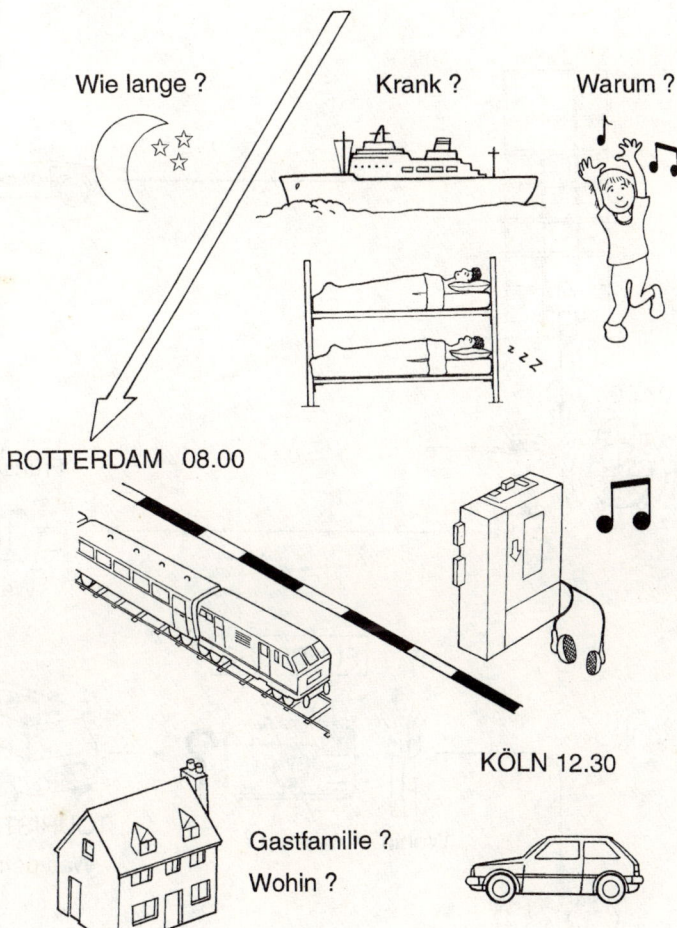

Abfahrt – Wann ? Datum ? Uhrzeit ?

M62

Wie ?

Wohin ?

HULL 17.30

Wie lange ?   Krank ?   Warum ?

ROTTERDAM 08.00

KÖLN 12.30

Gastfamilie ?

Wohin ?

148 Chapter 9 Speaking: Higher Tier – role-plays

▶ Role-play K

Situation: Below are notes giving an outline of a holiday you had in Switzerland. Tell the examiner what happened during the holiday. Answer his/her questions and respond to any comments he/she makes.

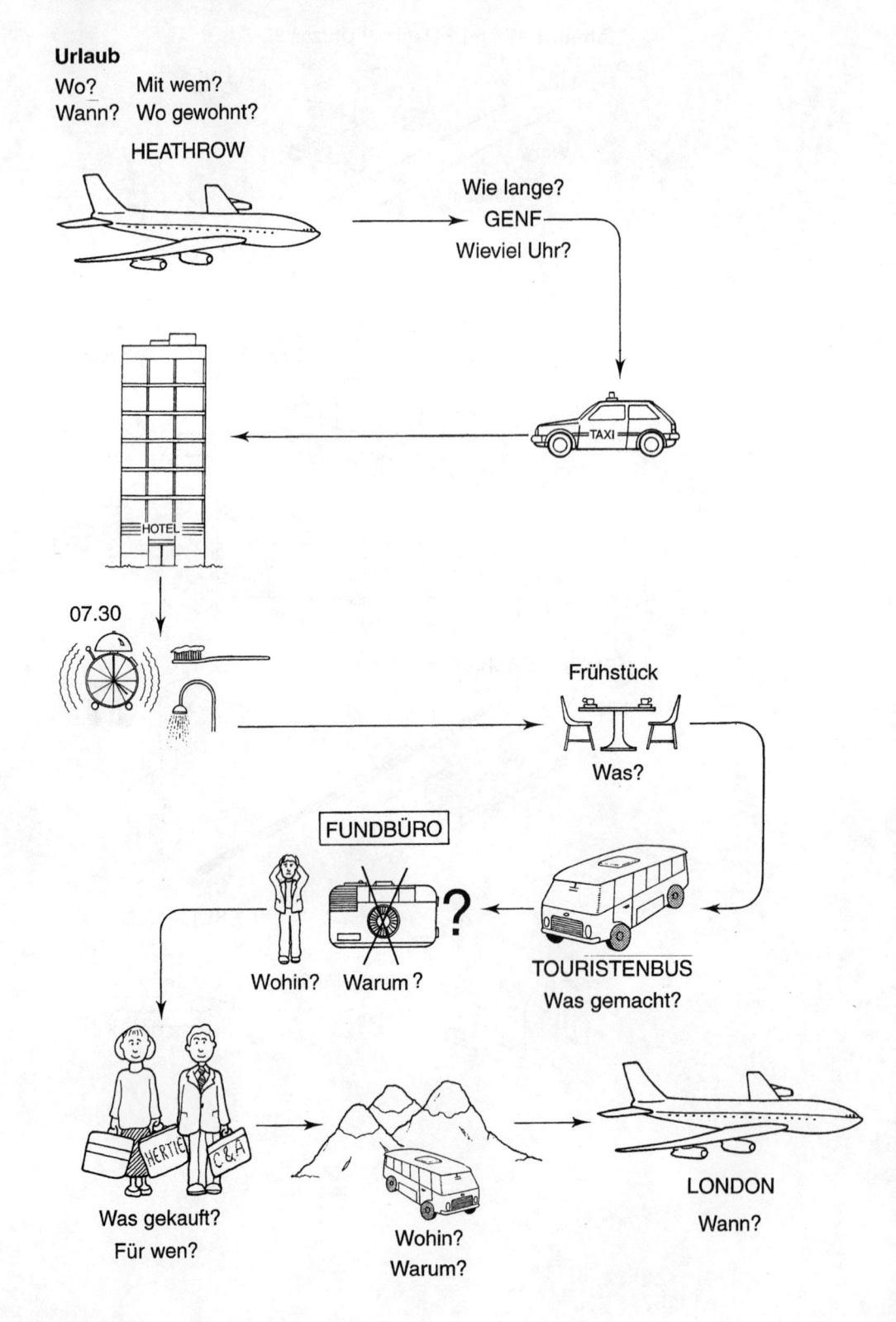

Urlaub
Wo? Mit wem?
Wann? Wo gewohnt?

HEATHROW

Wie lange?
→ GENF
Wieviel Uhr?

TAXI

HOTEL

07.30

Frühstück
Was?

FUNDBÜRO
Wohin? Warum?

TOURISTENBUS
Was gemacht?

Was gekauft?
Für wen?

Wohin?
Warum?

LONDON
Wann?

Role-play L

Situation: Below are notes giving an outline of an accident you witnessed while visiting your pen-friend in Germany. Tell the examiner what happened. Answer his/her questions and respond to any comments he/she makes.

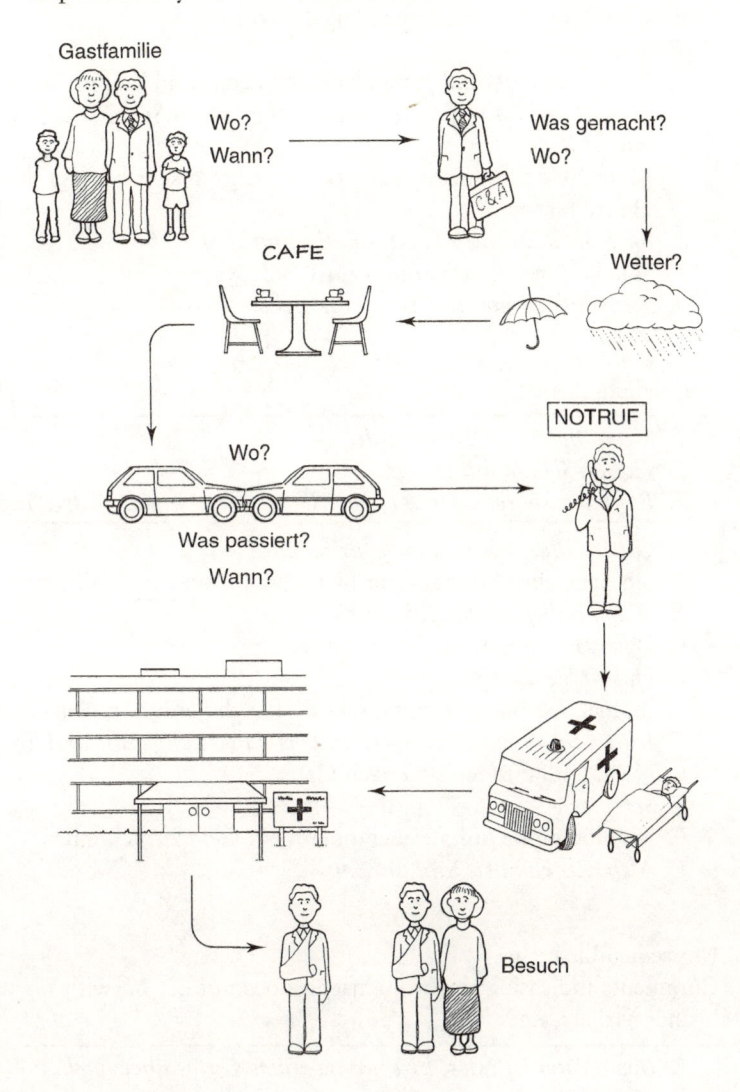

Gastfamilie — Wo? Wann? — Was gemacht? Wo? — Wetter? — CAFE — Wo? Was passiert? Wann? — NOTRUF — Besuch

EXAMINATION ANSWERS

Role-play A

Unpredictable items:

> E *Was für eine Schule besuchst du?*
> E *Was machst du nächstes Jahr?*

E *Was für eine Schule besuchst du?*
C Ich gehe auf eine Gesamtschule.
E *Wie findest du die Schule?*
C Ich mag die Schule nicht so gern, weil sie zu groß ist.
E *Schade. Was machst du nächstes Jahr?*
C Ich gehe in die Oberstufe.
E *Schön. Was lernst du am liebsten?*
C Mein Lieblingsfach ist Deutsch, weil ich es einfach finde.
E *Du kannst schon gut Deutsch.*
C Wie sind die Schulen hier in Deutschland?
E *Die meisten Schulen hier in der Stadt sind gut.*

Role-play B

Unpredictable items:

> E *Wo und wann haben Sie das verloren?*
> E *Was war darin?*

Chapter 9 Speaking: Higher Tier – role-plays

    E *Wie kann ich Ihnen helfen?*
    C Ich habe mein Portemonnaie verloren.
    E *Wo und wann haben Sie es verloren?*
    C Ich glaube, heute morgen am Marktplatz.
    E *Wie sieht es aus?*
    C Es ist viereckig und ganz klein, aus Leder und braun. Mein Name ist in Gold darauf.
    E *Das ist nicht abgegeben worden, aber füllen Sie bitte ein Formular aus. Was war darin?*
    C Mein Geld und meine Scheckkarte. Ich bin sehr besorgt, weil ich übermorgen nach Hause fahren
    E *Sie sollen das auch bei der Polizei melden.*
    C Wie komme ich am besten zur Polizeiwache?
    E *Sie ist gleich hier rechts um die Ecke.*

▶ Role-play C   Unpredictable items:

> E *Wann haben Sie sie gekauft?*
> E *Haben Sie die Quittung?*
> E *Ich kann sie reparieren lassen. Das dauert ungefähr drei Tage. Ist das in Ordnung?*

    E *Guten Tag. Was kann ich für Sie tun?*
    C Ich habe eine Armbanduhr hier gekauft, und sie funktioniert nicht.
    E *Wann haben Sie sie gekauft?*
    C Das war vorgestern. Am Nachmittag.
    E *Haben Sie die Quittung?*
    C Ja, hier. Ich bin sehr enttäuscht und auch verärgert, weil die Armbanduhr so teuer war.
    E *Ich kann sie reparieren lassen. Das dauert ungefähr drei Tage. Ist das in Ordnung?*
    C Nein. Ich fahre morgen nach Hause.
    E *Schwierig.*
    C Ich möchte sie umtauschen oder mein Geld zurückhaben.
    E *Also, ich kann sie umtauschen.*

▶ Role-play D   Unpredictable items:
Comments indicating that your friend does not get on with his parents/has problems with his/her parents, e.g.

> E *Mein Vater ist mies. Er sagt nie etwas Gutes über mich.*
> E *Meine Eltern meckern immer, daß ich nicht fleißig in der Schule bin.*
> E *Die Eltern erlauben mir nie auszugehen.*

    C Wie kommst du mit deinen Eltern aus?
    E *Ach! Gar nicht gut. Ich komme eigentlich schlecht mit ihnen aus. Und du? Wie sind deine Eltern.*
    C Ich habe ein gutes Verhältnis zu meinen Eltern. Meine Mutter ist immer guter Laune, und mein Vater ist sehr verständnisvoll.
    E *Du hast Glück!*
    C Ich finde meine Eltern gut, weil sie immer Zeit für mich haben.
    E *Meine Eltern meckern immer, daß ich nicht fleißig genug in der Schule bin.*
    C Sie wollen vielleicht nur helfen, damit du gute Noten bekommst.

▶ Role-play E   Unpredictable items:
Opinions that the rules you mention are stupid etc., e.g.

> E *Ich finde das blöd!*
> E *Das hat doch keinen Sinn.*
> E *Das finde ich gar nicht nötig.*

    C Sind die Regeln in deiner Schule streng?
    E *Nicht besonders. Es gibt eigentlich nicht so viele Regeln bei uns in der Schule.*
    C Bei uns darf man absolut nicht rauchen, und essen im Klassenzimmer ist auch verboten.

E *Das finde ich blöd! Wir haben ein Raucherzimmer für diejenigen, die rauchen wollen. Und warum soll man im Klassenzimmer nicht essen, wenn man hungrig ist?*
C Ich finde es gut, daß man nicht rauchen darf. Und meiner Meinung nach ist es sinnvoll, daß man im Klassenzimmer nicht essen darf.
E *Ich verstehe das nicht. Das hat doch keinen Sinn.*
C Rauchen ist schlecht für die Gesundheit, auch für die Schüler, die nicht rauchen. Der Zigarettenrauch ist überall. Und wenn die Schüler im Klassenzimmer essen, gibt es zu viel Abfall.
E *Ja, ich sehe ein, daß dann vielleicht alles sauberer ist.*

▷ Role-play F

Unpredictable items:
Comments to the effect that your friend is uninterested in environmental issues or doesn't do anything for the environment, e.g.

> E *Ich finde Umweltfragen langweilig.*
> E *Ich tue nichts für die Umwelt. Ein Mensch kann alleine nichts machen.*
> E *Das geht mich nichts an.*
> E *Das macht zu viel Mühe.*

C Was denkst du über Umweltfragen?
E *Ich finde Umweltfragen eigentlich langweilig.*
C Bei uns zu Hause recyceln wir alles, Papier, Glas, Bioabfälle.
E *Ach! Das alles macht zu viel Mühe.*
C Wir machen das, weil wir es sinnvoll finden.
E *Das geht mich nichts an. Ich tue nichts für die Umwelt. Ein Mensch kann alleine nichts machen.*
C Du kannst aber dabei Geld sparen! Wenn du Lichter und das Fernsehen ausschaltest, sparst du Strom und Geld. Das ist gut für die Umwelt und gut für dich!
E *Ja, natürlich, das kann ich einsehen.*

▷ Role-play G

Unpredictable elements:

> E *Wie wollen Sie reisen?*
> E *Wie lange wollen Sie bleiben?*

E *Guten Tag. Was kann ich für Sie tun?*
C Ich möchte in die Schweiz reisen.
E *Wohin möchten Sie genau fahren?*
C Ich möchte am nächsten Wochenende nach Genf fahren.
E *Gut. Wie lange wollen Sie bleiben?*
C Ein Wochenende, zwei oder drei Nächte. Ich möchte in einem Hotel wohnen.
E *Wie wollen Sie reisen?*
C Gerne mit dem Flugzeug.
E *Prima. Ich kann ihnen zwei Nächte im Hotel mit Flug zu DM 290 anbieten.*
C Ich möchte auch die Sehenswürdigkeiten sehen.
E *Sie können hier eine Stadtrundfahrt buchen, wenn Sie wollen.*

▷ Role-play H

Unpredictable items:

> E *Ich habe eine Ohrenentzündung gehabt. Also darf ich leider nicht ins Wasser.*
> E *Wo essen wir?*

E *Was willst du denn morgen machen?*
C Ich möchte das Vergnügungszentrum in Helmstedt besuchen.
E *Naja! Ich habe eine Ohrenentzündung gehabt. Also darf ich leider nicht ins Wasser.*
C Das ist O.K. Wir können auch Tennis oder Squash dort spielen.
E *Na schön.*
C Wir können mit dem Bus dorthin fahren.
E *Alles klar! Aber wo essen wir?*
C Wir können ein Picknick mitnehmen, wenn du willst.
E *Ja, gute Idee! Das machen wir.*

Role-play I

Unpredictable items:

> E *Leider ist es ausgebucht.*
> E *Wo würden Sie gerne sitzen?*

E *Hallo. Schauspielhaus.*
C Ich möchte drei Karten für La Bohème am 12. Juni, bitte.
E *Leider ist es ausgebucht.*
C Haben Sie Plätze für Norma am 14. Juni?
E *Ja, das geht. Wo würden Sie gerne sitzen?*
C Im zweiten Rang vielleicht.
E *Also, drei Plätze im zweiten Rang. Das geht.*
C Was kosten die Karten?
E *Insgesamt DM 75.*
C Gut. Wann beginnt die Aufführung?
E *Um neunzehn Uhr dreißig.*

Role-play J

Unpredictable items:
It is obviously difficult to decide what exactly the unpredictable items would be in the kind of test we see here in J, K and L. The examiner may ask you about anything depicted in the diagram and which you have not already mentioned. It is very likely that you will be asked about your feelings and/or opinions and asked to say why you felt or thought that way. The following are only ideas of how role-plays J, K and L, might go.

C Ich habe letzten September an einem Austausch teilgenommen. Ich bin mit dem Bus nach Hull gefahren.
E *Um wieviel Uhr sind Sie losgefahren?*
C So um 14.00 Uhr. Wir sind um 17.30 Uhr in Hull angekommen und mit der Fähre nach Rotterdam gefahren.
E *Was haben Sie im Bus gemacht?*
C Ich habe ein Buch gelesen. Das war ein Krimi. Er war gut für die Reise, weil er lang war.
E *Und wie lange hat die Fahrt auf der Fähre gedauert?*
C Die hat lange gedauert. Wir mußten auf dem Schiff übernachten. Wir sind in die Disco gegangen, und dann haben wir geschlafen.
E *Wie war die Überfahrt?*
C Sie war nicht so gut für mich, weil ich seekrank war. Es war sehr stürmisch.
E *Schade. Wie sind Sie von Rotterdam weitergefahren.*
C Wir sind mit dem Zug von Rotterdam nach Köln gefahren. Ich habe unterwegs Musik gehört. Wir sind um 12.30 Uhr in Köln angekommen und haben unsere Gastfamilie getroffen. Dann sind wir mit dem Auto zum Haus meines Freundes gefahren.
E *Wie haben Sie die Reise gefunden?*
C Es war eigentlich zu lang und für mich ermüdend. Der Bus und der Zug waren langweilig, weil es nicht viel gab, was man tun konnte.
E *Und die Fähre?*
C Ich habe die Fähre prima gefunden, weil es eine Disco gab.

Role-play K

C Ich habe letztes Jahr in der Schweiz Urlaub gemacht, mit meiner Familie. Wir sind von London geflogen.
E *Wie haben Sie den Flug gefunden?*
C Nicht gut. Ich fliege nicht gern, weil ich dann immer krank bin. Aber der Flug dauerte nur neunzig Minuten. Also war es nicht so schlimm. Dann sind wir mit dem Taxi zum Hotel gefahren.
E *Und wohin sind Sie genau gefahren?*
C Wir sind nach Genf gefahren und haben dort eine Woche verbracht.
E *Wie war das Hotel?*
C Ich habe das Hotel prima gefunden, weil es sehr bequem und luxuriös war. Wir hatten ein Zimmer mit Dusche im vierten Stock. Von dort hatten wir eine schöne Aussicht.

    E *Was haben Sie alles gemacht?*
    C Am ersten Tag bin ich um 7.30 Uhr aufgestanden. Ich habe geduscht und zum Frühstück Kaffee getrunken und Müsli gegessen. Dann haben wir am Vormittag eine Stadtrundfahrt gemacht. Am Nachmittag haben wir die Sehenswürdigkeiten gesehen.
    E *Was für eine Stadt ist Genf?*
    C Ich habe Genf sehr schön gefunden, weil alles sehr sauber war. Das ist eine interessante Stadt. Leider habe ich aber meinen Fotoapparat verloren, und wir mußten zum Fundbüro gehen. Ich habe ihn nicht wieder zurückbekommen.
    E *Schade. Was haben Sie später gemacht?*
    C Wir haben eingekauft und auch einen Ausflug in die Berge gemacht.
    E *Wie war das?*
    C Prima! Ich habe die Landschaft wunderschön gefunden, weil es so anders als bei uns ist.

▶ **Role-play L**
    C Ich habe letzten Monat eine Woche bei meinem Austauschpartner in Berlin verbracht.
    E *Was haben Sie während der Woche gemacht?*
    C An einem Tag sind wir einkaufen gegangen. Wir sind mit der S-Bahn in die Stadtmitte gefahren.
    E *Was haben Sie gekauft?*
    C Ich habe Andenken für meine Familie gekauft. Für meinen Vater einen Bierkrug, für meine Mutter eine Kette und für meinen Bruder ein Poster.
    E *Wie war das Wetter?*
    C Es war nicht so gut. Es hat geregnet, und es war kalt. Wir sind also in ein Café gegangen, um etwas zu trinken. Als wir im Café waren, haben wir einen Unfall gesehen.
    E *Was ist passiert?*
    C Zwei Autos sind zusammengestoßen. Es war eine Einbahnstraße, also ist ein Auto falsch gefahren.
    E *Was haben Sie gemacht?*
    C Ich habe sofort einen Notruf gemacht. Ich habe die Polizei und den Krankenwagen angerufen.
    E *War jemand verletzt?*
    C Ja, ein Fahrer war verletzt. Man hat ihn mit dem Krankenwagen ins Krankenhaus gebracht, weil er den Arm gebrochen hatte.
    E *Wie haben Sie sich gefühlt?*
    C Ich war zunächst schockiert. Ich hatte auch Angst, weil ein Fahrer verletzt war. Ich habe ihn später im Krankenhaus besucht, und ihm ist es besser gegangen.

▶ A STEP FURTHER

There is really only one way to practise role-play and that is to act it out with a partner. No doubt you have plenty of opportunity to do this in the classroom, but with a bit of initiative you could easily organise it for yourselves. There are lots of role-play situations in most course books and there are many in this book too.

If you are working with a friend on the same course, I suggest you go about it in a business-like way.

1. Decide who is going to play which part.
2. Read the parts through as a dialogue.
3. Repeat, but this time, instead of actually reading word by word, glance at the phrase you have to say, and then look up and say it.
4. This time try to say it by heart.
5. Now, finally, leave this book on the table, stand up and act it out, putting in *Guten Tag, danke, auf Wiedersehen* and so on as appropriate.

You may need several attempts at some of the stages, but you will improve in this kind of learning very quickly. When you are satisfied, change parts.

This is a much better way of learning than just reading the parts through. With this method you will really make the words and phrases part of your own language repertoire and you will be able to use them in a variety of situations both in the examination and in Germany.

There is an alternative method if you have not got a partner. That is to record on tape the part played by the examiner, leaving a suitable gap for your own part. Then play it over again and again, putting in your own part, gradually making yourself less and less dependent on the book. Finally, do it while walking round the room, with appropriate gestures and facial expressions. (Don't worry. No one is looking!)

Chapter 10

Speaking: Foundation and Higher conversation, presentation and coursework

> ## GETTING STARTED

At GCSE you will be required, in addition to the role-plays, to have a short conversation with your teacher. This takes place immediately after you have completed the role-plays. The length of the conversation varies from examining group to examining group and is longer at Higher Tier than at Foundation Tier. You should expect about 5–7 minutes at Foundation Tier and 8–10 at Higher. Check the exact requirements of the group you are studying for. (See also Table 1.1 in Chapter 1). The conversation topics are taken from the five Areas of Experience of the National Curriculum and are usually listed in the examining groups' syllabuses. Examples are given later in this chapter. Remember you will have to do a conversation whether you do Foundation or Higher Tier. Some examining groups also require a short presentation and discussion before the general conversation.

> ## WHAT YOU NEED TO KNOW

> ### The test – Foundation Tier

The topics to be covered by the general conversation will be chosen either by your teacher/examiner from alternatives supplied by the examining group, or by you, using cards with the topics printed on them. You may have to choose a certain card or cards, but you will not be able to see what is on them! The general conversation will cover a number of topics taken from the National Curriculum Areas of Experience, usually two (three for MEG). The teacher/examiner may have to cover, say, two conversation topics from a total of three (three from five for MEG). If you are studying for London the conversation will cover two topics, the first of which you may choose in advance from a list supplied by London and prepare. You can take a visual stimulus (e.g. a photo or map) and brief notes into the exam. (See also the 'Presentation' section later in this chapter on page 159). The second topic will be chosen by the teacher/examiner at the time of the test. In essence, you will be asked some 10–20 questions depending on the length of the test and how much you say in reply, and you will be expected to provide fairly straightforward answers, perhaps including references to past and future as well as present, and giving simple opinions.

The marks awarded will again depend on your ability to make yourself understood, to **communicate** some meaning. Your teacher will be trying to help you by taking the role of a sympathetic native speaker, and if there is something he or she does not understand then he or she will react just as if it were a real-life situation. For instance, in reality, if you met a German teenager at a party and asked how old he or she was and you got the reply 'forty', you wouldn't just leave it there and go on to another question! You would probably express surprise (!) and say something like 'Forty? I'm sure you don't mean that!' The German teenager would then have a chance to correct the previous answer: 'No, I mean fourteen'. This is what happens in natural conversation, and your teacher will be trying to make this part of the test as natural as possible. Try to be as natural as you can, too!

The conversation is not a cross-examination! The idea is not to probe into your secrets, but simply to assess your ability to speak German. The conversation in German will be based on the material you have covered throughout your course. The questions and topic areas covered will sample what you have been doing all along in your oral work in class and at home. Your teacher will not be trying to 'trick' you or catch you out. Remember, also, you do not have to tell the truth, just speak good German to impress the examiner.

Given that you now know that every effort is made to help you, make sure you help yourself by being prepared to **say something**!

155

The **topics** you are likely to be asked about will include:

- yourself, your home, family and friends
- your home town, village or area
- your school
- your interests and hobbies
- your leisure activities
- your daily routines
- your holidays
- your visits abroad
- your future plans

A conversation is a **two-way** affair, and you need to play your part. You will not be expected to give long, elaborate answers at this level, but you will be expected to say more than *ja* and *nein*! If, for instance, you are asked *Siehst du gern fern?*, then don't just say *ja* or *nein*, but volunteer some other information, e.g. *Mein Lieblingsprogramm ist East-Enders*. Most of the questions asked will in fact give you an opportunity to say a few words or a couple of sentences. Remember, this part of the examination assesses your ability to speak German, so **you must speak!** You may be asked to talk about the past, present and future and to give simple opinions.

The questions you will be asked are questions with which you should be familiar, but if there is a question you do not understand, don't panic. Ask the teacher to repeat the question: *Wie bitte?* or *Noch einmal, bitte*. Make sure you have a few phrases 'up your sleeve' to help you out of such difficulties.

The test – Higher Tier

The main difference between the Foundation Tier and Higher Tier conversation is that you are expected to **say more!** The initiative lies with you much more than it does with the examiner. The questions asked will require more than a brief response. Your teacher, as the examiner, will ask questions of a more open nature, giving you a cue to talk on a particular topic. An example could be something like 'You say you are very interested in sport. Can you tell me more?' This question form is a clear invitation to you to say what you can, so at this level you must be prepared to string a number of sentences together on a variety of themes.

Another important feature will be the actual language you use. Communication will still be very important, but this is the chance for you to really 'show off' what you know. You should be looking to make your answers **interesting** in terms of content, vocabulary, idiom, structure. Remember, if you don't use it, you cannot be awarded credit for knowing it!

As stated earlier, the topic areas covered will be much the same as for Foundation Tier (see above). The conversation will cover a range of these topics and will usually follow a fairly logical sequence. You are likely to be asked two or three questions on one topic area before going on to a different one.

Approaching the test

Students have often claimed that it is not possible to revise or prepare for an oral examination, but that simply is not true.

Once you have checked the **topic areas**, you can work out small groups of questions for each topic area and make sure that you can answer them. The **vocabulary** and **language tasks** in Chapter 3 will help you to do so. See also the examples given in the next section.

The first thing to do is pick out areas of **special interest** to you. After all, if you are interested in something, you are likely to have something to say! You should then prepare these topics thoroughly. The conversation will not be very long, but it's a good idea to string together some notes and sentences so that you can talk confidently on the individual subjects for about a minute. In the examination you will not be allowed to give a pre-learnt talk, but you will be expected to volunteer ideas and information.

Next you should concentrate on the **other possible themes** which are perhaps of less interest to you. Remember, though, that you should aim to be interesting yourself in the examination, so pretend! Think of ways to convey enthusiasm, e.g. by using particular items of vocabulary or idioms. I remember planning my own Advanced Level French oral as a student. I had recently spent a very enjoyable term at a school in Germany and it seemed a good idea to talk about it. I began by mentioning the channel crossing, but instead of just saying the French equivalent of 'the journey was good', I said enthusiastically, 'the crossing was superb!' The effect on the examiner was very positive. You are advised to think of similar 'tricks', so instead of *die Fahrt war gut*, say something like *die Überfahrt war wirklich toll, obwohl es ein bißchen stürmisch war*.

EXAMINATION QUESTIONS – FOUNDATION TIER

Here are some examples of the kind of questions you can expect in this part of the examination. As most of these questions will be familiar to you, we have not added the English equivalent. However, if you have difficulty understanding you could:

- ask a friend or relative
- look up words in the vocabulary list (Chapter 16)
- ask your teacher.

Yourself, your home, family and friends

Wie heißt du?
Wie alt bist du?
Wann hast du Geburtstag?
Hast du Geschwister?
Wie ist dein Bruder?
Wie ist deine Schwester?
Wie heißt dein bester Freund/deine beste Freundin?
Wie ist er/sie?

Wo wohnt er/sie?
Warum hast du ihn/sie gern?
Was macht ihr gern zusammen?
Hast du Haustiere?
Was ist dein Vater von Beruf?
Was ist deine Mutter von Beruf?
Wie ist dein Haus?
Beschreibe bitte dein Haus.

Your home town village or area

Wo wohnst du?
Wo ist Great Staughton?
Ist das eine Stadt?
Ist das ein Dorf?

Wohnst du gern in Great Staughton?
Was gibt es in Great Staughton zu sehen?
Was kann man in Great Staughton machen?
Wie lange wohnst du schon in Great Staughton?

Your school

Wie kommst du in die Schule?
Um wieviel Uhr gehst du in die Schule?
Wie ist deine Schule?
Was lernst du in der Schule?
Was ist dein Lieblingsfach?

Seit wann lernst du Deutsch?
Was machst du in der Pause?
Wo ißt du zu Mittag?
Welchen Sport treibst du in der Schule?

Your interests and hobbies

Was sind deine Hobbys?
Was machst du nach der Schule?
Wo machst du es?
Wie oft machst du es?

Wo spielst du Tischtennis?
Mit wem spielst du Tennis?
Ist das teuer?
Spielst du ein Instrument?

Your leisure activities

Was machst du in deiner Freizeit?
Siehst du gern fern?
Was siehst du gern im Fernsehen? Warum?
Was ist deine Lieblingssendung? Warum?
Was für Musik hörst du gern?
Wer ist dein Lieblingssänger?

Wo kannst du tanzen?
Was machst du am Wochenende?
Liest du auch gern?
Was liest du gern?
Bekommst du viel Taschengeld?
Was machst du mit deinem Taschengeld?

Your daily routine

Um wieviel Uhr stehst du gewöhnlich auf?
Was machst du dann?
Was ißt du zum Frühstück?
Wer bereitet das Frühstück bei euch vor?
Um wieviel Uhr verläßt du morgens das Haus?

Um wieviel Uhr ißt du abends?
Wann gehst du gewöhnlich ins Bett?
Wie hilfst du zu Hause?
Hilfst du gern zu Hause?
Um wieviel Uhr stehst du sonntags auf?

Your holidays

Wohin fährst du in Urlaub?
Mit wem fährst du in Urlaub?
Wie lange bleibst du dort?
Wie fährst du dorthin?
Fliegst du gern?
Gefällt dir Blackpool? Warum (nicht)?
Was machst du nächstes Jahr?

Was machst du gern im Urlaub?
Was machst du abends?
Was hast du im letzten Urlaub gemacht?
Wie war dein letzter Urlaub?
Was machst du diesen Sommer?
Wohin bist du letztes Jahr gefahren?

▷ **Your visits abroad**
Bist du schon einmal nach Deutschland gefahren?
Kennst du Deutschland?
Wo warst du?
Wann war das?
Hast du in einem Hotel gewohnt?
Was hat dir (nicht so) gut gefallen?
Bist du schon einmal ins Ausland gefahren?
War das mit einem Austausch?
Möchtest du in Deutschland wohnen? Warum (nicht)?
Warum gefällt dir Frankreich?

As you can see, there is a good deal of overlap in terms of the type of question to expect, but your teacher will use a mixture. In order to give you a chance of achieving grades D or C, you can expect some questions needing answers in the past, present and future. You should also expect to have to give simple opinions. There are many other possible questions. Make sure you check what you cover during your lessons and listen carefully to what your teacher says about preparation for this part of the examination.

Other examination questions

In some cases the format of an interview may be used as a basis for conversation. This applies to SEG but it is also possible for other groups to adopt this format. An example is included here, together with possible teacher/examiner questions.

You have applied for a job in Germany during the summer holidays through an agency. You have to go for an interview.

GESUCHT

Campingplatz Sonnenberg

Junge/Mädchen als Gehilfe/Gehilfin
16–19 Jahre
1. Juli–6. September

(Name?)   (Alter?)
(Wohnort?)   (Job?)
(Schule?)   (Fächer?)
(Freizeit?)   (Charakter?)

Possible teacher/examiner questions:

1 Für welchen Job interessieren Sie sich?
2 Wie heißen Sie?
3 Wie alt sind Sie?
4 Wo wohnen Sie?
5 Geben Sie mir bitte Ihre Adresse und Telefonnummer.
6 Wo gehen Sie auf die Schule?
7 Was studieren Sie?
8 Was haben Sie für einen Charakter?
9 Wann können Sie beginnen?

EXAMINATION QUESTIONS – HIGHER TIER

As mentioned earlier, the questions asked at Higher Tier will be of a much more open nature – an invitation to talk, to express ideas and opinions. The questions will fall into two main categories:

- The questions may simply follow up something you have already mentioned, e.g. *Du hast gesagt, du magst London (nicht) gern. Warum eigentlich (nicht)?*
- The questions may pick up something quite new, e.g. *Welche Pläne hast du für die Zukunft?*

In both examples, you have been given the 'green light', so take the opportunity!
The following are further examples of the kind of question to expect:

Du hast viele Geschwister. Wie findest du das?
Beschreibe mir ein bißchen dein Haus.
Wohnst du gern in deinem Haus?
Welche Vorteile/Nachteile hat das Leben in der Stadt?
Warum möchtest du auf dem Lande wohnen?
Warum gefällt dir die Schule (nicht)?
Warum gefällt dir die Schuluniform (nicht)?
Was trägst du gern am Wochenende, und warum?
Was machst du gewöhnlich am Samstagabend?
Was machst du mit deinem Taschengeld?
Bist du schon einmal nach Deutschland gefahren?
Wie war der Austausch?
Bist du schon einmal ins Ausland gefahren?
Würdest du gern im Ausland wohnen?
Welche Länder möchtest du besuchen?
Warum bleibst du auf der Schule?
Was für eine Stelle suchst du (nachher)?
Welche Ferienpläne hast du für den Sommer?

You can expect to have to talk about the past, present and future as well as give full opinions and justify them.

Other examination questions

In some cases, as at Foundation Tier, the format of an interview may be used as a basis for conversation. For instance, at Higher Tier the SEG conversation would have the same stimulus as at Foundation Tier (e.g. a job advertisement), but there would be no prompt questions on your conversation card. You therefore have to reply to unexpected questions, examples of which might be:

1. Warum haben Sie diesen Job gewählt?
2. Was denken Sie über den Job?
3. Möchten Sie mir Fragen stellen?
4. Arbeiten Sie im Moment?
5. Welche Pläne haben Sie für nächstes Jahr?
6. Warum suchen Sie einen Job in Deutschland?

PRESENTATION

If you are studying for MEG or NEAB, you are required to give a short presentation lasting about one minute. This serves as an introduction to some questions from the teacher/examiner about the subject matter of your presentation, which in turn leads on to the general conversation. If you are doing the London GCSE then the first of the two conversation topics is in effect a presentation, since you choose it in advance and can use brief notes and/or a visual stimulus in the exam.

You can choose the subject of your presentation from the list of topics covering the five Areas of Experience of the National Curriculum. For NEAB you may also make use of a stimulus. This might be, for instance, a photograph. You will have a short time to introduce your chosen topic and talk about it. There will then be a discussion about it with your teacher/examiner, who will ask further questions appropriate to either Foundation or Higher Tier (see examples of conversation questions above). Your presentation should not be a pre-learned speech. You choose the subject and prepare it in plenty of time beforehand, but it should sound spontaneous, as though you are speaking freely. For MEG you are allowed to take cue cards into the test with up to five short headings. Here are some examples of subjects you might choose and cue card headings you could take into the exam with you:

Mein Haus: Wo?   Zimmer?   Garten?   gern/nicht gern?   mein Zimmer?
Meine Hobbys: Sport?   Wo?/Wie oft?   Interessen?
Meine letzten Ferien: Wohin gefahren?   Wetter?   Wo gewohnt?   Was gemacht?   gut?/nicht gut?/Warum?
Meine Schule: Gesamtschule/Wo?   Fächer/Lieblingsfach?   Lehrer/Lehrerinnen?   Schulregeln, gut oder schlecht?   Ich hasse die Schule! Warum?

You should note that for MEG the questions on the three conversation topics covered by the general conversation will not include questions on the same topic as your presentation. Check the exact requirements of your examining group with your teacher. For London you may also take brief notes into the exam.

▶ SPEAKING COURSEWORK

▶ **SEG** Modules 1 and 3 of the SEG GCSE course contain speaking assessments. You have to make a short tape-recorded presentation on one of the aspects of the module laid down by SEG. Here is an example of the type of task you will find for the Module 1 assessment:

Der Jugendklub im Dorf deines Brieffreundes/deiner Brieffreundin würde gern eine Tonbandaufnahme von dir haben.
    Du sollst über die folgenden Sachen sprechen:

1 dich selbst
2 deine Familie
3 deinen Wohnort
4 deine Hobbys
5 deine Schule.

Du sollst ungefähr 3 Minuten sprechen.

You should note that at the beginning of the tape you will be expected to record your name, your candidate number, the name of your school, the centre number of your school and the date.
    You may prepare your presentation beforehand, but you may not read from a script during the recording. When preparing you can use a dictionary and during the recording itself you may refer to any prompt material supplied by SEG. The recording must be made at one sitting, though you are allowed to pause the tape at intervals, so that you can gather your thoughts. The recording will be marked at the tier you are entered for and that is most appropriate for you. Here is another example task, this time for Module 3:

Du sollst eine Tonbandaufnahme über einen Urlaub machen. Du könntest über einen Familienurlaub oder eine Schulfahrt sprechen.
    Du könntest etwas über die folgenden Sachen sagen:

1 Wo?
2 Wann?
3 Mit wem?
4 Wo hast du übernachtet?
5 Wetter?
6 Sehenswürdigkeiten?
7 Aktivitäten?

▶ **London** If you are studying for the London GCSE, one option is to do speaking coursework instead of a final speaking exam. If you opt for this you will have to produce **three units** of work. This may be spread out over the whole course, but must be completed by the end of the first week of May in the year in which you do the exam. Each unit of work must include **at least four** activities. The activities must include role-playing type tasks as well as conversation/presentation type tasks, some of which may involve work in pairs or groups. The **three units** of work must be based on three of the five Areas of Experience of the National Curriculum, i.e.

A Everyday Activities
B Personal and Social Life
C The World Around Us
D The World of Work
E The International World

One of the units of work must be based on *either* Area D *or* Area E. Some tasks, but not all, will have to be recorded. In practice your teacher may decide to record everything, since it will probably be easier to mark the work if it is recorded.

The types of task you have to do could include any of the role-play tasks covered in Chapters 8 and 9, depending on which tier you are attempting, a presentation on any of the topics like those described for MEG and SEG earlier in this chapter, and/or conversation with your teacher on similar topics. The possibilities might include:

Foundation Tier

Area A   A role-play in a café
Area B   A presentation about your family using a photograph
Area C   A role-play asking for directions
Area D   A basic job interview
Area E   A radio presentation about an aspect of life in Germany

Higher Tier

Area A   A radio presentation about students' rights (school rules etc.)
Area B   Negotiate with a friend to arrange to go out (i.e. open-ended role-play)
Area C   A presentation about a local place of interest using a photograph
Area D   Leave an answerphone message answering a job advertisement
Area E   A radio presentation about a world event (sporting, entertainment)

As you will see from the above examples the types of task, and therefore the language needed, are similar to those encountered in a final exam, although the context and format of the task may be slightly different, and you will have to do more tasks! If you work through the example role-plays in Chapters 8 and 9 (for Higher Tier) and also work your way through the conversation section of this chapter, you will have covered most of what you need.

▶ **A STEP FURTHER**

The German word for language is *Sprache*, which also means 'speaking'. This reminds us of the obvious fact that in a normal day we use language more for speaking than for reading or writing. Speaking is also the criterion by which people will normally judge your ability in a language. They will say 'Oh, you are learning German, are you? Go on, say something in German!' And later on, when working, a colleague may say, 'Oh, you did German at school, didn't you? Can you deal with this visitor or customer?'

So in reality it is our speaking of the language which is likely to be put to the test most often. Anyway, most of us like talking, so let us think of ways of improving our conversation skills.

First ask yourself this question. If you had a conversation with a non-English-speaking visitor, would you prefer that his English should be lively, interesting, with plenty of mistakes and a funny accent, or that he should speak slowly and laboriously but correctly? The answer is obvious. A slow conversation with long pauses is boring in the extreme, so make up your mind that this is not for you!

A German conversation should ideally take place in Germany, Austria or Switzerland with a German-speaking person. A satisfactory alternative would be a conversation with a

German in this country, or with your teacher. But in the real world this is not often possible in the limited time available, so we shall have to think of other ways of practising.

If you have a good friend with whom you can work, then this will be fine, but let us think of the many times when you are having to revise on your own.

▷ **Reading**   A language is for speaking out loud, and your accent and fluency will not improve until you get into the habit of reading or speaking German out loud as a regular thing. If you are learning a part for a play, you know that it really only works if you say it out loud. So start by **reading** German out loud to yourself. If this embarrasses you at first, then put your elbows on the table and your hands over your ears and read it quietly.

▷ **Speaking**   Take a topic from the list – say, 'yourself, your home, family and friends' – and think for a few minutes of how you might talk about it to someone who doesn't know you. When you feel ready, try talking for a minute fairly fluently. Use an alarm clock or a watch if you wish, and if possible record what you say on cassette. Make it sound chatty and interesting. **Don't** make it sound as though you are reading it or as if you have learnt it off by heart. If you are not satisfied, do it again. To make it more interesting, tell a pack of lies, exaggerating your own skills, explaining how your mother is a lead singer in a pop group and your father plays in goal for West Ham. But if you don't tell the truth in the exam at least make it believable.

Of course this exercise would be much better if you could turn it into a conversation. One way of getting round the problem would be to record a series of questions on cassette, leaving a gap after each question long enough for a full answer. Your teacher or German assistant might do it for you, but you could always do it yourself.

▷ **Topics**   Use your topic lists in the following way to help you with your conversation work. Take a piece of paper for each topic and make a list of 10–15 words or phrases to remind you of what you are able to say. For example, for the topic 'yourself, your home, family and friends' you could write these key words:

- Name
- Wie alt?
- Wohnen?
- Mutter, Vater
- Geschwister
- Haustiere
- Haus
- Schlafzimmer
- Hobbys
- Freunde, Freundinnen
- Ferien
- Schule

▷ **Partners**   Do you have a dog or a cat or a baby in the house? If so, you probably talk to them quite frequently without expecting much of a response. Try talking to your dog or cat in German: *Hallo, Mitzi. Wie geht es dir? Hast du Hunger? Was willst du trinken? Milch? Tee? Whisky? Oh, so ist es besser, nicht wahr?* and so on. The dog or cat won't mind and at least it will give you the feeling that you are talking to someone, even if the response is limited!

▷ **Exercise into conversation**   Making an exercise sound like a conversation is really a very tricky thing to do. You should, particularly if you are doing the Higher Tier, be aware of the many little words and phrases that the Germans put into their speech, which make it sound like authentic German. Here is an example of how a native German might respond to the questions on the topic of 'your leisure activities', with an explanation of the idiomatic phrases used.

Your leisure activities

E *Was machst du in deiner Freizeit?*
C Ja, *das ist schwer zu sagen. Momentan* habe ich nicht viel Freizeit. Aber ich spiele gern Fußball, und ich gehe manchmal ins Kino.
E *Siehst du gern fern?*
C Ja, sehr gern, wenn ich Zeit habe.

E *Was siehst du gern im Fernsehen? Warum?*
C Erstens Sport. Ich finde das sehr interessant, und dann Filme, weil sie oft sehr gut sind. Es ist auch billiger als im Kino!
E *Was für Musik hörst du gern?*
C Ja, meistens Popmusik, aber auch *ab und zu* Jazz oder klassische Musik.
E *Was machst du am Wochenende?*
C *Das kommt darauf an.* Wenn das Wetter schön ist, gehe ich aus. Oder ich fahre in die Stadt und treffe meine Freunde.
E *Liest du auch gern?*
C Ja, *besonders* spät am Abend, wenn ich im Bett bin.
E *Was liest du gern?*
C Na ja, *das ist verschieden*. Krimis, Science Fiction und auch die Zeitung. Und Sie? Was lesen Sie gern?
E *Ich? O ja, ich lese auch gern, meistens Romane. Und bekommst du viel Taschengeld?*
C Nein! Viel zu wenig. Aber ich habe einen Job in einem Schuhgeschäft.
E *Was machst du mit deinem Taschengeld?*
C Ich kaufe Schallplatten oder gehe ins Kino. Ich glaube, das ist alles.

das ist schwer zu sagen	that is hard to say
momentan	at the moment
ab und zu	now and then
das kommt darauf an	that depends
besonders	especially
das ist verschieden	that varies

All these phrases could be used in almost any conversation and they add a lot of colour and interest. Note how the candidate often went further than just an answer to the question given. He even at one point turned the tables and asked the examiner a question! This gives an excellent impression.

This conversation is of course of a very high standard, but it gives you something to aim for.

Chapter 11

Writing: Foundation Tier

GETTING STARTED

Everyone who does GCSE German will have to show that they can write in German. You must do *either* Foundation Tier *or* Higher, but, as with the other skills tested, you may *not* do *both*. If you do Foundation Tier, the highest grade you can achieve on this part of the exam is a C. As with the speaking tests the main aim is that you should be able to put your message across, not that you should be able to write fault-free German. If you are studying for the MEG, NEAB, London or WJEC GCSE you can opt to do coursework for this part of the exam instead of a final examination, if your centre will allow this. The details of the coursework option for writing are dealt with in Chapter 13. For SEG you will do some written coursework assessments in Module 3 together with an end of course test. Even if you are doing the SEG course or coursework for other examining groups that offer it, you should work through this chapter, as the tasks you will have to do are similar to those for the examination questions.

WHAT YOU NEED TO KNOW

Requirements

In many cases you will have to do the kinds of things you will have done to help you with the other skills. The tasks are designed to be fairly straightforward and predictable, and Foundation Tier writing is not intended to be more difficult than any other of the Foundation Tier tests.

As with Foundation and Higher Tier speaking, **you do not have to produce perfect German in order to score full marks.** The more accurate you are, however, the more marks you will gain. Again, you must do *either* Foundation or Higher, but not both.

The writing tasks vary somewhat between the different examining groups, and you will need to check carefully which topic areas you are expected to cover and which exercises you are required to do. There is, however, major agreement in that you may be required:

- to write **simple lists**, e.g. a shopping list
- to write **simple messages,** e.g. a note left for a friend (20–40 words)
- to write **a postcard**, e.g. to a German pen friend, possibly in reply to a postcard received by you (20–40 words)
- to **complete a given form**, e.g. an application form
- to write a **simple letter, formal** or **informal,** in response to a letter in German or instructions in German or English (60–100 words)

In all exercises there will be clear instructions in German or perhaps English (e.g. scene setting) as to what you should include. If there is an indication of the number of words to be written, this is only a guide. The important thing is that you cover all the tasks.

We will look at the different kinds of question later in the chapter, in the section 'Examination questions' (see page 169).

You may be required to write a reply to a stimulus letter or card written in German and addressed to you. It is important for you to **practise reading and understanding German handwriting.** Your course book will no doubt contain examples. If you have a German pen friend or exchange partner then note how he/she forms the individual letters. Some examples are provided in the sections on reading comprehension in Chapters 6 and 7 as well as in the chapters on writing.

In general you will be required to do three tasks at Foundation Tier and the final most difficult task also forms the first (or easiest) Higher Tier question. For MEG you will have to do four tasks, and if you are doing the SEG modular course there is one Foundation Tier task to do in the end of course examination in Module 4. The tasks will usually be completion of a list, followed by another short task such as a postcard or message. Then there will be a little longer, but straightforward letter or article/report to write. You may be offered a choice of tasks for the final question. For MEG you have two of the easier list-type short tasks.

▶ Approaching the questions

1. You will need to communicate the information required in such a way that the person for whom the list/message/postcard/letter is intended can understand clearly what you mean. Clear handwriting is also an obvious advantage! If you do notice a mistake and want to correct it, then do so clearly and neatly. You will not be credited for anything an examiner cannot decipher!
2. You do not have to write perfect German in order to put your meaning across, but do try to be as accurate as possible.
3. You must make sure that you include all the relevant information required by the tasks. Make sure you do all the tasks.
4. Try to keep within any word limits for the question, though these are only a guide. The main thing is to do all the tasks.
5. Think carefully about what you are going to write before starting your answer. This is especially important if you have to write your answer in a limited space, e.g. on a blank notepad or postcard. There should be room on the exam paper for rough work or spare paper available in the examination room.
   (a) Make notes in German, using vocabulary and expressions with which you are familiar.
   (b) Always build on German that you know. Do not rely on the use of a dictionary, which will waste too much time. It is a good idea to learn and remember vocabulary and grammar in a set phrase as a kind of building block. If you know that *'Ich möchte'* means 'I would like', and that *'Ich möchte ein Kilo Äpfel'* means 'I would like a kilo of apples', then you can go on to use *ich möchte* . . . to say what else you would like.
   (c) Try to use interesting material wherever you can, but make sure it is relevant. Which of the following do you think is likely to create a better impression?
   – *es war gut*
   – *es war sehr gut*
   – *es war wirklich gut*
   – *es war einfach klasse/toll*
   (d) Beware the so-called 'false friends'; that is, German words which are spelt or sound similar to English words and vice-versa, but which actually have a different meaning. Have you heard the German teacher's standard joke? 'A German tourist goes into a butcher's in England, and, getting rather fed up with waiting his turn, calls out: "When do I become a sausage?"' Ugh, but perhaps it will help you to remember the problem of become/*bekommen*.
   (e) Although it is sometimes tempting, don't think of what you want to say in English and then try to translate it into German. Just look at what can happen. The task is to explain that you hope your friend is coming.
   – *Ich hoffe, du bist kommen(d).*   This is the sort of writing that has driven many a teacher or examiner prematurely bald!
   – *Ich hoffe, (daß) du kommst.*   This is fine.
   – *Hoffentlich kommst du.*   A fine alternative correct formulation.
   (f) There are many different ways of saying the same thing in English, and it is just the same with German (consider again the example above). You might, for instance, want to find out if there is a swimming pool nearby. It would be equally possible and equally acceptable to write:
   – *Gibt es dort in der Nähe ein Schwimmbad?*
   – *Ist dort in der Nähe ein Schwimmbad?*
   – *Habt ihr dort in der Nähe ein Schwimmbad?*
   – *Ist dort ein Schwimmbad? Ist es weit?*
   It's important, then, for you to think: 'How can I say that in German and make myself understood? What useful words and expressions do I know?' If you use a dictionary make sure any word you look up is the right one for the context. If in doubt, don't use it!
6. Make sure you check your work thoroughly. In particular, check spellings, genders, cases, verbs, and – above all else – that you have done all that is required of you. If, for example, there are five tasks, make sure that you have included them all.

There is a comprehensive checklist in the next chapter which can be used and adapted to suit your needs (see page 181).

The information provided by the examining groups will tell you which topics will be examined and what vocabulary and grammar you need to know. You will find helpful details elsewhere in the book on these subjects. It is up to you to prepare fully, so that you are not caught out by something unexpected.

You must also ensure that you get enough practice in the different exercises that may appear in the examination. Here are some suggestions which you may find practical and of benefit.

▶ Vocabulary

- You cannot suddenly expect to sit down and learn 1500–2000 words. Be systematic and learn vocabulary regularly and in short bursts. 'Little but often' is a sensible approach.
- Get the vocabulary habit! 10 minutes twice a day soon builds up, but make sure you test yourself or get someone else to test you. Check spellings and try not to make the same mistakes next time.
- Try and think of some novel ways to help you to make learning items less boring.
- Set yourself realistic targets and allow yourself small rewards for the successful completion of a target.
- I have a friend who wrote out short lists which she left in prominent places, where she couldn't help seeing them: next to the mirror, by the radio, by the record-player, by the kettle, etc.
- Think of a topic area, give yourself a time limit and then see how many words you can write down in the time allowed.
- Think of a word and then see what new word comes into your head next, e.g. *Tisch, Tennis, Sommer, Sonne, Ferien, keine Schule* and so on (good fun with a friend).

You must have plenty of other ideas.

▶ Practice in writing

- If you have contacts in or from Germany, Austria or Switzerland, then use them. Exchange letters and postcards, swap language, ask for help, make notes of vocabulary and expressions you think may help you.
- Go over as many specimen questions as you can. There will be many exercises in your course books similar to those which occur in the GCSE examination.
- Go over and revise exercises you have written in the past and try to do them again, only this time see if you can improve on your previous performance.
- Try to make note of any particular weaknesses which occur/have occurred regularly in your writing and try to do something about it. Ask your teacher for help if you don't understand or can't see why you often make the same mistake.

▶ Types of writing task

We shall now look at each type of writing task you are likely to meet.

Writing lists
Writing a list is really not much more than showing that you have learnt certain items of vocabulary. Check the topic areas to be tested and learn the vocabulary! You can help yourself learn the vocabulary by actually testing yourself regularly. You can also devise your own test lists to fit in with the kind of exercise you may have to complete in this section of the examination.

The sort of list you will be required to write is likely to centre on the topic areas of **shopping** and **holidays, clothing** and **personal belongings**, though these may not be the only topics tested. Possible lists could be:

- shopping for food and drink, e.g. for a party or picnic
- shopping for presents, e.g. to take home from Germany, Austria, Switzerland
- describing the contents of a lost bag or case.

Apart from knowing the individual words, you may be required to give further information, e.g. stating an **appropriate quantity** or **amount** (for food and drink), or using **adjectives of size, colour and age**, e.g. to describe clothing.

Remember to make sure that what you include in your list makes sense for the task. For instance, if you are writing a shopping list for a picnic, it is unlikely that you would wish to take *Bratkartoffeln*! Nor is it likely that you would wish to take ten different things to drink and nothing to eat!

Writing messages

The messages you have to write may not involve you needing to write in complete sentences – simple notes may be sufficient. Be careful, as always, to check all the instructions very carefully and cover all the tasks.

Again, refer to the topic areas tested in this section by your examining group. Some obvious possible messages/notes could include:

▶ leaving **instructions for a German-speaking visitor** explaining to him/her how to get to a particular place
▶ leaving a **telephone message**, e.g. 'Klaus rang up, he wants to go to the cinema tonight, the film is great, can you ring him at 6.30?'
▶ explaining **why you have gone out** and where, when you will be back, etc.
▶ **making arrangements** for some kind of activity, e.g. planning a trip to town or to a concert, football match, etc.

In order to be able to leave the right kind of message or note, you will need to be able to give details about:

▶ **directions and places:**	first left, straight on, at the café etc.
	die erste Straße links, geradeaus, im Café, usw.
▶ **methods of transport:**	on foot, by bus/train/taxi etc.
	zu Fuß, mit dem Bus/Zug/Taxi, usw.
▶ **times and dates:**	half past four, in the evening, on Friday etc.
	halb fünf, am Abend, am Freitag, usw.
▶ **duration of time:**	five minutes, half an hour etc.
	fünf Minuten, eine halbe Stunde, usw.
▶ **activities of interest:**	cinema, concert, theatre, swimming etc.
	Kino, Konzert, Theater, Schwimmen, usw.
▶ **simple instructions/**	Can you come to the party?
suggestions:	*Kannst du zu der Party kommen?*

The above is not intended to be a complete list, but rather to show some examples of the kind of message to expect.

Writing postcards

As before, check all the instructions fully. You may have to write your answer on a blank postcard provided. This means you have to plan what you are going to write very carefully, and stick closely to the word limits.

As with writing a letter, there are some standard things you will be expected to know how to do:

1 state where you are writing from, and the date
2 start a postcard
3 end a postcard
4 write a German-style address.

You may not be required to show you can do all of these in any one postcard, but you should be prepared.

1 You should not write the full postal address. The standard way to state where you are writing from and the date is as follows:
 – *Cambridge, den 4. Mai*
 – *Marbella, den 11. August* etc.
2 You can begin either with a greeting from wherever you are, or by greeting the person to whom you are writing, e.g.
 – *Viele Grüße aus Blackpool, Frankreich* etc.   *or*

– *Lieber Bernd, Jochen, Dieter* etc.
– *Liebe Sonja, Marianne, Inge* etc.

You can also write *Lieber Bernd!* using the exclamation mark, but then the first word of your postcard must be written with a capital letter. Otherwise the first word of your postcard should be written with a small letter unless it is a name.

3 There are a number of different ways of ending a card. You could choose from the following:
– *viele Grüße* (but best avoided if you have begun with *Viele Grüße aus . . .*)
– *Dein* (if you are male) or *Deine* (if female) and your first name.

For example:
viele Grüße
Dein Brian/Deine Sarah

4 There are some important points to remember when addressing cards or letters to Germany/Austria/Switzerland:
– *Herr* becomes *Herrn* for Mr . . .
– the street is followed by the house number
– the post code *(Postleitzahl)* comes before the name of the town/village.

For example
Herrn Rainer Hohenner
Am Glaskopf 36
60322 Frankfurt am Main

It is a sensible idea to try to learn some addresses for possible inclusion. It could be the address of a pen friend or an imaginary one.

Filling in forms

The types of form you may be required to fill in could include the following:

▶ Booking forms for hotels, campsites etc.
▶ Forms for a school exchange (with a view to matching you to a suitable partner)
▶ Forms for a pen friend agency.

Most forms will include obvious personal details such as name and address and possibly, age, sex and marital status, and even physical appearance. Dates and times are also frequently needed. Remember that not all the information will be required in German. You cannot write your name and address in German! Make sure you do not leave any gaps. Fill in everything you are asked for, even if you are not certain. Most of what you have to write in German will be single words, but there may be parts of the form where a phrase or short sentence will be more appropriate, for instance where you have to give details of your interests. If you have to write dates or times in German, make sure you have used the correct notation. Write numbers as figures and not as words, since there is less scope for error this way.

Writing letters

You may be asked to write a short formal letter (e.g. to a hotel) or informal letter (e.g. to a pen friend). There may be a letter for you to read and reply to or alternatively there may be a situation described and a list of tasks for you to do. This is what you should do.

▶ Decide whether you are to write a formal or informal letter. Generally if you are writing to a hotel or company (people you do not know) the letter will be formal. If you are writing to someone you know, or who is roughly your own age (a pen friend, whom you have or have not met), the letter will be informal. This is important because you must begin and end the letter appropriately. Formal letters begin; *Lieber Herr Schmidt* or *Liebe Frau Braun*. Alternatively you could use *Sehr geehrter Herr, Sehr geehrte Dame* or *Sehr geehrte Damen und Herren*. A formal letter usually ends with *Hochachtungsvoll* or *Mit freundlichem Gruß*. Informal letters usually begin; *Lieber Helmut* or *Liebe Birgit* and end with *Bis bald, Dein/Deine. . . .* Other possibilities are given in the vocabulary sections.

▶ Remember that all words appearing in a letter that mean '**you**' or '**your**' must be written with a capital letter in German:
  Du, Dich, Dir, Dein
  Sie, Ihnen, Ihr
  Ihr, Euch, Euer

- If there is a stimulus letter to which you must reply, make sure you cover all the points raised by the letter, replying to any questions asked and giving the information required. Likewise, if there is a list of tasks to do, make sure you include all the tasks in your answer.
- Remember that if you are given a number of words to write, this is only a guide. The important thing is to cover all the tasks appropriately. You may be able to do this adequately in less than the stated number of words or more. Try to avoid including lots of irrelevant material, however. For the most part one or two sentences will be enough to do each task.

EXAMINATION QUESTIONS

On the following pages you will find a variety of examples of tests for Foundation Level writing. Possible answers have been provided in the 'Examination answers' section at the end of the chapter (see page 173). But do it yourself first!

Question 1 Du fliegst nach Deutschland. Am Flughafen in Frankfurt kannst du deinen Koffer nicht finden. Was ist im Koffer? Schreibe eine Liste.

(a) ....
(b) ....
(c) ....
(d) ....
(e) ....
(f) ....
(g) ....
(h) ....
(i) ....
(j) ....

Question 2 You plan a trip to the countryside with your German friends and will take a picnic. Add **six** more items to this shopping list **in German**.

(a) Coca Cola
(b) Brot
(c) ....
(d) ....
(e) ....
(f) ....
(g) ....
(h) ....

Chapter 11 Writing: Foundation Tier

Question 3 Du schreibst eine Liste für deine deutsche Freundin mit allem, was du am Wochenende machst. Schreibe **fünf** Dinge.
Beispiel: Ich mache Einkäufe.

....

....

....

Question 4 Du bist eine Woche bei deinem Brieffreund in Deutschland. Was machst du und wo machst du es? Fülle das Tagebuch aus.

Tag	Was machst du?	Wo machst du es?
Sonntag	Ankunft	Flughafen
Montag		
Dienstag		
Mittwoch		
Donnerstag		
Freitag		
Samstag		

Question 5 Du bist im Urlaub. Du schreibst eine Ansichtskarte an einen Brieffreund/eine Brieffreundin in Österreich. Schreibe nicht mehr als 40 Wörter.

Wo?
Wie lange?
Wetter?
Was machst du?
Wann nach Hause?

POSTKARTE

Question 6 You are on holiday in Spain. You send a postcard to a friend in Germany.

Beschreibe: das Hotel
   das Wetter
   das Essen.
Sage: wie du nach Spanien gefahren bist
   was du jeden Tag machst.

▷ **Question 7** Brieffreunde

> Hallo Freunde! Ich, Helmut (15), suche interessante Brieffreunde/Brieffreundinnen aus aller Welt. Wenn Ihr Lust habt, schreibt mit Foto an: Helmut Rheinberger, Knackertstraße 88, 60322 Frankfurt am Main, Deutschland

Schreibe eine Postkarte an Helmut und gib die folgenden Informationen:
Name, Alter, Wohnort, Interessen, Charaktereigenschaften (ungefähr 30 Wörter).

Lieber Helmut,

....

....

....

.... *Helmut Rheinberger*

.... *Knackertstr. 88*

.... *60322 Frankfurt/Main*

....

....

Tschüß, ...

▷ **Question 8** Du schreibst an einen Freund aus Österreich einen Brief über deine Schule. Im Brief beantwortest du folgende Fragen:

(a) Was für eine Schule besuchst du?
(b) Wann beginnt die Schule?
(c) Welche Fächer magst du am liebsten?
(d) Wie ist die Uniform?
(e) Wie sind die Lehrer?

▷ **Question 9** Sie schreiben einen Brief an ein Hotel in der Schweiz. Sie wollen Zimmer reservieren. Die folgenden Punkte müssen im Brief stehen:

▶ Ankunftsdatum
▶ wie lange Sie bleiben
▶ wieviele Leute mit Ihnen fahren
▶ was für Zimmer Sie genau wollen.

Sie müssen nach den folgenden Informationen fragen:

▶ Preise
▶ Freizeitmöglichkeiten in der Nähe.

▷ **Question 10** Sie müssen für die Schülerzeitung einen Artikel über Ihren Austausch schreiben. Schreiben Sie 100 Wörter **auf deutsch**.

Austauschprogramm

Samstag	Ankunft in Heilbronn
	Begrüßung im Rathaus
Sonntag	frei
Montag	Stadtrundfahrt
Dienstag	Tag in der Schule
Mittwoch	Dombesichtigung und danach
	Ausflug in den Odenwald
Donnerstag	Abschiedsdisco

▷ **Question 11** You have sent your name and address to an agency in Germany which was advertising for English teenagers to write to German children of the same age, and they have sent you the following form to fill in. Answer each point **in German** giving details of your family, school subjects and interests as requested.

Name: _____ Vorname: _____
Alter – Jahre: _____ Monate: _____
Familie: _____
_____
_____
Haustiere: _____
Schule: _____
Schulfächer: _____
_____
Fremdsprachen: _____
_____
Freizeitbeschäftigung: _____
Sport: _____
Andere Interessen: _____
_____
Datum: _____ Unterschrift: _____

▷ **Question 12** Schreibe auf deutsch einen Brief an einen deutschen Brieffreund oder an eine deutsche Brieffreundin. Schreibe 100 Wörter.

Beschreibe: deine Familie
dein Haus
dein Schlafzimmer
deinen Wohnort

Frage deinen Freund/deine Freundin nach seinem/ihrem Haus und Wohnort.

▷ **Question 13** Du hast diesen Brief von deinem Brieffreund bekommen. Schreibe eine Antwort. Schreibe ungefähr 70 Wörter.

> Tag!
>
> Danke vielmals für Deinen letzten Brief. Ich freue mich, daß Du wieder nach so langer Zeit geschrieben hast! Wie geht's?
>
> Im Moment muß ich viel im Haus helfen weil meine Mutter krank ist. Mußt Du auch helfen? Ich hasse das! Wie ist es bei Dir?
>
> In den Sommerferien haben wir Urlaub in Österreich gemacht. Das war furchtbar! Was hast Du gemacht? Hast Du schon Pläne für nächstes Jahr? Also jetzt muß ich schon Schluß machen.
>
> Schreib bald wieder!
>
> Dein Gerd

▷ **Question 14** Sie haben in den Sommerferien einen Job gehabt. Sie schreiben einen Brief an einen deutschen Freund. Beschreiben Sie folgendes:

- ▶ was Sie in dem Job gemacht haben
- ▶ was Sie verdient haben
- ▶ was Ihnen gefallen hat
- ▶ was Ihnen nicht gefallen hat.

▷ **EXAMINATION ANSWERS**

▷ **Answer 1** (a) eine Jeans (b) ein Pullover (c) ein Hemd
(d) Unterhosen (e) eine Zahnbürste (f) ein Geschenk
(g) Trainingsschuhe (h) eine Jacke (i) eine Krawatte
(j) Seife

▷ **Answer 2** (a) eine Tüte Chips (b) Margarine (c) Schinken
(d) Wurst (e) Erdbeerkuchen (f) Limonade

▷ **Answer 3** Ich spiele Fußball.
Ich mache meine Hausaufgaben.
Ich gehe in die Stadt.
Ich treffe mich mit meinen Freunden.
Ich wasche den Wagen für meinen Vater.

▷ **Answer 4**

Montag	schwimmen	Freibad
Dienstag	Fußball spielen	Sportzentrum
Mittwoch	einkaufen	Stadtmitte
Donnerstag	fernsehen	zu Hause
Freitag	tanzen	in der Disco
Samstag	wandern	im Wald

▷ **Answer 5** **Student answer**

> Liebe Brünhilde,
> ich bin auf Urlaub in Frankreich. Ich verbringe hier zwei Wochen. Das Wetter ist toll! Ich schwimme jeden Tag. Ich fahre am 20. August nach Hause.
> Bis bald,
> Deine Diane

Examiner's comment
Excellent! The beginning and ending are good. All the tasks have been done. The sentences are short and clear. Some words from the question itself have been well incorporated.

▷ **Answer 6** **Student answer**

> Lieber Richard,
> hier in Spanien für eine Woche. Wetter sehr heiß! Hotel wunderschön! Das Essen schmeckt gut, viel Fisch. Ich bin mit dem Zug nach Spanien gefahren. Ich gehe jeden Tag zum Strand. Tschüß!
> Dein Peter

Examiner's comment
Peter has not written in full sentences all the time. This is fine for postcards. Everything is clear. Another excellent answer.

▷ **Answer 7** **Student answer**

> Lieber Helmut,
> ich heiße Anita. Ich bin sechzehn Jahre alt und wohne in Bolton.
> Meine Hobbys sind Schwimmen und Musikhören. Ich bin sympathisch und immer guter Laune.
> Tschüß, Anita

Examiner's comment
Again, the answer is full and accurate. The tasks have been dealt with in order.

Answer 8 Student answer

> Ich gehe auf eine Gesamtschule.
> Die Schule beginnt um neun Uhr.
> Meine Lieblingsfächer sind Mathe und Chemie.
> Wir tragen eine Jacke. Die ist blau. Die Krawatte ist rot und schwarz.
> Die meisten Lehrer sind sympathisch, aber manche sind streng.

Examiner's comment
In the last two tasks the candidate has kept things straightforward by not putting the describing words in front of the nouns, where they would have needed correct endings.

Answer 9 Student answer

> Sehr geehrter Herr!
>
> Ich möchte zwei Doppelzimmer mit Bad in Ihrem Hotel reservieren. Wir sind vier Personen. Wir kommen am 12. Juni an und möchten vier Nächte bleiben.
> Was kostet das pro Nacht? Was kann man in der Nähe machen? Gibt es ein Schwimmbad?
>   Vielen Dank im voraus.
>
> Ihr
>
> Peter Smith

Examiner's comment
This is an ideal answer at this tier. It is to the point, with all tasks done logically, though not in the same order as in the question. The candidate has remembered to include a **formal** beginning and ending.

Answer 10 Student answer

> Wir kamen am Samstag, dem 13. März an. Es gab eine Begrüßung im Rathaus. Das war prima! Der Bürgermeister war dort. Wir hatten Sonntag frei, und das war gut so. Ich war sehr müde. Die Reise war lang! Am Montag machten wir eine Stadtrundfahrt. Wir sahen den Dom und die Stadtmitte. Die Dombesichtigung war am Mittwochvormittag. Der Dom ist sehr schön und alt. Am Nachmittag fuhren wir mit dem Bus in den Odenwald, wo wir eine Wanderung machten. Das beste war am Donnerstag, dem letzten Tag. In der Schule gab es eine Abschiedsdisko. Wir tanzten viel, bis spät.

Examiner's comment
The candidate successfully uses words and phrases from the stimulus. He/she has chosen to write in the imperfect tense, though the perfect or present would have done equally well. It is good to see so many simple opinions. Not every day is covered, but this does not matter, as the correct number of words has been written and most of the programme dealt with. There is one more complex sentence with *wo* and the correct word order for good measure!

Answer 11

Name:	CLARKESON	Vorname:	CHRISTOPHER
Alter – Jahre:	15	Monate:	10

Familie: 2 Brüder

Haustiere: Keine

Schule: Smithills School – Gesamtschule

Schulfächer: Englisch Mathe Chemie Biologie Erdkunde Geschichte

Fremdsprachen: Deutsch Französisch

Freizeitbeschäftigung: Briefmarken sammeln

Sport: Fußball Eishockey

Andere Interessen: Musik Kino

Datum: 10.1.97   Unterschrift: C. J. Clarkeson

Answer 12 Student answer

> Liebe Bärbel,
>
> wie geht's? Mir geht's gut.
> In meiner Familie gibt es fünf Personen, meine Eltern natürlich, und ich habe zwei Brüder. Meine Brüder sind jünger als ich.
>
> Wir wohnen in einem Doppelhaus in Wigan. Ich finde das Haus schön und bequem. Unten gibt es ein Wohnzimmer, ein Eßzimmer und eine große Küche. Wir haben auch einen tollen Garten hinter dem Haus. Das ist ein Glück! Oben haben wir vier Schlafzimmer und das Badezimmer.
>
> Ich habe ein eigenes Schlafzimmer mit einem Schreibtisch, einem Fernseher und einer Stereoanlage. Mein Zimmer ist ein bißchen klein, aber ich mag es gern.
>
> Wigan liegt in Nordwestengland. Es ist sehr alt und interessant! Was für ein Haus hast Du? Ist es groß? Wo wohnst Du, in einer Stadt oder einem Dorf?
>
> Schreib bald wieder!
>
> Deine Sabeena

Examiner's comment

This goes over the word count. It can be quite difficult to keep to the count if you can remember plenty of German! It isn't a problem here, but don't write massively more than you should, especially if you are using up time that could be devoted to other questions. All the tasks are done and there is a good range of vocabulary and use of prepositions.

Answer 13 Student answer

> Lieber Gerd,
>
> danke für den Brief. Mir geht's gut.
>
> Ich muß ab und zu im Haus helfen. Ich wasche einmal in der Woche ab und wasche auch das Auto für meinen Vater. Ich mache das nicht gern, aber ich bekomme Geld dafür.
>
> Wir sind in den Ferien nach Spanien gefahren. Das Wetter war phantastisch, und wir sind jeden Tag zum Strand gegangen. Nächstes Jahr fahren wir nach Amerika. Ich möchte nach Disneyland in Florida.
>
> Bis bald!
>
> Dein William

Examiner's comment

Words and phrases from the stimulus letter are well used for the candidate's own purposes without being copied. There are some simple opinions and all the tasks are covered. Good use of inverted word order.

Answer 14 Student answer

> Lieber Hans,
>
> in den Sommerferien habe ich in einem Büro für meinen Onkel gearbeitet. Ich habe das ganz interessant gefunden. Ich mußte jeden Tag die Post aufmachen und sortieren. Am Nachmittag bin ich auf die Post gegangen, um Briefmarken zu kaufen und die Briefe zu verschicken. Ich habe auch viele Tassen Tee und Kaffee für die Sekretärinnen im Büro gemacht!
>
> Ich habe hundert Pfund pro Woche verdient. Das war phantastisch, weil ich für meinen Urlaub gespart habe.
>
> Einmal mußte ich staubsaugen, und das habe ich nicht gern gemacht. Die Sekretärinnen haben mir gut gefallen, weil sie sehr freundlich waren.
>
> Schreib bald wieder,
>
> Dein Michael

Examiner's comment

All the tasks are done. Good vocabulary is used including some things from the question adapted for use in the answer. There are opinions and simple reasons and also some complicated sentences with 'weil' and the correct word order.

TESTS WITH STUDENT ANSWERS

Here you will find further examples of tests for the Foundation Tier, which have been done by a candidate. An examiner has marked them and added comments.

Test 1

Du bist auf Urlaub. Du schreibst eine Postkarte an deinen deutschen Freund/deine deutsche Freundin. Schreibe ungefähr 30 Wörter.

Wo?
Wetter?
Was machst du tagsüber?
Was machst du abends?

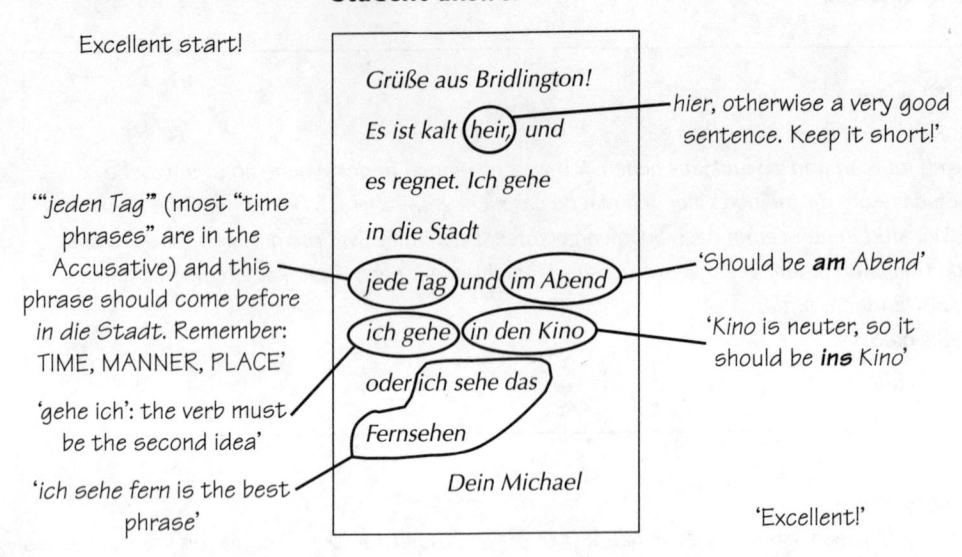

Chapter 11 Writing: Foundation Tier

Student answer

> Grüße aus Bridlington!
> Es ist kalt (*heir*), und es regnet. Ich gehe in die Stadt (*jede Tag*) und (*im Abend*) *ich gehe* (*in den Kino*) oder *ich sehe das Fernsehen*
> Dein Michael

- Excellent start!
- '*hier*, otherwise a very good sentence. Keep it short!'
- '"jeden Tag" (most "time phrases" are in the Accusative) and this phrase should come before *in die Stadt*. Remember: TIME, MANNER, PLACE'
- 'Should be **am** Abend'
- '*gehe ich*: the verb must be the second idea'
- 'Kino is neuter, so it should be **ins** Kino'
- '*ich sehe fern* is the best phrase'
- 'Excellent!'

'As you see, quite a few small mistakes, but you have answered all the points required, have made yourself totally clear, and have a very good start and end to the card. This would be given a high mark. Well done!'

▶ **Test 2** Du bist bei deiner deutschen Brieffreundin. Du willst ein Picknick machen. Schreibe eine Einkaufsliste. Du brauchst **zehn** Sachen.

Student answer

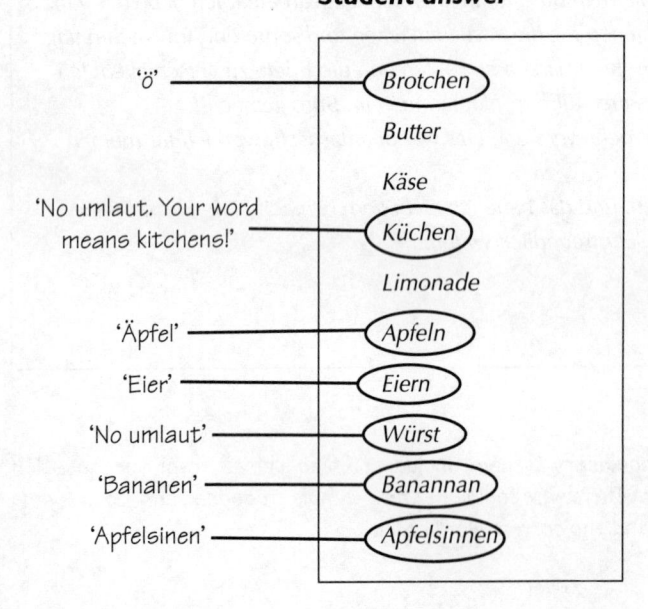

> Brotchen
> Butter
> Käse
> Küchen
> Limonade
> Apfeln
> Eiern
> Würst
> Banannan
> Apfelsinnen

- 'ö'
- 'No umlaut. Your word means kitchens!'
- 'Äpfel'
- 'Eier'
- 'No umlaut'
- 'Bananen'
- 'Apfelsinen'

'An excellent list of which a dietician would approve! It would provide a well-balanced meal!'

'As you can see, some spelling mistakes in common words (often umlauts) but the meaning is totally clear.'

▶ **Test 3** Schreiben Sie einen Brief an einen deutschen Brieffreund/eine deutsche Brieffreundin.

Schreiben Sie ungefähr 60 Wörter.

Beschreiben Sie: Ihre Hobbys
einen typischen Abend
ein typisches Wochenende.

Fragen Sie: nach seinen/ihren Wochenenden.

Student answer

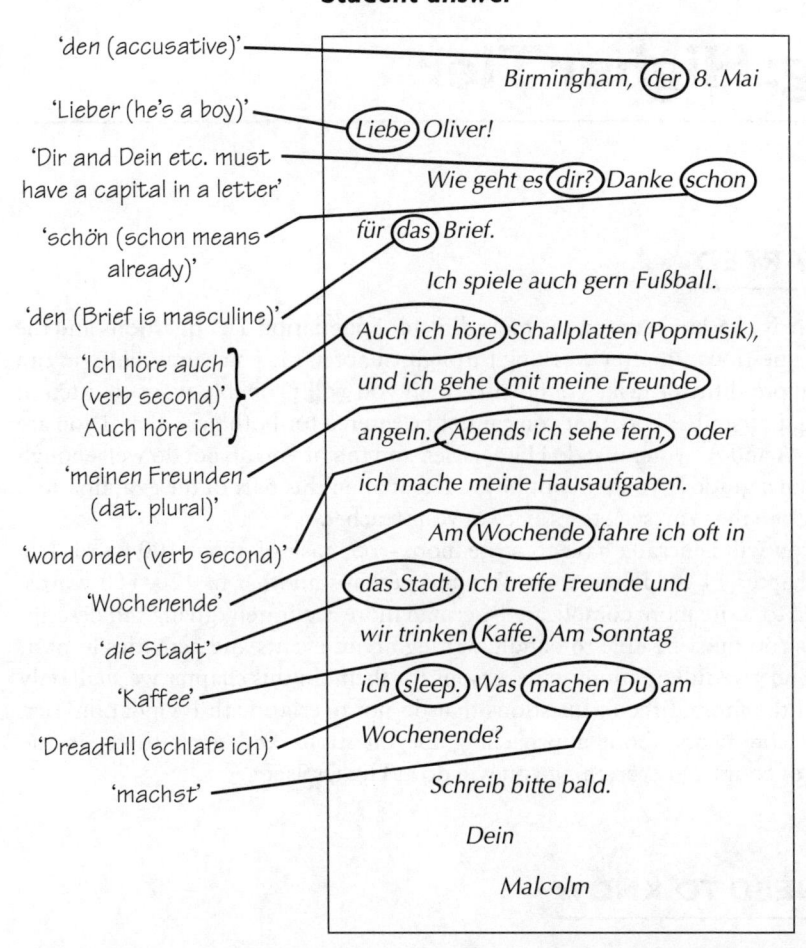

Birmingham, (der) 8. Mai

(Liebe) Oliver!

Wie geht es (dir?) Danke (schon) für (das) Brief.

Ich spiele auch gern Fußball.

(Auch ich höre) Schallplatten (Popmusik), und ich gehe (mit meine Freunde) angeln. (Abends ich sehe fern,) oder ich mache meine Hausaufgaben.

Am (Wochende) fahre ich oft in (das Stadt.) Ich treffe Freunde und wir trinken (Kaffe.) Am Sonntag ich (sleep.) Was (machen Du) am Wochenende?

Schreib bitte bald.

Dein

Malcolm

Annotations (left margin):
- 'den (accusative)'
- 'Lieber (he's a boy)'
- 'Dir and Dein etc. must have a capital in a letter'
- 'schön (schon means already)'
- 'den (Brief is masculine)'
- 'Ich höre auch (verb second)' / Auch höre ich
- 'meinen Freunden (dat. plural)'
- 'word order (verb second)'
- 'Wochenende'
- 'die Stadt'
- 'Kaffee'
- 'Dreadful! (schlafe ich)'
- 'machst'

'Although at first sight there appear to be a lot of mistakes in this letter, there is also much to commend.
(a) Communication is fine. Everything is easily understood.
(b) The letter is well set out. The beginning and the end are good although there are errors.
(c) There are some good phrases, e.g. Wie geht es Dir?, Ich spiele auch gern Fußball, Ich höre Schallplatten, Ich mache meine Hausaufgaben, Ich treffe Freunde, abends, am Sonntag.

'However, there are errors which could have been avoided:
(a) three spelling mistakes: schon, Wochende (spelt correctly later on!) and Kaffe.
(b) ich sleep is unforgivable and creates a very poor impression. If you cannot remember the correct word, think of something else to say. You did not have to say anything about sleeping. This is an unforced error!
(c) There are errors of word order, case endings, gender and verb endings. Clearly these areas need revision.'

'In general terms this is a good piece of work at Foundation Tier, but would be inadequate for a high mark at Higher Tier.'

You will find further practical suggestions for improving your written German at the end of the next chapter (see page 190).

Chapter 12

Writing: Higher Tier

GETTING STARTED

Remember that there is overlap between the most difficult Foundation Tier questions and the easiest Higher Tier questions. If, after working through Chapter 11, you think that you can handle the longer, more difficult tasks confidently, then you will probably want to attempt Higher Tier Writing. Remember, too, that you cannot be entered for both tiers, that if you are aiming for grades B, A and A* you must do Higher Tier, and that if you do not do well enough at Higher Tier to gain a grade D you will not be graded at all in this part of the examination. It is important therefore that you seek the advice of your teacher.

At Higher Tier you will generally have to write more – one task of about 100 words like those covered in Chapter 11 for Foundation Tier and perhaps another of 120–150 words. You will be expected to write more complicated German more accurately, giving full descriptions and accounts. You must be able to handle writing about events and activities in past, present and future and give full opinions with reasons for them. In this chapter we shall only look at examples of the more difficult questions that do not overlap with Foundation Tier, though the general comments about approaching the questions and what to do in the examination apply, of course, to everything you will do at Higher Tier.

WHAT YOU NEED TO KNOW

Find out exactly what your examining group requires.

- How much time is allowed?
- How many words are you expected to write?
- What kind of writing are you expected to produce?
- How many pieces will you have to write?
- Is there a choice?
- What questions are you best at if there is a choice?

The following is a basic indication of what each group stipulates for Higher Tier **including the overlap question with Foundation Tier** (examples in Chapter 11). It should help answer some of the above questions. Examining groups usually say that the number of words is a guide only and that the exact number you write is irrelevant **provided that all the tasks are done.**

MEG One task of approx. 100 words (overlap question) from a choice of two.
+
One task of approx. 150 words from a choice of two.

NEAB One task of approx. 90 words (overlap question). No choice.
+
One task of approx. 120 words. No choice.

NICCEA One task (overlap question, perhaps a letter). No choice.
+
One task (longer letter, report or account). No choice.

SEG (Module 4 end of course examination)

One task of approx. 120 words (letter, article or report). No choice.

London

One task of approx. 70 words (overlap question). No choice.
+
One task of approx. 150 words from a choice of two.

WJEC

One task (overlap question, perhaps a letter) from a choice of two.
+
One task of approx. 120 words (letter, account, picture essay) from a choice of three.

Times allowed are given in Table 1.1 in Chapter 1. If you are in any doubt at all about what to expect, check with your teacher or the examining group.

Mark schemes/criteria for assessment

At Higher Level the examination groups seek to reward answers by marking positively across three main areas. In some cases the emphasis is slightly different, and the three areas listed below are sometimes merged to form just two areas. Find out exactly what your examining group is doing! The three main areas are:

1 Communication
2 Accuracy
3 Quality of expression

It is worth considering these aspects in more detail.

1 Communication

This refers to the extent to which the relevant information is conveyed to the reader. Do you cover all the tasks and make yourself understood?

2 Accuracy

This refers to the extent to which grammatical accuracy helps to convey the relevant information. Do you just manage to get the message across, or are you able to get the message across clearly in largely correct German?

3 Quality of expression

This refers to the extent to which the language you use helps to make your writing interesting and appropriate to the task. Do you use a variety of vocabulary, idioms, tenses, grammatical structures? Does your writing show coherence as a whole?

Approaching the examination

- Check the topic areas to be tested in Higher Tier writing.
- Learn the vocabulary and structures required.
- Study as many specimen papers and past examination papers as possible.
- Devise a checklist which suits you, to help you to check your work for accuracy/mistakes before and during the examination.
- Write as many practice essays/letters as you can before the examination. Work to the times allowed in the examination and use your checklist.

Devising a checklist

It is important that the **checklist** you adopt is simple but thorough, and also suits you. Outlined below is an example checklist for you to consider.

1 Have you answered the question including all the relevant information?
2 Have you kept within the word limits?
3 Have you checked your work for accuracy?

Verbs

- Do subjects and verbs agree in number?
  der Mann kam ✓   *der Mann kamen* ✗
- Have you chosen the right form of the verb?
  die Frau sagte ✓   *die Frau sagtest* ✗
- Have you chosen the right auxiliary verb (*haben* or *sein*) with the perfect and pluperfect tense?
  ich bin nach Bonn gefahren ✓   *ich habe nach Bonn gefahren* ✗
- Have you chosen the right tense?
  als ich in die Schule ging ✓   *als ich in die Schule gehe* ✗

Genders

- Do articles agree with the nouns in number and gender? (It is surprising how often very common words are used with the wrong gender.)
  die Bücher ✓   *das Bücher* ✗
  das Mädchen ✓   *die Mädchen* (in the singular) ✗
- Do pronouns agree with the nouns they replace in number and gender?
  der Mann – er
  die Frau – sie
  das Buch – es

Adjectives

- Do adjectives have the right endings?

Cases

- Are all subjects in the nominative case?
- Are all direct objects in the accusative case?
- Are all indirect objects in the dative case?
- Have you chosen the right case after prepositions?
  Remember there are four main groups of prepositions:
  – those followed by the accusative
  – those always followed by the dative
  – those followed by the accusative *or* dative:
    'motion towards' + accusative
    'no motion towards/position' + dative
  – those always followed by the genitive.

Word Order

Have you chosen the correct word order?

- Adverbs: Time/Manner/Place (TMP)
- Nouns: Subject/Verb/Indirect Object/Direct Object
- Pronouns: Direct Object/Indirect Object
  Pronouns always come before nouns
- Inversion of verb + subject, e.g. after *dann, plötzlich*
- Verbs at end of subordinate and relative clauses, e.g. *das Wohnzimmer, wo wir jeden Abend sitzen, . . .*
- Past participles at end of clause, e.g. *Ich habe die Zeitung noch nicht gelesen.*
- Position of infinitives, e.g. *Er muß morgen früh zur Arbeit gehen.*

Spellings

- Do your nouns begin with a capital letter?
- Have you used correct plural forms?
- Have you used umlauts where necessary?
- Have you used ß where necessary?

For more information see Chapter 14, which deals with grammar.

> **In the examination**

It is helpful to have a plan of action for the things to do once you have been told that you may start the examination. Your teacher will certainly have discussed the importance of this, but here again are some useful reminders and suggestions that are worth considering.

1. Make a quick note of any memory aids or checklists you may wish to refer to. These may be in the form of mnemonics, e.g. VZ BANS GAME (initial letters of prepositions always followed by the dative case), or tables, e.g.
   Nom. *der/die/das*
   Acc. *den/die/das*
   Gen. *des/der/des*
   Dat. *dem/der/dem*
2. Read the instructions on the question paper carefully, and make a sensible choice (where appropriate) from the questions available.
3. Plan what you are going to write before you launch into the answer proper. Make a note of key vocabulary and expressions to be included.
4. Allow enough time for each question.
5. Allow enough time to re-read and check your work.
6. Write clearly and legibly. A well-presented script creates a favourable impression on examiners and is easier for them to mark.
7. Make sure that what you write is relevant to the question. Reproducing material learnt by heart, however correct, will lose you marks if it is not relevant to the question.
8. Only use German that you know. Don't plan an answer in English and then try to translate it into German. That's a recipe for disaster! Draw on the vocabulary, idioms, phrases and constructions that you are familiar with. On the other hand, it is important to 'show off' what you do know. The examiner can only award marks for what you have written, so make sure you reveal as full a range of your knowledge as you possibly can, i.e. a range of vocabulary, idiom, construction etc.
9. Check that you have answered all aspects of the question.
10. Check that you have kept within the word limits.
11. Last but by no means least: *check your work carefully for accuracy* – use your checklist (see Chapter 15)!

▶ EXAMINATION QUESTIONS

Here we provide a variety of examples of the most difficult tests for Higher Tier writing. Remember that there is overlap between the tiers and that the easier questions for Higher Tier are also the most difficult for Foundation Tier. Examples of these will be found in Chapter 11. A star against the number of the item indicates that a corrected version of a candidate's answer has been provided at the end of the tests in the section 'Outline answers'. But attempt the questions yourself first!

Writing letters

Letter-writing is a possibility for the more difficult questions at Higher Tier. You may have to write an informal letter to a pen friend, for example, or a formal one, perhaps to a hotel, information office or prospective employer.

Whatever you have to write it is important to make sure that you include all the information required. The first step is, therefore, to establish just what tasks or areas you have to cover. Consider the following examples, and try to work out what you need to include in your letter before reading the suggestions at the end of this section.

> **Example 1**

Eine deutsche Freundin/ein deutscher Freund von dir hat im Moment Probleme mit ihren/seinen Eltern. Du schreibst an sie/ihn einen Brief darüber. Du sollst etwa 120 Wörter schreiben. Vergiß nicht folgende Punkte!

Sage: wie du über die Probleme deiner Freundin/deines Freunds denkst und warum?

Erkläre: ob du Probleme mit deinen Eltern hast.
wenn ja, warum?
wenn nein, warum nicht?
Beschreibe: was deine Freundin/dein Freund machen könnte, deiner Meinung nach.
Versuche: deine Freundin/deinen Freund zu überzeugen, daß die Probleme vielleicht nicht so schlimm sind.

▷ **Example 2** You have recently returned from a holiday in Austria with your family. Your parents are furious about the hotel and the problems you had there. They give you the hotel's business card and ask you to write a letter of complaint to the manager.

HOTEL FRIEDENHOF

Altgasse 8, Klagenfurt.

Herr Norbert Strauß wünscht Ihnen einen angenehmen Aufenthalt.

Ruhig in der Stadtmitte gelegen

Don't forget to:

▶ say why you are writing.
▶ describe the problems.
▶ say what you think about them and why.
▶ tell the manager what you require.
▶ explain what you will do if not satisfied.

Some letter writing tasks may be very open and allow you greater scope to do your own thing! Always look for ways of making your work better by being imaginative. This letter provides a loose framework with plenty of possibilities for a lively response.

▷ **Example 3*** Du bist bei der Familie deines deutschen Austauschpartners/deiner deutschen Austauschpartnerin in Deutschland. Du verbringst einen Tag mit der Mutter deines Partners/deiner Partnerin an ihrem Arbeitsplatz. Du schreibst einen Brief darüber an einen deutschen Freund/eine deutsche Freundin. Schreibe ungefähr 100 Wörter.

Beschreibe: den Arbeitsplatz.
die Leute am Arbeitsplatz.
die Arbeit, die du gemacht hast.
Sage: deine Meinung dazu.
Erkläre: die Vorteile/Nachteile des Tages.

▷ **Example 4** You have received this letter on the Internet. Reply to Bodo **in German**.

```
Hello!

I am called Bodo. My English teacher has given me your
e-mail address and so I think it is good if we can
```
(continued)

(continued)

```
write each other. I want to practise my English and
maybe you can write me in German.
      I am going to a grammar school in Würzburg.
There are about 800 pupils at the school and I think
there are about fifty teachers. Can you tell me of your
school? What sort of school is it? My school is very
old but we are enjoying lots of facilities. For
example we have a language laboratory and for my
favourite subjects, sciences, we have new
laboratories. I think this is very important if we
want to do well. I do not know much of schools in your
country. Can you tell me if you have good
opportunities? We have to go to school on Saturday
morning but only every two weeks. I have no school
after 2 o'clock in the afternoon. Do you have to spend
all day in school? I think that is better, what do you
think? I am interested to learn everything you tell me
about your school. In your letter you can ask me more
about my school. It will be my turn to answer your
questions.

Best wishes from your new friend,
                                        Bodo
```

▶ **Example 5** This example is not as open. You must read the extract and instructions carefully in order to find out exactly what to do.

Sie lesen diesen Text in einem deutschen Magazin:

> Tabak ist gesundheitsschädlich!
> Alkohol ist gesundheitsschädlich!
> Pommes frites sind gesundheitsschädlich!
> Rindfleisch ist gesundheitsschädlich!
> Sonnenschein ist gesundheitsschädlich!
> Sogar Fernsehen ist gesundheitsschädlich!
>
> Alles was man genießen kann, ist schlecht für die Gesundheit.
>
> Stimmen Sie damit überein?
> Schreiben Sie an die Redaktion!

Sie schreiben an die Redaktion des Magazins:
Schreiben Sie ungefähr 150 Wörter.

Beschreiben Sie: was Sie täglich essen und trinken.
Sagen Sie: ob Sie es für gesund halten. Warum (nicht)?
　　　　　　　ob Sie mit dem Text in dem Magazin übereinstimmen.
Erklären Sie: ob Sie etwas anders machen würden, um gesünder zu sein. Was? Warum? Wenn nicht, warum nicht?

Reports, narratives and accounts

You will almost certainly have to do at least one piece of writing (maybe two) at Higher Tier in the form of a report, narrative (story) or account. In effect any of the previous five examples could have been presented in this form rather than as a letter, and answered as a report or article rather than in letter form. The types of thing you will have to write about will generally be similar in an account or report, but the presentation of the question and the form of the answer will be slightly different. There may be instructions in German or English or a visual or written stimulus of some kind. As with letter-writing, however, you must make sure that you include all the necessary details and that your answer is a genuine response to the question.

▷ **Example 6*** Du hast zwei Wochen bei einer Familie in Deutschland verbracht. Dein Freund Jürgen will, daß du für seine Schülerzeitung etwas darüber schreibst. Du mußt etwa 150 Wörter schreiben. Vergiß nicht folgende Punkte:

▶ Sage, was du alles gemacht hast.
▶ Beschreibe deine Eindrücke von Deutschland.

▷ **Example 7** Ergänzen Sie den folgenden Brief an eine deutsche Freundin/einen deutschen Freund:

> Liebe Katharina,
> Als ich am letzten Mittwoch von der Schule zurückkam, habe ich einen furchtbaren Unfall gesehen....

Beschreiben Sie: was passiert ist.

die Verunglückten.

die Konsequenzen.

was Sie gemacht haben.

wie Sie sich gefühlt haben.

▷ **Example 8** Die Sprachschule 'Macmillan School' will Studenten aus Deutschland dafür gewinnen, Englisch in Großbritannien zu lernen.

Schreiben Sie den Text einer Broschüre für die Sprachschule 'Macmillan School' in der Nähe von Ihnen. Schreiben Sie etwa 150 Wörter. Vergessen Sie nicht folgende Punkte:

- Für wen ist die 'Macmillan School' gut?
- Vorteile, in Großbritannien zu studieren.
- Die beste Jahreszeit und warum?
- Aufenthalt in Familien. Eine gute Sache? Warum?
- Was gibt es in der Region für Deutsche?
- Freizeitmöglichkeiten.
- Wie kann man von Deutschland aus anreisen?

▷ **Example 9** Schreibe einen Bericht über eine Reise nach Deutschland.

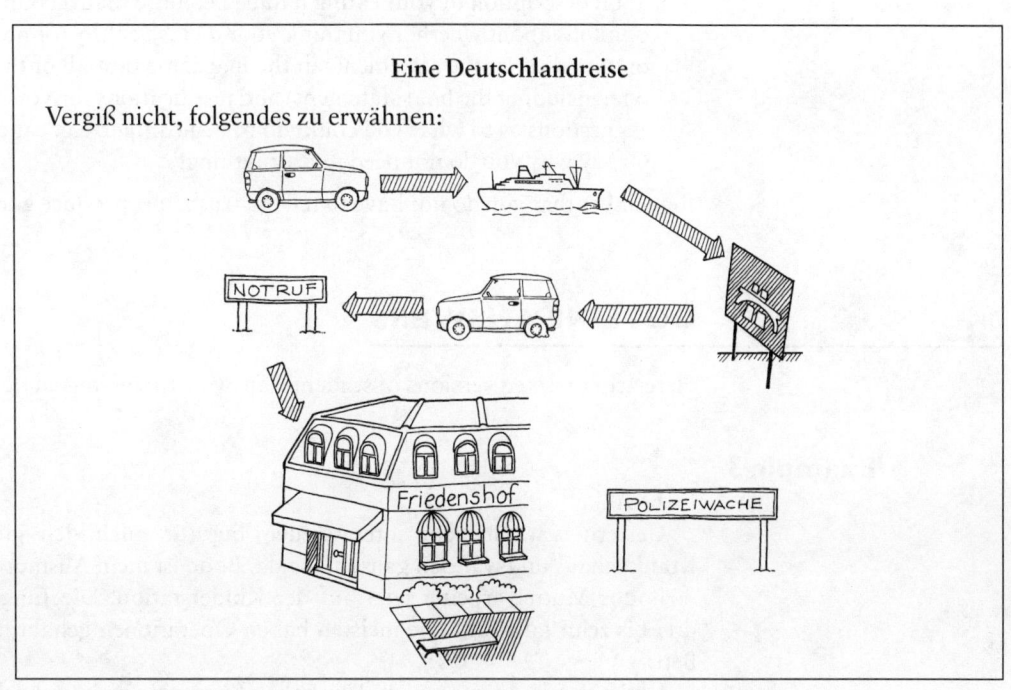

Eine Deutschlandreise

Vergiß nicht, folgendes zu erwähnen:

▷ **Example 10** Sie haben zu Hause eine Party gefeiert. Beschreiben Sie, was passiert ist.

HINTS FOR EXAMPLES 1–5

▷ **Example 1** Here you would need to include the following:

- Think of a suitable beginning and ending. The instruction to write a letter is in the introduction, not in the list of points not to forget.
- Say how you feel about your friend's problems, e.g. express sympathy and give a reason.
- Explain if you have similar problems or not (you don't have to tell the truth, just say what's easiest in German for you) and say why, e.g. describe the problems or lack of them and give a reason, e.g. a description of your parents' characters.
- Suggest what your friend could do to make things better.
- Be sympathetic! Try to convince your friend that things are not so bad.

Remember to try and use sentences with *weil* to give reasons.

▷ **Example 2**
- Include a formal beginning and ending.
- Say you are writing for your parents and when you were at the hotel etc.
- Describe more than one problem.
- Give feelings, opinions and reasons.
- Ask for some money back or for the hotel to make good in some other way.
- Say you will complain/write to the tourist office in Klagenfurt if you are still not satisfied.

▷ **Example 3**   An example answer is given in the section 'Outline answers'.

▷ **Example 4**   Here you could:
- thank Bodo for his letter
- give a full and detailed description of your school, including type, routine, facilities etc.
- give opinions of your school and justify them
- make some comparisons between your school/English schools and what you know/Bodo tells you of German schools (e.g. uniform)
- say what you think about Bodo's school from what he tells you
- ask Bodo as much about his school/German schools as you can.

▷ **Example 5**   You need to include:
- a full description of your eating habits, i.e. more than a couple of sentences
- opinions about whether you think your diet is healthy (or not) and reasons
- opinions about the statements in the magazine (not all of them, but certainly more than one, including the final statement) and justifications for your opinions
- suggestions as to what you could do to be healthier, e.g. eat differently, give up smoking. Or say why you do not need to do anything!

Remember that you do not have to tell the truth, just produce good German!

▷ OUTLINE ANSWERS

Here are corrected versions of students' answers to the starred questions.

▷ **Example 3**

Krefeld, den 8. April

Liebe Anke!

Gestern war ein sehr interessanter Tag für mich. Ich ging mit Bodos Mutter ins Krankenhaus und war den ganzen Tag da. Bodo ist mein Austauschpartner.

Bodos Mutter arbeitet jetzt auf der Kinderstation. Die Jungen und Mädchen sind von drei bis zehn Jahre alt. Die meisten haben Operationen gehabt, aber sie sind nicht mehr im Bett.

Ich habe mit ihnen gespielt. Wir haben Karten gespielt und gebastelt. Ein Junge plauderte die ganze Zeit, aber ich habe nicht viel verstanden. Er kommt aus der Türkei.

Nach dem Mittagessen haben die Kinder geschlafen, und ich habe mein Buch gelesen. Dann habe ich einen kleinen Spaziergang mit zwei Mädchen gemacht. Sie waren sehr nett.

Am Abend war ich sehr müde. Ich möchte auch Krankenschwester werden, aber die Arbeit ist schwer. Der Tag war eine gute Erfahrung für mich.

Herzliche Grüße,
Deine Ruth

Examiner's comments
At first this question might seem a bit daunting.
But Ruth has successfully managed to avoid difficulties by sticking to the German that she knows, and using it in simple and accurate sentences.

▷ **Example 6**   Hallo! Ich bin David Bennett, und ich komme aus Exeter in Südwestengland. Ich verbringe zwei Wochen hier in Detmold bei Jürgen, meinem Brieffreund.

Es gefällt mir sehr gut hier. Das Wetter ist etwas wärmer als in England, und wir sind fast die ganze Zeit im Freien.

Wir sind einmal zum Hermannsdenkmal gewandert, und das war sehr interessant. Es ist so groß! Und der Wald ist wirklich schön – so ruhig und kühl. Man kann so lange wandern, ohne andere Leute zu sehen. Auf dem Trimm-dich-Pfad haben wir viel Spaß gehabt. Das gibt es nicht so oft bei uns. Ich bin nicht so fit, wie ich dachte!

Das Freibad in der Stadt finde ich auch toll. Das Wasser ist schön warm, und die Wellen sind sehr gut!

Es gefällt mir auch, durch die Stadt zu bummeln. Die Geschäfte in der Fußgängerzone sind erstklassig. Aber wo sind die neuesten Schlager? Ich finde sie nicht.

Schon zweimal haben wir Kaffee und Kuchen gehabt. Das ist fantastisch! Und so viel Schlagsahne! Ich darf aber nicht so viel essen! Sonst schimpft meine Mutter, wenn ich nächste Woche wieder zu Hause bin!

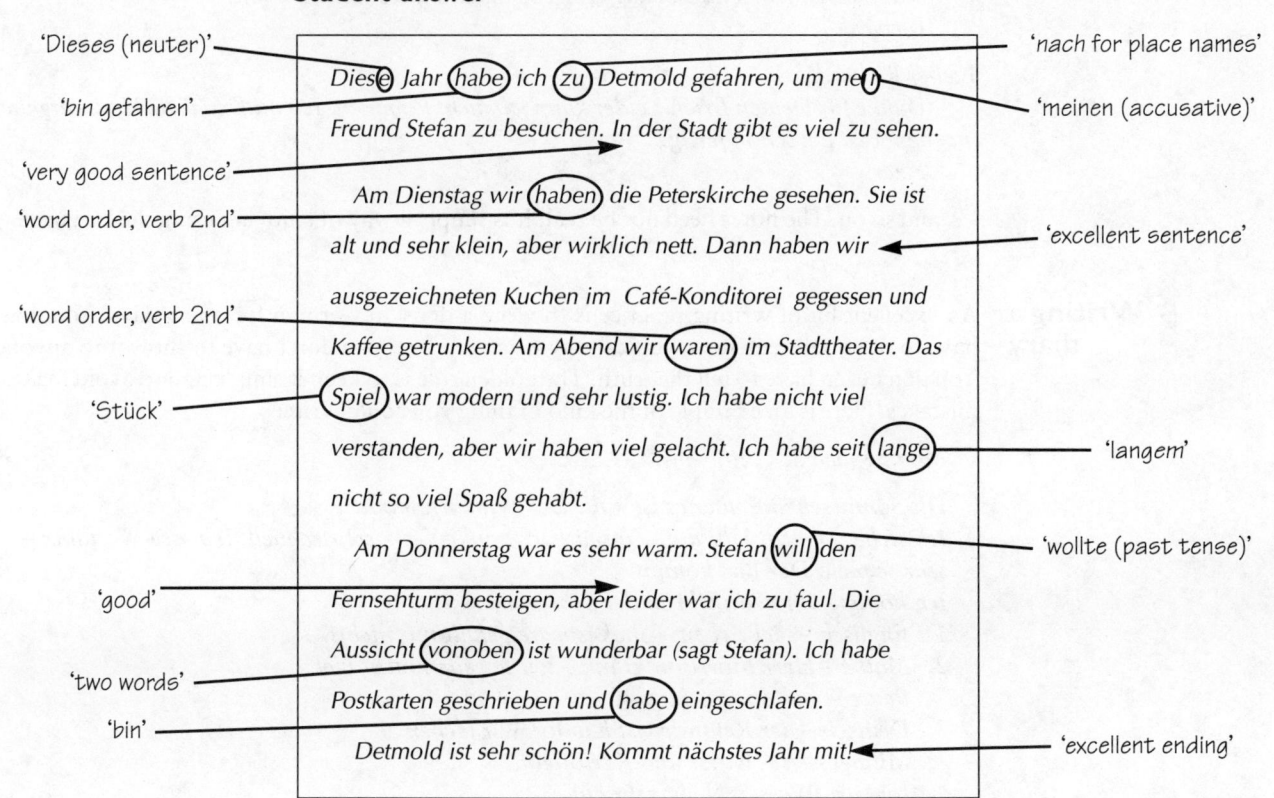

Examiner's comments

The candidate has made a really good job of this. The subject clearly suited him and gave him the opportunity to write about a part of Germany that he has visited. Notice that several of his sentences end with an exclamation mark and some even contain no verb. This gives a lively tone to the writing and is not at all difficult to do. He has also put in a question. This too is an excellent idea.

As with other candidates he too has kept his German simple and sentences short. If you ever get in a tangle with a sentence, split it into two or more. If it is difficult for you to write then it will be difficult for others to read! And that defeats the object of the exercise.

TEST WITH STUDENT ANSWER

Here is a model question for the Higher Tier Writing examination, which has been answered by a student. It has been marked by an examiner, who has added comments.

Du hast sechs Tage bei deiner deutschen Freundin/deinem deutschen Freund verbracht. Du hast Notizen in ein Tagebuch geschrieben und willst jetzt einen Bericht für die Schülerzeitung deiner Freundin/deines Freundes schreiben. Schreibe etwa 120 Wörter. Schaue ins Tagebuch.

Sonntag	Ankunft
Montag	Kirchenbesuch
Dienstag	Kaffee und Kuchen
Mittwoch	Theater
Donnerstag	Fernsehturm
Freitag	Abfahrt

Student answer

Dieses Jahr habe ich zu Detmold gefahren, um mein Freund Stefan zu besuchen. In der Stadt gibt es viel zu sehen.

Am Dienstag wir haben die Peterskirche gesehen. Sie ist alt und sehr klein, aber wirklich nett. Dann haben wir ausgezeichneten Kuchen im Café-Konditorei gegessen und Kaffee getrunken. Am Abend wir waren im Stadttheater. Das Spiel war modern und sehr lustig. Ich habe nicht viel verstanden, aber wir haben viel gelacht. Ich habe seit lange nicht so viel Spaß gehabt.

Am Donnerstag war es sehr warm. Stefan will den Fernsehturm besteigen, aber leider war ich zu faul. Die Aussicht vonoben ist wunderbar (sagt Stefan). Ich habe Postkarten geschrieben und habe eingeschlafen.

Detmold ist sehr schön! Kommt nächstes Jahr mit!

Annotations:
- 'Dieses (neuter)' — Diese[s]
- 'bin gefahren' — habe
- 'very good sentence'
- 'word order, verb 2nd' — Am Dienstag wir haben
- 'word order, verb 2nd' — Am Abend wir waren
- 'Stück' — Spiel
- 'good'
- 'two words' — vonoben
- 'bin' — habe (eingeschlafen)
- 'nach for place names' — zu
- 'meinen (accusative)' — mein
- 'excellent sentence'
- 'langem' — lange
- 'wollte (past tense)' — will
- 'excellent ending'

Examiner's comments

In spite of a number of mistakes this is a reasonable piece of work at Higher Tier. You have clearly studied the question very carefully before writing. You have also included a variety of vocabulary and expressions (as requested) and all your material was relevant (also as requested).

Your main errors were in the fields of word order, verbs with *sein* and case endings. Otherwise your work is fairly accurate and would achieve a creditable mark at Higher Tier.

A STEP FURTHER

Much of the writing work which you will need to do in preparation for the exam will be done in class and homework time and much of it will be marked and corrected by your teacher. But his or her time is limited, so it is worthwhile considering a number of ways in which you can help yourself to improve your writing skills.

Accuracy

First of all take care that everything you write in German is spelt correctly, no matter how rough the work may be. Remember, accuracy includes all the umlauts and capital letters. (Remember, too, that punctuation is more important in German than in English, and that there are strict rules which you should keep to.) Mistakes in **spoken** German are not so serious, but mistakes in the written part of the paper can count against you, particularly if you are hoping for a high grade.

Letter-writing

In your vocabulary book or in your note book collect together all the phrases you can find which can be used in a variety of different letters. Beginnings and endings are particularly important. Look carefully at any letters which you may receive from a pen friend or which you come across in books, and learn their beginnings and endings and use them in your own work.

Notes

If you have a like-minded friend, then try exchanging notes with him or her in German. For example:

Lieber Peter!
  Was machst Du heute abend? Ich gehe ins Kino. Kommst Du mit?
  Richard

Lieber Richard!
  Danke für Deinen Brief. Leider kann ich nicht kommen. Ich muß zu viele Hausaufgaben machen. Bist Du schon fertig?
  Peter

. . . and so on. The notes need not be real. It is simply a way of enjoying using the language.

Writing a diary

An excellent bit of writing practice is to write a diary in German for a few days. You don't have to write full sentences, you can say what you like, you don't have to show it to anyone. You don't even have to tell the truth. The golden rule is to keep it simple and to avoid making mistakes. Here is an example of the kind of thing you could write:

Montag, den 3. Oktober

Die Sonne scheint, aber es ist kalt. Der Winter kommt!
Ich stehe um acht Uhr auf. Zu spät! Ich trinke Tee – sehr schnell. Ich esse Weetabix – sehr schnell. Der Bus kommt.
Ich komme um neun Uhr in der Schule an.
1 *Englisch – viel Arbeit – Shakespeare gefällt mir nicht!*
2 *Mathe – Herr Morrison krank – wir arbeiten nicht viel.*
  Pause – gut, aber es regnet.
3 *Deutsch – der Rekorder ist kaputt! Wir lachen.*
  Mittagessen – Wurst und Kartoffeln.
  Joghurt. Wasser. Nicht sehr gut.

4 Erdkunde – langweilig.
5 Sport – es regnet nicht mehr. Fußball – sehr gut, aber ich bin schmutzig!
Ich gehe um halb fünf nach Hause. Eine Tasse Tee. Wie sagt man 'biscuits' auf Deutsch?!
Hausaufgaben (Englisch und Deutsch)
Fernsehen – Fußball – England gegen Holland. England gewinnt 2–0!!
Ich lese und gehe ins Bett. Gute Nacht!

There! That is all very easy German, isn't it, and just the sort of thing you could do yourself.

▶ **Double translation**

This is a somewhat intellectual exercise which may appeal to those of you who are tackling Higher Tier in writing.

Take a paragraph of four or five lines of fairly straightforward German from your course book or from a similar source. Translate it into English, close the book and then translate it back into German again. Check with the original. How did you get on? If you are not satisfied, do it again, at least in part.

Chapter 13

Writing: Coursework

▷ GETTING STARTED

If you are studying for the SEG Modular GCSE you will have to do written coursework in Module 3 of the course. If you are doing the MEG, NEAB, London or WJEC GCSE you can opt to do written coursework instead of the final writing examination. For London, however, you cannot opt for both spoken and written coursework. You will have to choose one option. Your being allowed to do coursework will also depend on whether your school or college is prepared to enter you for coursework. If you are an external candidate, that is if you are entering yourself for the GCSE and just going along to a convenient examination centre to sit the exams, you cannot do coursework. This chapter is intended as a general oversight of what coursework involves. To gain practice in the specific writing skills required you should work through Chapters 11 and 12 as appropriate, since the tasks you will do as coursework will be broadly similar to answers required for examination questions.

▷ WHAT YOU NEED TO KNOW

▷ **Requirements** The requirements of the different examining groups regarding the submission of written coursework are all broadly similar, since they all have to comply with the same regulations. In general you will have to be assessed on three pieces of written work, though you may decide to do more pieces of work than this and submit the best three to count towards your grade. If you are doing the SEG Modular GCSE you will have to submit only two pieces of coursework, done during Module 3 of the course. You also have to do one written task in the SEG final examination, so in effect you will be assessed on three pieces like all the other candidates from other examining groups.

The work can be done at any time during the two-year GCSE course, though the standard for marking is the same whenever you do it. That is to say that you will not be treated more leniently at the start of the course than at the end. Usually the pieces of work counting towards your final grades must be sent to the relevant examining group by the end of April or beginning of May in the year that you sit the rest of the examination. For SEG this may be earlier, perhaps in December, as Module 3 would usually be done in the autumn term of the second year of the course. To achieve grade C you should be able to write about events in the past, present and future and express straightforward opinions. Tasks will be set and marked by your teacher, perhaps from a bank of suggestions from the examining group. For the most part they will be similar to the Foundation and Higher Tier examination questions found in Chapters 11 and 12.

The following paragraphs look in more detail at the requirements of the four examining groups offering a written coursework option.

MEG

You will be assessed on the marks of three pieces of work, one of which must have been done under controlled conditions. In effect this means in class under examination conditions. The pieces must be based on work from a range of National Curriculum Areas of Experience. The length of each piece will vary according to the task and the grade you are aiming at. For grades G, F, and E, for example, pieces of about 40 words would be appropriate, for D and C pieces of 100 words, and for B, A and A* pieces of 150 words.

NEAB

Three pieces of work will be assessed and count towards your grade. You and your teacher will choose the tasks from a bank of suitable tasks supplied by NEAB. Each piece must be based on a different National Curriculum Area of Experience. The three pieces must be sent to NEAB by 30 April in the year you sit the rest of the examination. At Foundation Tier the total number of words for all three pieces of work must be 200–300. At Higher Tier the total for the three must be 300–500.

SEG

You will have to submit two pieces of work from Module 3, Holidays and Travel. A variety of assessment tasks is sent to schools by SEG. Your teacher will give you appropriate tasks to do. At Foundation Tier you must produce one piece of work of about 30 words (e.g. a postcard, message or completed form), and one piece of 100–120 words (e.g. a formal or informal letter). At Higher Tier you have to submit two pieces each of 100–120 words (e.g. formal or informal letters, reports, articles). All the tasks will be based on the module's theme of Holidays and Travel.

London

You will be assessed on three units of work covering three different National Curriculum Areas of Experience, one of which must be Area D (The World of Work) or Area E (The International World). Each unit of work may be made up of one or more individual pieces. Candidates aiming at grades G to D will need to have done 250–350 words in total, and those aiming at grades C to A* 500–600 in total. At least one third of the work must be completed under controlled conditions, that is one complete unit of work or a third of the total amount.

WJEC

You will do five pieces of coursework under controlled conditions and a selection from them will be made by your teacher and sent to the examining group. Usually three pieces will be selected representing the top, middle and bottom marks out of the five pieces. The coursework tasks are set by WJEC and sent to schools. You are not allowed to see them before you do them, but your teacher will have given you plenty of opportunities to practise similar tasks. The tasks must cover a range of National Curriculum Areas of Experience.

▶ Types of coursework task

You may be given coursework tasks to do by your teacher, who will have checked that they are suitable and will result in the best possible end result for you. One advantage of coursework, however, is that you can discuss with your teacher what pieces of work you would like to do. As long as the pieces you end up with for assessment and submission to the board cover the required Areas of Experience and are suitable in length and content, this is fine. In practice the sorts of task you do probably will not be very different from the tests from the Foundation and Higher Tier final examination papers, examples of which we have seen in Chapters 11 and 12. Since, however, you or your teacher have more control over the task set, there is more scope for originality and for you to do something more personal.

Below are some examples of the type of task that would be suitable for candidates aiming at certain grades. The examples are intended to be representative of the kind of tasks which could be done regardless of the examining group you are studying for. The list is not exhaustive, however, and there are always other possibilities.

Foundation Tier grades G, F, E

- Design an advertising poster for a product or service.
- Write a diary of a week's activities at school or perhaps on holiday.
- Fill in a form, e.g. hotel booking form.
- Fill in a job application form or make a curriculum vitae using an example as a model.
- Perhaps using a brochure as a source, write a short letter asking for tourist (or other) information about a country where German is spoken.

Foundation/Higher Tier grades D and C

- Write a description of local attractions, facilities etc. for an exchange school.

- Write a letter asking for information about a holiday job using an advertisement as a stimulus.
- Write a diary of leisure and free time activities.
- Write a short article about a celebrity, perhaps based on notes taken from an interview read or heard.
- Write a song or poem about school, your home town, a member of your family.

Remember that for grade C and above you should be able to write about past, present and future events and activities and give simple opinions.

Higher Tier grades B, A and A*

- Write a review of a book, film, play, concert, television or radio programme.
- Write an article or letter about an environmental issue giving your point of view and your reasons.
- Write a letter of complaint to a hotel, campsite, holiday company or airline.
- Write an article about your home town including its history and perhaps how you see it developing in the future.
- Write an account of your own work experience, relating how you felt about it and giving advantages and disadvantages.

Remember that for these grades you should be able to write about past, present and future events, give detailed accounts and descriptions using more complex language with greater accuracy as well as give full opinions and reasons for them.

Approaching coursework

Choice of assignments

Sometimes this will be easy, as the choice will be made wholly or partly for you. Your teacher may simply tell you what assignments are to be completed and provide source/stimulus material. NEAB provide a list of coursework assignments for you and your teacher to choose from. In Module 3 of the SEG course materials will have been supplied to the school. However, there will still be some scope for negotiation about what exactly you are going to do. It is important to listen to the advice of your teacher who will be familiar with your capabilities. Do not be overambitious in your choice of assignment, but on the other hand make sure you are doing something suited to the grade you are aiming for and that will stretch you. If you want to use source materials, you will have to consider what is available. Here is a list of some possible sources:

- books about Germany and life in Germany
- German magazine or newspaper articles or advertisements
- radio and television programmes in German
- material such as interviews gathered while on an exchange visit.

Remember that you do not need to have all these things available. They are just ideas. It is also possible to produce excellent coursework pieces with little or no source material. The choice is largely yours, subject to any requirements your teacher may make.

Preparation, supervision and teacher help

For any pieces of coursework done under controlled conditions in class you should follow the advice given for the writing tests in Chapters 11 and 12. Other pieces may be done in class or outside, or indeed in a combination of the two. The following hints may be useful:

- Decide whether you need any source material or not. If you do, make sure it is to hand and check with your teacher that it is suitable.
- Always make sure you have plenty of time. You may need to speak to your teacher about when a particular assignment should be completed. Do not leave everything until the last minute.
- Make some rough notes as a first step and then perhaps select things from your notes that are going to be the most useful.
- Make a plan of your piece of work and show it to your teacher, who may well make useful general advice at this stage.

- Do a first draft and again have your teacher comment. Your teacher will not be allowed to actually correct things but may draw your attention to general points, e.g. check spellings, verb endings. He/she may comment that some part of the content is missing or unbalanced.
- Go away and, bearing in mind any advice, write the final piece to be submitted. Once you have started this your teacher will not be able to give you any further help.

Authenticity

Your teacher must guarantee that the final pieces of work in your coursework folder that are sent to the examining group are entirely your own work. Obviously your teacher will be very familiar with the standard and style of your work, so it will be pointless to try and cheat by giving in work by an older brother or sister, or a German pen-friend or exchange partner. All the examining groups take this extremely seriously and if you are found to have broken any of the rules you will not only lose you German GCSE, but they also reserve the right to disqualify you in all your subjects! This is an eventuality best avoided!

▶ SAMPLE COURSEWORK WITH TEACHER COMMENTS

The following is an example of what might have been shown as first draft of a piece of coursework at Foundation Tier (grades G, F and E). A teacher has made general comments about it to help you before you write the final version for submission to the examining group.

> Birmingham der 8. Mai
>
> *Liebe Oliver!*
>   *Wie geht es dir? Danke schon für das Brief.*
>   *Ich spiele auch gern Fußball. Auch ich höre Schallplatten (Popmusik) und ich gehe mit meine Freunde angeln. Abends ich sehe fern oder mache meine Hausaufgaben.*
>   *Am Wochende fahre ich oft in das Stadt. Ich treffe Freunde und wir trinken Kaffe. Am Sonntag ich sleep. Was machen Du am Wochenende?*
>   *Schreib bitte bald.*
>   *Dein*
>   *Malcolm*

Teacher's comments
- Check spellings.
- Check your verb endings.
- Have you thought about giving some opinions to make the letter more interesting?
- Perhaps you could make it a bit longer by including something about last weekend.

Chapter 14

Grammar

▶ GETTING STARTED

It is generally accepted that real competence in a foreign language depends on an understanding of grammar. This does not apply to our own language, where we depend more on our long experience of the language to determine the correctness of what we say and write. Some students of German at GCSE level may have lived in Germany or may have had extensive experience of the language to give them a real feeling for the sound of German. But for most of us there is no easy short cut.

Do not forget that a language grows by itself and is constantly changing. The 'rules' have been thought up to make some sort of sense out of an already established language. Much of the grammar in this chapter will be familiar to you. It is intended as a reference section, but there are areas where you are recommended to learn phrases by heart, and to use them wherever possible in a practical situation.

▶ Nouns and articles

Recognition

One of the most encouraging aspects of learning German is that many German nouns are instantly **recognisable** to English-speaking people. If you knew no German at all you would have no difficulty in understanding *Mann, Haus, Garten, Hand, Finger, Hammer, Familie*. And even *Buch, Schule, Stuhl, Büro, Mantel* would pose few problems.

Cases

However, each German noun has to be learnt with its gender and its plural form, and also in the four separate **case** forms. This sounds a daunting task, but with a little patience and application it should not prove to be too difficult.

Let us look at the familiar tables:

	Masculine	**Feminine**	**Neuter**	**Plural**
Nominative	der Mann	die Frau	das Kind	die Leute
Accusative	den Mann	die Frau	das Kind	die Leute
Genitive	des Mannes	der Frau	des Kindes	der Leute
Dative	dem Mann	der Frau	dem Kind	den Leuten

	Masculine	**Feminine**	**Neuter**	**Plural**
Nominative	ein Mann	eine Frau	ein Kind	keine Leute
Accusative	einen Mann	eine Frau	ein Kind	keine Leute
Genitive	eines Mannes	einer Frau	eines Kindes	keiner Leute
Dative	einem Mann	einer Frau	einem Kind	keinen Leuten

You will see that there are six words for 'the' and five words for 'a'. But the differences between the two tables are confined to *der – ein* and *das – ein*. Otherwise the case endings of the articles are identical in the two tables. This makes it much more manageable.

Patterns

The next point to remember is that the following words follow the **pattern** of *der*:

dieser	*this*	solcher	*such*
jener	*that*	welcher	*which*
jeder	*each*	mancher	*many a*

and these words follow the pattern of *ein*:

kein	*no, not a*		
mein	*my*	unser	*our*
dein	*your*	euer	*your*
sein	*his*	Ihr	*your*
ihr	*her*	ihr	*their*

Gender

There are **some** rules of **gender** but they are only a rough guide and provide no substitute for the grim fact that all genders must be learnt with each noun. Nevertheless these guidelines should help:

Masculine nouns include:

- all seasons, months and days, e.g. *der Frühling, der Mai, der Sonntag*
- all words denoting a male being, e.g. *der Mann, der Bäcker, der Bruder*.

Feminine nouns include:

- all words ending with *-ung, -heit, -ei, -schaft*, e.g. *die Zeitung, die Krankheit, die Bäckerei, die Freundschaft*
- almost all words denoting a female being, e.g. *die Frau, die Lehrerin, die Schwester*
- many words ending with *-e*, e.g. *die Straße, die Vase, die Tasse*.

Neuter nouns include:

- all nouns formed from the infinitive of verbs, e.g. *das Fischen, das Essen*
- most names of countries (but not *die Schweiz* or *die Türkei*)
- all nouns ending with *-chen* and *-lein*, e.g. *das Mädchen, das Fräulein*
- most words of foreign origin, e.g. *das Auto, das Hotel, das Taxi*.

Plurals

Plurals are equally tricky. There are at least nine ways of forming plurals in German and the plural should be learnt with each noun as well as the gender. Experience will show you, however, that some plurals are much more common than others. For instance, *Eier* and *Kartoffeln* are more often found in the plural than in the singular, whereas the plural of *die Welt* is comparatively rare.

Here are a few hints to help you learn the plurals:

- Most nouns ending in *-er* or *-el*, do not change in the plural, or they take an umlaut, e.g. *Brüder, Löffel, Messer, Onkel*.
- Most feminine nouns take *-n* or *-en*, e.g. *Vasen, Frauen, Zeitungen*.
- Most foreign words take *-s*, e.g. *Autos, Taxis, Sofas*.

Weak masculine nouns

These are oddities because they take an *-n* or *-en* in every case except the nominative singular, e.g.

	Singular	**Plural**
Nominative	der Mensch	die Menschen
Accusative	den Menschen	die Menschen
Genitive	des Menschen	der Menschen
Dative	dem Menschen	den Menschen

Some common weak masculine nouns are:

Junge	*boy*	Prinz	*prince*
Löwe	*lion*	Franzose	*Frenchman*
Neffe	*nephew*	Matrose	*sailor*
Schotte	*Scotsman*	Soldat	*soldier*

Bauer	*farmer*	Student	*student*
Russe	*Russian*	Polizist	*policeman*
Kunde	*customer*		

Don't forget *Herr* (sir, Mr, gentleman) which takes *-n* in the singular and *-en* in the plural.

Points to remember

▶ Leave out the article when giving someone's profession, e.g. *Mein Vater ist Polizist* – My father is a policeman.

▶ Leave out the articles when using *weder ... noch ...*, e.g. *Ich habe weder Brot noch Käse* – I have neither bread nor cheese.

▶ Use the definite article in German for expressions using parts of the body or clothes, e.g.
Er wäscht sich die Hände (*not* seine Hände).
Er hob den Kopf (*not* seinen Kopf).
Sie hatte den Koffer in der Hand (*not* ihren Koffer in ihrer Hand).

▶ Certain idiomatic phrases have no article and they should be learnt by heart, e.g.

er hat Fieber *he has a temperature*
ich habe Kopfschmerzen *I have a headache*
es ist schade *it is a pity*
wir haben Besuch *we have visitors*

TEST YOURSELF (1)

(a) Give the genders of these words: *Onkel, Wohnung, Restaurant, Büchlein, Schneider, Engländerin, Laufen, Vater, Bluse, Mutter*
and these trickier ones: *Park, Name, Person, Balkon, Tür, Käse, Butter, Mädchen, Fräulein, Klub.*

(b) Give the plural of these words: *Wagen, Bluse, Ausstellung, Café, Zimmer, Hotel, Traube, Tür, Radio, Kellner*
and these trickier ones: *Kartoffel, Nacht, Nummer, Freundin, Autobus, Schwester.*

(c) Translate into German:
 (i) We have neither a cat nor a dog.
 (ii) Herr Rabowski is a dentist.
 (iii) The cars are not here.
 (iv) I am brushing my teeth.
 (v) She is my sister.
 (vi) Our grandpa is at home.
 (vii) These people are hungry.
 (viii) Which boy can you see?
 (ix) He's got toothache.
 (x) Switzerland is beautiful.

Now look up the answers at the end of this chapter (page 216).

▶ Adjectives

Separation

The easiest way to use an adjective in German is to separate it from the noun it describes, e.g. *Unser Haus ist groß*. In this way the adjective does not have to agree with the noun, and thus all problems are avoided. So if you are not sure of the correct endings in a sentence like *Wir haben ein großes Haus*, you could say *Wir haben ein Haus. Es ist sehr groß*, which avoids the necessity for an agreement.

Agreement

However, there are times when you will have to put the adjective in front of the noun and it is then that you will have to know this table:

	Masculine	Feminine	Neuter
Nominative	der große Baum / ein großer Baum	die große Stadt. / eine große Stadt	das große Haus / ein großes Haus
Accusative	den großen Baum	die große Stadt	das große Haus / ein großes Haus
Genitive	des großen Baumes	der großen Stadt	des großen Hauses
Dative	dem großen Baum	der großen Stadt	dem großen Haus

	Plural
Nominative	die großen Häuser
	meine großen Häuser
Accusative	die großen Häuser
Genitive	der großen Häuser
Dative	den großen Häusern

Assuming that you have already learnt the correct articles and genders, the adjectives should not present a great problem. Let us look at the facts from a different point of view.

▶ After *der*, *die* and *das*, and *eine* the adjective ends in *-e*. (Be careful with the exceptions in the feminine genitive and dative cases, and in the plural.)
▶ After *ein* the adjective ends in *-er* or *-es*.
▶ Otherwise the adjective ends in *-en*.

That surely reduces the problem a little.

Use as noun

You can use an adjective as a noun, e.g.

der Arme   *the poor boy or poor man*
die Alte   *the old woman*
das Beste   *the best thing*
ein Deutscher   *a German (man or boy)*

Gender

Notice that each gender has a characteristic letter:

Masculine = R
Feminine = E
Neuter = S

and this letter should wherever possible be apparent, eg:

der kleine Stuhl	ein kleiner Stuhl
die weiße Bluse	eine weiße Bluse
das kleine Kind	ein kleines Kind

Omission of article

In the same way, if the **article** is omitted, then the **adjective** should show the gender or number of the noun, e.g.

guter Wein
klassische Musik
frisches Obst
schöne Trauben

Points to remember

▶ The characteristic letter (R, E and S) for the genders must only appear once in the masculine and neuter forms. So *der langer Garten* is definitely wrong and so is *das kleines Kind*!
▶ The adjective only agrees if it precedes the noun.
▶ The key letter for each gender can help you decide the gender of a word you do not know. For instance, *ein neues Geschäft* is clearly neuter.

TEST YOURSELF (2)   Translate into German:

(a) the red bus
(b) a red bus
(c) the narrow street
(d) a narrow street
(e) the small village
(f) a small village

(g) the white mountains
(h) white mountains
(i) cold weather
(j) We have a large garden.
(k) the old man
(l) Our cat is stupid.
(m) My poor head!

Comparatives and superlatives

Formation

The comparatives and superlatives of adjectives are formed in much the same way as in shorter English adjectives. Just as 'small' becomes 'smaller' and 'smallest', so *klein* becomes *kleiner* and *kleinst*. Some adjectives take an umlaut.

Adjective	Comparative	Superlative
klein	kleiner	kleinst
jung	jünger	jüngst
alt	älter	ältest
neu	neuer	neuest
modern	moderner	modernst
schön	schöner	schönst
groß	größer	größt

and a few irregulars:

gut	besser	best
nah	näher	nächst
hoch	höher	höchst
viel	mehr	meist

Agreement

Do not forget that a comparative or a superlative must agree with the noun in the familiar way, e.g.

der kleinste Junge *the smallest boy*
mein jüngerer Bruder *my younger brother*
die längste Straße *the longest street*

Examples

Look at the following examples and learn them by heart:

Ich bin größer als du. *I am bigger than you.*
Herr Schneider ist (eben)so alt wie Herr Rabowski. *Herr Schneider is as old as Herr Rabowski.*
Sabine ist nicht so alt wie Richard. *Sabine is not as old as Richard.*
Das Wetter wird immer kälter. *The weather gets colder and colder.*
Je mehr es regnet, desto lieber bleibe ich zu Hause. *The more it rains, the more I prefer staying at home.*

Points to remember

▶ Do not use *mehr* to translate 'more boring'. The German is *langweiliger*.
▶ Do not use *meist* to translate 'most interesting'. The German is *interessantest*.

TEST YOURSELF (3) Translate into German:

(a) my older sister
(b) the longest month
(c) the most boring lesson
(d) She is older than me.
(e) It is not as cold as yesterday.
(f) The nights are becoming shorter and shorter.
(g) the best films
(h) next year
(i) a more modern school
(j) most people

▶ Verbs *Endings*

Most people shudder at the thought of verbs, and in some languages they do present serious problems. But in German, although there is much to learn, verbs are not a major stumbling block.

Every sentence contains a verb, so we must be prepared to use verbs as accurately as possible.

First of all, let us look at a straightforward present tense of a verb:

wohnen *to live*

ich wohne	*I live*	wir wohnen	*we live*
du wohnst	*you live*	ihr wohnt	*you live*
er, sie, es wohnt	*he, she, it lives*	Sie wohnen	*you live*
		sie wohnen	*they live*

These verb endings are the endings for the great majority of German verbs in every tense. Once you have learnt them you should never make mistakes such as *ich wohnen* or *er wohne*.

Types of verbs

German verbs can be divided into four groups:

▶ **weak verbs** like *wohnen* which are regular and which form the majority of German verbs
▶ **strong verbs** which are irregular and which must be learnt
▶ **mixed verbs** which are also irregular and must be learnt
▶ **modal verbs** which consist of six very common irregular verbs.

There is a list of strong and mixed verbs at the end of the section on verbs (see page 206).

Weak verbs

The present tense of *wohnen* has already been given. The **imperfect** (or **simple past**) tense follows much the same pattern:

ich wohnte *I lived, I used to live*	wir wohnten
du wohntest	ihr wohntet
er, sie, es wohnte	Sie wohnten
	sie wohnten

The **perfect tense** uses the present tense of *haben* and the past participle of *wohnen*:

ich habe gewohnt *I lived, I have lived*	wir haben gewohnt
du hast gewohnt	ihr habt gewohnt
er, sie, es hat gewohnt	Sie haben gewohnt
	sie haben gewohnt

All other tenses can now be formed without further difficulty. This will be explained below.

Strong verbs

These verbs are irregular but often follow a common pattern, so they usually pose little problem to learners. Here is an example using **sehen** *to see*.

Present tense

ich sehe *I see, etc.*	wir sehen
du siehst	ihr seht
er, sie, es sieht	Sie sehen
	sie sehen

Imperfect tense

ich sah *I saw, etc.*	wir sahen
du sahst	ihr saht
er, sie, es sah	Sie sahen
	sie sahen

Perfect tense

ich habe gesehen	*I saw, have seen, etc.*	wir haben gesehen
du hast gesehen		ihr habt gesehen
er, sie, es hat gesehen		Sie haben gesehen
		sie haben gesehen

Mixed verbs

These few verbs have characteristics of both weak and strong verbs and are listed in the verb table at the end of this section.

Modal verbs

There are six modal verbs and they are normally used with other verbs. They are:

| dürfen | *to be allowed to* | mögen | *to like to* | sollen | *to be supposed to* |
| können | *to be able to* | müssen | *to have to* | wollen | *to wish/want to* |

The **present tense** of these verbs is irregular as follows:

ich	darf	kann	mag	muß	soll	will
du	darfst	kannst	magst	mußt	sollst	willst
er, sie, es	darf	kann	mag	muß	soll	will
wir	dürfen	können	mögen	müssen	sollen	wollen
ihr	dürft	könnt	mögt	müßt	sollt	wollt
Sie	dürfen	können	mögen	müssen	sollen	wollen
sie	dürfen	können	mögen	müssen	sollen	wollen

The **imperfect tense** of these verbs is:

| ich | durfte | konnte | mochte | mußte | sollte | wollte |

In the **perfect tense** the past participle is rarely used, the infinitive is used instead, e.g.

Ich habe nicht arbeiten können.   *I have not been able to work.*

Now let us look at each tense in more detail.

The tenses

The present tense
This tense, e.g. *ich wohne*, translates 'I live', 'I do live' and 'I am living'. Be careful therefore not to think in English when writing German. If you think in terms of 'I am going to town' as *Ich bin . . .* then you are doomed to disaster. Think of 'I am going' as one idea for which the German is *Ich gehe . . .*

The imperfect tense (simple past)
This tense, e.g. *ich wohnte*, means 'I lived', 'I was living' or 'I used to live'. Here again the German is simpler than the English form. This tense is used extensively in narrative German (story telling) and sometimes in spoken German. However, in speech the perfect tense is more commonly used for describing events in the past.

The perfect tense
This tense, e.g. *ich habe gewohnt*, means 'I lived' or 'I have lived'. For most German verbs the perfect tense is formed with the present tense of *haben*. But some require *sein* instead (e.g. *ich bin gefahren* – I travelled) and these verbs must be learnt from the verb table. Remember that the past participle must go to the end of the sentence or clause, e.g. *Ich <u>habe</u> ein neues Motorrad im Park <u>gesehen</u>.*

The pluperfect tense
This translates 'I had . . .' and uses the **imperfect** tense of *haben* or *sein* with the past participle, e.g.

Ich hatte den Film schon gesehen.   *I had already seen the film.*
Er war zu Hause geblieben.   *He had stayed at home.*

The future tense
This is formed by the present tense of *werden* with the infinitive of the main verb at the end of the sentence, e.g.

Ich werde nächstes Jahr ein Auto kaufen.   *Next year I will buy a car.*

But remember that for events in the immediate future the present tense may be used, just as in English, e.g.

Ich fahre heute nachmittag in die Stadt   *I am going to town this afternoon.*

The conditional tense
This translates 'would' in a sentence such as 'If it wasn't raining I would play tennis'. 'Would' is translated by *würde* (the imperfect subjunctive of *werden*) with the infinitive at the end of the sentence, e.g.

Ich würde Tennis spielen, wenn ...   *I would play tennis if ...*
Was würdest du mit so viel Geld tun?   *What would you do with so much money?*

The passive
You are unlikely to use the passive at this stage but you should be able to recognise it. It is formed with *werden* and the past participle of the main verb. Here are some examples:

Die Tür wird gestrichen   *The door is being painted.*
Er wurde durch einen Tunnel geführt.   *He was led through a tunnel.*
Es wird oft gesagt ...   *It is often said ...*
Das Auto wurde verkauft.   *The car was sold.*

The subjunctive
This also needs to be recognised but does not need to be used at this stage. It is used mainly in reported speech, e.g.

Er sagte, er habe wenig Geld.   *He said he had little money.*
Sie sagt, sie sei krank.   *She says she is ill* (sei *comes from* sein).

It is also used after *als ob* (as if), e.g.

Er lief so schnell, als ob er Angst hätte.   *He ran so fast, as if he were afraid.*

The modal verbs and *haben* and *sein* are often found in the subjunctive. Look at these examples:

Ich könnte nicht schlafen.   *I wouldn't be able to sleep.*
Er müßte nach Hause gehen.   *He would have to go home.*
Ich möchte bitte ...   *I would like ...*
Ich dürfte nicht bleiben.   *I would not be allowed to stay.*
Ich hätte gern ...   *I would like ...*
Das wäre nett.   *That would be nice.*

Points to remember
▶ Some phrases use a different tense in German from English, e.g.

Ich wohne seit zwei Jahren in Hamm.   *I have been living in Hamm for two years.*
Er lernte seit sechs Wochen Deutsch.   *He had been learning German for six weeks.*

▶ Some verbs do not take *ge-* in their past participle:
– those verbs beginning with *be-, ge-, er-, ver-, zer-, emp-, ent-* (*besuchen, gewinnen, erkennen, verlieren, zerbrechen, empfehlen, entscheiden*)
– those verbs ending in *-ieren* (*reparieren*).

▶ Modal verbs rarely use their past participles but use the infinitive instead, e.g.

Ich habe schwer arbeiten müssen.   *I have had to work hard.*

TEST YOURSELF (4)   (a)   Translate into English:
(i) Er stand vor dem Kino.
(ii) Der Zug war schon angekommen.
(iii) Es wird bald regnen.
(iv) Das Buch wurde sehr schnell geschrieben.
(v) Er sagte, er könne nicht arbeiten.

(vi) Ich wäre sehr dankbar.
(vii) Das würde DM 200 kosten.
(viii) Wohin bist du gelaufen?
(ix) Er bekam zwei Briefe.
(x) Er tat, als ob er nichts kaufen wolle.

(b) Translate into German:
(i) He is learning Italian.
(ii) We used to live in Austria.
(iii) I would like some tomatoes, please.
(iv) Have you bought the house?
(v) I had already left.
(vi) Are you reading the paper?
(vii) I would stay at home, if . . .
(viii) They are tired.
(ix) We had already eaten.
(x) What did you find?

Imperatives

Imperatives are used for giving commands. Here are the normal forms for the verb *arbeiten* – to work:

Arbeite! *work!* (du *form*)
Arbeitet! *work!* (ihr *form*)
Arbeiten Sie! *work!* (Sie *form*)
Arbeiten wir! *let us work!* (wir *form*)

You will notice that only the *du* form is different from the present tense. The *-st* is dropped and so frequently is the *-e* in more common verbs. Study the examples of the *du* form:

Gib mir dein Buch! *Give me your book!*
Steh auf! *Stand up! (or: Get up!)*
Komm mal her! *Come here!*
Geh weg! *Go away!*
Putz dir die Zähne! *Brush your teeth!*

Reflexive verbs

Pronoun

These are normal verbs which add a reflexive pronoun, e.g. *sich waschen* – to wash oneself.

Present tense

ich wasche mich	*I get washed (literally: I wash myself)*	wir waschen uns	*we get washed*
du wäschst dich	*you get washed*	ihr wascht euch	*you get washed*
		Sie waschen sich	*you get washed*
er, sie, es wäscht sich	*he, she gets washed*	sie waschen sich	*they get washed*

Points to remember

▶ In the perfect tense reflexive verbs use *haben*.
▶ In certain phrases, e.g. *ich wasche mir die Hände*, the reflexive pronoun becomes **dative**, because it is now the **hands** you are washing. In such cases the only changes are *mich* to *mir* and *dich* to *dir*. The other pronouns remain the same.

Common reflexive verbs
Some common reflexive verbs are:

sich ängstigen	*to become anxious*	sich setzen	*to sit down*
sich beeilen	*to hurry*	sich vorstellen	*to introduce oneself, imagine*
sich erholen	*to recover*		
sich erinnern an	*to remember*	sich bemühen	*to take the trouble*
sich erkälten	*to catch cold*	sich anziehen	*to get dressed*
sich interessieren für	*to be interested in*	sich ausziehen	*to get undressed*
sich rasieren	*to shave*	sich entscheiden	*to decide*
sich umziehen	*to get changed*	sich unterhalten	*to converse*

Separable verbs

Prefix

These verbs have a **prefix** which can be separated from the main part of the verb. Study these examples of the verb *ausgehen* – to go out:

Present tense: Ich gehe jeden Abend aus. *I go out every evening.*
Perfect tense: Ich bin gestern ausgegangen. *I went out yesterday.*
Future tense: Morgen abend werden wir ausgehen. *We will go out tomorrow evening.*
Infinitive with *zu*: Meine Schwester hatte vor, auszugehen. *My sister planned to go out.*

Common separable verbs

These are some of the commonest separable verbs which you should be able to recognise and use:

ausgehen	*to go out*	umsteigen	*to change (trains)*
ankommen	*to arrive*	umziehen	*to move house*
abfahren	*to depart*	sich anziehen	*to dress*
weggehen	*to go away*	sich ausziehen	*to undress*
aufstehen	*to get up*	sich umziehen	*to change (clothes)*
aufwachen	*to wake up*	fernsehen	*to watch TV*
aufhören	*to stop (doing something)*	zurückkommen	*to come back*
teilnehmen	*to take part*	stattfinden	*to take place*
einsteigen	*to get in*	mitteilen	*to inform*
aussteigen	*to get out*	vorhaben	*to have in mind*
anfangen	*to begin*	zuhören	*to listen*

Points to remember

▶ Do not confuse *umziehen* with *sich umziehen*.
▶ When hearing German or reading German watch out for the separable prefix at the end of the sentence. It can totally change the meaning of a sentence.

Impersonal verbs

These verbs or idiomatic phrases can only be used in the *es* form. Here are some examples:

es regnet	*it's raining*	es tut mir weh	*it hurts (me)*
es schneit	*it's snowing*	es gefällt mir	*I like it (it pleases me)*
es friert	*it's freezing*	es fällt mir ein	*it occurs to me*
es blitzt	*there's lightning*	es gelingt mir	*I succeed, I manage*
es donnert	*it's thundering*	es ist mir kalt	*I'm cold*
es tut mir leid	*I'm sorry*	es geht mir gut	*I'm well*

TEST YOURSELF (5) This covers the last few sections. Translate into German:

(a) Go home! (all three forms)
(b) Don't drive so fast! (all three forms)
(c) Wash your hands! (all three forms)
(d) Let's stay at home!
(e) She's getting changed.
(f) He's shaving.
(g) We are chatting.
(h) I get up at seven o'clock.
(i) We watched TV last night.
(j) What have you got in mind today?
(k) How are you?
(l) I don't feel so good.

Table of strong and mixed verbs

This list gives the third person singular (*er*, *sie*, *es* form) of all the common strong and mixed verbs. Candidates aiming for Higher Tier should be able to recognise and use most of these verbs. Foundation Tier candidates should concentrate on those marked with an asterisk.

Infinitive	Meaning	Present	Imperfect	Perfect
backen	to bake	bäckt	backte	hat gebacken
befehlen	to command	befiehlt	befahl	hat befohlen
*beginnen	to begin	beginnt	begann	hat begonnen
beißen	to bite	beißt	biß	hat gebissen
*bekommen	to get, obtain	bekommt	bekam	hat bekommen
biegen	to bend	biegt	bog	hat gebogen
*bieten	to offer	bietet	bot	hat geboten
binden	to bind, tie	bindet	band	hat gebunden
*bitten	to ask, beg	bittet	bat	hat gebeten
blasen	to blow	bläst	blies	hat geblasen
*bleiben	to remain	bleibt	blieb	ist geblieben
*brechen	to break	bricht	brach	hat gebrochen
*brennen	to burn	brennt	brannte	hat gebrannt
*bringen	to bring	bringt	brachte	hat gebracht
*denken	to think	denkt	dachte	hat gedacht
dringen	to pierce, penetrate	dringt	drang	ist gedrungen
*einladen	to invite	lädt ein	lud ein	hat eingeladen
*empfehlen	to recommend	empfiehlt	empfahl	hat empfohlen
erlöschen	to die down, go out (of fire, light)	erlischt	erlosch	ist erloschen
*erschrecken	to be frightened	erschrickt	erschrak	ist erschrocken
*essen	to eat	ißt	aß	hat gegessen
*fahren	to drive, ride	fährt	fuhr	ist gefahren
*fallen	to fall	fällt	fiel	ist gefallen
*fangen	to catch	fängt	fing	hat gefangen
*finden	to find	findet	fand	hat gefunden
*fliegen	to fly	fliegt	flog	ist geflogen
fliehen	to flee	flieht	floh	ist geflohen
*fließen	to flow	fließt	floß	ist geflossen
*fressen	to eat (of animals)	frißt	fraß	hat gefressen
*frieren	to freeze	friert	fror	hat gefroren
*geben	to give	gibt	gab	hat gegeben
*gehen	to go	geht	ging	ist gegangen
*gelingen	to succeed	gelingt	gelang	ist gelungen
*genießen	to enjoy	genießt	genoß	hat genossen
*geschehen	to happen	geschieht	geschah	ist geschehen
*gewinnen	to gain, win	gewinnt	gewann	hat gewonnen
gießen	to pour	gießt	goß	hat gegossen
gleichen	to resemble	gleicht	glich	hat geglichen
gleiten	to glide	gleitet	glitt	ist geglitten
graben	to dig	gräbt	grub	hat gegraben
*greifen	to seize	greift	griff	hat gegriffen
*haben	to have	hat	hatte	hat gehabt
*halten	to hold, stop	hält	hielt	hat gehalten
*hängen	to hang, be suspended	hängt	hing	hat gehangen
heben	to lift	hebt	hob	hat gehoben
*heißen	to be called	heißt	hieß	hat geheißen
*helfen	to help	hilft	half	hat geholfen
*kennen	to know	kennt	kannte	hat gekannt

Infinitive	Meaning	Present	Imperfect	Perfect
*klingen	to sound	klingt	klang	hat geklungen
*kommen	to come	kommt	kam	ist gekommen
kriechen	to creep	kriecht	kroch	ist gekrochen
*lassen	to let	läßt	ließ	hat gelassen
*laufen	to run	läuft	lief	ist gelaufen
*leiden	to suffer	leidet	litt	hat gelitten
leihen	to lend	leiht	lieh	hat geliehen
*lesen	to read	liest	las	hat gelesen
*liegen	to lie	liegt	lag	hat gelegen
lügen	to tell lies	lügt	log	hat gelogen
meiden	to avoid	meidet	mied	hat gemieden
messen	to measure	mißt	maß	hat gemessen
*nehmen	to take	nimmt	nahm	hat genommen
*nennen	to name, call	nennt	nannte	hat genannt
*raten	to advise, guess	rät	riet	hat geraten
reiben	to rub	reibt	rieb	hat gerieben
*reißen	to tear	reißt	riß	hat gerissen
*reiten	to ride	reitet	ritt	hat geritten
*rennen	to run	rennt	rannte	ist gerannt
*riechen	to smell	riecht	roch	hat gerochen
*rufen	to call	ruft	rief	hat gerufen
*scheinen	to appear, shine	scheint	schien	hat geschienen
*schieben	to shove, push	schiebt	schob	hat geschoben
*schießen	to shoot	schießt	schoß	hat geschossen
*schlafen	to sleep	schläft	schlief	hat geschlafen
*schlagen	to strike, hit	schlägt	schlug	hat geschlagen
schleichen	to creep	schleicht	schlich	ist geschlichen
*schließen	to shut	schließt	schloß	hat geschlossen
schmelzen	to melt	schmilzt	schmolz	ist geschmolzen
*schneiden	to cut	schneidet	schnitt	hat geschnitten
*schreiben	to write	schreibt	schrieb	hat geschrieben
*schreien	to cry out, shout	schreit	schrie	hat geschrie(e)n
schreiten	to stride	schreitet	schritt	ist geschritten
*schweigen	to be silent	schweigt	schwieg	hat geschwiegen
*schwimmen	to swim	schwimmt	schwamm	ist geschwommen
schwingen	to swing	schwingt	schwang	hat geschwungen
schwören	to swear	schwört	schwor	hat geschworen
*sehen	to see	sieht	sah	hat gesehen
*sein	to be	ist	war	ist gewesen
*singen	to sing	singt	sang	hat gesungen
*sinken	to sink	sinkt	sank	ist gesunken
*sitzen	to sit	sitzt	saß	hat gesessen
*sprechen	to speak	spricht	sprach	hat gesprochen
*springen	to spring, jump	springt	sprang	ist gesprungen
*stehen	to stand	steht	stand	hat gestanden
*stehlen	to steal	stiehlt	stahl	hat gestohlen
*steigen	to climb	steigt	stieg	ist gestiegen
*sterben	to die	stirbt	starb	ist gestorben
*stoßen	to push, knock, bump	stößt	stieß	hat gestoßen
*streichen	to paint, spread	streicht	strich	hat gestrichen
*streiten	to argue, fight	streitet	stritt	hat gestritten
*tragen	to carry, wear	trägt	trug	hat getragen
*treffen	to hit, meet	trifft	traf	hat getroffen
*treiben	to drive	treibt	trieb	hat getrieben
*treten	to step, kick (football)	tritt	trat	hat getreten
*trinken	to drink	trinkt	trank	hat getrunken
*tun	to do	tut	tat	hat getan

Infinitive	Meaning	Present	Imperfect	Perfect
*verbieten	to forbid	verbietet	verbot	hat verboten
verderben	to spoil	verdirbt	verdarb	hat verdorben
*vergessen	to forget	vergißt	vergaß	hat vergessen
*verlieren	to lose	verliert	verlor	hat verloren
*verschwinden	to disappear	verschwindet	verschwand	ist verschwunden
*verzeihen	to pardon	verzeiht	verzieh	hat verziehen
*wachsen	to grow	wächst	wuchs	ist gewachsen
*waschen	to wash	wäscht	wusch	hat gewaschen
weisen	to show/point	weist	wies	hat gewiesen
*werden	to become	wird	wurde	ist geworden
*werfen	to throw	wirft	warf	hat geworfen
wiegen	to weigh	wiegt	wog	hat gewogen
*wissen	to know	weiß	wußte	hat gewußt
*ziehen	to draw, pull	zieht	zog	hat gezogen
zwingen	to force	zwingt	zwang	hat gezwungen

▶ Cases and prepositions

The four cases – nominative, accusative, genitive and dative – cause difficulties for English students of German. Your course book will no doubt deal with them thoroughly, and you will have had frequent practice in using the cases. This section summarises the main rules, and gives examples of the use of the different cases, often with prepositions, with a recommendation that some of the phrases should be learnt by heart and used wherever possible both in spoken and in written German.

The cases

Nominative
The **Nominative** case is the starting point. It is the case given in vocabularies and dictionaries. It is used for the **subject** of the verb.

Accusative
The **Accusative** is used:

▶ for the *direct object* of the verb, e.g. *Ich habe einen Bruder; Kannst du die Berge sehen? Er hat seine Jacke verloren.*
▶ after the following prepositions: *für, um, durch, gegen, entlang, bis, ohne.*
▶ after the following prepositions when **motion towards** is indicated: *in, an, auf, über, vor, hinter, unter, neben, zwischen.*
▶ in many time phrases, e.g. *letztes Jahr, guten Morgen, nächste Woche, diesen Dienstag, den ganzen Tag.*

Genitive
The **Genitive** case is used:

▶ for possession, e.g. *das Zimmer meiner Eltern* – my parents' room, *ein Freund meines Bruders* – a friend of my brother.
▶ after the following prepositions: *wegen, während, trotz, anstatt, statt, außerhalb, innerhalb.*

Dative
The **Dative** case is used:

▶ for the **indirect object** of the verb, e.g. *Ich gebe meinem Vater* (i.e. **to** my father) *den Brief; Du sagst mir* (i.e. **to** me) *nichts.*
▶ after the following prepositions: *aus, bei, mit, nach, seit, von, zu, gegenüber.*
▶ after the following prepositions when **no motion towards** but rather **position** is indicated: *in, an, auf, über, vor, hinter, unter, neben, zwischen.*

Points to remember
▶ The only difference in form between the nominative case and the accusative case is in the masculine *(der – den, ein – einen).*
▶ The preposition *entlang* **follows** the noun.

▶ *Gegenüber* often appears after the noun, and **always** after a prounoun, e.g. *dem Rathaus gegenüber, mir gegenüber*.
▶ The genitive case is slowly (very slowly) becoming less used, so that one sometimes hears *während den Ferien* (dative). Some people also avoid using the genitive by using a dative with *von* instead, e.g. *das Zimmer von meinen Eltern* rather than *das Zimmer meiner Eltern*.
▶ The accusative prepositions are best learned in the order given, which provides the word FUDGEBO!
▶ The dative prepositions are best learned as written, in alphabetical order, in the following jingle:

Aus, bei, mit, nach, seit, von, zu
All take the dative and *gegenüber* too!

The prepositions

These words frequently indicate the position of objects. Their use is often idiomatic and you should therefore learn by heart the phrases given here as examples. Many of them you will know already!

Accusative
Accusative only:

für	*for*	Das ist für mich. Das ist für meinen Bruder.
um	*round, at*	um die Ecke, um den Tisch, um 8 Uhr
durch	*through*	durch den Garten, durch die Stadt, durch das Haus
entlang	*along*	die Straße entlang
bis	*until*	Bis nächsten Monat! Bis morgen!
ohne	*without*	ohne meine Bücher

Genitive
Genitive only:

wegen	*because of*	Wegen des Regens kann er nicht kommen.
während	*during*	Während der Mittagspause hat es geregnet.
trotz	*in spite of*	Trotz des schlechten Wetters ist es warm.
anstatt/statt	*instead of*	statt meines Freundes
außerhalb	*outside*	außerhalb des Dorfes
innerhalb	*inside*	innerhalb der Stadt

Dative
Dative only:

aus	*out of, from, made of*	Er ging aus der Küche. Ich komme aus Schottland. Ein Bett aus Holz
bei	*at the home of, near, at*	bei meiner Freundin, bei Köln, beim Frühstück, bei schönem Wetter
mit	*with, by*	mit meinen Freunden, mit dem Rad
nach	*to, after*	nach Spanien, nach Ulm, nach dem Mittagessen, meiner Meinung nach
seit	*since*	seit den Olympischen Spielen, seit drei Jahren
von	*of, from*	das Haus von meiner Oma Der Zug fährt von Bonn nach Bingen.
zu	*to, at*	ich gehe zum Bahnhof, zu Weihnachten, zum Geburtstag, eine Briefmarke zu 90 Pfennig
gegenüber	*opposite*	gegenüber der Kirche, ihm gegenüber

Accusative or dative
Prepositions taking accusative or dative:

in	*into, in*	Acc.	Er ging in die Stadt. *(into)*
		Dat.	Er arbeitet in der Stadt. *(in)*

an	*to, at*	Acc.	Wir fahren ans Meer. *(to)*
		Dat.	Kiel liegt am Meer. *(at, on)*
auf	*onto, on*	Acc.	Die Katze sprang auf den Tisch. *(onto)*
		Dat.	Meine Sachen liegen auf dem Tisch. *(on)*
über	*over, above*	Acc.	Lauf schnell über die Straße! *(over)*
		Dat.	Die Lampe hängt über der Straße. *(above)*

The remaining prepositions in this group are nearly always followed by the **dative** case:

vor	*in front of, before*	vor dem Kino, vor dem Frühstück
hinter	*behind*	hinter der Garage
unter	*under, below*	unter dem Sofa
neben	*near*	neben der Schule
zwischen	*between*	zwischen der Post und dem Rathaus

Useful prepositional phrases

Other useful prepositional phrases to learn:

bis zum Ende *right to the end*
Tag für Tag *day after day*
er geht nach Hause *he's going home*
sie bleibt zu Hause *she's staying at home*
Geh zu Bett! *go to bed!*
zu Fuß *on foot*
zum Glück *fortunately*
am zweiten April *on the second of April*
Frankfurt am Main *Frankfurt on the Main*
Der Spiegel ist an der Wand *The mirror is on the wall.*
am Himmel *in the sky*
Wir fahren aufs Land. *We're going into the country.*
Der Bauernhof ist auf dem Land. *The farm is in the country.*
auf diese Weise *in this way*
auf jeden Fall *in any case*
auf dem Markt *in the market*
Ich gehe auf die Bank. *I'm going to the bank.*
Fahren Sie in die Schweiz? *Are you going to Switzerland?*
Ich gehe ins Kino / Theater / Konzert / in die Disco. *I'm going to the cinema / the theatre / a concert / the disco.*
in der Nähe von Dortmund *near Dortmund*
im Freien *in the open air*
im ersten Stock *on the first floor*
im Fernsehen *on TV*
über Rotterdam *via Rotterdam*
vor drei Wochen *three weeks ago*
vor allem *above all*
er hat Angst vor Spinnen *he's afraid of spiders*
unter meinen Freunden *among my friends*

Points to remember

The word 'to' can be translated by *nach, zu, in, an* or *auf*!
Check carefully before making a wild guess.

▶ *nach* is used for place names of towns or countries
▶ *zu* is the most general word otherwise
▶ *in* means going **into** (*in die Schule, ins Büro*)
▶ *an* means going up to, but not into (*an den Fluß, ans Meer*)
▶ *auf* means going on to (*auf den Markt, auf das Land*).

TEST YOURSELF (6) Translate into German:

(a) by train
(b) in the country
(c) to Belgium
(d) to the Black Forest

(e) opposite you
(f) at half past six
(g) on Friday
(h) see you soon!
(i) on the wall
(j) made of plastic
(k) at our house
(l) at Easter
(m) through the window
(n) after lunch
(o) at home
(p) 10 years ago
(q) on the radio
(r) in English
(s) in Switzerland
(t) to Turkey

Pronouns

Common pronouns

The table which follows reminds you of the pronouns with which you are already familiar:

	I	you	he	she	it	we	you	you	they
Nominative	ich	du	er	sie	es	wir	ihr	Sie	sie
Accusative	mich	dich	ihn	sie	es	uns	euch	Sie	sie
Dative	mir	dir	ihm	ihr	ihm	uns	euch	Ihnen	ihnen

Patterns

A quick count will show you that there are seven different words for 'you'! But having digested this unpleasant fact, there are two reassuring features of the table:

▶ The words for 'he', 'she', 'it' and 'they' follow exactly the pattern of the definite articles, *der*, *die*, *das* and *die*.
▶ The word for 'we' is always *wir* and the word for 'us' is always *uns*.

Points to remember

▶ When writing a letter *Du*, *Dich* and *Dir* must be written with a capital letter. Similarly *Ihr* and *Euch*.
▶ 'In it' is not translated by *in ihm*, but by *darin*. Similarly *darauf*, *daran*, *damit*, *darüber* and so on.
▶ Do not forget the prounoun *man*, which is common in German, e.g. *Hier spricht man Englisch* – English spoken here.
▶ 'It's me' is translated by *Ich bin's*.

TEST YOURSELF (7) Translate into German:

(a) for me
(b) with you
(c) without us
(d) against it.
(e) without him
(f) for her
(g) at your house
(h) with her
(i) with me
(j) on it
(k) in front of it

Relative pronouns

Nominative

Der Mann, der dort allein sitzt, ist mein Lehrer. *The man who is sitting there alone, is my teacher.*

The word *der* which is underlined is a relative pronoun meaning 'who'. It is *der* because it relates back to a masculine noun (*der Mann*) and because it is the **subject** of its own verb (*sitzt*).

Accusative

Der Mann, den du dort siehst, ist mein Lehrer. *The man whom you see there is my teacher.*

This time the relative pronoun is *den* because it is the **object** of the verb in the clause (*siehst*).

Dative

Der Mann, mit dem du sprichst, ist mein Lehrer.   *The man with whom you are speaking is my teacher.*

Here *dem* is dative following the word *mit*.

Summary
Here is the table for relative pronouns:

	Masculine	Feminine	Neuter	Plural
Nominative	der	die	das	die
Accusative	den	die	das	die
Genitive	dessen	deren	dessen	deren
Dative	dem	der	dem	denen

You will see that there are a few new words, but that most relative pronouns are the same as the definite articles.

Examples
Die Kinder, die hier wohnen, kommen aus Schottland.   *The children who live here come from Scotland.*
Die Freunde, mit denen ich Tennis spiele, kommen später nach Hause.   *The friends with whom I play tennis are coming home later.*
Der Mann, dessen Sohn im Krankenhaus liegt, heißt Müller.   *The man whose son is in hospital is called Müller.*

Here is an example of a different kind of relative pronoun:

Hier ist die Küche, wo wir gewöhnlich essen.   *Here is the kitchen where we usually eat.*

Points to remember
- Remember that the relative pronoun sends the verb to the end of the clause.
- Be prepared to recognise these words both in reading and in listening.
- Only use them if you feel confident you can do so correctly. Two short sentences would often do just as well.

▶ Adverbs

Comparison with adjectives

Many adverbs in German are the same as the adjective. For instance, in the sentence *Er ist ein guter Arbeiter* the word *gut* is an adjective. But it can also be used as an adverb in the sentence *Er arbeitet sehr gut* (He works very **well**).

Superlative

The superlative of adverbs, however, needs some attention. 'He runs the fastest' is translated as *Er läuft am schnellsten*. At this stage this form is largely for understanding only, apart from the phrase *am liebsten* (best of all), e.g.

Ich esse gern Erbsen, aber am liebsten esse ich Bohnen.   *I like eating peas but I like eating beans best of all.*

Common adverbs

Many adverbs are easy to use but are often forgotten by candidates in German. Here are a few which you will know, but which you may not often put to active use. Make a serious effort to introduce them sensibly into your written and spoken work.

auch	*also*	kaum	*hardly*
bald	*soon*	lange	*for a long time*
dann	*then*	leider	*unfortunately*
damals	*at that time*	manchmal	*sometimes*
eben	*just*	normalerweise	*normally, usually*
erst	*not until*	nur	*only*
(e.g. erst morgen	*not until tomorrow*)	oft	*often*

fast *almost*
ganz *quite, completely*
genug *enough*
gerade *just*
glücklicherweise *luckily*
immer *always*
jetzt *now*

schon *already*
sogar *even*
sonst *otherwise*
vielleicht *perhaps*
wohl *I suppose*
ziemlich *fairly, rather*

Conjunctions

Uses of conjunctions

Conjunctions are words which join clauses together to make them longer and more complex. A few do not alter the word order:

und *and*
oder *or*
aber *but*

denn *for, because*
sondern *but (on the contrary)*

Others send the verb to the end of the clause. The most common examples of these are:

als *when, as*
bis *until*
bevor *before*
da *as, since*
daß *that*
falls *in case, if*
indem *while*
nachdem *after*
damit *in order that*

ob *whether, if*
obwohl *although*
seitdem *since*
sobald *as soon as*
so daß *so that*
während *while*
wenn *when, if*
weil *because*

Als ich jung war, ... *When I was young ...*
Bevor wir das Haus verließen, ... *Before we left the house ...*
Nachdem wir gefrühstückt hatten, ... *After we had had breakfast ...*
Obwohl es sehr kalt war, ... *Although it was very cold ...*
Wenn ich Zeit habe, ... *When (if) I have time ...*
Weil ich momentan kein Geld habe, ... *Because I haven't any money at the moment ...*

Points to remember

▶ Using these conjunctions makes the sentence more complex. If you are unsure of what you are doing, divide your sentence into two simpler sentences. For example:

Ich werde Tennis spielen, weil das Wetter schön ist.
Das Wetter ist schön. Ich werde Tennis spielen.

▶ *Bis* and *während* are also prepositions, but as such have a different meaning. Do not confuse their use as a conjunction and as a preposition.
▶ Do not confuse *nachdem* with *nach dem*.
▶ *Da* (as, since) also has other meanings.

TEST YOURSELF (8) Translate into German:

(a) Because it's raining today ...
(b) Before I go to bed ...
(c) Although my mother is ill ...
(d) While you are doing your homework ...
(e) If the sun is shining ...
(f) I don't know if he is coming today.
(g) As it is already nine o'clock ...
(h) I know that the film is good.
(i) As soon as the train arrives ...
(j) Since we have been living here ...

Interrogatives

Question words

Questions in German are easy. All question words begin with 'w'.

was? *what?*

wer? *who?*

wo? *where?*
woher? *where from?*
wohin? *where to?*
wie? *how?*
wieviele? *how many?*
warum? *why?*
welcher...? *which...?*

wen? *whom?*
wessen? *whose?*
wem? *whom?*
wieviel? *how much?*
was für...? *what sort of...?*
womit? wovon? *with what? of what?*

Examples:

Woher kommst du? *Where do you come from?*
Wohin fährt dieser Zug? *Where is this train going?*
Wie ist Ihr Hund? *What is your dog like?*
Was für einen Lehrer habt ihr? *What sort of a teacher do you have?*
Mit wem hast du gesprochen? *Who(m) did you speak with?*
Womit schreiben Sie? *What are you writing with?*
Welches Buch hast du da? *What (which) book have you got there?*
Warum muß man immer arbeiten? *Why does one always have to work?*
Wessen Schuhe sind die? *Whose shoes are these?*

Points to remember

▶ *mit wem?* means 'with whom?' (i.e. a person)
  womit? means 'with what?' (i.e. a thing)
▶ *woher* and *wohin* can separate, e.g. Wo gehst du hin? Wo kommst du her?

TEST YOURSELF (9) Translate into German:

(a) How much does that cost?
(b) Why are you so tired?
(c) What sort of a book is it?
(d) How many people are here?
(e) Where does this bus go?
(f) What's the weather like?
(g) Which lessons have we got?
(h) What are you standing on?
(i) Who is that?
(j) Who(m) do you play tennis with?

▶ Negatives *Beginnings*

Negatives should cause little problem in German. Almost all negative words begin with the letter 'n'.

nicht *not*
nie *never*
nein *no*
nichts *nothing*
niemand *no one*
nirgendwo *nowhere*
nicht mehr *no longer*

noch nie *never yet*
noch nicht *not yet*
nicht wahr? *isn't it? don't you? etc.*
gar nicht *not at all*
weder...noch *neither...nor*
kein *no, not a*

Examples:

Meine Arbeit ist noch nicht fertig. *My work is not yet finished.*
Ich war noch nie in der Schweiz. *I have never been to Switzerland (yet).*
Da war nichts zu sehen. *There was nothing to see.*
Es regnet nicht mehr. *It's stopped raining.*
Ich lerne weder Physik noch Biologie. *I don't learn either physics or biology.*
Heute abend müssen wir keine Hausaufgaben machen. *We haven't any homework tonight.*

Points to remember

▶ 'not a' or 'no' is *kein, keine*, etc.
▶ 'not anything' is the same as 'nothing' (*nichts*)
▶ 'not ever' is the same as 'never' (*nie*)

TEST YOURSELF (10) Translate into German:

(a) She doesn't love me any more.
(b) It's not yet 9 o'clock.
(c) I haven't got a brother.
(d) He hasn't eaten anything.
(e) I'm right, aren't I?
(f) I have nothing at all to say.
(g) Nobody knows.
(h) It is nowhere to be found.
(i) Never again.
(j) Haven't you got a dog?

▶ Word order

Basic rules

1. The basic rule for word order is that the **verb** should stand as the **second idea** in the sentence. Look at the following sentences:

   Mein Vater fährt am Donnerstag nach Berlin.
   Am Donnerstag fährt mein Vater nach Berlin.

   Although the order of the phrases has changed, the verb remains in the second place.

2. This rule holds for the perfect tense when the auxiliary verb is in second place with the past participle at the end:

   Wir haben den Kuchen schon gegessen.
   Den Kuchen haben wir schon gegessen.

3. This also applies when a subordinate clause begins the sentence, as in:

   Da er kein Geld hatte, blieb er zu Hause.

   If we count *Da er kein Geld hatte* as the first idea, then *blieb* as the main verb is still in second place.

4. Past participles and infinitives go to the end, e.g.

   Ich kann dieses Lied nicht leiden.
   Warum hast du die Platte gekauft?

5. In questions or commands the verb is often first, e.g.

   Kommst du heute abend oder nicht?
   Geh schnell nach Hause zurück!

6. If you have a number of phrases in a sentence, remember the order of TIME, MANNER, PLACE, e.g.

   Wir fahren morgen früh   mit dem Wagen   nach Basel.
                TIME   MANNER   PLACE

Points to remember

▶ If you have too many phrases in your sentence, it is often easier to start with a time phrase, e.g. *Am Donnerstag fahre ich mit dem Zug nach Lübeck*. This does not in any way alter the meaning of the sentence.

▶ Try reading out loud the sentences you write. If a sentence sounds wrong, think again. This is the test which we subconsciously apply to our own language.

TEST YOURSELF (10) Rewrite these sentences with the words in the correct order:

(a) muß mit Dover morgen fahren dem ich nach Schiff
(b) einen es kalt wenn trage ich Pullover ist
(c) schon es Uhr acht ist?
(d) sieben Film um an fängt der
(e) einen heute gekauft Rock Sabine Bluse hat und eine
(f) Straße nicht Lärm macht so viel der auf!
(g) am in Stadt wirst Samstag du die fahren?
(h) fährt entlang die die schnell Straßenbahn Straße
(i) kommt uns Briefträger heute zu der nicht
(j) wissen der ist kaputt daß wir Plattenspieler

Numbers, quantity and time

Cardinal and ordinal numbers

Cardinal numbers

1	eins	21	einundzwanzig		
2	zwei	22	zweiundzwanzig		
3	drei	30	dreißig		
4	vier	40	vierzig		
5	fünf	50	fünfzig		
6	sechs	60	sechzig		
7	sieben	70	siebzig		
8	acht	80	achtzig		
9	neun	90	neunzig		
10	zehn	100	hundert		
11	elf	120	hundertzwanzig		
12	zwölf	1,000	tausend		
13	dreizehn	1,000,000	eine Million		
14	vierzehn				
15	fünfzehn				
16	sechzehn				
17	siebzehn				
18	achtzehn				
19	neunzehn				
20	zwanzig				

Ordinal numbers

1st	der erste
2nd	der zweite
3rd	der dritte
4th	der vierte
5th	der fünfte
20th	der zwanzigste

Time

Wieviel Uhr ist es? } *What time is it?*
Wie spät ist es?

Es ist ein Uhr. *It's one o'clock.*
Es ist zwei Uhr *etc.*
um sechs Uhr *at six o'clock*
gegen sieben Uhr *about seven o'clock*
Es ist Viertel nach zwei. *It's a quarter past two.*
Es ist halb drei. *It's half past <u>two</u>.*
Es ist Viertel vor drei. *It's a quarter to three.*
Es ist fünf (Minuten) nach acht. *It's five past eight.*
Es ist fünf nach halb zehn. *It's twenty-five to ten.*

Days and months

Days of the week
Sonntag, Montag, Dienstag, Mittwoch, Donnerstag, Freitag, Samstag (*or* Sonnabend)
Months of the year
Januar, Februar, März, April, Mai, Juni,
Juli, August, September, Oktober, November, Dezember

ANSWERS TO 'TEST YOURSELF'

1. (a) der Onkel, die Wohnung, das Restaurant, das Büchlein, der Schneider, die Engländerin, das Laufen, der Vater, die Bluse, die Mutter
der Park, der Name, die Person, der Balkon, die Tür, der Käse, die Butter, das Mädchen, das Fräulein, der Klub
(b) die Wagen, Blusen, Ausstellungen, Cafés, Zimmer, Hotels, Trauben, Türen, Radios, Kellner
die Kartoffeln, Nächte, Nummern, Freundinnen, Autobusse, Schwestern
(c) (i) Wir haben weder Katze noch Hund.
(ii) Herr Rabowski ist Zahnarzt.
(iii) Die Autos (Wagen) sind nicht hier.
(iv) Ich putze mir die Zähne.
(v) Sie ist meine Schwester.
(vi) Unser Opa ist zu Hause.
(vii) Diese Leute sind hungrig.

Answers to 'test yourself' 217

    (viii) Welchen Jungen kannst du sehen?

2. (a) der rote Bus
   (b) ein roter Bus
   (c) die enge Straße
   (d) eine enge Straße
   (e) das kleine Dorf
   (f) ein kleines Dorf
   (g) die weißen Berge
   (h) weiße Berge
   (i) kaltes Wetter
   (j) Wir haben einen großen Garten.
   (k) der Alte
   (l) Unsere Katze ist dumm.
   (m) Mein armer Kopf!

    (ix) Er hat Zahnschmerzen.
    (x) Die Schweiz ist schön

3. (a) meine ältere Schwester
   (b) der längste Monat
   (c) die langweiligste Stunde
   (d) Sie ist älter als ich.
   (e) Es ist nicht so kalt wie gestern.
   (f) Die Nächte werden immer kürzer.
   (g) die besten Filme
   (h) nächstes Jahr
   (i) eine modernere Schule
   (j) die meisten Leute

4. (a) (i) He stood outside the cinema.
      (ii) The train had already arrived.
      (iii) It will rain soon.
      (iv) The book was written very quickly.
      (v) He said he couldn't work.
      (vi) I would be very grateful.
      (vii) That would cost DM 200.
      (viii) Where did you run to?
      (ix) He received two letters.
      (x) He acted as if he did not want to buy anything.

  (b) (i) Er lernt Italienisch.
      (ii) Wir wohnten in Österreich.
      (iii) Ich möchte bitte Tomaten.
      (iv) Haben Sie das Haus gekauft?
      (v) Ich war schon weggefahren.
      (vi) Lesen Sie die Zeitung?
      (vii) Ich würde zu Hause bleiben, wenn ...
      (viii) Sie sind müde.
      (ix) Wir hatten schon gegessen.
      (x) Was haben Sie gefunden?

5. (a) Geh nach Hause! Geht nach Hause! Gehen Sie nach Hause!
   (b) Fahr (Fahrt, Fahren Sie) nicht so schnell!
   (c) Wasch dir (Wascht euch, Waschen Sie sich) die Hände!
   (d) Bleiben wir zu Hause!
   (e) Sie zieht sich um.
   (f) Er rasiert sich.
   (g) Wir unterhalten uns.
   (h) Ich stehe um sieben Uhr auf.
   (i) Wir haben gestern abend ferngesehen.
   (j) Was haben Sie heute vor?
   (k) Wie geht es dir?
   (l) Es geht mir nicht so gut.

6. (a) mit dem Zug
   (b) auf dem Lande
   (c) nach Belgien
   (d) in den Schwarzwald
   (e) dir gegenüber
   (f) um halb sieben
   (g) am Freitag
   (h) bis bald!
   (i) an der Wand
   (j) aus Plastik
   (k) bei uns
   (l) zu Ostern
   (m) durch das Fenster
   (n) nach dem Mittagessen
   (o) zu Hause
   (p) vor zehn Jahren
   (q) im Radio
   (r) auf englisch
   (s) in der Schweiz
   (t) in die Türkei

7. (a) für mich
   (b) mit dir
   (c) ohne uns
   (d) dagegen
   (e) ohne ihn
   (f) für sie
   (g) bei dir
   (h) mit ihr
   (i) mit mir
   (j) darauf
   (k) davor

8. (a) Weil es heute regnet, ...
   (b) Bevor ich ins Bett gehe, ...
   (c) Obwohl meine Mutter krank ist, ...
   (d) Während du deine Hausaufgaben machst, ...
   (e) Falls die Sonne scheint, ...
   (f) Ich weiß nicht, ob er heute kommt.
   (g) Da es schon neun Uhr ist, ...
   (h) Ich weiß, daß der Film gut ist.
   (i) Sobald der Zug ankommt, ...
   (j) Seitdem wir hier wohnen, ...

9 (a) Wieviel kostet das?
  (b) Warum bist du so müde?
  (c) Was für ein Buch ist es?
  (d) Wieviele Leute sind hier?
  (e) Wohin fährt dieser Bus?
  (f) Wie ist das Wetter?
  (g) Welche Stunden haben wir?
  (h) Worauf stehen Sie?
  (i) Wer ist das?
  (j) Mit wem spielen Sie Tennis?

10 (a) Sie liebt mich nicht mehr.
   (b) Es ist noch nicht neun Uhr.
   (c) Ich habe keinen Bruder.
   (d) Er hat nichts gegessen.
   (e) Ich habe recht, nicht wahr?
   (f) Ich habe gar nichts zu sagen.
   (g) Niemand weiß.
   (h) Es ist nirgendwo zu finden.
   (i) Nie wieder.
   (j) Hast du keinen Hund?

11 (a) Morgen muß ich mit dem Schiff nach Dover fahren.
   (b) Wenn es kalt ist, trage ich einen Pullover.
   (c) Ist es schon acht Uhr?
   (d) Der Film fängt um sieben an.
   (e) Sabine hat heute eine Bluse und einen Rock gekauft.
   (f) Macht nicht so viel Lärm auf der Straße!
   (g) Wirst du am Samstag in die Stadt fahren?
   (h) Die Straßenbahn fährt schnell die Straße entlang.
   (i) Der Briefträger kommt heute nicht zu uns.
   (j) Wir wissen, daß der Plattenspieler kaputt ist.

Chapter 15

A checklist of language tasks

GETTING STARTED

It is very important that you should keep a record of the work that you do, and this chapter is designed to help you do so. Each Area of Experience is divided up into topics. Tasks preceded by 'H' are required at Higher Tier only. On the right-hand side of each page are two blank columns. These are for you to use. You should indicate that you have learnt each topic (first square) and that you have tested it satisfactorily (second square). You may even feel it wise to add a third square for a final revision check. You could write the date in the square or you could colour it in. You will see that the responsibility for this work is entirely yours, but it should allow you (if tackled properly) to approach the examination with maximum confidence.

WHAT YOU NEED TO KNOW

Area of Experience A: Everyday activities

Language of the classroom, courtesies and conversation skills

You should be able to:

Learnt   Tested

▶ Greet and say goodbye to a German speaker.

▶ Ask how people are and express suitable feelings.

▶ Understand classroom instructions and make requests.

▶ Say whether or not you understand and ask for repetition and spellings.

▶ Ask someone to speak more slowly.

▶ Ask if someone speaks English or German.

▶ Say you speak German and how well.

▶ Ask whether others speak German and how well.

▶ Ask what things are in English or German and what they mean.

▶ Ask/state whether something is correct/incorrect.

[H] ▶ Ask for explanations and pronunciation.

▶ Say if you agree/disagree and ask others.

School

You should be able to **give** and **ask for information** and **opinions** about:

Learnt   Tested

▶ Your school/college and its facilities.

▶ The type, size and location of your school and its buildings.

▶ Daily routines: when school begins and ends, how many lessons there are and how long they last, break times and lunch times.

▶ Homework.

- How you travel to and from school.
- Your school year and holidays.
- The subjects studied and your preferences.
- Clubs, sports, trips and other activities.
- Your progress at school.
- School meals.
- [H] Other types of school, making comparisons.
- The disadvantages/advantages of mixed schools/colleges.
- School rules

Home life

You should be able to discuss where and under what conditions you and others live. In particular you should be able to do the following:

Learnt   Tested

- Say whether you live in a house, flat etc. and ask others the same.
- Describe your house, flat etc. and its location.
- Find out about and give details of rooms, garage, garden etc. as appropriate.
- Mention or enquire about the essential pieces of furniture, amenities, services etc.
- Say what jobs you do around the home and whether you like or dislike them.
- [H] Discuss how much other members of your family help at home.
- Offer and ask for help with household tasks.
- Ask and say where places and things are in the house.
- Say you need and ask others if they need soap, toothpaste, towel etc.
- Ask about taking a bath/shower.
- Describe daily routines at home on working days and weekends.
- Give and ask for information about meals and meal times.
- [H] Express opinions about typical meals, meal times and eating habits.
- Talk about pocket money and how it is earnt/spent.
- [H] Discuss the responsibilities of running a home and compare your home to others.

Media

You should be able to:

Learnt   Tested

- Understand simple information about television programmes, films, radio, music and performers.
- State which programmes, films, music or performers you have recently seen or heard.
- Express simple opinions about television and radio programmes, films, books, magazines and music.

- Ask permission to use the telephone, radio or watch television.
- [H] Understand and narrate plots/themes of books, television/radio programmes, films and simple news items.
- Ask for and give opinions about newspapers, magazines, books, television and radio programmes, music and performers and give reasons.

Health and fitness, well-being

General

Learnt Tested

- State how you feel (well, ill, better, hot, cold, tired).
- Ask others how they feel.
- Refer to parts of the body where you are in pain or discomfort.
- Call for help.
- Warn about danger.
- Say if you have any allergies.
- [H] Discuss healthy and unhealthy lifestyles.

Illness and injury

Learnt Tested

- Report minor ailments (e.g. temperature, cold, sunburn).
- Say you have lost a filling.
- Ask for items in a chemist's and ask if they have anything for a particular ailment.
- Respond to an enquiry as to how long an ailment or symptom has persisted.
- Say you would like to see a doctor or a dentist.
- [H] Make an appointment to see a doctor, dentist or chemist.
- Report injuries.
- Deal with contact with the medical services.
- Say whether you take medicine regularly and, if so, what.
- [H] Ask advice about medicines and understand instructions about them.
- Tell others about medical facilities and surgery hours.
- Say if you are insured.

Accident

Learnt Tested

- [H] Describe an accident and say if anyone is hurt or injured and how.
- Report that there has been an accident.
- Ask or say whether it is serious.
- Ask or advise someone to telephone for the police, doctor, ambulance or fire brigade.

Food and drink

General

	Learnt	Tested
▶ Discuss your likes, dislikes and preferences and those of others.	☐	☐
▶ Discuss your typical meals, meal times and eating habits.	☐	☐
▶ Buy food and drink (see also Shopping).	☐	☐
▶ Explain what a dish is or contains.	☐	☐
[H] ▶ Discuss dietary requirements and the preparation of specific dishes.	☐	☐

Café, restaurant and other public places

	Learnt	Tested
▶ Attract the attention of the waiter/waitress.	☐	☐
▶ Order a drink or snack.	☐	☐
▶ Order a meal.	☐	☐
▶ Ask for a particular fixed price menu.	☐	☐
[H] ▶ Say how many there are in your group.	☐	☐
▶ Ask for a table (for a certain number) and generally make enquiries about seating and state seating requirements or preferences	☐	☐
▶ Ask about the availability of certain dishes and drinks.	☐	☐
▶ Ask the cost of dishes and drinks.	☐	☐
▶ Ask for an explanation or description of something on the menu.	☐	☐
▶ Express opinions about a meal or dish.	☐	☐
[H] ▶ Express appreciation and pay compliments.	☐	☐
▶ Make a specific complaint and give reasons.	☐	☐
▶ Accept or reject suggestions.	☐	☐
▶ Ask if the service charge is included.	☐	☐
▶ Ask about the location of facilities (e.g. toilets, telephone).	☐	☐

At home

	Learnt	Tested
▶ Ask about the time and place of meals.	☐	☐
▶ Ask for food and table items (e.g. more, a little, fork, knife, salt, pepper etc.).	☐	☐
▶ React to offers of food (accept, decline, apologise, express pleasure).	☐	☐
▶ Express likes, dislikes and preferences.	☐	☐
▶ Respond to a toast, e.g. *Prost*.	☐	☐

▶ **Area of Experience B: Personal and social life**

Self, family and friends/personal relationships

You should be able to **give information** about **yourself** and **others** (e.g. members of your family or host family, friends) and **ask for information** from others on the following points:

	Learnt	Tested
▶ Names (including spellings).	☐	☐
▶ Address (including spellings).	☐	☐

- ▶ Telephone numbers. ☐ ☐
- ▶ Ages and birthdays. ☐ ☐
- ▶ Nationality. ☐ ☐
- ▶ General descriptions (including sex, marital status, physical appearance, character or disposition of yourself and others). ☐ ☐
- ▶ Occupations. ☐ ☐
- ▶ Pets. ☐ ☐
- ▶ How you get on with people. ☐ ☐
- ▶ Likes and dislikes (with regard to other people and other topic areas in the syllabus). ☐ ☐
- [H] ▶ Feelings about others. ☐ ☐

You should also be able to:

- ▶ Greet people and respond to greetings both formally and informally. ☐ ☐
- ▶ Make and understand introductions. ☐ ☐

Free time, leisure and entertainment, holidays and special occasions

Learnt   Tested

- ▶ State your hobbies, leisure activities and interests. ☐ ☐
- ▶ Give simple opinions about hobbies, leisure activities and interests. ☐ ☐
- ▶ Ask about the hobbies and interests of other people. ☐ ☐
- [H] ▶ Discuss your interest and involvement in clubs or societies. ☐ ☐
- ▶ Agree or disagree with **other people's** opinions. ☐ ☐
- ▶ Describe and comment on the leisure facilities in your area. ☐ ☐
- ▶ Buy entry tickets for cinema, theatre, concert, swimming pool, sports centre, football match and leisure facilities. ☐ ☐
- ▶ Find out about the cost of seats or entry and about starting and finishing times. ☐ ☐
- ▶ Understand explanations of activities and invitations to participate. ☐ ☐
- ▶ Give explanations of activities and invite others to participate. ☐ ☐
- ▶ Describe recent holiday or leisure activities. ☐ ☐
- [H] ▶ Express and understand more detailed opinions about leisure activities. ☐ ☐
- ▶ Discuss preferences and alternatives for going out. ☐ ☐
- ▶ Give and ask for information about excursions and visits. ☐ ☐
- ▶ Discuss and express opinions about watching and participating in sporting events. ☐ ☐

Arranging a meeting, activity or to go out

Learnt   Tested

- ▶ Make simple suggestions for going out. ☐ ☐
- ▶ Invite someone to go out. ☐ ☐
- ▶ Accept or decline an invitation. ☐ ☐

- Ask about, suggest or confirm a time and place to meet. ☐ ☐
- [H] Find out whether a particular activity or facility is available and discuss options. ☐ ☐
- Negotiate arrangements for a meeting or activity. ☐ ☐

▶ Area of Experience C: The world around us

Home town, local area and customs, people and places

You should be able to **give information** and **simple opinions** about your home town or village and surrounding areas, and **ask for information** from others, with respect to:

Learnt Tested

- Location. ☐ ☐
- Character. ☐ ☐
- Amenities, attractions, features of interest. ☐ ☐
- Population. ☐ ☐
- Climate. ☐ ☐
- Local history, customs, festivals etc. ☐ ☐

You should also be able to:

- Understand weather predictions and descriptions and describe weather conditions.
- [H] Give weather predictions and understand forecasts. ☐ ☐
- Understand and make comparisons between your home and a German-speaking country: towns, regions, climate and geographical features. ☐ ☐
- Name parts of Germany, Austria and Switzerland or the UK you know, and talk about them. ☐ ☐
- Understand references to countries where German is spoken. ☐ ☐

Finding the way

You should be able to:

Learnt Tested

- Attract the attention of a passer-by. ☐ ☐
- Ask or state where a place is. ☐ ☐
- Ask how to get to a place. ☐ ☐
- Ask or state if a place is near or far. ☐ ☐
- Understand directions. ☐ ☐
- Express thanks. ☐ ☐
- [H] Ask for and give detailed directions to a specific place. ☐ ☐

Shopping

- You should be able to:

Learnt Tested

- Ask where specific shops are. ☐ ☐
- Ask about opening and closing times. ☐ ☐
- Ask for specific items mentioning colour, size, who it's for. ☐ ☐

- ▶ Express the quantity required: weight, volume, container. ☐ ☐
- ▶ Ask and understand about availability/non-availability. ☐ ☐
- ▶ Understand the question 'Is that all?' and reply to it. ☐ ☐
- ▶ Express opinions about clothes. ☐ ☐
- ▶ Say you will/will not buy something. ☐ ☐
- [H] ▶ Find specific goods and departments in a store. ☐ ☐
- ▶ Discuss shopping habits, preferences and facilities. ☐ ☐
- ▶ Give reasons for buying/not buying things. ☐ ☐
- ▶ Return unsatisfactory goods giving reasons, and ask for a refund. ☐ ☐
- ▶ Understand information about discounts, special offers, reductions and sales. ☐ ☐

Public services

Post office
You should be able to:

Learnt Tested

- ▶ Ask where a post office or letter box is. ☐ ☐
- ▶ State you would like to send letters/postcards to your home country and ask what it costs. ☐ ☐
- ▶ Ask for stamps of particular values. ☐ ☐
- ▶ Ask if there is a telephone nearby. ☐ ☐
- [H] ▶ Ask about sending letters and post cards or parcels to a specific country or within the country. ☐ ☐

Banks/currency exchange

Learnt Tested

- ▶ Say and understand numbers from 1–1000. ☐ ☐
- ▶ Find out when banks are open. ☐ ☐
- ▶ Exchange money or traveller's cheques. ☐ ☐
- ▶ Enquire about rates of exchange. ☐ ☐
- [H] ▶ Enquire about commission charges and the acceptability of eurocheques and credit cards. ☐ ☐
- ▶ Ask for coins or notes of a particular denomination. ☐ ☐

Lost property and theft

Learnt Tested

- ▶ Ask where a loss should be reported. ☐ ☐
- ▶ Report loss stating what you have lost, when and where it was lost or stolen and describing the item (what it is made of, size, shape, colour, make, contents). ☐ ☐
- [H] ▶ Report the theft of an item and give the above details. ☐ ☐

Hire services
You should be able to:

Learnt Tested

- ▶ Obtain information about the hire of specific items (car, bicycle, wind surfing board, sun lounger etc.). ☐ ☐
- ▶ Understand replies to the above and fill in a relevant form. ☐ ☐

Cleaning and repairs

You should be able to:

	Learnt	Tested
▶ Find out where something can be cleaned/repaired.	☐	☐
▶ Ask for something to be cleaned/repaired.	☐	☐
▶ Find out when an item will be ready for collection.	☐	☐
▶ Find out the cost.	☐	☐

Getting around

You should be able to:

	Learnt	Tested
▶ Give and understand information on how to get into town (means of transport, directions).	☐	☐
▶ Ask if there is a bus, tram, train to a particular place.	☐	☐
▶ Understand simple signs and notices.	☐	☐
▶ Ask about the location of facilities: bus/tram stops, platforms, ticket machines, toilets etc.	☐	☐
▶ Buy tickets, stating: destination, single or return, class, day of travel.	☐	☐
▶ Ask and tell someone about times of departure and arrival.	☐	☐
▶ Respond to ticket checks.	☐	☐
[H] ▶ Ask for and give information about travel by public transport.	☐	☐
▶ Make arrangements for travel by public transport.	☐	☐
▶ Discuss common forms of transport.	☐	☐
▶ Buy fuel and obtain services at a petrol station.	☐	☐
▶ Report the location and basic details of a breakdown.	☐	☐
▶ Report the location and basic details of an accident.	☐	☐

▶ Area of Experience D: The world of work

Further education and training

You should able to:

	Learnt	Tested
▶ Understand, ask and give information about future plans.	☐	☐
▶ Say what subjects/courses are available and state preferences.	☐	☐
[H] ▶ Understand information about different types of further education and training.	☐	☐
▶ Understand and discuss others' descriptions of their education/training.	☐	☐

Careers and employment

	Learnt	Tested
▶ Give information about travel to and from work.	☐	☐
▶ Understand and say that someone is unemployed.	☐	☐
▶ Understand details about and discuss jobs, weekend jobs and work experience.	☐	☐
▶ Say if you have a spare time job and give details.	☐	☐
▶ Give simple opinions about jobs.	☐	☐

- State occupation of self and family.
- Understand the names of common occupations.
- [H] Ask about and give reasons for future study choices.
- Express hopes for the future and describe plans.
- Enquire about the availability of work.
- Ask about people's occupations.
- [H] Discuss the advantages and disadvantages of different occupations.

Language and communication in the workplace

You should be able to:

Learnt Tested

- Ask for and give telephone numbers.
- Answer the telephone.
- Make telephone calls and ask to speak to someone in particular.
- Take or leave a telephone message: name, numbers, time to ring back.
- Ask about delivery and collection times.
- [H] Make arrangements to contact and be contacted by telephone, fax or E-mail.
- Obtain coins or a phone card.
- Describe local industries and employment opportunities.

Advertising and publicity

You should be able to do the following:

Learnt Tested

- Understand simple opinions about particular advertisements.
- Understand simple publicity about leisure activities and public events.
- [H] Give opinions about particular advertisements.

▶ Area of Experience E: The international world

Life in other countries/communities

You should be able to:

Learnt Tested

- Understand money including written and printed prices.
- [H] Discuss typical foods and how to prepare them.
- Discuss important social conventions such as forms of address and eating habits.

Tourism at home and abroad

You should be able to

Learnt Tested

- Talk and ask about holidays in general with regard to:
  - where you normally spend your holidays.
  - how long they last.

- with whom you go.
- what you do.

▶ Understand others giving this information.

▶ Describe a previous holiday, saying:
- where you went.
- how you went.
- with whom you went.
- for how long.
- where you stayed.
- what the weather was like.
- what you saw and did.
- what your general impressions were.

▶ Give simple opinions about excursions and places of interest.

[H] ▶ Ask for and give information about excursions: cost, time, location.

▶ Ask for tourist information, e.g. maps, town plans, brochures, prospectuses etc.

▶ Discuss past and future holidays.

▶ Express preferences and opinions about types of holiday, excursions and places of interest.

Accommodation

With reference to **hotels, youth hostels and campsites** you should be able to:

Learnt Tested

▶ Ask if accommodation is available.

▶ Say when you require accommodation and for how long.

▶ Say what sort of accommodation you require.

▶ Ask the cost per person per night.

▶ Accept or reject the accommodation offered.

▶ Identify yourself.

▶ Ask about your key and the location of your room.

▶ Ask where facilities are: dining room, toilet, showers, bathroom, games room.

▶ Ask about meal times.

▶ Say you would like to pay.

▶ Make reservations.

[H] ▶ Ask for and understand information about rules and regulations.

▶ Arrange accommodation for other people.

▶ Ask about reduced rates for students/groups.

▶ Make complaints, request alternative accommodation and give reasons.

▶ Give and ask about opinions and preferences regarding types of holiday accommodation.

The wider world, world events and issues

You should be able to:

Learnt *Tested*

▶ Understand the names of countries and nationalities commonly encountered. ☐ ☐

▶ Understand the discussion of current issues and events of general news value and of interest to 16-year-old students, e.g. conservation, nature, lifestyles. ☐ ☐

▶ Express a reaction to such items. ☐ ☐

▶ Discuss environmental issues of personal interest, e.g. pollution, recycling, nature, equal opportunities. ☐ ☐

H ▶ Understand opinions and information about global issues. ☐ ☐

▶ Discuss any part of a German-speaking country you know about and describe it (e.g. its history, geography, current and future developments) ☐ ☐

▶ Give opinions about religion, politics and society. ☐ ☐

▶ Compare UK lifestyles with those of German-speaking countries. ☐ ☐

Chapter 16

Vocabulary

▷ **GETTING STARTED**

The German word for 'vocabulary' is *Wortschatz* – a treasury of words. And that is just what this chapter is. It is a treasury of all the valuable words which you need to know. Do you know, for instance, what a *Hubschrauber* is? Or a *Schiedsrichter*? And do you know how to say in German 'congratulations' or 'good luck'? Well, it is all here!

The German–English list is **comprehensive**, covering the words required by all the examining groups. The English–German list which follows is **selective**, covering commonly used terms. There is also, in Chapter 3, a detailed breakdown of German words by **topic area** that can guide you when you are seeking the translation of a particular English word.

Und wir wünschen dir viel Spaß und alles Gute!

▷ **KEY TO SYMBOLS AND ABBREVIATIONS**

Plurals of nouns are indicated by (-), (-e), (¨e), (¨er), (-n), (-en), (-s), (-se) as appropriate.

(*sep.*) indicates a separable verb.

Further explanations in English are given in brackets where relevant to clarify meanings, e.g. ausgeben *to spend (money)*.

▷ **GERMAN–ENGLISH VOCABULARY (COMPREHENSIVE)**

The list which follows is based on a detailed analysis of the vocabulary listed by the individual examining groups. The list I have drawn up is comprehensive at both Tiers and should serve you well. It is intended primarily as a reference list and a means of cross-checking against vocabulary contained in the individual topic areas.

ab *from*
abbauen (*sep.*) *to take down, dismantle; mine*
abbiegen (*sep.*) *to turn off (directions)*
der Abend (-e) *evening*
das Abendbrot *evening meal (cold: bread+. . .)*
das Abendessen (-) *evening meal (hot)*
abends *in the evening*
aber *but*
abfahren (*sep.*) *to depart, leave*
die Abfahrt (-en) *departure*
der Abfall (¨e) *rubbish*
der Abfalleimer (-) *rubbish bin*
abfliegen (*sep.*) *to fly, take off*
der Abflug (¨e) *departure (of flights)*
abgeben (*sep.*) *to hand/give in (lost property)*
abgemacht *agreed*
abhängen (*sep.*) von+*dat to depend on*
es hängt von ihm ab *it depends on him*
abheben (*sep.*) *to take off (hat, lid, cover)*
abholen (*sep.*) *to collect, meet (e.g. at station)*
das Abitur *Advanced Level examination*
ablehnen (*sep.*) *to decline, reject*
abräumen (*sep.*) *to tidy up, clear away/up*
abschleppen (*sep.*) *to tow away, drag away*
der Abschleppdienst *breakdown service*
der Abschleppwagen (-) *breakdown vehicle*
abschließen (*sep.*) *to lock (up)*
die Abschlußprüfung (-en) *school-leaving examination*
abschreiben (*sep.*) *to copy (cheat), write down*
der Absender (-) *sender (of letter)*
Abs. *abbreviation for Absender*
abspülen (*sep.*) *to wash up*
Abstand halten *to keep one's distance (driving)*
abstellen (*sep.*) *to turn off (motor, engine)*
das Abteil (-e) *compartment (of train)*
die Abteilung (-en) *department (in shop, office)*
abtrocknen (*sep.*) *to dry up*
abwaschen (*sep.*) *to wash up*
achten auf+*acc. to pay attention to, look after*
Achtung! *look out! watch out! take care!*
ADAC *German AA motoring equivalent*
die Adresse (-n) *address*
der Affe (-n) *ape, monkey*
ähnlich *similar*
die Ahnung (-en) *idea*
(ich habe) keine Ahnung *I've no idea, I haven't a clue*
aktuell *current, currently, topical*
all- *every, all*
alle sein *to be all gone*
mein Geld ist alle *my money is all gone*
allein *alone*
die Allergie (-n) *allergy*

alles *everything*
alles Gute! *all the best!*
als *when (conj.), than (comparison)*
also *so, therefore*
alt *old*
älter *older*
das Alter *age*
altmodisch *old-fashioned*
die Altstadt (¨e) *old town*
am (an dem) *at the, on the*
Amerika *America*
der Amerikaner (-) *American (person)*
amerikanisch *American*
die Ampel (-n) *traffic lights*
an *at, on*
an . . . vorbei *past (e.g. to go past)*
an der Kirche vorbei *past the church*
an Bord *on board*
an sein *to be on (e.g. TV)*
anbieten (*sep.*) *to offer*
das Andenken (-) *souvenir*
ander- *other*
anders (als) *different (from)*
anderthalb *one and a half*
anderthalb Stunden *one and a half hours*
der Anfang (¨e) *beginning*
anfangen (*sep.*) *to begin*
das Angebot (-e) *offer*
angeln *to fish*
die Angelrute (-n) *fishing rod*
angenehm *pleasant; pleased to meet you!*
der/die Angestellte (-n) *employee*
die Angst (¨e) *fear*
anhaben (*sep.*) *to have on, wear*
per Anhalter fahren *to hitch-hike*
ankommen (*sep.*) *to arrive*
die Ankunft *arrival*
die Anlage (-n) *system, installation; park*
anlassen (*sep.*) *to start (car, engine)*
Anlieger frei *residents only (road sign)*
anmachen (*sep.*) *to turn on (e.g. light)*
sich anmelden (*sep.*) *to book in, report, enrol*
die Anmeldung (-en) *booking, enrolment, registration*
annehmen (*sep.*) *to accept*
der Anorak (-s) *anorak*
anprobieren (*sep.*) *to try on*
der Anruf (-e) *telephone call*
anrufen (*sep.*) *to telephone, make a phone call*
ans (an das) *to the*
der Ansager (-) *announcer (e.g. TV/radio)*
(sich anschnallen (*sep.*) *to fasten (one's) seat belt*
die Anschrift (-en) *address (e.g. on letter)*
ansehen (*sep.*) *to watch, look at*
die Ansichtskarte (-n) *postcard*
anstreichen (*sep.*) *to paint*

anstrengend *exhausting, hard work*
die Antwort (-en) *answer, reply*
antworten (auf+*acc.*) *to answer, reply (to)*
(sich) anziehen (*sep.*) *to put on, to dress/(get dressed)*
der Anzug (¨e) *suit*
der Apfel (¨) *apple*
der Apfelsaft (¨e) *apple juice*
die Apfelsine (-n) *orange*
die Apotheke (-n) *chemist's*
der Apotheker (-) *chemist*
der Apparat (-e) *telephone, camera, set, machine*
am Apparat *on the telephone, speaking*
der Appetit *appetite*
guten Appetit *enjoy your meal! bon appétit!*
der April *April*
die Arbeit (-en) *work*
arbeiten *to work*
der Arbeiter (-) *worker*
der Arbeitgeber (-) *employer*
der Arbeitnehmer (-) *employee*
arbeitslos *out of work, unemployed*
(sich) ärgern *to annoy/(get annoyed)*
arm *poor*
der Arm (-e) *arm*
das Armband (¨er) *bracelet*
die Armbanduhr (-en) *wrist watch*
die Armee (-n) *army*
die Armut *poverty*
der Artikel (-) *article, item*
der Arzt (¨e) *doctor (male)*
die Ärztin (-nen) *doctor (female)*
der Aschenbecher (-) *ashtray*
atemlos *breathless*
die Atmosphäre *atmosphere*
die Atomkraft *atomic energy*
auch *also, too*
auf *on, onto, to*
auf dem Lande *in the country*
auf deutsch *in German*
auf die Toilette gehen *to go to the toilet*
auf Wiederhören! *goodbye! (on telephone)*
auf Wiedersehen! *goodbye!*
aufbauen (*sep.*) *to build up*
der Aufenthalt (-e) *stay*
die Aufführung (-en) *performance, production*
die Aufgabe (-n) *exercise (school)*
aufgeben (*sep.*) *to give up, to set/assign (homework)*
aufheben (*sep.*) *to pick up (e.g. from the ground)*
die Aufheiterung (-en) *bright period (weather)*
aufhören (*sep.*) *to stop, give up, cease*
der Aufkleber (-) *sticker*
aufmachen (*sep.*) *to open*
die Aufnahme (-n) *photo, recording*
aufpassen (*sep.*) *to pay attention*
aufräumen (*sep.*) *to tidy up, clear away/up*

aufschlagen (*sep.*) *to open; to pitch (tent)*
der Aufschnitt *cold meat(s)*
aufstehen (*sep.*) *to get up, stand up*
aufwachen (*sep.*) *to awake, wake up*
der Aufzug (¨e) *lift, elevator*
das Auge (-n) *eye*
der Augenblick (-e) *moment*
der August *August*
die Aula (die Aulen) *(assembly) hall, lecture theatre*
aus *out, out of, from, made of*
der Ausdruck (¨e) *expression*
die Ausfahrt (-en) *exit, drive (motoring)*
ausfallen (*sep.*) *to be cancelled*
der Ausflug (¨e) *excursion, trip*
ausfüllen (*sep.*) *to fill out, complete (forms)*
der Ausgang (¨e) *way out, exit*
ausgeben (*sep.*) *to spend (money)*
ausgehen (*sep.*) *to go out*
ausgezeichnet *excellent*
die Auskunft (¨e) *information*
das Ausland *abroad*
der Ausländer (-) *foreigner*
ausmachen (*sep.*) *to turn off/out (e.g. light); to arrange, make (appointment)*
auspacken (*sep.*) *to unpack*
der Auspuff *exhaust*
die Auspuffgase (-n) *exhaust fumes*
ausreichend *satisfactory (German school grade)*
sich ausruhen (*sep.*) *to relax, rest*
ausschalten (*sep.*) *to switch off (e.g. TV/radio)*
aussehen (*sep.*) *to look, appear*
Außen- *outside . . .*
außer *apart from, besides, except*
außer Betrieb *out of order, out of action*
außerdem *besides*
äußerst *extremely, exceptionally*
die Aussicht (-en) *view, outlook*
aussprechen (*sep.*) *to express, pronounce*
aussteigen (*sep.*) *to get off/out*
die Ausstellung (-en) *exhibition*
der Ausstieg (-e) *exit (e.g. on bus, train)*
austragen (*sep.*) *to deal with, cancel*
der Austausch (-e) *exchange (school visit)*
der Austauschpartner (-) *exchange partner*
austrinken (*sep.*) *to drink up*
der Ausverkauf *clearance sale (reduced price)*
ausverkauft *sold out*
die Auswahl *selection, choice*
der Ausweis (-e) *identity card, papers*
sich ausziehen (*sep.*) *to get undressed*
das Auto (-s) *car*
die Autobahn (-en) *motorway*
das Autobahndreieck (-e) *motorway merging point*
das Autobahnkreuz (-e) *motorway intersection*

die Autofähre (-n) *car ferry*
der Automat (-en) *vending machine*
die Autowäsche (-n) *car wash*
das Baby (-s) *baby*
der Bach (¨e) *stream, brook*
backen *to bake*
der Bäcker (-) *baker*
die Bäckerei (-en) *baker's*
das Bad (¨er) *bath, bathroom*
der Badeanzug (¨e) *swimsuit*
die Badehose (-n) *swimming trunks*
die Bademütze (-n) *bathing hat*
baden *to bath, bathe, have a bath*
das Badetuch (¨er) *bath(ing) towel*
die Badewanne (-n) *bath, bath tub*
das Badezimmer (-) *bathroom*
Badminton *badminton*
die Bahn (-en) *railway, track*
der Bahnhof (¨e) *railway station*
der Bahnsteig (-e) *platform (at station)*
der Bahnübergang (¨e) *level crossing*
bald *soon*
der Balkon (-s) *balcony*
der Ball (¨e) *ball*
die Banane (-n) *banana*
die Bank (-en) *bank (of money)*
die Banknote (-n) *bank note*
die Bar (-s) *bar, pub*
der Bart (¨e) *beard*
basteln *to make models, do handicraft, etc.*
die Batterie (-n) *battery*
der Bauch (¨e) *stomach*
Bauchschmerzen *stomach ache*
bauen *to build*
der Bauer (-n) *farmer*
der Bauernhof (¨e) *farm*
der Baum (¨e) *tree*
die Baumwolle *cotton*
die Baustelle (-n) *building site, roadworks*
der Beamte (-n) *official, civil servant*
beantworten *to answer*
sich bedanken *to say thank you, express gratitude*
bedauern *to regret*
bedeckt *cloudy (of sky)*
bedienen *to serve, wait on*
sich bedienen *to serve/help oneself*
die Bedienung (-en) *service*
sich beeilen *to hurry*
sich befinden *to be situated, to be*
der Beginn (-e) *beginning, start*
beginnen *to begin, start*
begleiten *to accompany*
begrüßen *to greet*
behandeln *to treat (e.g. a patient)*
behilflich *helpful, of assistance*
bei *at (the house of), near, on*
beide *both*
beilegen (sep.) *to enclose*
beim (bei dem) *at the, near the*
das Bein (-e) *leg*
das Beispiel (-e) *example*
beißen *to bite*
bekannt *well known, famous*
der/die Bekannte (-n) *acquaintance*
sich beklagen *to complain*
bekommen *to get, receive*

ein belegtes Brot (-e) *open sandwich, bread and . . .*
Belgien *Belgium*
der Belgier *Belgian (person)*
belgisch *Belgian (adjective)*
beliebt *popular, liked*
bellen *to bark*
bemerken *to notice*
benutzen *to use*
das Benzin *petrol*
beobachten *to watch, observe*
bequem *comfortable*
der Berg (-e) *mountain*
bergsteigen *to climb, go mountaineering*
der Bericht (-e) *report*
der Beruf (-e) *profession*
die Berufsberatung *careers advice*
die Berufsschule (-n) *technical college*
berufstätig *in paid work, employed*
berühmt *famous*
beschäftigt *busy, occupied*
der Bescheid (e) *information, notification*
Bescheid sagen *to let someone know, tell someone*
beschließen *to decide*
beschreiben *to describe*
die Beschreibung (-en) *description*
sich beschweren *to complain*
besetzt *occupied, taken; engaged (phone)*
besichtigen *to visit, see (sights)*
die Besichtigung (-en) *visit*
besonder(s) *special/(especially)*
besorgen *to obtain*
besser *better*
die Besserung *improvement, recovery*
gute Besserung! *get well soon!*
best- *best*
das Besteck (-e) *cutlery, place setting (at table)*
bestehen (aus) *to exist; consist (of)*
bestellen *to order (food, books, etc.)*
bestimmt *definite(ly), certain(ly)*
bestrafen *to punish*
der Besuch (-e) *visit*
besuchen *to visit*
betreten *to enter; step on (e.g. grass)*
der Betrieb (-e) *firm, factory, works*
außer Betrieb *out of order, not working*
die Betriebsferien *works' holidays*
betrunken *drunk*
das Bett (-en) *bed*
ins Bett/zu Bett gehen *to go to bed*
die Bettdecke (-n) *blanket*
die Bettwäsche *bed linen*
bevor *before (conjunction)*
sich bewegen *to move*
beweisen *to prove*
bewölkt *cloudy*
die Bewölkung *clouding over, becoming cloudy; cloud*
bezahlen *to pay (for)*
die Bibliothek (-en) *library*
das Bier (-e) *beer*
bieten *to offer, provide*

das Bild (-er) *picture*
billig *cheap*
binden *to tie, bind, unite*
Biologie *Biology*
die Birne (-n) *pear; light-bulb*
bis *until, as far as; by (of time)*
bis bald *see you soon!*
bis gleich *see you soon/shortly!*
bis morgen *until/see you/by tomorrow*
bis später *see you later!*
bis zu *as far as*
ein bißchen *a little, a bit*
bitte *please; that's all right, here*
bitte nochmals *again please, same again please*
bitte schön *here you are, that's all right*
bitte sehr *here you are, that's all right*
bitten *to ask, request*
die Blaskapelle (-n) *brass band*
blaß *pale*
das Blatt (¨er) *leaf (of tree), page (of book), sheet (of paper)*
blau *blue; drunk (slang)*
bleiben *to stay, remain*
bleifrei *lead free (petrol)*
der Bleistift (-e) *pencil*
der Blick (-e) *view, look*
blind *blind*
der Blitz (-e) *flash (photo), flash of lightning*
blitzen *to flash (of photo or lightning)*
der Block (¨e) *block (of houses, flats)*
die Blockflöte (-n) *recorder (instrument)*
blöd *mad, stupid*
der Blödsinn *madness, nonsense, stupidity*
blond *blond, fair*
die Blume (-n) *flower*
der Blumenkohl *cauliflower*
die Bluse (-n) *blouse*
das Blut *blood*
bluten *to bleed*
die Bockwurst *sausage (large Frankfurter)*
der Boden *floor, ground*
der Bodensee *Lake Constance*
die Bohne (-n) *green bean*
das/der Bonbon (-s) *sweet*
das Boot (-e) *boat*
böse *angry, cross; naughty*
braten *to fry, roast*
der Braten *roast (a roast dish)*
das Brathähnchen (-) *roast chicken*
die Bratkartoffel (-n) *fried potato*
die Bratwurst (¨e) *fried sausage*
brauchen *to need*
braun *brown*
brav *good, well behaved*
die BRD (Bundesrepublik Deutschland) *FRG (Federal Republic of Germany)*
brechen *to break*
breit *broad, wide*
die Bremse (-n) *brake*
bremsen *to brake*
das Brett (-er) *board, shelf; stage (slang)*

der Brief (-e) *letter*
der Brieffreund (-e) *pen friend*
der Briefkasten (⸚) *letter box*
die Briefmarke (-n) *stamp*
die Brieftasche (-n) *wallet*
der Briefträger (-) *postman*
der Briefumschlag (⸚e) *envelope*
die Brille (-n) *(pair of) glasses*
bringen *to bring*
die Broschüre (-n) *brochure*
das Brot (-e) *bread, loaf of bread*
das Brötchen (-) *bread roll*
die Brücke (-n) *bridge*
der Bruder (⸚) *brother*
die Brust (⸚e) *breast, chest*
das Buch (⸚er) *book*
buchen *to book*
die Bücherei (-en) *library*
buchstabieren *to spell*
die Buchhandlung (-en) *bookshop*
der Buddhismus *Buddhism*
bügeln *to iron*
die Bühne (-n) *stage (of theatre, concert)*
bummeln *to wander, stroll (in town)*
die Bundesliga *German football league*
die Bundesrepublik *The Federal Republic*
der Bungalow (-s) *bungalow*
bunt *bright, brightly coloured*
die Burg (-en) *castle*
der Bürgermeister (-) *mayor*
der Bürgerkrieg *civil war*
der Bürgersteig (-e) *pavement*
das Büro (-s) *office*
die Bürste (-n) *brush*
sich bürsten *to brush (oneself)*
der Bus (-se) *bus*
der Busbahnhof (⸚e) *bus station*
die Bushaltestelle (-n) *bus stop*
die Butter *butter*
das Butterbrot (-e) *sandwich*
bzw. *(short for beziehungsweise) respectively; that is (to say)*

das Café (-s) *café*
der Campingkocher (-) *camping stove*
der Campingplatz (⸚e) *campsite*
der CD-Spieler (-) *CD Player*
Celsius *centigrade, Celsius*
der Champignon (-s) *mushroom*
der Chef (-s) *boss, head*
Chemie *Chemistry*
Chips *crisps*
der Chor (⸚e) *choir*
das Christentum *Christianity*
die /das Cola (-s) *coke*
der Computer (-) *computer*
der Cousin (-s) *cousin (male)*
die Cousine (-n) *cousin (female)*
die Currywurst (⸚e) *curried sausage*

da *there*
da *since (conjunction)*
das Dach (⸚er) *roof*
der Dachboden *attic*
dagegen *against (it/something)*
damals *then, at that time*
die Dame (-n) *lady*

Damen or D *Ladies (on public toilets)*
damit *with it; so that*
der Dampfer *steamer*
danach *afterwards*
der Dank *thanks*
vielen Dank *thanks a lot*
dankbar *grateful*
danke *thank you*
danke schön/sehr *thank you very much*
danken *to thank*
dann *then*
das geht *that's all right/OK*
daß *that (conjunction)*
das Datum (Daten) *date*
dauern *to last*
der Daumen (-) *thumb*
die DB (Deutsche Bundesbahn) *German Federal Railway*
die DDR (Deutsche Demokratische Republik) *GDR (German Democratic Republic)*
die Decke (-n) *ceiling; blanket, cover (on bed)*
decken *to cover; lay (table)*
dein *your*
denken *to think*
das Denkmal (⸚er) *monument*
denn *for, because*
deutlich *clear, clearly*
deutsch *German*
die Deutsche Bundesbahn *German Federal Railway*
der}
die} Deutsche (-n) *German (person)*
deutsches Beefsteak *German beefsteak*
Deutschland *Germany*
die deutsche Mark *German Mark, Deutschmark*
der Dezember *December*
das Dia (-s) *slide (photo)*
dick *fat*
der Dieb (-e) *thief*
dienen *to serve*
der Dienst (-e) *service*
der Dienstag *Tuesday*
Diesel *diesel*
dieser *this*
diesmal *this time*
das Ding (-er) *thing*
direkt *direct, non-stop, without changing*
der Direktor *director, headmaster*
die Diskothek (-en) *discotheque*
DJH *German Youth Hostel Association*
DM or D-Mark (deutsche Mark) *German Mark, Deutschmark*
doch *but, however*
der Dom (-e) *cathedral*
die Donau *The Danube*
der Donner (-) *thunder*
donnern *to thunder*
der Donnerstag *Thursday*
doof *stupid, mad*
das Doppelhaus (⸚er) *semi-detached house*
das Doppelzimmer (-) *double room*
das Dorf (⸚er) *village*
dort *there*

dort drüben *over there*
die Dose (-n) *tin, can, jar*
der Dosenöffner (-) *tin-opener*
dransein (*sep.*) *to have one's turn/go*
ich bin dran *it's my turn/go*
dreckig *dirty*
dringend *urgent*
dritte *third*
die Drogerie (-n) *drugstore, chemist*
der Drogist *chemist*
drohen *to threaten*
drüben *over there*
drücken *to press, push*
dumm *stupid*
dunkel *dark*
dünn *thin*
durch *through*
der Durchfall *diarrhoea*
durchfallen (*sep.*) *to fail (test, examination*
Durchgang verboten *no thoroughfare*
der Durchgangsverkehr *through traffic*
dürfen *to be allowed*
der Durst *thirst*
durstig *thirsty*
die Dusche (-n) *shower*
duschen *to shower*
duzen *to use du when talking to (somebody)*
der D-Zug (⸚e) *express train*

der E111-Schein *E111 form (health insurance)*
eben *just, flat*
ebenso *just as*
echt *genuine, real*
die Ecke (-n) *corner*
egal *equal, same*
das ist mir egal *it's all the same to me*
die Ehe (-n) *marriage*
die Ehefrau (-en) *married woman, wife*
der Ehemann (⸚er) *married man, husband*
das Ehepaar (-e) *married couple*
ehrlich *genuine, honest*
das Ei (-er) *egg*
eigen *own, of one's own*
die Eile *hurry*
eilen *to hurry*
der Eilzug (⸚e) *fast train*
ein paar *a few*
ein wenig *a little*
die Einbahnstraße (-n) *one-way street/road*
einbrechen (*sep.*) *to break in*
der Einbrecher (-) *burglar*
der Eindruck (⸚e) *impression*
einfach *simple, easy; single*
die Einfahrt (-en) *entry, entrance*
das Einfamilienhaus (⸚er) *detached house*
der Eingang (⸚e) *entry, entrance*
einige *a few, some*
die Einkäufe machen *to shop, do the shopping*
einkaufen (*sep.*) *to shop, do the shopping*

der Einkaufskorb (¨e) *shopping basket*
der Einkaufswagen (-) *shopping trolley*
das Einkaufszentrum (-tren) *shopping centre*
einladen *(sep.)* *to invite*
die Einladung (-en) *invitation*
einlösen *(sep.)* *to cash (cheques)*
einmal *once, single, one portion of*
einordnen *(sep.)* *to put in order; get into lane*
einpacken *(sep.)* *to pack*
einreiben *(sep.)* *to rub in*
einreichen *(sep.)* *to hand in*
einschalten *(sep.)* *to switch on*
einschenken *(sep.)* *to pour (in)*
einschl. (einschließlich) *inclusive, included*
einschlafen *(sep.)* *to fall asleep*
einschließlich *inclusive, included*
einsteigen *(sep.)* *to get on/in*
der Einstieg (-e) *entry, entrance (bus, tram, etc.)*
der Eintritt (-e) *admission*
die Eintrittskarte (-n) *entrance ticket (e.g. to concert)*
einverstanden *agreed*
einwerfen *(sep.)* *to post, put in slot*
der Einwohner (-) *inhabitant*
der Einwurf (¨e) *slit for inserting coins/letters*
die Einzelheiten *details*
die Einzelkarte (-n) *single ticket*
das Einzelkind (-er) *only child*
das Einzelzimmer (-) *single room*
das Eis (-e) *ice-cream; ice*
der Eisbecher (-) *ice-cream sundae*
die Eisenbahn (-en) *railway*
der Elefant (-en) *elephant*
der Elektriker (-) *electrician*
elektrisch *electric*
Elektro- *electric . . .*
die Elektrizität *electricity*
die Eltern *parents*
der Empfang (¨e) *reception*
die Empfangsdame (-n) *receptionist (female)*
empfehlen *to recommend*
das Ende *end*
enden *to end*
endlich *at last, finally*
das Endspiel (-e) *final (of competition)*
die Energie *energy*
eng *narrow; close (of friendship)*
England *England*
der Engländer (-) *Englishman*
die Engländerin (-nen) *Englishwoman*
englisch *English (thing/language)*
der Enkel (-) *grandchild, grandson*
die Ente (-n) *duck*
entfernt *distant, away, far (away)*
entlang *along*
(sich) entscheiden *to decide*
entschuldigen *to forgive, excuse*
sich entschuldigen *to apologise*
die Entschuldigung (-en) *apology, excuse*

Entschuldigung! *excuse me!*
enttäuscht *disappointed*
entweder *either*
der Entwerter (-) *(ticket) cancelling machine*
die Erbse (-n) *pea*
die Erdbeere (-n) *strawberry*
die Erde *earth, ground*
das Erdgeschoß *ground floor*
Erdkunde *Geography*
erfahren *to learn, experience*
die Erfahrung (-en) *experience*
der Erfolg (-e) *success*
Erfrischungen *refreshments*
das Ergebnis (-se) *result*
erhalten *to receive, get*
erhältlich *obtainable*
sich erholen *to recover, get better*
sich erinnern *to remember*
sich erkälten *to catch a cold*
erkältet sein *to have a cold*
die Erkältung (-en) *cold (illness)*
erkennen *to recognise*
erklären *to explain*
sich erkundigen *to enquire*
erlauben *to allow*
die Erlaubnis (-se) *permission*
die Ermäßigung (-en) *reduction (of cost)*
ernst *serious*
erreichen *to reach, catch (train/bus)*
das Ersatzteil (-e) *spare part*
erscheinen *to appear, come into view*
erschrecken *to frighten*
erschrocken *frightened*
erst *first, firstly*
erst (um) *not until, only (of time)*
erste *first (adjective)*
die Erste Hilfe *first aid*
erstaunt *surprised*
der Erwachsene (-n) *adult, grown-up*
erwarten *to expect*
erzählen *to tell, relate*
es freut mich *I'm pleased*
es geht *(it's) all right*
es gibt+acc. *there is, there are*
es ist mir egal *I don't mind*
es macht nichts *it doesn't matter*
es tut mir leid *I'm sorry*
das Essen *food, meal*
essen *to eat*
das Eßzimmer (-) *dining room*
die Etage (-n) *floor, storey*
etwa *about, approximately, somewhat*
etwas *something*
die EU/Europäische Union *EU/European Union*
euer *your*
Europa *Europe*
evangelisch *Protestant*
das Examen (-) *examination*

die Fabrik (-en) *factory*
der Fabrikarbeiter (-) *factory worker*
das Fach (¨er) *subject (school)*
die Fachhochschule (-n) *technical college*
die Fachschule (-n) *technical school*
der Fahrausweis (-e) *ticket*

die Fähre (-n) *ferry*
fahren *to go, travel, drive*
der Fahrer (-) *driver*
der Fahrgast (¨e) *passenger*
die Fahrkarte (-n) *ticket*
der Fahrkartenschalter (-) *ticket office*
der Fahrplan (¨e) *timetable (of transport)*
der Fahrpreis (-e) *fare*
das Fahrrad (¨er) *bicycle*
der Fahrschein (-e) *ticket*
der Fahrstuhl (¨e) *lift, elevator*
die Fahrt (-en) *journey*
das Fahrzeug (-e) *vehicle*
der Fall (¨e) *case, event*
auf keinen Fall *in no way*
fallen *to fall*
fallen lassen *to drop*
falls *in case*
falsch *false, incorrect, wrong*
die Familie (-n) *family*
der Familienname (-n) *surname*
der Fan (-s) *fan*
der Fanatiker (-) *fan(atic)*
fangen *to catch*
die Farbe (-n) *colour*
der Fasching *Carnival*
fast *almost, nearly*
faul *lazy*
der Februar *February*
Federball *badminton*
das Federbett (-en) *quilt, duvet*
fehlen *to be missing/absent*
der Fehler (-) *mistake*
die Feier (-n) *celebration, party*
der Feierabend *end of work, evening*
feiern *to celebrate*
der Feiertag (-e) *public holiday*
das Feld (-er) *field*
das Fenster (-) *window*
die Ferien *holidays*
das Ferngespräch (-e) *long-distance call*
der Fernsehapparat (-e) *television set*
fernsehen *(sep.)* *to watch television*
der Fernseher (-) *television set*
der Fernsprecher (-) *(public) telephone*
fertig *ready*
das Fest (-e) *celebration, party*
festhalten *(sep.)* *to hold onto/fast*
fett *fat*
feucht *damp*
das Feuer (-) *fire*
Feuer haben *to have a light (colloquial)*
der Feuerlöscher (-) *fire extinguisher*
die Feuerwehr *fire brigade*
der Feuerwehrwagen (-) *fire engine*
das Feuerzeug (-e) *cigarette lighter*
das Fieber *temperature*
der Film (-e) *film*
der Filzstift (-e) *felt-tip pen*
finden *to find*
der Finger (-) *finger*
die Firma (Firmen) *firm, company*
der Fisch (-e) *fish*
fit *fit*
flach *flat*
die Flasche (-n) *bottle*

der Flaschenöffner (-) bottle-opener
das Fleisch meat
der Fleischer (-) butcher
die Fleischerei (-en) butcher's shop
fleißig hard-working, industrious
die Fliege (-n) fly
fliegen to fly
fließen to flow
fließend flowing, running (water)
die Flöte (-n) flute
der Flug (¨e) flight
der Fluggast (¨e) passenger (on flight)
der Flughafen (¨) airport
der Flugplatz (¨e) airport
das Flugzeug (-e) aeroplane
der Flur (-e) corridor, hall
der Fluß (Flüsse) river
folgen to follow
folgend following
die Forelle (-n) trout
das Formular (-e) form (to be completed)
der Forst (-en) forest
der Fortschritt (-e) progress
das Foto (-s) photo
der Fotoapparat (-e) camera
fotografieren to take a photo
die Frage (-n) question
eine Frage stellen to ask a question
fragen to ask
der Franken Swiss franc
Frankreich France
der Franzose (-n) Frenchman
die Französin (-nen) Frenchwoman
französisch French (adjective)
die Frau (-en) woman
Frau ... Mrs ...
das Fräulein (-) girl, waitress
Fräulein! waitress!
Fräulein ... Miss ...
frech cheeky
frei free, open, not taken
das Freibad (¨er) open-air swimming pool
freihalten (sep.) to keep clear/free (e.g. drive)
der Freitag Friday
die Freizeit free time
die Freizeitbeschäftigung (-en) leisure activity
das Freizeitzentrum leisure centre
fremd strange, foreign
der Fremde (-n) stranger, foreigner
das Fremdenzimmer (-) room (in guest house)
die Fremdsprache (-n) foreign language
fressen to eat (of animals)
sich freuen to be pleased
der Freund (-e) friend
freundlich friendly
der Frieden peace
der Friedhof (¨e) cemetery, graveyard
frieren to be cold, freeze
die Frikadelle (-n) rissole
frisch fresh
der Friseur/Frisör hairdresser (male)
die Friseuse/Frisörin hairdresser (female)
die Frisur (-en) haircut, style
froh happy, glad

frohe Ostern Happy Easter
frohe Weihnachten Happy/Merry Christmas
frohes Neujahr Happy New Year
fröhlich happy, cheerful
früh early
früher earlier, previously
der Frühling Spring
das Frühstück breakfast
frühstücken to have breakfast
sich fühlen to feel
führen to lead, take
der Führerschein (-e) driving licence
die Führung (-en) guided tour; lead
füllen to fill
der Füller (-) fountain pen
das Fundbüro (-s) lost property office
funktionieren to function
für for (preposition)
furchtbar terrible
der Fuß (Füsse) foot
zu Fuß on foot, walking
der Fußball (¨e) football
der Fußballplatz (¨e) football ground/pitch
der Fußballspieler (-) footballer
der Fußboden floor (opposite of ceiling)
der Fußgänger (-) pedestrian
die Fußgängerzone (-n) pedestrian zone
das Futter food (for animals)
füttern to feed (animals)

die Gabel (-n) fork (cutlery)
der Gang (¨e) corridor; gear (of car)
die Gans (¨e) goose
ganz quite, very (adverb); all (adjective)
die Ganztagsschule (-n) all-day school
gar kein no, none at all
gar nicht not at all
gar nichts nothing at all
die Garage (-n) garage
die Garderobe (-n) wardrobe; cloakroom
die Gardine (-n) curtain
der Garten (¨) garden
das Gas gas
Gas geben to accelerate
der Gast (¨e) guest
das Gasthaus (¨er) restaurant, inn
der Gasthof (¨e) restaurant, inn
die Gaststätte (-n) restaurant
gebacken baked
das Gebäck biscuits
das Gebäude (-) building
geben to give
das Gebiet (-e) area, region
das Gebirge (-) mountains, mountain range
geboren born
gebraten roast, baked, fried
gebrauchen to use
die Gebrauchsanweisung (-en) instructions for use
gebraucht used, second-hand
die Gebühr (-en) fee, charge
gebührenpflichtig fee payable, chargeable
die Geburt (-en) birth
das Geburtsdatum (-en) date of birth

der Geburtsort (-e) place of birth
der Geburtstag (-e) birthday
geduldig patient
die Gefahr (-en) danger
gefährlich dangerous
gefallen to please
es gefällt mir I like it
das Gefängnis (-se) prison
gegen against, towards; about (time)
die Gegend (-en) area, neighbourhood
das Gegenteil (-e) opposite
gegenüber opposite (preposition)
der Gehalt (-e) content
das Gehalt (¨er) salary
gehen to go
gehören (+dat.) to belong (to)
die Geige (-n) violin
gelaunt tempered
gut/schlecht gelaunt good/bad-tempered, in a good/bad mood
gelb yellow
das Geld (-er) money
der Geldbeutel (-) purse
die Geldbörse (-n) purse
die Geldstrafe (-n) fine (e.g. for motoring offence)
der Geldwechsel (-) exchange (of currency)
die Gelegenheit (-en) opportunity, occasion
gelegentlich occasional(ly)
gelingen (impersonal) to succeed
es gelingt mir I succeed
gemischt/gem. mixed
das Gemüse vegetables
der Gemüsehändler (-) greengrocer
gemütlich cosy
genau exact(ly), precise(ly)
genug enough
genügen to be enough, suffice
geöffnet open
Geographie Geography
das Gepäck luggage
die Gepäckannahme left-luggage deposit
die Gepäckaufbewahrung left-luggage office
die Gepäckaufgabe left-luggage deposit
die Gepäckausgabe left-luggage collection area
das Gepäcknetz (-e) luggage rack/net
die Gepäckrückgabe left-luggage return area
der Gepäckträger (-) porter
gerade straight, just
geradeaus straight on, straight ahead
das Gerät (-e) piece of equipment, appliance
das Gericht (-e) court (of law); course/dish (meal)
gern(e) willingly, gladly
gern geschehen my pleasure
gernhaben (sep.) to like
ich hätte gern I would like
die Gesamtschule (-n) comprehensive school
das Geschäft (-e) shop, business
der Geschäftsmann (¨er) businessman

die Geschäftszeiten *opening/business hours*
geschehen *to happen*
das Geschenk (-e) *present*
Geschichte *History*
die Geschichte (-n) *story, tale*
geschieden *divorced, separated*
das Geschirr (-e) *crockery*
das Geschlecht (-er) *sex*
geschlossen *closed, shut*
der Geschmack (¨-e) *taste*
die Geschwindigkeit (-en) *speed*
die Geschwister *brothers and sisters*
das Gesicht (-er) *face*
gesperrt *closed, blocked (of road)*
das Gespräch (-e) *conversation*
gestatten *to allow, permit*
gestattet *allowed, permitted*
gestern *yesterday*
gestrichen *painted*
  frisch gestrichen *wet paint*
gesund *healthy*
die Gesundheit *health*
Gesundheit! *bless you! (after sneeze)*
das Getränk (-e) *drink*
die Getränkekarte (-n) *drinks menu/list*
getrennt *separate(ly) (of paying a bill)*
das Gewicht *weight*
gewinnen *to win*
gewiß *certain(ly), definite(ly)*
das Gewitter (-) *thunderstorm*
sich gewöhnen an+acc. *to get used to*
gewöhnlich *usually, usual*
der Gipfel (-) *summit, top*
der Gips (-e) *plaster cast*
die Gitarre (-n) *guitar*
das Glas (¨-er) *glass*
glauben *to think, believe*
gleich *immediately, straightaway; same*
  es ist mir gleich *it's all the same to me*
gleichfalls *the same to you (polite)*
das Gleis (-e) *platform, track (railway)*
das Glück *luck, good fortune*
glücklich *happy, fortunate, lucky*
glücklicherweise *fortunately*
der Glückwunsch (¨-e) *congratulation*
das Gold *gold*
der Goldfisch (-e) *goldfish*
der Gott (¨-er) *God*
der Grad (-e) *degree (of temperature)*
das Gramm (-e) *gram(me)*
das Gras *grass*
gratulieren *to congratulate*
grau *grey*
die Grenze (-n) *border, boundary, limit*
grillen *to grill, have a barbecue*
die Grippe *influenza*
der Groschen (-) *10 Pfennig coin; Austrian currency*
groß *big, large, tall*
großartig *wonderful, superb*
die Großeltern *grandparents*
die Großmutter (¨-) *grandmother*

die Großstadt (¨-e) *large city*
der Großvater (¨-) *grandfather*
großzügig *generous*
die Größe (-n) *size*
grün *green*
grüne Karte *green card (motoring)*
die Grundschule (-n) *primary school*
die Gruppe (-n) *group*
der Gruß (¨-e) *greeting*
grüß dich! *greetings! hello!*
grüß Gott! *hello! (South Germany/Austria)*
grüßen *to greet*
gucken *to look*
der/das Gulasch (-e) *goulash*
die Gulaschsuppe (-n) *goulash soup*
gültig *valid (e.g. of tickets)*
der/das Gummi *rubber*
günstig *favourable, good value*
die Gurke (-n) *cucumber*
der Gürtel (-) *belt, seat-belt*
gut *good*
gut gelaunt *in a good mood, good-tempered*
gute Besserung! *get well soon*
gute Fahrt! *safe/good journey!*
gute Heimfahrt! *safe/good journey home!*
gute Nacht! *goodnight!*
gute Reise! *have a good journey!*
guten Abend! *good evening!*
guten Appetit! *enjoy your meal! bon appétit!*
guten Morgen! *good morning!*
guten Tag! *hello! good day!*
das Gymnasium (-ien) *grammar school*

das Haar (-e) *hair*
die Haarbürste (-n) *hairbrush*
das Haarshampoo *shampoo*
der Haartrockner (-) *hairdrier*
das Haarwaschmittel (-) *shampoo*
haben *to have*
der Hafen (¨-) *port*
der Hagel *hail (weather)*
hageln *to hail (weather)*
das Hähnchen (-) *chicken*
halb *half*
die Halbpension *half-board*
die Hälfte (-n) *half*
die Halle (-n) *hall*
das Hallenbad (¨-er) *indoor swimming pool*
Hallo! *hello! (also to attract attention)*
der Hals (¨-e) *neck, throat*
der Halsschmerzen *sore throat*
halten *to hold, keep, store, stop*
die Haltestelle (-n) *stop (of bus, tram)*
der Hamster (-) *hamster*
die Hand (¨-e) *hand*
die Handarbeit *needlework*
der Handball (¨-e) *handball*
sich handeln um *to be about (e.g. film, book)*
der Händler (-) *tradesman, dealer*
die Handlung (-en) *action, deed; business, trade*
der Handschuh (-e) *glove*

die Handtasche (-n) *handbag*
das Handtuch (¨-er) *handtowel*
Hannover *Hanover*
hart *hard*
hassen *to hate*
häßlich *ugly*
der Hauptbahnhof (¨-e) *main station*
die Hauptschule (-n) *secondary modern school*
die Hauptstadt (¨-e) *capital city*
die Hauptstraße (-n) *main road*
das Haus (¨-er) *house*
die Hausaufgabe (-n) *homework*
die Hausfrau (-en) *housewife*
der Haushalt (-e) *household*
der Hausmeister (-) *caretaker*
die Hausnummer (-n) *house number*
das Haustier (-e) *pet*
heben *to lift, pick up*
das Heft (-e) *exercise book*
das Heftpflaster (-) *sticky plaster*
der Heilige Abend *Christmas Eve*
die Heimat (-en) *home country*
die Heimfahrt (-en) *homeward journey*
Heimweh haben *to be homesick*
heiraten *to marry*
heiß *hot*
heißen *to be called*
heiter *bright (of weather)*
heizen *to heat*
die Heizung *heating*
helfen *to help*
hell *bright, light (of colours)*
das Hemd (-en) *shirt*
her- *(towards the speaker)*
herein (etc.) *come in (etc.)*
die Herbergseltern *wardens of hostel*
der Herbergsvater (¨-) *hostel warden (male)*
die Herbergsmutter (¨-) *hostel warden (female)*
der Herbst *autumn*
der Herd (-e) *cooker, stove*
herein! *come in!*
der Herr (-en) *gentleman, sir*
Herr... *Mr...*
Herren or H *Gentlemen (on public toilets)*
Herr Ober! *Waiter!*
die Herrenmode *menswear*
herrlich *wonderful*
herstellen (sep.) *to produce*
das Herz (-en) *heart*
herzlich *warm, sincere*
herzliche Grüße *kind regards, warm greetings*
herzlichen Glückwunsch! *congratulations!*
heute *today*
heute abend *this evening*
heutzutage *nowadays, currently*
hier *here*
die Hilfe (no plural) *help, aid*
Erste Hilfe *first aid*
Hilfe! *help!*
die Himbeere (-n) *raspberry*
der Himmel *sky; Heaven*
hin- *(away from the speaker)*
hinaus! (etc.) *get out! (etc.)*
hin und zurück *return*
hinauslehnen (sep.) *to lean out*

sich hinlegen (*sep.*) *to have a lie down, rest*
sich hinsetzen (*sep.*) *to sit down*
hinten *behind (adverb)*
hinter *behind (preposition)*
die Hit (-s) *hit (success)*
die Hitparade (-n) *hit parade*
die Hitze *heat*
hitzefrei *time off school because of heat*
die Hitzewelle (-n) *heat-wave*
das Hobby (-s) *hobby*
hoch *high, tall*
hochachtungsvoll *yours faithfully*
der Hochdruck *high pressure (weather)*
die Hochgarage (-n) *multi-storey car park*
das Hochhaus (¨er) *high-rise/multi-storey building*
die Hochschule (-n) *technical college, university*
die Höchstgeschwindigkeit (-en) *maximum speed*
die Höchsttemperatur (-en) *maximum temperature*
die Hochzeit (-en) *wedding*
der Hof (¨e) *yard, courtyard, playground (school)*
hoffen *to hope*
hoffentlich *it is to be hoped, I hope, etc.*
die Hoffnung (-en) *hope*
höflich *polite*
holen *to fetch, get, collect*
Holland *Holland*
der Holländer (-) *Dutchman*
die Holländerin (-nen) *Dutchwoman*
holländisch *Dutch (adjective)*
das Holz (¨er) *wood (material)*
der Honig *honey*
hören *to hear, listen to*
der Hörer (-) *receiver (telephone)*
die Hose (-n) *(pair of) trousers*
das Hotel (-s) *hotel*
der Hubschrauber (-) *helicopter*
hübsch *pretty*
der Hügel (-) *hill*
der Hund (-e) *dog*
der Hunger *hunger*
Hunger haben *to be hungry*
hungrig *hungry*
husten *to cough*
der Hut (¨e) *hat*
die Hütte (-n) *hut*

die Idee (-n) *idea*
ihr *her (possessive)*
ihr *you (plural of* du*)*
ihr *their (possessive)*
Ihr *your (polite form possessive)*
die Illustrierte (-n) *magazine*
im (in dem) *in the*
im Freien *in the open*
der Imbiß (-sse) *snack*
die Imbißhalle (-n) *snackbar*
die Imbißstube (-n) *snackbar*
immer *always*
immer noch *still*
in *in*
inbegriffen/inbegr. *inclusive, including*

die Industrie (-n) *industry*
der Ingenieur (-e) *engineer*
inklusiv *inclusive*
das Inland *domestic, home, inland*
innen *inner*
die Innenstadt (¨e) *town centre, city centre*
ins (in das) *into*
das Insekt (-en) *insect*
die Insel (-n) *island*
das Instrument (-e) *instrument*
intelligent *intelligent*
der Inter-City-Zug (¨e) *Inter-City train*
interessant *interesting*
das Interesse (-n) *interest*
interessieren *to interest*
sich interessieren für *to be interested in*
irgend *some or other*
irgendwann *sometime or other*
irgendwas *something or other*
irgendwie *somehow or other*
irgendwo *somewhere or other*
der Islam *Islam*
Italien *Italy*
der Italiener (-) *Italian (man)*
die Italienerin (-nen) *Italian (woman)*
italienisch *Italian (adjective)*

ja *yes*
die Jacke (-n) *jacket*
jagen *to hunt*
der Jäger (-) *hunter*
das Jahr (-e) *year*
die Jahreszeit (-en) *season (of year)*
das Jahrhundert (-e) *century*
jährlich *annual, annually*
der Januar *January*
die Jeans (*singular & plural*) *jeans*
jeder *every*
jedesmal *every time*
jedoch *but, however*
jemand *someone, somebody*
jener *that*
jetzt *now*
der Job (-s) *job*
joggen *to jog*
Jogging *jogging*
der/das Joghurt (-s) *yoghurt*
die Jugend (*no plural*) *young people, youth (collective)*
der Jugendclub (-s) *youth club*
die Jugendherberge (-n) *youth hostel*
der Jugendliche (-n) *young person, youth*
das Jugendzentrum (-tren) *youth centre*
der Juli *July*
jung *young*
der Junge (-n) *boy*
jünger *younger*
der Juni *June*

die Kabine (-n) *cabin; booth (e.g. of telephone)*
der Kaffee (-s) *coffee*
die Kaffeekanne (-n) *coffee pot*
der Käfig (-e) *cage*
der Kai (-e or -s) *quay, waterfront*
der Kakao (-s) *cocoa*
das Kalbfleisch *veal*

der Kalender (-) *calendar*
kalt *cold*
kalte Platte (-n) *cold meal*
die Kälte (-n) *cold (weather)*
die Kamera (-s) *camera*
der Kamin (-e) *fireplace, fireside, chimney*
der Kamm (¨e) *comb*
sich kämmen *to comb one's hair*
der Kampf (¨e) *fight, struggle*
kämpfen *to fight, struggle*
der Kanal (¨e) *channel, English Channel*
das Kaninchen (-) *rabbit*
das Ännchen (-) *little pot (for tea/coffee)*
die Kantine (-n) *canteen*
die Kapelle (-n) *band; chapel*
kapieren *to understand (colloquial)*
kaputt *broken*
die Karotte (-n) *carrot*
die Karriere (-n) *career*
die Karte (-n) *card, ticket, map*
die Kartoffel (-n) *potato*
der Kartoffelbrei *mashed potato*
Kartoffelchips *potato crisps*
das Kartoffelmus *purée of potato*
der Kartoffelsalat *potato salad*
der Käse (-) *cheese*
der Käsekuchen *cheesecake*
die Kasse (-n) *box office, till, check-out*
der Kassenzettel (-) *till receipt*
die Kassette (-n) *cassette*
der Kassettenrecorder (-) *cassette recorder*
der Kater (-) *tom cat*
einen Kater haben *to have a hangover*
die Kathedrale (-n) *cathedral*
der Katholik (-en) *Roman Catholic (person)*
katholisch *Catholic (adjective)*
die Katze (-n) *cat*
kauen *to chew*
der Kauf (¨e) *purchase*
kaufen *to buy*
das Kaufhaus (¨er) *department store*
der Kaufmann (¨er) *businessman, merchant*
der Kaugummi *chewing gum*
kaum *hardly, scarcely*
kegeln *to bowl (10-pin, skittles)*
kein *no, not any*
der Keks (-e) *biscuit*
der Keller (-) *cellar*
der Kellner (-) *waiter*
kennen *to know (people, places)*
kennenlernen (*sep.*) *to get to know*
der Kerl (-e) *chap, guy; character*
die Kerze (-n) *candle*
die Kette (-n) *chain, necklace, bracelet*
das Kilo (*plural not much used* -s) *kilo*
der Kilometer (-) *kilometre*
das Kind (-er) *child*
der Kindergarten (¨) *kindergarten, nursery*
der Kinderteller (-) *child's portion/dish*

das Kino (-s) *cinema*
der Kiosk (-e) *kiosk*
die Kirche (-n) *church*
die Kirmes (-sen) *fair, funfair*
die Kirsche (-n) *cherry*
das Kissen (-) *cushion*
klappbar *folding, collapsible*
klappen *to fold, collapse; work out well*
der Klappstuhl (¨e) *folding chair*
der Klapptisch (-e) *folding table*
klar *clear, evident, obvious*
klasse *great, terrific, first class*
die Klasse (-n) *class (first, school)*
die Klassenarbeit (-en) *class test (formal)*
das Klassenbuch (¨er) *form book*
die Klassenfahrt (-en) *class trip*
der Klassenlehrer (-) *form/class/ teacher*
der Klassensprecher (-) *class speaker/representative*
das Klassenzimmer (-) *classroom*
klassisch *classical*
klauen *to steal, pinch, nick (slang)*
das Klavier (-e) *piano*
kleben *to stick*
das Kleid (-er) *dress; plural also=clothes*
die Kleider *clothes*
der Kleiderschrank (¨e) *wardrobe*
die Kleidung *clothing, clothes*
klein *small, little*
das Kleingeld *(small) change (of money)*
klettern *to climb, clamber*
das Klima (-s) *climate*
klingeln *to ring (of bell, phone)*
die Klinik (-en) *clinic; hospital*
die Klippe (-n) *cliff*
das Klo (-s) *toilet, loo (colloquial)*
klopfen *to knock, beat, hit*
der Klub (-s) or der Club (-s) *club*
klug *clever*
die Kneipe (-n) *pub, tavern*
das Knie (-n) *knee*
knipsen *to photograph*
der Knödel (-) *dumpling*
der Knopf (¨e) *button, knob*
der Koch (¨e) *cook*
kochen *to cook, boil*
Kochen *Cookery, Domestic Science*
der Koffer (-) *case, suitcase*
der Kofferkuli (-s) *luggage trolley*
der Kofferraum (¨e) *boot (of car)*
der Kohl (-e) *cabbage*
die Kohle (-n) *coal*
Köln *Cologne*
komisch *amusing, funny, strange*
kommen *to come*
die Komödie (-n) *comedy*
kompliziert *complicated*
der Kompost (-e) *compost*
kompostieren *to compost*
das Kompott (-e) *stewed fruit*
die Konditorei (-en) *cake shop, pâtisserie*
die Konfektion *clothing/wear*
Damenkonfektion *ladies' wear*

der König (-e) *king*
können *to be able*
das Konto (Konten or -s) *account*
die Kontonummer (-n) *account number*
die Kontrolle (-n) *check, control (e.g. customs)*
kontrollieren *to check, control*
das Konzert (-e) *concert*
der Kopf (¨e) *head*
das Kopfkissen (-) *pillow*
der Kopfsalat (-e) *lettuce*
Kopfschmerzen haben *to have a headache*
die Kopie (-n) *copy, duplicate*
kopieren *to copy, duplicate*
der Korb (¨e) *basket*
der Körper (-) *body*
körperbehindert *disabled*
korrigieren *to correct*
kostbar *expensive, dear*
kosten *to cost*
die Kosten (*plural*) *cost(s)*
kostenlos *free*
das Kostüm (-e) *costume, suit*
das Kotelett (-e) *chop, cutlet*
der Krach *big noise, din, racket*
die Kraft (¨e) *strength*
kräftig *hearty, strong*
krank *ill*
das Krankenhaus (¨er) *hospital*
die Krankenkasse (-n) *health insurance (company)*
der Krankenpfleger (-) *male nurse*
der Krankenschein (-e) *medical insurance record card*
die Krankenschwester (-n) *female nurse*
der Krankenwagen (-) *ambulance*
die Krankheit (-en) *illness*
die Krawatte (-n) *tie*
die Kreide (-n) *chalk*
der Kreis (-e) *circle; district*
das Kreuz (-e) *cross*
die Kreuzung (-en) *crossing*
der Krieg (-e) *war*
kriegen *to get (colloquial)*
der Krimi (s-) *mystery, thriller (book or film)*
der Kriminalfilm (-e) *thriller*
die Küche (-n) *kitchen; cooking*
der Kuchen (-) *cake*
die Kuckucksuhr (-en) *cuckoo clock*
der Kugelschreiber (-) *biro, ballpoint pen*
die Kuh (¨e) *cow*
kühl *cool*
der Kühlschrank (¨e) *refrigerator*
der Kuli (-s) (Kugelschreiber) *biro*
der Kunde (-n) *client, customer*
Kunst *Art*
der Künstler *artist*
künstlich *artificial*
der Kunststoff (-e) *synthetic material*
die Kur (-en) *health cure; diet*
der Kurort (-e) *spa, health resort*
der Kurs (-e) *course; rate of exchange*
die Kurve (-n) *curve, bend*
kurz *short*
die Kusine (-n) *female cousin*
der Kuß (¨sse) *kiss*

küssen *to kiss*
die Küste (-n) *coast*

das Labor (-s or -e) *laboratory*
lächeln *to smile*
lachen *to laugh*
der Laden (¨) *shop*
die Lage (-n) *position, situation*
das Lamm (¨er) *lamb*
die Lampe (-n) *lamp*
das Land (¨er) *country; state (of Germany)*
landen *to land*
die Landkarte (-n) *map*
die Landschaft (-en) *countryside*
die Landstraße (-n) *country road*
lang *long*
lange *for a long time*
die Langeweile *boredom*
langsam *slow, slowly*
die Langspielplattte (-n) *LP record*
sich langweilen *to be bored*
langweilig *boring*
der Lappen (-) *cloth, rag*
der Lärm (*no plural*) *noise*
lassen *to let, allow*
der Lastwagen (-) *lorry*
Latein *Latin*
laufen *to run, go by foot*
die Laune (-n) *mood*
laut *loud*
läuten *to sound, ring*
leben *to live*
das Leben *life*
die Lebensgefahr *danger to life*
die Lebensmittel (*plural*) *food/groceries*
das Lebensmittelgeschäft (-e) *grocer's shop*
die Leber (-n) *liver*
die Leberwurst (¨e) *liver sausage*
lebhaft *lively*
lecker *delicious*
das Leder *leather*
ledig *single*
leer *empty*
leeren *to empty*
die Leerung (-en) *collection (post)*
legen *to lay*
sich legen *to lie down*
der Lehnstuhl (¨e) *armchair*
die Lehre (-n) *apprenticeship*
der Lehrer (-) *teacher*
lehren *to teach*
das Lehrerzimmer (-) *staffroom*
der Lehrling *apprentice*
leicht *light, easy*
die Leichtathletik *athletics*
leid tun *to make one feel sorry, to hurt*
es tut mir leid *I am sorry*
leiden *to suffer*
leiden können *to bear*
ich kann ihn nicht leiden *I can't bear him*
leider *unfortunately*
leihen *to lend*
leise *softly, gently*
die Leistung (-en) *achievement, performance*
leiten *to lead*
der Leiter (-) *leader*

German–English vocabulary

die Leitung (-en) *guidance, direction*
das Lenkrad (¨-er) *steering wheel*
lernen *to learn*
lesen *to read*
letzt *last*
die Leute *people*
das Licht (-er) *light*
lieb *dear*
   liebe Birgit *dear (in letter)*
   lieber Franz *dear (in letter)*
die Liebe (-n) *love*
lieben *to love*
lieber *rather*
   lieber haben *to prefer*
Lieblings- *favourite . . .*
das Lieblingsfach (¨-er) *favourite subject*
am liebsten *best of all, most of all*
das Lied (-er) *song*
liefern *to deliver*
der Lieferwagen (-) *delivery van*
liegen *to lie*
liegenlassen (*sep.*) *to leave around/behind*
der Liegestuhl (¨-e) *deckchair*
der Liegewagen (-) *sleeping car*
der Lift (-e or -s) *lift*
die Limonade (-n) *lemonade*
das Lineal (-e) *ruler*
die Linie (-n) *line*
linke *left*
links *on the left*
die Liste (-n) *list*
der/das Liter (-) *litre*
der LKW (LKWs) *lorry*
loben *to praise*
das Loch (¨-er) *hole*
der Löffel (-) *spoon*
der Lohn (¨-e) *reward; wage*
los *loose, off*
löschen *to extinguish*
der Löscher (-) *blotter, extinguisher*
lösen *to cash, buy (tickets)*
der Löwe (-n) *lion*
die Luft *air*
der Luftdruck *air pressure*
die Luftmatratze (-n) *airbed*
die Luftpost *airmail*
die Luftverschmutzung *air pollution*
die Luftwaffe *airforce*
lügen *to tell a lie*
die Lust *wish*
   Lust haben (auf+*acc.*) *to feel like*
lustig *amusing*

machen *to do, make*
das Mädchen (-) *girl*
der Mädchenname (-n) *girl's/maiden name*
das Magazin (-e) *magazine*
der Magen *stomach*
Magenschmerzen *stomach ache*
mager *thin*
mähen *to mow*
die Mahlzeit (-en) *meal time, meal*
der Mai *May*
der Main *Main (river)*
mal *just*
   Ruf mal an! *Just ring up!*

das Mal (-e) *time*
malen *to paint*
man *one*
manchmal *sometimes*
mangelhaft *defective, lacking, weak*
der Mann (¨-er) *man, husband*
männlich *masculine, male*
die Mannschaft (-en) *team*
der Mantel (¨) *coat*
die Mappe (-n) *briefcase, satchel*
die Margarine *margarine*
die Marine *navy*
die Mark *Mark (currency)*
das Markstück (-e) *Mark coin*
der Markt (¨-e) *market*
der Marktplatz (¨-e) *marketplace*
die Marmelade (-n) *jam*
der März *March*
die Maschine (-n) *machine, aeroplane*
Mathe *Maths*
Mathematik *Mathematics*
der Matrose (-n) *sailor*
die Mauer (-n) *wall*
die Maus (¨-e) *mouse*
der Mechaniker (-) *mechanic*
die Medikamente (*plural*) *medicine*
die Medizin (*no plural*) *medicine*
das Meer (-e) *sea*
das Meerschweinchen (-) *guinea pig*
mehr *more*
mehrere *several*
die Mehrfahrtenkarte (-n) *ticket valid for a number of journeys*
mehrmals *often*
die Mehrwertsteuer *VAT*
die Meile (-n) *mile*
mein *my*
meinen *to mean, think*
die Meinung (-en) *meaning, opinion*
   meiner Meinung nach *in my opinion*
meist *most*
meistens *mostly*
die Meisterschaft (-en) *championship*
sich melden *to report, answer (phone)*
die Menge (-n) *crowd*
der Mensch (-en) *person, man*
das Menü (-s) *set menu*
merken *to notice*
merkwürdig *remarkable*
die Messe (-n) *mass, trade fair*
messen *to measure*
das Messer (-e) *knife*
der/das Meter (-) *metre*
der Metzger (-) *butcher*
die Metzgerei (-en) *butcher's shop*
die Miete (-n) *rent*
mieten *to rent, hire*
die Milch *milk*
die Milchbar (-) *milk bar*
mild *mild*
mindestens *at least*
das Mineralwasser (-) *mineral water*
die Minute (-n) *minute*
das Mißverständnis (-se) *misunderstanding*
mit *with*
mitbringen (*sep.*) *to bring (with you)*

das Mitglied (-er) *member*
mitkommen (*sep.*) *to come along with, to accompany*
das Mitleid *sympathy*
mitmachen (*sep.*) *to join in*
mitnehmen (*sep.*) *to take with you*
   zum Mitnehmen *to take away*
mitspielen (*sep.*) *to play with, to join in*
der Mittag (-e) *midday*
das Mittagessen (-) *midday meal, lunch*
die Mittagspause (-n) *midday break*
die Mitte (-n) *middle*
mitteilen (*sep.*) *to communicate, tell*
das Mittel (-) *means*
mittelgroß *middle-sized, average*
das Mittelmeer *Mediterranean*
mitten *middle, in the middle*
Mitternacht *midnight*
der Mittwoch *Wednesday*
die Möbel (*plural*) *furniture*
möbliert *furnished*
die Mode (-n) *fashion*
modern *modern*
modisch *in fashion, fashionable*
das Mofa (-s) *moped*
mogeln *to cheat*
mögen *to like*
möglich *possible*
die Möglichkeit (-en) *possibility*
die Möhre (-n) *carrot*
die Molkerei (-en) *dairy*
der Moment (-e) *moment*
Moment! *just a mo!*
der Monat (-e) *month*
monatlich *monthly*
der Mond (-e) *moon*
der Montag *Monday*
morgen *tomorrow*
morgen früh *tomorrow morning*
der Morgen *morning*
die Morgenpause (-n) *morning break*
morgens *in the mornings*
die Mosel *Moselle (river)*
der Moselwein *Moselle wine*
der Motor (-en) *engine*
das Motorboot (-e) *motor boat*
das Motorrad (¨-er) *motorbike*
die Mücke (-n) *mosquito, gnat*
müde *tired*
München *Munich*
der Mund (¨-er) *mouth*
mündlich *oral*
die Münze (-n) *coin*
das Museum (Museen) *museum*
die Musik *music*
der Musiker (-) *musician*
müssen *to have to*
der Mut *courage*
mutig *courageous, brave*
die Mutter (¨) *mother*
die Muttersprache (-n) *mother tongue*
Mutti *mum, mummy*
die Mütze (-n) *cap*
die MWSt (Mehrwertsteuer) *VAT*

nach *after, to, according to*

der Nachbar (-n) *neighbour*
nachdem *after*
nachdenken (*sep.*) *to think, reflect*
nachgehen (*sep.*) *to follow*
nachher *afterwards*
der Nachmittag (-e) *afternoon*
nachmittags *in the afternoons*
die Nachmittagspause (-n) *afternoon break*
der Nachname (-n) *surname*
die Nachrichten (*plural*) *news*
nachschlagen (*sep.*) *to look up (a word)*
nachsehen (*sep.*) *to check*
nachsitzen (*sep.*) *to be kept in*
die Nachspeise (-n) *dessert*
nächst *next*
die Nacht (¨e) *night*
der Nachteil (-e) *disadvantage*
der Nachtisch (-e) *dessert*
nachts *at night*
nah(e) *near*
die Nähe *vicinity*
in der Nähe (von) *near (to)*
nähen *to sew*
Nähen *Needlework*
der Nahverkehrszug (¨e) *local train*
der Name (-n) *name*
der Namenstag (-e) *name day*
die Nase (-n) *nose*
naß *wet*
die Näße *dampness, wetness*
die Natur *Nature*
natürlich *of course, naturally*
Naturwissenschaften *Natural Sciences*
der Nebel (-) *fog*
neben *near*
nebenan *nearby, next door*
das Nebenfach (¨er) *subsidiary subject*
die Nebenstraße (-n) *side street*
neblig *foggy*
nee *no (colloquial)*
der Neffe (-n) *nephew*
nehmen *to take*
nein *no*
nennen *to name, call*
nervös *nervous*
nett *nice*
das Netz (-e) *net*
neu *new*
neugierig *curious, inquisitive*
das Neujahr *New Year*
neulich *recently*
die Neustadt (¨e) *new town*
nicht *not*
nicht mehr *no longer*
nicht wahr *isn't it?*
die Nichte (-n) *niece*
der Nichtraucher *non-smoker*
nichts *nothing*
nichts zu danken *that's all right*
nie *never*
die Niederlande *Netherlands*
der Niederschlag (¨e) *knock-out, precipitation (e.g. rain, snow)*
niedrig *low*
niemals *never*
niemand *no one*
nirgends *nowhere*
niesen *to sneeze*

noch *still, yet*
noch einmal *once again*
noch etwas *a bit more*
noch mal *again*
noch nicht *not yet*
Nord- *north . . .*
der Norden *north*
in den Norden *to the north*
im Norden *in the north*
nördlich *northerly*
die Nordsee *North Sea*
normal *normal*
normalerweise *usually*
die Not *need, emergency*
der Notausgang (¨e) *emergency exit*
der Notdienst (-e) *emergency service*
die Note (-n) *mark*
der Notruf (-e) *emergency call*
nötig *necessary*
notwendig *necessary*
der November *November*
die Nudeln (*plural*) *noodles*
null *nil, zero*
die Nummer (-n) *number*
nun *now, well*
nur *only*
die Nuß (¨sse) *nut*
nützen *to be of use*
nützlich *useful*

ob *if, whether*
oben *above, upstairs*
nach oben *upstairs, upwards*
der Ober (-) *head waiter*
Herr Ober! *waiter!*
das Obergeschoß (-sse) *upper floor*
die Oberstufe (-n) *sixth form*
obgleich *although*
das Obst (*no plural*) *fruit*
der Obstbaum (¨e) *fruit tree*
die Obsttorte (-n) *fruit flan or gateau*
obwohl *although*
die Ochsenschwanzsuppe (n) *oxtail soup*
oder *or*
der Ofen (¨) *stove, oven, cooker*
offen *open*
öffentlich *public*
öffnen *to open*
die Öffnungszeiten (*plural*) *opening times*
oft *often*
ohne *without*
das Ohr (-en) *ear*
der Oktober *October*
das Öl *oil*
die Oma (-s) *granny*
das Omelett (-e or -s) *omelette*
der Onkel (-) *uncle*
der Opa (-s) *grandpa*
die Operation (-en) *operation (medical)*
operieren *to operate (medical)*
die Orange (-n) *orange*
der Orangensaft (¨e) *orange juice*
das Orchester (-) *orchestra*
ordentlich *tidy*
die Ordnung (-en) *order, tidiness*
in Ordnung *in order, OK*
Ordnung machen *to tidy up*
organisieren *to organise*
der Ort (-e) *place*

das Ortsgespräch (-e) *local call (telephone)*
Ost- *east . . .*
der. Osten *east*
in den Osten *to the east*
im Osten *in the east*
Ostern *Easter*
Österreich *Austria*
der Österreicher *Austrian (man)*
österreichisch *Austrian (adjective)*
östlich *easterly*
die Ostsee *Baltic Sea*
der Ozean (-e) *Ocean*
das Ozonloch *hole in the ozone layer*
der Ozonschicht *ozone layer*

ein paar *a few*
das Paar *pair*
das Päckchen (-) *packet*
packen *to pack, wrap*
das Paket (-e) *parcel*
die Packung (-en) *packet*
paniert *in bread crumbs*
die Panne (-n) *breakdown*
das Papier (e-) *paper*
das Parfum (-s) *perfume*
das Parfüm (-e or -s) *perfume*
der Park (-s) *park*
die Parkanlage (-n) *parkland*
parken *to park*
das Parkett *stalls (cinema)*
das Parkhaus (¨er) *multi-storey car park*
der Parkplatz (¨e) *car park*
der Parkschein (-e) *parking ticket*
die Parkuhr (-en) *parking meter*
das Parkverbot *no parking*
das Parterre *ground floor*
der Partner *partner*
die Partnerstadt (¨e) *twin town*
die Party (-ys or ies) *party*
der Paß (Pässe) *pass, passport*
der Passagier (-e) *passenger*
passen *to suit*
passieren *to happen*
die Paßkontrolle (-n) *passport control*
der Patient (-en) *patient*
die Pause (-n) *pause, break*
Pech haben *to have bad luck*
peinlich *painful, embarrassing*
die Pension *guest house*
per Anhalter *by hitch-hiking*
die Person (-en) *person*
der Personalausweis (-e) *personal identity card*
der Personenzug (¨e) *passenger train*
persönlich *personally, in person*
der Pfad (-e) *path*
der Pfadfinder (-) *scout*
der Pfannkuchen (-) *pancake*
der Pfeffer *pepper*
die Pfeife (-n) *pipe*
der Pfennig (-e) *Pfennig*
das Pferd (-e) *horse*
Pfingsten *Whitsun*
der Pfirsich (-e) *peach*
die Pflanze (-n) *plant*
pflanzen *to plant*
das Pflaster (-) *pavement, plaster*
die Pflaume (-n) *plum*
pflegen *to nurse, look after*

die Pflicht (-en) *duty*
das Pflichtfach (¨er) *compulsory subject*
das Pfund *pound*
Physik *Physics*
das Picknick (-e or -s) *picnic*
die Pille (-n) *pill*
das Pils (-) *beer (Pils)*
der Pilz (-e) *mushroom*
der Pkw (-s) *private car*
das Plakat (-e) *poster*
der Plan (¨e) *plan*
planen *to plan*
planmäßig *according to plan/timetable*
das Plastik *plastic*
die Platte (-n) *record*
der Plattenspieler (-) *record player*
der Platz (¨e) *place, square*
Platz nehmen *to sit down, take a seat*
die Platzkarte (-n) *seat ticket*
plaudern *to chat*
plötzlich *suddenly*
der Pokal (-e) *cup*
die Politik *politics*
der Politiker (-) *politician*
die Polizei (*no plural*) *police*
die Polizeiwache (-n) *police station*
der Polizist (-en) *policeman*
Pommes frites *chips*
die Popmusik *pop music*
das Portemonnaie (-s) *purse*
der Portier (-s) *porter*
die Portion (-en) *portion*
die Post *post, post office*
das Postamt (¨er) *post office*
die Postanweisung (-en) *postal order*
das Poster (- or -s) *poster*
die Postleitzahl (-en) *post code*
das Postwertzeichen (-) *stamp*
praktisch *practical, convenient*
die Praline (-n or -s) *praline, chocolate*
der Preis (-e) *price, prize*
preiswert *cheap, good value*
die Presse (-n) *press*
prima! *great!*
pro *per*
probieren *to try*
das Problem (-e) *problem*
der Profi (-s) *professional*
das Programm (-e) *programme*
der Prospekt (-e) *prospectus, brochure*
Prosit! *cheers!*
Prost! *cheers!*
protestieren *to protest*
prüfen *to test, check*
die Prüfung (-en) *test, examination*
der Pudding (-s) *pudding, dessert*
der Pulli (-s) *pullover*
der Pullover (-) *pullover*
das Pult (-e) *desk*
der Punkt (-e) *point, full stop*
pünktlich *punctual*
die Puppe (-n) *doll*
putzen *to clean*

der Quadratmeter (-) *qm square metre*
die Qualität (-en) *quality*
Quatsch! *rubbish!*
die Querstraße (-n) *cross street*

die Quittung (-en) *receipt*

der Rabatt (-e) *discount*
das Rad (¨er) *wheel, bicycle*
radfahren (*sep.*) *to cycle*
der Radfahrer (-) *cyclist*
der Radiergummi (*India*) *rubber, eraser*
das Radio (-s) *radio*
der Rand (¨er) *edge*
der Rang (¨e) *circle (in theatre)*
der Rasen (-) *lawn*
der Rasierapparat (-e) *razor, shaver*
sich rasieren *to shave*
das Rasthaus (¨er) *hotel*
der Rasthof (¨e) *service station*
der Rastplatz (¨e) *service area, parking area*
die Raststätte (-n) *service station*
der Rat (Ratschläge) *advice*
raten *to advise*
das Rathaus (¨er) *town hall*
der Ratskeller (-) *town hall cellar (restaurant)*
der Räuber (-) *robber*
rauchen *to smoke*
der Raucher (-) *smoker*
der Raum (¨e) *room, space*
die Realschule (-n) *secondary school*
rechnen *to count, reckon, calculate*
die Rechnung (-en) *bill*
recht haben *to be right*
recht *right (adjective)*
rechts *on the right*
recyceln *to recycle*
das Recycling *recycling*
die Rede (-n) *speech*
das Regal (-e) *shelf*
die Regel (-n) *rule*
regelmäßig *regular(ly)*
der Regen *rain*
der Regenmantel (¨) *raincoat*
der Regenschirm (-e) *umbrella*
der Regenwald (¨er) *rain forest*
die Regierung (-en) *government*
regnen *to rain*
regnerisch *rainy*
reiben *to rub, grate*
reich *rich*
reichen *to reach, be sufficient, pass*
der Reifen *tyre*
der Reifendruck *tyre pressure*
die Reifenpanne (-n) *puncture*
die Reihe (-n) *row*
das Reihenhaus (¨er) *terraced house*
rein *clean, pure*
reinigen *to clean*
reinigen lassen *to have cleaned*
die Reinigung (-en) *cleaning*
der Reis *rice*
die Reise (-n) *journey*
das Reiseandenken (-) *souvenir*
die Reiseauskunft *travel information*
das Reisebüro (-s) *travel agent*
der Reiseführer (-) *guidebook*
der Reiseleiter (-) *guide*
reisen *to travel*
der Reisende (-n) *traveller*
der Reisepaß (¨sse) *passport*
der Reisescheck (-s) *travellers' cheque*

der Reißverschluß (¨sse) *zip*
reiten *to ride*
die Reklame (-n) *advertisement*
die Religion *religion*
rennen *to run*
der Rentner (-) *pensioner*
die Reparatur (-en) *repair*
die Reparaturwerkstatt (¨e) *repair workshop*
reparieren *to repair*
reparieren lassen *to have repaired*
der Reporter (-) *reporter*
reservieren *to reserve*
reserviert *reserved*
die Reservierung (-en) *reservation*
das Restaurant (-s) *restaurant*
retten *to save, rescue*
sich retten *to save oneself*
die Rettung (-en) *rescue*
die Rettungsaktion (-en) *rescue action*
das Rettungsboot (-e) *rescue boat*
der Rettungsdienst (-e) *rescue service*
der Rettungsgürtel (-) *safety strap/belt*
das Rezept (-e) *recipe, prescription*
der Rhein *Rhine (river)*
richtig *correct*
die Richtung (-en) *direction*
riechen *to smell*
das Rindfleisch *beef*
der Ring (-e) *ring*
der Rock (¨e) *skirt*
die Rolle (-n) *role*
der Roller (-) *scooter*
das Rollo (-s) *roller blind*
der Rollschuh (-e) *rollerskate*
die Rolltreppe (-n) *moving staircase, escalator*
der Roman (-e) *novel*
romantisch *romantic*
rosa *pink*
der Rotkohl *red cabbage*
der Rotwein *red wine*
der Rücken *back*
die Rückfahrkarte (-n) *return ticket*
die Rückfahrt (-en) *return journey*
die Rückgabe *return (of luggage)*
das Rückgespräch (-e) *reversed charge call (telephone)*
der Rucksack *rucksack*
rückwärts *backwards*
das Ruderboot (-e) *rowing boat*
rudern *to row*
der Ruf (-e) *call, shout, reputation*
rufen *to call, to shout*
die Ruhe *peace, quietness*
ruhen *to rest*
der Ruhetag (-e) *rest day, holiday*
ruhig *quiet, peaceful*
das Rührei (-er) *scrambled egg*
die Ruine (-n) *ruin*
rund *round*
die Rundfahrt (-en) *tour*
der Rundfunk *radio (station)*
russisch *Russian (adjective)*
rutschen *to slip*

SB *self-service*
die S-Bahn *urban railway*
der Saal (Säle) *hall*
die Sache (-n) *thing, affair*
der Saft (¨e) *juice*
sagen *to say*

die Sahne *cream*
die Saison *season*
der Salat (-e) *salad, lettuce*
das Salz *salt*
die Salzkartoffel (-n) *boiled potato*
  sammeln *to collect*
die Sammlung (-en) *collection*
der Samstag *Saturday*
der Sand (-e) *sand*
die Sandale (-n) *sandal*
das Sandwich (-es or -s) *sandwich*
der Sänger (-) *singer*
  satt *full up, satisfied*
  sauber *clean*
  sauber machen *to clean*
  sauer *sour*
das Sauerkraut *pickled cabbage*
  saurer Regen *acid rain*
das Sauwetter *awful weather*
  SB-tanken *self-service (petrol)*
das Schach *chess*
die Schachtel (-n) *box*
  schade *pity*
  wie schade! *what a shame!*
  schaden *to damage*
das Schaf (-e) *sheep*
der Schaffner (-) *ticket collector*
der Schal (-e) *shawl, scarf*
die Schale (-n) *bowl*
  schälen *to peel*
die Schallplatte (-n) *record*
der Schalter (-) *counter, box office*
  sich schämen *to be ashamed*
  scharf *sharp, hot (spicy)*
der Schatten (-) *shadow, shade*
  schauen *to see, look*
der Schauer (-) *shower*
das Schaufenster (-) *shop window*
das Schauspiel (-e) *play*
der Schauspieler (-) *actor*
der Scheck (-s) *cheque*
das Scheckbuch (¨er) *cheque book*
die Scheckkarte (-n) *cheque card*
die Scheibe (-n) *slice*
der Scheibenwischer (-) *windscreen wiper*
der Schein (-e) *note, banknote*
  scheinen *to seem, appear, shine*
der Scheinwerfer (-) *headlight*
  schellen *to ring out, ring the bell*
die Schenke (-n) *bar, public house*
  schenken *to give as a present*
  schick *smart*
  schicken *to send*
  schieben *to push*
der Schiedsrichter (-) *referee*
  schief *crooked*
  schießen *to shoot*
das Schiff (-e) *ship*
die Schildkröte (-n) *tortoise*
der Schilling (-e) *schilling*
der Schinken *ham*
der Schirm (-e) *umbrella, shade*
der Schlafanzug (¨e) *pyjamas*
  schlafen *to sleep*
  schlaflos *sleepless*
der Schlafraum (¨e) *dormitory*
der Schlafsack (¨e) *sleeping bag*
der Schlafwagen (-) *sleeping car*
das Schlafzimmer (-) *bedroom*
  schlagen *to hit, strike, beat*
der Schläger (-) *racket, bat, stick*

der Schlager (-) *'hit', pop tune*
die Schlagsahne *whipped cream*
das Schlagzeug *drums, percussion*
die Schlange (-n) *snake, queue*
  Schlange stehen *to stand in a queue*
  schlank *slim*
  schlau *clever, cunning*
  schlecht *bad*
    schlecht gelaunt *in a bad mood*
  schließen *to close, finish*
das Schließfach (¨er) *PO box/left luggage locker*
  schließlich *finally, in the end*
  schlimm *bad*
der Schlips (-e) *tie*
der Schlittschuh (-e) *ice skate*
  Schlittschuh laufen (sep.) *to go iceskating*
das Schloß (¨sser) *castle; lock*
  schlucken *to swallow*
der Schluß *end*
  Schluß machen *to finish*
der Schlüssel (-) *key*
der Schlüsselring (-e) *key ring*
der Schlußverkauf *final sale, closing-down sale*
  schmal *narrow*
  schmecken *to taste (good)*
    hat's geschmeckt? *did you like it?*
  Schmerzen (plural) *pain*
  schmerzen *to hurt*
der Schmuck *jewellery*
  schmutzig *dirty*
der Schnaps (¨e) *schnaps, spirits*
der Schnee *snow*
  schneiden *to cut*
  schneien *to snow*
  schnell *fast*
der Schnellimbiß *snack*
die Schnellreinigung *quick cleaning*
der Schnellzug (¨e) *express (train)*
das Schnitzel (-) *cutlet*
der Schnupfen *cold*
der Schnurrbart (¨e) *moustache*
die Schokolade *chocolate*
  schon *already*
  schonen *to protect*
  schön *beautiful*
der Schotte (-n) *Scotsman, Scot*
die Schottin (-nen) *Scotswoman, Scot*
  schottisch *Scottish*
  Schottland *Scotland*
der Schrank (¨e) *cupboard*
  schrecklich *awful*
  schreiben *to write*
die Schreibmaschine (-n) *typewriter*
das Schreibpapier *writing paper*
der Schreibtisch (-e) *desk*
die Schreibwaren (plural) *stationery*
der Schreibwarenhändler (-) *stationer*
die Schreibwarenhandlung (-en) *stationery shop*
  schreien *to shriek, shout*
  schriftlich *in writing*
der Schritt (-e) *step, pace*
  Schritt fahren *to drive at walking speed*
  schüchtern *shy*
der Schuh (-e) *shoe*
  Schul- *school . . .*

das Schulbuch (¨er) *schoolbook*
  schuld sein *to be guilty*
  schuldig *guilty*
die Schule (-n) *school*
der Schüler (-) *schoolboy*
die Schülerin (-nen) *schoolgirl*
  schulfrei *day off school*
der Schulhof (¨e) *playground*
das Schuljahr (-e) *school year*
der Schulleiter (-) *head teacher*
die Schulmappe (-n) *school bag*
das Schulsystem (-e) *school system*
der Schultag *school day*
die Schulter (-n) *shoulder*
die Schuluniform (-en) *school uniform*
der Schulweg (-e) *the way to school*
die Schüssel (-n) *dish*
  schütteln *to shake*
  schützen *to protect*
  schwach *weak*
der Schwager (¨) *brother-in-law*
der Schwamm (¨e) *sponge*
  schwänzen *play truant*
  schwarz *black*
das Schwarzbrot *dark bread*
  schweigen *to be silent*
das Schwein (-e) *pig*
das Schweinefleisch *pork*
die Schweiz *Switzerland*
der Schweizer (-) *Swiss (man)*
  schweizerisch *Swiss (adjective)*
  schwer *heavy, difficult*
die Schwester (-n) *sister*
  Schwieger- *-in-law*
  schwierig *difficult*
die Schwierigkeit (-en) *difficulty*
das Schwimmbad (¨er) *swimming pool*
  schwimmen *to swim*
  schwindlig *dizzy*
  schwül *sultry*
der See (-n) *lake*
die See (-n) *sea*
  seekrank *seasick*
die Seekrankheit *seasickness*
  Segel- *sail . . .*
das Segelboot (-e) *sailing boat*
  segeln *to sail*
  sehen *to see*
  sehenswert *worth seeing*
die Sehenswürdigkeit (-en) *attraction, thing worth seeing*
  sehr *very*
  sehr geehrte Frau . . . *Dear Mrs . . .*
  sehr geehrte Herren *Dear Sirs*
  sehr geehrter Herr . . . *Dear Mr . . .*
  sehr gut *very good*
  sehr verehrter Herr/verehrte Frau *Sir/Madam (more formal)*
die Seide (-n) *silk*
die Seife *soap*
die Seilbahn (-en) *cablecar*
  sein *his*
  sein *to be*
  seit *since (preposition)*
die Seite (-n) *page, side*
  seitdem *since (conjunction)*
der Sekretär (-e) *secretary (male)*
die Sekretärin (-nen) *secretary (female)*

der Sekt (-e) *champagne*
die Sekunde (-n) *second*
selber *even, oneself*
selbst *oneself*
selbständig *independent*
die Selbstbedienung *self-service (cafeteria, supermarket)*
das Selbsttanken *self-service (petrol station)*
selbstverständlich *of course*
selten *rare(ly)*
das Semester (-) *term (of 6 months)*
die Sendefolge (-n) *episode (of series)*
senden *to send*
die Sendereihe (-n) *series (of broadcasts)*
die Sendung (-en) *broadcast, programme*
der Senf (-e) *mustard*
der September *September*
der Sessel (-) *armchair*
sich setzen *to sit down*
das Shampoo *shampoo*
sicher *sure, certain, safe*
die Sicherheit *safety*
der Sicherheitsgurt (-e) *safety belt*
sichtbar *visible*
der Sieg (-e) *victory*
siezen *to say Sie to someone*
das Silber (*no plural*) *silver*
der das Silvester *New Year's Eve*
singen *to sing*
sinken *to sink*
sitzen *to sit*
sitzenbleiben (*sep.*) *to remain seated, to repeat a year (school)*
der Ski (-er) *ski*
skifahren (*sep.*) *to go skiing*
so *so, thus, like this, well*
so viel *so much*
sobald *as soon as*
die Socke (-n) *sock*
das Sofa (-s) *sofa*
sofort *straight away*
sogleich *straight away*
der Sohn (¨e) *son*
die Solarzelle (-n) *solar cell/panel*
der Soldat (-en) *soldier*
sollen *to be supposed to, to ought to*
der Sommer *summer*
die Sommerferien (*plural*) *summer holidays*
der Sommerschlußverkauf *end of summer sale*
das Sonderangebot (-e) *special offer*
sondern *but*
der Sonderpreis (-e) *special price*
die Sonne (-n) *sun*
sich sonnen *to sunbathe*
die Sonnenbrille (-n) *sunglasses*
die Sonnencreme *suncream*
die Sonnenmilch *suntan lotion*
das Sonnenöl *suntan oil*
der Sonnenschein *sunshine*
sonnig *sunny*
der Sonntag *Sunday*
sonst *otherwise; once (in the past)*
sonst noch etwas? *anything else?*
die Sorge (-n) *care, worry*
sorgen *to care (for)*

die Sorte (-n) *sort, kind*
die Soße (-n) *sauce*
das Souvenir (-s) *souvenir*
soviel *as much, so much*
sowieso *anyway, in any case*
sowohl . . . als auch . . . *both . . . and . . .*
Sozialkunde *Social Studies*
Spanien *Spain*
der Spanier (-) *Spaniard (male)*
die Spanierin (-nen) *Spaniard (female)*
spanisch *Spanish*
spannend *exciting*
sparen *to save*
die Sparkasse (-n) *savings bank*
der Spaß *fun*
viel Spaß *have fun!*
Spaß haben *to have fun, enjoy yourself*
spät *late*
spazieren *to walk*
spazierengehen (*sep.*) *to go for a walk*
der Spaziergang (¨e) *walk*
die Speisekarte (-n) *menu*
der Speisesaal (-säle) *dining hall/room*
der Speisewagen (-) *restaurant car*
die Spende (-n) *donation*
spenden *to donate*
die Sperre (-n) *barrier*
die Spezialität (-en) *speciality*
der Spiegel (-) *mirror*
das Spiegelei (-er) *fried egg*
das Spiel (-e) *game, match*
spielen *to play*
der Spieler (-) *player*
der Spielplatz (¨e) *playground*
das Spielzeug (-e) *toy*
die Spitze (-n) *summit, top*
der Sport *sport*
der Sportplatz (¨e) *sports field*
die Sprache (-n) *language*
das Sprachlabor (-e or -s) *language laboratory*
sprechen *to speak*
die Sprechstunde (-n) *consulting hours, surgery*
springen *to jump*
die Spritze (-n) *injection*
der Sprudel (-) *mineral water/lemonade*
spucken *to spit*
spülen *to rinse, wash up*
die Spülmaschine (-n) *dishwasher*
das Spülmittel (-) *washing-up liquid*
der Staat (-en) *state*
die Staatsangehörigkeit (-en) *nationality*
das Stadion (Stadien) *stadium*
die Stadt (¨e) *town*
der Stadtbummel *stroll through town*
die Stadtmauer (-n) *town wall*
die Stadtmitte (-n) *town centre*
der Stadtplan (¨e) *town plan*
der Stadtrand (¨er) *edge of town, outskirts*
das Stadtteil (-e) *part of town, quarter*
das Stadtzentrum (-ren) *town centre*
der Stahl *steel*
der Stall (¨e) *stable*

stammen (aus) *to come (from)*
der Stammtisch (¨e) *regulars' table (public house)*
der Stand (¨e) *stand, stall; level*
stark *strong*
starten *to start (a car)*
die Station (-en) *station*
stattfinden (*sep.*) *to take place*
der Stau (-s) *traffic jam*
der Staubsauger (-) *vacuum cleaner*
die Steckdose (-n) *electric socket*
stehen *to stand*
die Stehlampe (-n) *standard lamp*
stehlen *to steal*
steigen *to climb*
steil *steep*
der Stein (-e) *stone*
die Stelle (-n) *place, position, job*
stellen *to place, put*
sterben *to die*
die Stereoanlage (-n) *stereo*
der Stern (-e) *star*
die Steuer (-n) *tax*
das Steuerrad (¨er) *steering wheel*
der Stiefel (-) *boot*
still *quiet*
die Stimme (-n) *voice*
stimmen *to be correct, to tune*
die Stimmung (-en) *mood, atmosphere*
der Stock (Stockwerke) *floor, storey*
der Stoff (-e) *material*
stolz *proud*
stören *to disturb*
die Strafarbeit (-en) *extra work (school)*
die Strafe (-n) *fine, punishment*
der Strand (¨e) *beach*
die Straße (-n) *street, road*
die Straßenbahn (-en) *tram*
das Streichholz (¨er) *match*
der Streik (-s) *strike*
streiten *to quarrel*
streng *severe, strict*
stricken *to knit*
der Strom *river, current; electricity*
der Strumpf (¨e) *stocking, long sock*
das Stück (-e) *piece, play (theatre)*
der Student (-en) *student*
studieren *to study*
die Studien (*plural*) *studies*
der Stuhl (¨e) *chair*
stumm *silent*
die Stunde (-n) *hour, lesson*
der Stundenplan (¨e) *timetable*
der Sturm (¨e) *storm*
stürmisch *stormy*
stürzen *to rush, fall*
suchen *to look for*
Süd- *south . . .*
der Süden *south*
in den Süden *to the south*
im Süden *in the south*
Super *4-star (petrol)*
der Supermarkt (¨e) *supermarket*
die Suppe (-n) *soup*
süß *sweet*
sympathisch *nice, kind*

das T-Shirt (-s) *T-shirt*
der Tabak *tobacco*
das Tablett (-s) *tray*

die Tablette (-n) *tablet*
die Tafel (-n) *board, blackboard*
der Tag (-e) *day*
die Tageskarte (-n) *day ticket*
die Tagesschau (-en) *news (TV)*
täglich *daily*
das Tal (¨er) *valley*
die Talsperre (-n) *dam*
tanken *to fill with petrol*
die Tankstelle (-n) *petrol station*
der Tankwart (-e) *petrol attendant*
der Tannenbaum (¨e) *fir tree, Christmas tree*
die Tante (-n) *aunt*
der Tanz (¨e) *dance*
das Tanzen *dancing*
tanzen *to dance*
die Tasche (-n) *bag, pocket*
das Taschenbuch (¨er) *paperback book*
der Taschendieb (-e) *pick-pocket*
das Taschengeld *pocket money*
das Taschentuch (¨er) *handkerchief*
die Tasse (-n) *cup*
die Tat *action, deed*
taub *deaf*
tauchen *to dive*
das Taxi (-s) *taxi*
der Tee *tea*
die Teekanne (-n) *teapot*
der TEE-Zug (¨e) *Trans-European express train*
das Teil (-e) *part*
teilen *to share*
teilnehmen (*sep.*) *to take part*
der Teilnehmer (-) *participant*
das Telefon *telephone*
der Telefonanruf (-e) *telephone call*
das Telefonbuch *telephone directory*
telefonieren *to phone*
telefonisch *on the phone, by phone*
die Telefonnummer (-n) *telephone number*
die Telefonzelle (-n) *telephone box*
das Telegramm (-e) *telegram*
der Teller (-) *plate*
die Temperatur (-en) *temperature*
Tennis *tennis*
der Tennisplatz (¨e) *tennis court*
der Tennisschläger (-) *tennis racquet*
der Teppich (-e) *carpet*
der Termin (-e) *appointment*
die Terrasse (-n) *terrace*
teuer *expensive*
das Theater (-) *theatre*
die Theke (-en) *counter*
tief *deep*
der Tiefdruck *low pressure (weather)*
die Tiefgarage (-n) *underground garage*
die Tiefkühltruhe (-n) *freezer*
die Tiefsttemperatur (-en) *lowest temperature*
das Tier (-e) *animal*
der Tierarzt (¨e) *vet*
der Tiger (-) *tiger*
der Tisch (-e) *table*
die Tischdecke (-n) *table cloth*
Tischtennis *table tennis*
die Tochter (¨) *daughter*
der Tod (-e) *death*

die Toilette (-n) *toilet*
das Toilettenpapier *toilet paper*
toll *mad; great*
die Tomate (-n) *tomato*
der Ton (¨e) *sound*
das Tonbandgerät (-e) *tape recorder*
der Topf (¨e) *pot, saucepan*
das Tor (-e) *gate, goal*
die Torte (-n) *flan, gateau*
tragbar *portable*
tragen *to carry, wear*
trainieren *to train*
der Trainingsanzug (¨e) *tracksuit*
trampen *to hitch-hike*
Transistor- *transistor...*
die Traube (-n) *grape*
träumen *to dream*
träume süß *sweet dreams!*
traurig *sad*
sich treffen *to meet*
der Treffpunkt *meeting point*
treiben *to do, drift*
die Treppe (-n) *stairs*
das Treppenhaus *staircase*
treten *to step*
trinken *to drink*
das Trinkgeld (-er) *tip*
das Trinkwasser *drinking water*
kein Trinkwasser *not drinking water*
trocken *dry*
trocknen *to dry*
die Trompete (-n) *trumpet*
trotz *in spite of*
trüb *gloomy*
Tschüß! *cheerio!*
das Tuch (¨er) *cloth*
tun *to do*
die Tür (-en) *door*
der Turm (¨e) *tower*
turnen *to do gymnastics*
Turnen *Gymnastics*
die Turnhalle (-n) *gymnasium*
die Tüte (-n) *bag*
typisch *typical*

die U-Bahn (-en) *underground railway*
übel *ill, evil*
üben *to practise*
über *over, above*
über Köln *via Cologne*
überall *everywhere*
überfahren *to run over*
die Überfahrt (-en) *crossing*
überfallen *to attack*
überhaupt *on the whole*
überhaupt nichts *nothing at all*
überholen *to overtake*
überlegen *to think about*
übermorgen *day after tomorrow*
übernachten *to spend the night*
die Übernachtung (-en) *overnight stay*
überqueren *to cross*
überraschen *to surprise*
überrascht *surprised*
die Überraschung (-en) *surprise*
übersetzen *to translate*
übertreiben *to exaggerate*
überzeugen *to convince*
übrig *left over*
übrigens *besides*

die Übung (-en) *exercise*
das Ufer (-) *river bank*
die Uhr (-en) *clock, time*
die Uhrzeit (-en) *clock time*
um *round, at*
die Umgebung (-en) *surroundings*
der Umkleideraum (¨e) *changing room*
umkommen (*sep.*) *to die*
die Umleitung (-en) *diversion*
ums Leben kommen *to die*
der Umschlag (¨e) *envelope*
umsonst *in vain, free*
umsteigen (*sep.*) *to change (trains etc.)*
der Umtausch *exchange*
umtauschen (*sep.*) *to exchange*
die Umwelt *environment*
die Umweltfrage (-n) *environmental issue*
sich umziehen *to change (clothes)*
unangenehm *unpleasant*
unbedingt *absolutely*
unbekannt *unknown*
unbeschränkt *unlimited*
und *and*
unentschieden *undecided, a draw*
der Unfall (¨e) *accident*
unfreundlich *unfriendly*
ungeduldig *impatient*
ungefähr *approximately*
ungenügend *unsatisfactory*
das Unglück (-e) *misfortune, accident*
unglücklich *unfortunate*
unglücklicherweise *unfortunately*
die Uni (-s) *university*
die Uniform (-en) *uniform*
die Universität (-en) *university*
unmöglich *impossible*
unrecht haben *to be wrong*
unruhig *restless*
unschuldig *innocent*
unser *our*
der Unsinn *nonsense*
unten *below, downstairs*
unter *under, below*
das Untergeschoß (-sse) *cellar, basement*
die Untergrundbahn (-en) *underground railway*
sich unterhalten *to chat*
die Unterkunft (¨e) *accommodation*
der Unterricht (*no plural*) *instruction*
der Unterschied (-e) *difference*
unterschiedlich *variable*
unterschreiben *to sign*
die Unterschrift (-en) *signature*
untersuchen *to examine*
die Untertasse (-n) *saucer*
die Unterwäsche *underclothes*
unterwegs *on the way*
unwahrscheinlich *improbable*
unzufrieden *dissatisfied*
der Urlaub (-e) *holiday, leave*
der Urlauber (-) *holidaymaker*
die Ursache (-n) *cause*

die Vanille *vanilla*
die Vase (-n) *vase*
der Vater (¨) *father*
Vati *dad*

der Vegetarier (-) *vegetarian (male)*
die Vegetarierin (-nen) *vegetarian (female)*
vegetarisch *vegetarian*
der Vegetarismus *vegetarianism*
sich verabreden *to make an appointment*
die Verabredung (-en) *appointment*
sich verabschieden *to leave*
die Veranstaltung (-en) *event*
der Verband (¨-e) *association, federation; bandage (medicine)*
verbessern *to improve*
verbinden *to connect*
die Verbindung (-en) *connection*
verboten *forbidden*
verbrauchen *to use up*
verbringen *to spend (time)*
verdienen *to earn*
der Verein (-e) *club*
die Vereinigten Staaten *USA*
vergebens *in vain*
vergessen *to forget*
der Vergleich (-e) *comparison*
vergleichen *to compare*
das Vergnügen (-) *pleasure*
das Verhältnis (-se) *relationship*
verheiratet *married*
verhungern *to starve*
sich verirren *to lose the way*
der Verkauf (¨-e) *sale*
verkaufen *to sell*
der Verkäufer (-) *salesman*
der Verkehr *traffic*
verkehren *to run (of transport)*
die Verkehrsampel (-n) *traffic lights*
das Verkehrsamt (¨-er) *tourist office*
der Verkehrsstau (-s) *traffic jam*
verlangen *to demand*
verlassen *to leave*
sich verlaufen *to lose the way*
sich verletzen *to get hurt*
verletzt *injured*
die Verletzung (-en) *injury*
sich verlieben *to fall in love*
verlieren *to lose*
verlobt *engaged*
der Verlobte (-n) *fiancé*
die Verlobte (-n) *fiancée*
vermeiden *to avoid*
vernünftig *reasonable*
verpassen *to miss*
verreisen *to go away (on a journey)*
verrenken *to twist*
verrückt *mad*
verschieden *different*
verschließen *to lock*
die Verschmutzung *pollution*
verschmutzen *to pollute*
verschwenden *to waste*
verschwinden *to disappear*
versetzen *to remove, transfer*
versichern *to insure, assure*
die Versicherung (-en) *insurance*
verspätet *delayed*
die Verspätung (-en) *delay*
versprechen *to promise*
verständlich *understandable*
verstehen *to understand*
die Verstopfung (-en) *constipation*
der Versuch (-e) *attempt*

versuchen *to try*
verteidigen *to defend*
die Verteidigung *defence*
sich vertragen *to get on/along (with a person)*
verunglücken *to have an accident*
verunglückt *injured*
der Verwandte (-n) *relative (male)*
die Verwandte (-n) *relative (female)*
verwundet *wounded*
verzeihen *to excuse*
Verzeihung! *sorry!*
um Verzeihung bitten *to apologise to (somebody)*
verzollen *to declare (customs)*
der Vetter (-) *cousin (male)*
Video- *video . . .*
das Videogerät (-e) *video recorder*
das Vieh *cattle*
viel *much*
viel Glück *good luck!*
viel Vergnügen *have a good time!*
viele *many*
vielen Dank *many thanks*
vielleicht *perhaps*
vielmals *many times*
vier *four*
viereckig *square, rectangular*
das Viertel (-) *quarter*
die Viertelstunde (-n) *quarter of an hour*
der Vogel (¨-) *bird*
voll *full*
Volleyball *volleyball*
völlig *completely*
vollkommen *completely*
Vollkornbrot *wholemeal bread*
die Vollpension *full board*
volltanken (sep.) *to fill up (petrol)*
vom (von dem) *from the, of the*
von *from, of*
von wo *where from*
von Zeit zu Zeit *from time to time*
vor *before, in front of*
vor allem *above all*
vor kurzem *a short time ago*
vorbei *past*
vorbeigehen (sep.) *to pass*
vorbeikommen (sep.) *to look in*
vorbereiten *to prepare*
Vorder- *front . . .*
die Vorfahrt *right of way*
vorgehen (sep.) *to go ahead*
vorgestern *day before yesterday*
vorhaben (sep.) *to plan*
der Vorhang (¨-e) *curtain*
vorher *previously*
die Vorhersage (-n) *forecast*
vorig *last (previous)*
vorkommen (sep.) *to happen*
vorläufig *provisional(ly)*
der Vormittag (-e) *morning*
vormittags *in the morning*
der Vorname (-n) *first name*
vorne *at the front*
der Vorort (-e) *suburb*
der Vorschlag (¨-e) *proposal, plan*
vorschlagen (sep.) *to propose*
die Vorsicht *caution*
vorsichtig *cautious*
die Vorspeise (-n) *starter (meal)*
die Vorstadt (¨-e) *suburb*

sich vorstellen (sep.) *to introduce (oneself)*
die Vorstellung (-en) *introduction, performance*
der Vorteil (-e) *advantage*
die Vorwahlnummer (-n) *code (telephone)*
vorwärts *forwards*
vorzeigen (sep.) *to show*
vorziehen (sep.) *to prefer*

wach *awake*
wachsen *to grow*
die Waffe (-n) *weapon*
der Wagen (-) *car*
die Wahl (-en) *choice*
wählen *to choose*
das Wahlfach (¨-er) *optional subject*
wahr *true*
während *during, while*
wahrscheinlich *probable(ly)*
der Wald (¨-er) *wood (trees)*
Wales *Wales*
der Waliser (-) *Welshman*
walisisch *Welsh*
die Wand (¨-e) *wall*
wandern *to hike*
die Wanderung (-en) *walk, hike*
wann *when*
die Ware (-n) *product, goods*
das Warenhaus (¨-er) *department store*
warm *warm*
warnen *to warn*
die Warnung (-en) *warning*
warten *to wait*
der Warteraum (¨-e) *waiting room*
der Wartesaal (-äle) *waiting room*
das Wartezimmer (-) *waiting room*
warum *why*
was *what*
was? *what?*
was fehlt? *what's up?*
was für? *what sort of?*
was für ein? *what sort of a?*
was gibt's? *what is there?*
was ist? *what is?*
was ist das? *what is that*
was ist los? *what's the matter?*
was läuft? *what's on?*
das Waschbecken (-) *wash basin*
die Wäsche *washing, laundry*
(sich) waschen *to wash*
die Wäscherei (-en) *laundry room*
die Waschmaschine (-n) *washing machine*
das Waschpulver *washing powder*
der Waschraum (¨-e) *washroom*
das Wasser *water*
Wasserball *water polo*
der Wasserfall (¨-e) *waterfall*
der Wasserhahn (¨-e) *water tap*
die Wasserverschmutzung *water pollution*
das WC (-s) *WC*
der Wechsel (-) *change*
der Wechselkurs (-e) *rate of exchange*
wechseln *to change*
die Wechselstube (-n) *bureau de change*
wecken *to wake*
der Wecker (-) *alarm clock*
weder *neither*

weder ...
   noch ... *neither ... nor ...*
der Weg (-e) *way, track*
weg *away*
wegen *because of*
weggehen (*sep.*) *to go away*
wegnehmen (*sep.*) *to take away*
der Wegweiser (-) *signpost*
wegwerfen (*sep.*) *to throw away*
der Wehrdienst *conscription*
wehtun (*sep.*) *to hurt*
weiblich *feminine, female*
weich *soft*
Weihnachten *Christmas*
weil *because*
die Weile *while*
der Wein (-e) *wine*
weinen *to cry, weep*
die Weinkarte (-n) *wine list*
der Weinkeller (-) *wine cellar*
die Weinliste (-n) *wine list*
die Weinprobe (-n) *wine-tasting*
die Weinstube (-n) *wine bar*
die Weintraube (-n) *grape*
die Weise (-n) *way*
weiß *white*
das Weißbrot *white bread*
der Weißwein (-e) *white wine*
weit *far*
weiter *further*
weiterfahren (*sep.*) *drive on*
weitergeben (*sep.*) *pass on*
weitergehen (*sep.*) *go on*
weiterhin *in future*
welcher *which*
der Wellensittich (-e) *budgerigar*
die Welt *world*
die Dritte Welt *the third world*
die Weltmeisterschaft (-en) *world cup*
wem *to whom*
wen *whom*
wenig *little*
ein wenig *a little*
wenige *few*
wenigstens *at least*
wenn *when, if*
wer *who*
die Werbung (-en) *advertising, advertisement*
werden *to become*
werfen *to throw*
die Werkstätte (-n) *workshop*
werktags *weekdays*
das Werkzeug (-e) *tool*
der Wert (-e) *value, worth*
wert *worth*
wertvoll *valuable*
die Wespe (-n) *wasp*
West- *west ...*
der Westen *west*
westlich *western*
das Wetter *weather*
der Wetterbericht (-e) *weather report*
die Wetterlage (-n) *weather conditions*
die Wettervorhersage (-n) *weather forecast*
wichtig *important*
wie *how*
wie bitte? *I beg your pardon?*
wie geht's? *how are you?*

wie komme ich am besten ...? *how do I get ...?*
wie schade! *what a pity!*
wieder *again*
wiederholen *to repeat*
wiederhören *to hear again*
   auf Wiederhören *goodbye (telephone)*
   auf Wiederschauen *goodbye*
wiedersehen *to see again*
   auf Wiedersehen *goodbye*
wiegen *to rock, cradle, weigh*
Wien *Vienna*
das Wiener Schnitzel (-) *Vienna cutlet*
die Wiese (-n) *meadow*
wieso? *how do you mean?*
wieviel(e)? *how much (many)?*
   der Wievielte? *what date?*
das Wildleder (-) *suede*
willkommen *to welcome*
das Willkommen (-) *welcome*
der Wind (-e) *wind*
windig *windy*
die Windschutzscheibe (-n) *windscreen*
winken *to wave*
der Winter *winter*
der Wintersport *winter sport*
wirklich *really*
die Wirklichkeit (-en) *reality*
die Wirtschaft (-en) *economy; inn*
das Wirtshaus (¨er) *public house, inn*
wissen *to know*
die Wissenschaften *sciences*
die Witwe (-n) *widow*
der Witwer (-) *widower*
wo? *where?*
wo ... her? *where from?*
die Woche (-n) *week*
das Wochenende (-n) *weekend*
wochentags *on weekdays*
wöchentlich *weekly*
woher? *where from?*
wohin? *where to?*
wohl *well, I suppose*
sich wohlfühlen (*sep.*) *to feel well*
der Wohnblock (¨e or -s) *block of flats*
wohnen *to live*
der Wohnort (-e) *domicile*
die Wohnung (-en) *flat, home*
der Wohnwagen (-) *caravan*
das Wohnzimmer (-) *living room*
die Wolke (-n) *cloud*
wolkenlos *cloudless*
wolkig *cloudy*
die Wolle *wool*
wollen *to want to*
das Wort (-e or ¨er) *word*
das Wörterbuch (¨er) *dictionary*
wunderbar *wonderful*
wunderschön *wonderful*
der Wunsch (¨e) *wish*
wünschen *to wish*
die Wurst (¨e) *sausage*
die Wurstbude (-n) *sausage stall*
das Würstchen (-) *small sausage*
die Wut *anger*
wütend *angry*

die Zahl (-en) *number*
zahlen *to pay*

zählen *to count*
der Zahn (¨e) *tooth*
Zahn- *tooth ...*
der Zahnarzt (¨e) *dentist*
die Zahnbürste (-n) *toothbrush*
die Zahnpasta *toothpaste*
die Zahnschmerzen (*plural*) *toothache*
die Zehe (-n)/der Zeh (-en) *toe*
zeichnen *to draw*
Zeichnen *drawing (activity)*
die Zeichnung (-en) *drawing*
zeigen *to show*
die Zeit (-en) *time*
die Zeitschrift (-en) *magazine*
die Zeitung (-en) *newspaper*
das Zeitungsgeschäft (-e) *paper shop*
der Zeitungskiosk (-e) *paper stall*
der Zeitungsstand (¨e) *paper stand*
das Zelt (-e) *tent*
zelten *to camp*
der/das Zentimeter *centimetre*
die Zentralheizung *central heating*
das Zentrum (-ren) *centre*
zerstören *to destroy*
der Zettel (-) *note*
das Zeug *thing*
der Zeuge (-n) *witness*
das Zeugnis (-se) *report (school)*
ziehen *to pull*
das Ziel (-e) *aim, destination, target*
ziemlich *fairly*
die Zigarette (-n) *cigarette*
das Zimmer (-) *room*
der Zimmernachweis (-e) *room indication*
die Zitrone (-n) *lemon*
zittern *to tremble*
der Zoll *customs*
der Zollbeamte (-n) *customs official*
zollfrei *duty free*
die Zollkontrolle (-n) *customs control*
der Zoo (-s) *zoo*
zornig *angry*
zu *to*
zu Fuß *on foot*
zu Mittag essen *to have lunch*
der Zucker *sugar*
zuerst *at first*
die Zufahrt (-en) *approach (road)*
zufrieden *satisfied*
der Zug (¨e) *train*
zugestiegen *got in (bus etc.)*
zuhören (*sep.*) *to listen*
die Zukunft *future*
zum (zu dem) *to the*
zum Wohl! *cheers!*
zumachen (*sep.*) *to close*
zunächst *at first, next*
zunehmen (*sep.*) *to increase, put on weight*
die Zunge (-n) *tongue*
zur (zu der) *to the*
zurück *back*
zurück- ... *back*
zurückfahren (*sep.*) *to return*
zurückgeben (*sep.*) *to give back*
zurückkehren (*sep.*) *to return*
zurückkommen (*sep.*) *to come back*
zusammen *together*

der	Zusammenstoß (¨e) *crash*	der	Zutritt *access*		zweifellos *without doubt*
der	Zuschauer (-) *spectator*		Kein Zutritt *no access*	die	Zwiebel (-n) *onion*
der	Zuschlag (¨e) *supplement*		zuviel *too much*		zwischen *between*
	zuschlagspflichtig *supplement obligatory*		zuviel (e) *too many*		zwo/zwei *two*
	zuschließen (*sep.*) *to close*	der	Zweck (-e) *aim, purpose*		
		der	Zweifel (-) *doubt*		

▶ ENGLISH–GERMAN VOCABULARY (SELECTIVE)

	able: to be able to *können*		breakfast *das Frühstück (-e)*		door *die Tür (-en)*
	about (=around) *um*+acc.	to	bring (with) *(mit)bringen*		back door *die Hintertür (-en)*
	about (with time) *gegen*+acc.		brother *der Bruder (¨)*		front door *die Haustür (-en)*
	above *über*+dat./acc.	to	build *bauen*		downstairs: to go downstairs
	abroad (adv.) *im Ausland*		building *das Gebäude (-)*		*nach unten gehen, die Treppe hinuntergehen*
	to go abroad *ins Ausland fahren*		bus *der (Auto)bus (-se)*		
	address *die Adresse (-n), die Anschrift (-en)*	to	buy *kaufen*	to	drink *trinken*
	afraid (adj.) *ängstlich*		by (prep.) *durch*+acc.; *von*+dat.	to	drive *fahren, führen*
	to be afraid of *Angst haben vor*+dat.		by train *mit dem Zug*		duck *die Ente (-n)*
	after (prep.) *nach*+dat.		café *das Café (-s)*		during (prep.) *während*+gen.
	after (adv.) *nachher*	to	call *rufen*; (on telephone) *anrufen*		Easter *Ostern*
	after (conj.) *nachdem*		camera *die Kamera (-s)*		at Easter *zu Ostern*
	again (adv.) *wieder*		campsite *der Campingplatz (¨e)*		Easter holidays *die Osterferien*
	against *gegen*+acc.		car *das Auto (-s), der Wagen (-)*	to	eat *essen*; (of animals) *fressen*
	ago (adv.) *vor*+dat.		card *die Karte (-n)*	to	eat up *aufessen, auffressen*
	alarm clock *der Wecker (-)*	to	cash (a cheque) *einlösen*		egg *das Ei (-er)*
	all *all, alle*		chair *der Stuhl (¨e)*		elder (adj.) *älter*
	all sorts of *allerlei*		cheque *der Scheck (-s)*		elsewhere *anderswo*
	allowed *erlaubt*		child *das Kind (-er)*		empty *leer*
	to be allowed to *dürfen*		Christmas *Weihnachten*		English *englisch* (adj.), (=language) *English*
	almost *fast, beinahe*		cinema *das Kino (-s)*		enough *genug*
	alone *allein*		clean *sauber*		evening *der Abend (-e)*
	already *schon*	to	clean *putzen*		everybody *jeder*
	although *obwohl, obgleich*		clear *klar*		everything *alles*
	always *immer*		coast *die Küste (-n)*		everywhere *überall*
	among *unter*+dat.		coffee *der Kaffee*		except *außer*+dat.
	and *und*		cold (noun) *die Kälte*; (=illness) *die Erkältung (-en)*		eye *das Auge (-n)*
	angry *böse*				
	angrily *zornig, wütend*		cold (adj.) *kalt*		face *das Gesicht (-er)*
to	arrive *ankommen*	to	come *kommen*		family *die Familie (-n)*
	as … as *so … wie*		comfortable *bequem*		far *weit, fern, entfernt*
	as (conj.) *während, indem*		counter (shop) *der Ladentisch (-e)*; (pub) *die Theke (-n)*; (bank) *der Kassenschalter(-)*		farm *die Bauernhof (¨e)*
to	ask *fragen, bitten*				fat *dick*
	at (prep.) (place) *in, an, bei*; (time) *um, zu*				father *der Vater (¨)*
	at last *endlich*		countryside *das Land*		favourite *Lieblings-*
	at least *wenigstens, mindestens*	to	cry (=shout) *schreien*; (=weep) *weinen*		favourite subject *das Lieblingsfach (¨er)*
	aunt *die Tante (-n)*				
			cup *die Tasse (-n)*		few *einige, ein paar, wenige*
	bad *schlecht, schlimm*		curtain (net) *die Gardine (-n)*; (heavy) *der Vorhang (¨e)*		film *der Film (-e)*
	bank *die Bank (-en)*			to	find *finden*
	bathroom *das Badezimmer (-)*	to	cut *schneiden*		first *erst*
to	be *sein*				at first *zuerst*
to	be situated *sich befinden*		dad *Vati*		fish *der Fische (-e)*
	because (conj.) *denn, weil*		date (time) *das Datum (Daten)*		flash: quick as a flash *blitzschnell*
	bed *das Bett (-en)*		daughter *die Tochter (¨)*		flat (adj.) *flach*
	bedroom *das Schlafzimmer (-)*		day *der Tag (-e)*		flat (noun) *die Wohnung (-en)*
	before, in front of *vor*+dat./acc.	to	decide *beschließen, sich entscheiden*		football *der Fußball (¨e)*
to	begin *beginnen, anfangen*				for (conj.) *denn*
	beginning *der Anfang (¨e)*		difficult *schwer, schwierig*		for (prep.) *für*+acc.
	behind (prep.) *hinter*+acc./dat.		dining room *das Eßzimmer (-), das Speisezimmer (-)*	to	forget *vergessen*
	below *unter*+dat./acc.				fork *die Gabel (-n)*
	beside *neben*+dat./acc.		dinner *das Abendessen (-)*		fortnight *vierzehn Tage*
	between *zwischen*+dat./acc.		directory (telephone) *das Telefonbuch (¨er)*		friend (male) *der Freund (-e)*; (female) *die Freundin (-nen)*
	big *groß*				
	black *schwarz*		dish *das Gericht (-e)*		friendly (adv.) *freundlich*
	book *das Buch (¨er)*		distance *die Ferne*		from (prep.) *von*+dat., *aus*+dat.
	bread *das Brot (-e or -sorten)*		in the distance *in der Ferne*		front: in front of (prep.) *vor*+dat./acc.
		to	do *machen, tun*		
			dog *der Hund (-e)*		

Chapter 16 Vocabulary

furniture *die Möbel* (plural)
garden *der Garten (-̈)*
gateau *die Torte (-n)*
Germany *(das) Deutschland*
to get (=become) *werden*
to get dressed *sich anziehen*
to get undressed *sich ausziehen*
to get changed *sich umziehen*
to get up/to stand up *aufstehen*
girl *das Mädchen (-)*
girlfriend *die Freundin (-nen)*
to give *geben*
glad *froh*
glass *das Glas (-̈er)*
to go *gehen, fahren*
to go back *zurückgehen, zurückfahren*
to go for a walk *einen Spaziergang machen*
good *gut*
grandmother *die Großmutter (-̈)*
granny *die Oma (-s)*
grapes *die Weintrauben*

half (adj.) *halb*
half (noun) *die Hälfte (-n)*
half an hour *eine halbe Stunde*
hand *die Hand (-̈e)*
to have to *müssen*
he *er*
to hear *hören*
to help *helfen+dat.*
her *ihr*
here *hier*
his *sein*
holiday *der Urlaub (-e)*
holidays *die Ferien* (plural)
home: to go home *nach Hause gehen*
hope: I hope that, etc. *hoffentlich*
to hope for *hoffen auf+acc.*
hospital *das Krankenhaus (-̈er)*
hotel *das Hotel (-s)*
hour *die Stunde (-n)*
house *das Haus (-̈er)*
how *wie*
how much *wieviel*
however *aber*
hungry *hungrig*
  to be hungry *Hunger haben*
husband *der Mann (-̈er)*

I *ich*
ice *das Eis (-e)*
idea *die Idee (-n)*
if (conj.) *wenn, ob*
ill *krank*
in (into) *in+dat./acc.*
inside *drinnen*
interested: to be interested in *sich interessieren für+acc.*
to invite *einladen*
island *die Insel (-n)*
it *es*

jam *die Marmelade (-n)*
juice *der Saft (-̈e)*
to jump *springen*
just (adv.) *eben*

kitchen *die Küche (-n)*
knife *das Messer (-)*

to knock at *klopfen an+acc.*
to know (a fact) *wissen;* (a person) *kennen*

lake *der See (-n)*
large *groß*
last *letzt*
late *spät*
to laugh *lachen*
to learn *lernen*
to leave *verlassen;* (=depart) *abfahren*
left *links*
less *weniger*
letter *der Brief (-e)*
to lie *liegen*
light *das Licht (-er)*
to light *anzünden*
to like *gern haben*
to listen *(zu)hören;* (=pay attention) *aufpassen*
little *klein*
to live *leben;* (=to dwell) *wohnen*
long *lang*
to look *blicken*
to look for *suchen*
to look (=appear) *aussehen*
to look forward (to) *sich freuen (auf+acc.)*
to lose *verlieren*
to lose one's way *sich verlaufen*
a lot *viel, viele*

man *der Mann (-̈er)*
many *viele*
marvellous *wunderbar*
meal *die Mahlzeit (-en)*
menu *die Speisekarte (-n)*
midday *(der) Mittag (-e)*
minute *die Minute (-n)*
to miss (e.g. a bus) *verpassen*
money *das Geld*
more *mehr*
morning *der Morgen (-)*
mother, mummy *die Mutter (-̈), Mutti*
mountain *der Berg (-e)*
  range of mountains *das Gebirge (-)*
much *viel*
my *mein*

near *nahe*
nearly *fast*
to need *brauchen*
new *neu*
newspaper *die Zeitung (-en)*
next *nächst*
nice *nett*
night *die Nacht (-̈e)*
no *nein*
nothing *nichts*
to notice *bemerken*
now *nun, jetzt*
number *die Nummer (-n)*

of course *natürlich*
old *alt*
on *auf+dat./acc.*
only *nur, erst*
open *offen*
to open *öffnen, aufmachen*
to order *bestellen*

other *ander*
our *unser*
out of *aus+dat.*
outside *draußen*
over there *dort drüben*
own *eigen*

parents *die Eltern* (plural)
park *der Park (-s)*
particularly *besonders*
to pass (of time) *vergehen*
passport *der Paß (Pässe)*
past: to go past *vorbeigehen (an+dat.)*
to pay for *bezahlen*
peas *Erbsen*
people *die Leute*
pepper *der Pfeffer*
perhaps *vielleicht*
person *die Person (-en)*
pet *das Haustier (-e)*
piece *das Stück (-e);* (of toast) *die Scheibe (-n)*
pipe *die Pfeife (-n)*
plan *der Plan (-̈e)*
please! *bitte!*
pleased: to be pleased (about) *sich freuen (über+acc.)*
poor *arm*
post office *das Postamt (-̈er), die Post*
present *das Geschenk (-e)*
pretty *hübsch*

quality *die Qualität*
quarter *das Viertel (-)*
quick *schnell, rasch*
quickly *schnell, rasch*
quite *ganz*

radio *das Radio (-s)*
railway *die Eisenbahn (-en)*
to reach *erreichen*
to read *lesen*
ready *fertig*
really *wirklich*
reception (desk) *die Rezeption (-en), der Empfang (-̈e)*
to remember *sich erinnern an+acc.*
to repair *reparieren*
to repeat *wiederholen*
to reply *antworten, erwidern*
reply *die Antwort (-en)*
to reserve *reservieren*
restaurant *das Restaurant (-s)*
to return *zurückgehen, zurückkommen*
right *recht, rechts*
right (correct) *richtig*
  to be right *recht haben*
to ring *klingeln, läuten*
room (single) *das Einzelzimmer (-)*
room (double) *das Doppelzimmer (-)*
to run *laufen*

sandwich *das Sandwich (-s or -es)*
to say *sagen*
scarcely *kaum*
school *die Schule (-n)*
sea *die See (-n), das Meer (-e)*
seaside: at the seaside *an der See*

to	see	*sehen*		tea	*der Tee*	
to	send	*schicken, senden*		telegram	*das Telegramm (-e)*	
	she	*sie*		telephone	*das Telefon (-e)*	
to	shine	*scheinen*	to	tell	*sagen, erzählen*	
	shopping: to go shopping	*die einkaufen (gehen)*		tent	*das Zelt (-e)*	
to	show	*zeigen*		terrible, terribly	*furchtbar, schrecklich*	
	shower	*die Dusche (-n)*		than (in comparison)	*als*	
	since (prep.)	*seit+dat.*		thanks	*der Dank* (no plural)	
	since (conj.)	*seitdem*		many thanks	*vielen Dank*	
	since (adv.)	*seither*		their	*ihr*	
	single	*einzeln;* (unmarried) *ledig*		then	*dann, denn, damals*	
	sister	*die Schwester (-n)*		there	*da, dort*	
	brothers and sisters	*die Geschwister*		thermos flask	*die Thermosflasche (-n)*	
				they	*sie*	
to	sit, be sitting	*sitzen*		thin	*dünn, mager*	
to	sit down	*sich setzen*		thing	*das Ding (-e)*	
	slice	*die Scheibe (-n)*	to	think	*denken, glauben*	
	slowly	*langsam*	to	think about/of	*halten von+dat.*	
	small	*klein*		through	*durch+acc.*	
to	smile	*lächeln*	to	throw	*werfen*	
	so	*so, also*		ticket	*die Fahrkarte (-n)*	
	some	*einige, wenige*		ticket office	*der Schalter (-), der Fahrkartenschalter (-)*	
	somebody	*jemand*				
	something	*etwas*		time	*die Zeit (-en)*	
	soon	*bald*		to (prep.)	*an+dat./acc., zu+dat.*	
	sorry!	*Verzeihung! es tut mir leid*		toast	*der Toast (-e)*	
to	speak	*sprechen*		today	*heute*	
to	spend (time)	*verbringen*		too (adv.)	*zu*	
	spring	*der Frühling (-e)*		too many, too much	*zuviel (-e)*	
	stamp	*die Briefmarke (-n)*		tooth	*der Zahn (¨e)*	
to	starve	*verhungern*		towards: he came towards me	*er kam auf mich zu*	
	station	*der Bahnhof (¨e)*				
	main station	*der Hauptbahnhof (¨e)*		town	*die Stadt (¨e)*	
				town hall	*das Rathaus (¨er)*	
to	stay	*bleiben, wohnen*		train	*der Zug (¨e)*	
	still (adv.)	*noch*		goods train	*der Güterzug (¨e)*	
to	stop	*anhalten;* (=to cease) *aufhören*		slow train	*der Personenzug (¨e)*	
				through/fast train	*der D-Zug (¨e)*	
	story	*die Geschichte (-n)*				
	straight away	*gleich*		traveller	*der/die Reisende (-n)*	
to	swim	*schwimmen*		travellers' cheque	*der Reisescheck (-s)*	
	sugar	*der Zucker (-)*				
	summer	*der Sommer (-)*	to	try	*versuchen*	
	sun	*die Sonne (-n)*				
	sure	*sicher*		uncle	*der Onkel (-)*	
				under (prep.)	*unter+acc./dat.*	
	table	*der Tisch (-e)*	to	understand	*verstehen*	
to	take	*nehmen*		until	*bis*	
to	talk	*sprechen*		upstairs	*oben*	

vegetable(s)	*das Gemüse*	
very	*sehr*	
view	*die Aussicht (-en)*	
village	*das Dorf (¨er)*	
vinegar	*der Essig*	
visit	*der Besuch (-e)*	
to visit	*besuchen*	
voice	*die Stimme (-n)*	
to wait (for)	*warten (auf+acc.)*	
waiter	*der Kellner (-), der Ober (-)*	
waitress	*die Kellnerin (-nen)*	
walk: to go for a walk	*einen Spaziergang machen, spazierengehen*	
to walk	*zu Fuß gehen*	
to want	*wollen*	
warden	*der Wärter (-)*	
to wash (oneself)	*(sich) waschen*	
washroom	*der Waschraum (¨e)*	
water	*das Wasser*	
we	*wir*	
weather	*das Wetter (-)*	
week	*die Woche (-n)*	
well: I am well	*es geht mir gut*	
when	*wann, wenn*	
where	*wo*	
while (conj.)	*während*	
after a while	*nach einer Weile*	
white	*weiß*	
why	*warum*	
window	*das Fenster (-)*	
wish	*der Wunsch (¨e)*	
to wish	*wünschen*	
with (prep.)	*mit+dat.*	
without (prep.)	*ohne+acc.*	
worry	*die Sorge (-n)*	
to write	*schreiben*	
year	*das Jahr (-e)*	
yellow	*gelb*	
yes	*ja, jawohl*	
yesterday	*gestern*	
yesterday evening	*gestern abend*	
yet	*doch*	
you	*du, ihr, Sie*	
young	*jung*	
your	*dein, Ihr, euer*	
youth hostel	*die Jugendherberge (-n)*	

▶ INSTRUCTIONS AND QUESTIONS

The following is a list of instructions that you may come across in the GCSE examination. Some examining groups favour the polite form in instructions, while others use the familiar form, so you will find a mixture of both in this list.

auf deutsch	*in German*
Ändere	*Change/alter*
Äußern Sie sich dazu	*Comment (on this)*
Beantworte (die Fragen)	*Answer (the questions)*
Begrüße	*Greet*
Beispiel	*Example*
Berichte	*Report*
Beschrifte	*Label (a picture/diagram)*
Beschreibe	*Describe*
Bitte (das Formular) ausfüllen	*Please fill in (the form)*

Bringen Sie die Sätze/Wörter in die richtige/eine sinnvolle Reihenfolge	Put the sentences/words into the correct/a sensible order
Danken Sie	Thank
entweder ... oder	either ... or
Erfinde	Make up/invent
Ergänze die Tabelle/den Stundenplan	Complete the grid/timetable
Erkläre	Explain
Ersetze	Replace
Erzähle	Tell (Give an account of)
Fange ... an	Begin ...
Finden Sie (die Wörter/Sätze)	Find (the words/sentences)
Frag(e) (nach)	Ask (about)
Füllen Sie (die Tabelle/das Formular/den Fragebogen/die Lücken) aus	Fill in (the table/form/questionnaire/gaps)
Gib Informationen über	Give information about
Hake ... an	Tick
Hör zu	Listen
jetzt	now
Kopiere	Copy
Korrigiere die folgenden Sätze	Correct the following sentences
Kreuze (das richtige/nur 5 Kästchen) an	Mark (the correct box/only 5 boxes) with a cross
Lies den Artikel/Brief/die Postkarte/Broschüre/Anzeige	Read the article/letter/potscard/brochure/advertisement
Lies den Text und füll die Lücken aus	Read the text and fill in the gaps
Machen Sie einen Kreis um Ja oder Nein	Circle Ja or Nein
Mache Notizen/eine Liste/ein Protokoll/ein Poster zum Thema ...	Make notes/a list/a report/a poster about ...
Markiere	Mark
Melden Sie sich	Say who you are (on the phone)
Nenne (zwei Dinge)	Name (two things)
Nimm Abschied von/Verabschiede dich von ...	Say goodbye to ...
Numeriere sie in der richtigen Reihenfolge	Number them in the correct order
Ordne die Sätze/Bilder	Put the sentences/pictures in order
Sag(e)	Say
Sag(e) deine Meinung über/zu ...	Give your opinion about ...
Schau ... an	Look at
Schlag(e) ... vor	Suggest ...
Schreibe positive/negative Sätze	Write positive/negative sentences
Schreibe an deinen Brieffreund/deine Brieffreundin	Write to your pen friend
Schreiben Sie den Buchstaben, der paßt	Write the letter that fits/matches.
Schreiben Sie in den Kalender	Write in the diary
Schreibe die richtige Nummer ...	Write the correct number ...
... auf den Plan	... on the map
... neben die Bilder hin	... next to the pictures
Schreibe einen Bericht über	Write a report about ...
Schreibe einen Brief an ...	Write a letter to ...
Schreibe deine Meinung zu/über ...	Write your opinion about ...
Sieh (die Notizen/Zeichnungen/Tabelle) an	Look at (the notes, drawings, table)
Stelle Fragen über ...	Ask questions about ...
Stellen Sie sich vor	Introduce yourself
Suche	Look for
Trage ... ein	Fill ... in
Unterstreiche	Underline
Verbinde	Connect/join up
Vergiß nicht ...	Do not forget ...
Vergleiche	Compare
Wähle	Choose

	Was bedeuten diese Symbole?	What do these symbols mean?
	Was ist richtig? Was ist falsch?	What is true? What is false?
	Was paßt zusammen?	What matches?
	Wiederholen Sie	Repeat
	Zeig(e)	Show
	zuerst	first
	in Ziffern	in numbers/figures
Questions	Was braucht man?	What is needed?
	Was fehlt (hier)?	What is missing (here)?
	Was paßt zusammen?	What matches?
	Was/welches Wort reimt sich?	What/which word rhymes?
	Was stimmt (nicht)?	What is (not) correct?
	Was trifft zu?	What is correct?
	Was wird angeboten?	What is being offered?
	Welche Person ist das?	Who is that/it?
	Wem gehört . . . ?	To whom does . . . belong?
	Wer ist das?	Who is that/it?
	Welche Nummer brauchst du?	Which number do you need?
	Welcher Satz ist richtig?	Which sentence is correct?
	Welche Zahl ist das?	Which number/figure is that/it?
	Welche . . . paßt zu welchem/welcher . . . ?	Which . . . matches which . . . ?
	Wer sagt das?	Who says that?
	Wie ist die richtige Reihenfolge?	What is the correct order?
	Worüber sprechen sie?	What are they talking about?

Index

accident 16, 70, 149, 186
accommodation 23–4
accounts 172, 186–7
accusative case 208–9
adjectives 198–200
  agreement of 198–9
adverbs 212–13
adverts 22, 64, 87, 90
Areas of Experience 11–12
articles 108, 116–17, 117–18, 172

banks 20, 130

café 17, 54, 56
campsites 23–4, 56, 127
cardinal numbers 216
careers 21–2
cases 196, 208–9
changing money 20, 130
checklist of language tasks 219–29
classroom language 14
commands 204
communication 13
comparatives 200
conditional tense 203
conjunctions 213
conversation skills 14
conversation
  a step further 161–3
  approaching the test 156
  Foundation Tier 155–6
  Foundation Tier questions, 157–8
  Higher Tier 156
  Higher Tier questions 159
coursework
  approaching writing 194–5
  requirements for writing 192–3
  sample of writing 195
  speaking 160–1
  teacher's role 194–5
  writing 192–5
  writing tasks 193–4
courtesies 14

dative case 208–9
days 216
definite article 196–8
dictionaries 8–9, 14
dry cleaning 21
dürfen 202

EDEXCEL Foundation 5
employment
  listening questions 72
  reading questions 116–17
  role-plays 130–1, 158
  tasks 21–2
  writing questions 173, 184
entertainment 18, 53, 70–1, 72, 146
everyday activities 14–17
exam group addresses 5–6
exam instructions and questions
    249–51
exam techniques 7–8

family 17–18, 88, 144, 183–4
finding the way 19, 53, 54, 56, 128
fitness 16–17
food and drink 17, 53, 54, 64, 91,
    128, 178
form filling 168, 172
free time
  reading questions 92, 109
  role-plays 125–6, 142–3, 146
  tasks 18
  writing questions 170
friends 17–18
future tense 203

GCSE
  aims of 1
  content 1, 11–13
  overview 1, 2–3
gender of nouns 197
genitive case 208–9
getting around 21, 87
going out 18–19, 65, 131, 132–3
grades 2, 4–5
grammar 196–218
  advice 7
  answers to tests 216–18

health 16–17, 54, 131–2, 134, 140–2
hiring 20
holidays
  listening questions 54, 71
  reading questions 96–7, 101–2,
      110–11
  role-plays 130, 145, 147–8
  tasks 18, 22–3
  writing questions 170, 177–8, 186,
      187, 189
home life
  listening questions 54, 56, 66
  reading questions 95, 111, 117–18
  tasks 15
  writing questions 178–9
home town 19, 172
hotels
  listening questions 57
  reading questions 99–100
  role-plays 123–4, 126–7
  tasks 23–4
  writing questions 171, 184

IGCSE 4, 6
illness 16, 69
imperatives 204
imperfect tense 201, 202
impersonal verbs 205
indefinite article 196–8
injury 16
interrogatives 213–14

jobs 21–2

Key Stage 4 1
können 202

language tasks 13
language tasks by topic 14–24
language of the classroom 14
leisure 18
letters 109, 168–9, 171, 172–3,
    183–5, 190
life in other countries 22, 112
listening
  a step further 80–2
  approaching the tests 46–8
  assessment objectives 46
  Foundation Tier 45–66
  Foundation Tier answers 60–2
  Foundation Tier questions 48–58
  Higher Tier 67–80
  Higher Tier answers 77–9
  Higher Tier questions 69–73
  Higher Tier themes 67–9
  preparation 7
  requirements 46, 67
  skills 45
  student answers 63–6, 79–80
  written version of extracts 58–60,
      73–7
lists 166–7, 169–70, 178
local area 19
London exams 5
lost property 20, 53, 133, 144

marking 181

meal times 17
media 15–16
MEG 5
memory aids 9
messages 69, 70, 167
mixed verbs 202, 206–8
modal verbs 202
modules 3
mögen 202
months 216
müssen 202
narratives 186–7
National Curriculum 1
NEAB 5
negatives 214
NICCEA 6
nominative case 208–9
nouns 196–8
numbers 216

ordinal numbers 216

passive voice 203
past tenses
perfect tense 201, 202
personal relationships 17–18
planning answers 10
pluperfect tense 202
plural of nouns 197
points 5
   conversion to grades 5
post office 20, 53, 55
postcards 167–8, 170–1
preparation 7–8
prepositions 209–11
present tense 201, 202
presentation 10
pronouns 211
public transport
   air 88–9, 138
   boat 55
   tasks 21
   train 52, 53, 54, 55, 105–7, 125, 127
publicity 22

question words 213–14

reading
   a step further 118–20
   approaching the tests 84–5
   assessment objectives 83–4
   exam hints 85–7
   Foundation Tier 83–102
   Foundation Tier answers 97–9
   Foundation Tier questions 87–97
   Foundation Tier themes 85
   Higher Tier 103–18
   Higher Tier answers 113–16
   Higher Tier questions 105–13
   Higher Tier requirements 103

Higher Tier themes 103–5
   preparation 7–8
   skills 83
   student answers 99–102, 116–18
reflexive verbs 204
relative pronouns 211–12
repairs 21
reports 186–7
restaurant 17, 88, 94–5, 122–3, 133–4
role-plays
   a step further 138, 153–4
   approaching the tests 122–6, 140–3
   format 122
   Foundation Tier 121–6
   Foundation Tier answers 135–8
   Foundation Tier questions 126–34
   Higher Tier 139–43
   Higher Tier answers 149–53
   Higher Tier questions 143–49
   situations 121–2
rubrics 249–51

school
   listening questions 48–52, 58
   reading questions 93, 112–13
   role-plays 144
   tasks 14–15
   writing questions 171, 184–5
SEG modular GCSE 3
self 17–18
separable verbs 205
shopping
   listening questions 53, 54, 56
   reading questions 87, 89–90, 91–2, 93–4
   role-plays 128–9, 144
   tasks 19–20
short courses 4
sollen 202
speaking
   coursework for London 161
   coursework for SEG 160
   Foundation Tier 121–38
   Foundation Tier requirements 121, 155–6
   Higher Tier 139–53
   Higher Tier requirements 139–40
   preparation 8
   presentation 159–60
   see also role-plays
special occasions 18
strong verbs 201–2, 206–8
subjunctive mood 203
superlatives 200

tasks
   accident 16
   accommodation 23–4
   adverts 22
   banks 20

café 17
campsites 23–4
careers 21–12
changing money 20
checklist 219–29
classroom language 14
conversation skills 14
courtesies 14
dry cleaning 21
employment 21–2
entertainment 18
family 17–18
finding the way 19
food and drink 17
free time 18
friends 17–18
getting around 21
going out 18–19
hiring 20
holidays 18, 22–3
home life 15
home town 19
hotels 23–4
illness 16
injury 16
jobs 21–2
leisure 18
life in other countries 22
local area 19
lost property 20
meal times 17
media 15–16
personal relationships 17–18
post office 20
public transport 21
publicity 22
repairs 21
restaurant 17
school 14–15
self 17–18
shopping 19–20
special occasions 18
telephoning 22
theft 20
weather 19
world events and issues 24
youth hostels 23–4
telephoning 22
theft 20, 108
time 216
time, manner, place 215
timing 10
topics *table 3.1*, 11–12
topics (SEG) *table 3.2*, 12–13

ULEAC 5

verbs 201–8
   conditional tense 203
   future tense 203

verbs *(continued)*
  impersonal 205
  mixed 201, 202, 206–8
  passive 203
  past tenses 202, 206–8
  present tense 201, 206–8
  reflexive 204
  strong 201–2, 206–8
  seperable 205
  subjunctive 203
  weak 201
vocabulary
  by topic areas 24–44
    accident 39
    addresses 24
    age 25
    air travel 34
    animals 28
    banks 43
    boat travel 34
    bus travel 34
    campsites 37
    clothes 40–1
    daily routine 27–8
    emergencies 39
    employment 30–1
    entertainment 32–3
    family 24, 25–6
    finding the way 33–4
    food and drink 41–2
    free time 31–3
    friends 24
    getting around 34
    health 38–9
    hobbies 31–3
    holidays 35–6
    home life 26
    hotels 36
    house 26, 28
    jobs 30–1
    letters 37
    lost property 43
    meeting people 37–8
    nationality 24
    people 25
    personal relationships 24
    post office 42–3
    postcards 37
    relatives 25–6
    road travel 35
    rooms 26–7
    rural surroundings 29
    school 29–30
    self 24
    shopping 40
    telephone 24, 37
    train travel 34
    urban surroundings 28–9
    weather 44
    world issues 44
    youth hostels 36–7
  English to German 247–9
  German to English 230–47
  learning 7, 84, 118–20, 166

weak nouns 197–8
weak verbs 201
weather 19, 52, 57, 70, 73
weil 213
well-being 16–17
WJEC 6
wollen 202

word order 215
world events and issues 24, 71, 73, 145
writing
  a step further 190–1
  accounts 186–7
  approaching the tests 165–6
  articles 172
  coursework 192–5, *see also* coursework
  different tasks 166–9
  form filling 168, 172
  Foundation Tier 164–79
  Foundation Tier answers 173–7
  Foundation Tier questions 169–73
  Foundation Tier requirements 164–5
  Higher Tier 180–91
  Higher Tier hints and answers 187–9
  Higher Tier questions 183–8
  Higher Tier requirements 180–1
  letters 168–9, 171, 172–3, 183–5, 190
  lists 166–7, 169–70
  messages 167
  narratives 186–7
  postcards 167–8, 170–1
  practice 166
  preparation 8
  reports 186–7
  student answers 177–9, 189–90

youth hostels 23–4, 129

Longman - for all your study guide needs

Addison Wesley Longman publishes a wide range of curriculum-related books to help you with your studies. If you have enjoyed using this book and have found it useful, you can now order others directly from us - simply follow the ordering instructions below.

Don't forget to tell your fellow students about *Longman Study Guides* - they might find them useful too!

HOW TO ORDER

A full list of titles is given overleaf. Decide which title(s) you require and then order in one of the following ways:

by post
Fill in the quantity alongside the title(s) you require, select your method of payment, complete your name and address details and return your completed order form and payment to:
Addison Wesley Longman Ltd
PO BOX 88
Harlow
Essex CM19 5SR

by phone
Call our Customer Information Centre on 01279 623923 to place your order, quoting mail number: HESG1

by fax
complete the order form overleaf and fill in your name and address details and method of payment, and fax it to us on 01279 414130.

by e-mail
E-mail your order to us on awlhe.orders@awl.co.uk listing title(s) and quantity required and providing full name and address details as requested here. Please quote mail number: HESG1. Please do not send credit card details by e-mail.

Mail no: HESG1

Your Name _____
Your Address _____
_____
Postcode _____ Telephone _____

Method of payment

☐ I enclose a cheque or a P/O for £ _____ made payable to Addison Wesley Longman Ltd
☐ Please charge my Visa/Access/AMEX/Diners Club card
Number _____ Expiry Date _____
Signature _____ Date _____
(please ensure that the address given above is the same as for your credit card)

Prices and other details are correct at time of going to press but may change without notice. All orders are subject to status.

☐ *Please tick this box if you would like a complete listing of York Notes Literature Guides (suitable for GCSE and A-level English students)*

LONGMAN   Addison Wesley Longman

LONGMAN HOMEWORK HANDBOOKS (KEY STAGE 3)
£7.99 each unless otherwise stated
QTY *(0582)*

1	_____ 29330 8	English (KS3)
2	_____ 29331 6	French (KS3)
3	_____ 30423 7	French pack*(KS3) (£12.99)
4	_____ 30425 3	French cassette (KS3) (£6.00)
5	_____ 29329 4	German (KS3)
6	_____ 30427 X	German pack*(KS3) (£12.99)
7	_____ 30428 8	German cassette (KS3) (£6.00)
8	_____ 29328 6	Mathematics (KS3)
9	_____ 29327 8	Science (KS3)

LONGMAN GCSE STUDY GUIDES
£9.99 each unless otherwise stated

10	_____ 30481 4	Biology
11	_____ 31538 7	Business Studies
12	_____ 30482 2	Chemistry
13	_____ 31539 5	Economics
14	_____ 30484 9	English
15	_____ 30483 0	English Literature
16	_____ 30485 7	French
17	_____ 03839 1	French pack* (£14.99)
18	_____ 03836 7	French cassette (£6.00)
19	_____ 30486 5	Geography
20	_____ 30487 3	German
21	_____ 03837 5	German pack* (£14.99)
22	_____ 03838 3	German cassette (£6.00)
23	_____ 30495 4	Higher Level Mathematics
24	_____ 30494 6	Information Technology (£10.99)
25	_____ 30496 2	Mathematics
26	_____ 30497 0	Music
27	_____ 31540 9	Physics
28	_____ 28700 6	Psychology
29	_____ 31542 5	Religious Studies
30	_____ 30498 9	Science (£10.99)
31	_____ 22651 1	Sociology
32	_____ 22652 X	Spanish
33	_____ 24509 5	Spanish pack* (£14.99)
34	_____ 24511 7	Spanish cassette (£6.00)
35	_____ 23771 8	Technology
36	_____ 30545 4	World History

LONGMAN GCSE EXAM PRACTICE KITS

37	_____ 30381 8	Biology £4.99)
38	_____ 30383 4	Business Studies (£4.99)
39	_____ 31191 8	English (£4.99)
40	_____ 30384 2	Geography (£4.99)
41	_____ 30385 0	Mathematics (£4.99)
42	_____ 30379 6	Physics (£4.99)
43	_____ 30380 X	Science (£5.99)

LONGMAN GCSE REFERENCE GUIDES *£6.99 each*

44	_____ 05788 4	Biology
45	_____ 05790 6	Chemistry
46	_____ 05072 3	English
47	_____ 05077 4	French
48	_____ 05074 X	Mathematics
49	_____ 05794 9	Physics
50	_____ 05076 6	Science

GCSE SURVIVAL GUIDE *£2.95*

51   _____ 05078 2

_____ **YORK NOTES LITERATURE GUIDES** *(see overleaf)*

LONGMAN A-LEVEL STUDY GUIDES
£9.99 each unless otherwise stated

52	_____ 22569 8	Accounting (£10.99)
53	_____ 31545 X	Biology
54	_____ 31652 9	Business Studies
55	_____ 31546 8	Chemistry
56	_____ 05782 5	Computer Science
57	_____ 27688 8	Economics (£10.99)
58	_____ 31656 1	English
59	_____ 05784 1	French
60	_____ 24495 1	French pack* (£14.99)
61	_____ 24497 8	French cassette (£6.00)
62	_____ 05173 8	Geography
63	_____ 31654 5	German
64	_____ 24498 6	German pack* (£14.99)
65	_____ 24508 7	German cassette (£6.00)
66	_____ 28702 2	Government and Politics (£10.99)
67	_____ 31549 2	Law (£10.99)
68	_____ 31550 6	Mathematics (£10.99)
69	_____ 31551 4	Modern History
70	_____ 27690 X	Physics
71	_____ 31655 3	Psychology
72	_____ 27691 8	Sociology

LONGMAN A-LEVEL EXAM PRACTICE KITS *£6.99 each*

73	_____ 30386 9	Biology
74	_____ 30387 7	Business Studies
75	_____ 30388 5	Chemistry
76	_____ 30389 3	Mathematics
77	_____ 30390 7	Psychology
78	_____ 30382 6	Sociology

LONGMAN A-LEVEL REFERENCE GUIDES *£6.99 each*

79	_____ 06394 9	Biology
80	_____ 06390 6	Chemistry
81	_____ 06396 5	English
82	_____ 06398 1	Mathematics
83	_____ 06392 2	Physics (£7.99)

LONGMAN HANDBOOKS *£7.99 each*

84	_____ 09965 X	Botany
85	_____ 08810 0	Chemistry

LONGMAN PARENT'S AND STUDENTS' GUIDES
£2.99 each

86	_____ 29971 3	Longman Parent's Guide to Pre-school Choices and Nursery Education
87	_____ 29975 6	Longman Parent's Guide to Key Stage 1 of the National Curriculum
88	_____ 29974 8	Longman Parent's Guide to Key Stage 2 of the National Curriculum
89	_____ 29973 X	Longman Parent's Guide to Key Stage 3 of the National Curriculum
90	_____ 29972 1	Longman Parent's Guide to GCSE and Key Stage 4 of the National Curriculum
91	_____ 29978 0	Longman A-level Survival Guide
92	_____ 29969 1	Longman Students' Guide to Vocational Education
93 to	_____ 29970 5	Longman Students' Guide to Returning Learning
94	_____ 29976 4	Longman Students' Guide to Higher Education

* *pack = book and cassette*